RUTH

WISDOM COMMENTARY

Volume 8

Ruth

Alice L. Laffey and
Mahri Leonard-Fleckman

Amy-Jill Levine
Volume Editor

Barbara E. Reid, OP
General Editor

A Michael Glazier Book

LITURGICAL PRESS
Collegeville, Minnesota

www.litpress.org

A Michael Glazier Book published by Liturgical Press

1 2 3 4 5 6 7 8 9

Library of Congress Cataloging-in-Publication Data

Names: Laffey, Alice L., 1944–, author. | Leonard-Fleckman, Mahri, author.
Title: Ruth / Alice L. Laffey and Mahri Leonard-Fleckman ; Amy-Jill Levine, volume editor, Barbara E. Reid, OP, general editor.
Description: Collegeville, Minnesota : Liturgical Press, 2017. | Series: Wisdom commentary ; Volume 8 | "A Michael Glazier book." | Includes bibliographical references and index.
Identifiers: LCCN 2017022473 (print) | LCCN 2017000814 (ebook) | ISBN 9780814681077 (hardcover) | ISBN 9780814681329 (ebook)
Subjects: LCSH: Bible. Ruth—Commentaries.
Classification: LCC BS1315.53 .L46 2017 (ebook) | LCC BS1315.53 (print) | DDC 222/.3507—dc23
LC record available at https://lccn.loc.gov/2017022473

Contents

Abbreviations

AB	Anchor Bible
ArBib	The Aramaic Bible
AYBRL	Anchor Yale Bible Reference Library
BA	*Biblical Archaeologist*
BibInt	Biblical Interpretation Series
BJS	Brown Judaic Studies
BLS	Bible and Literature Series
BT	*The Bible Translator*
CBQ	*Catholic Biblical Quarterly*
CF	Cistercian Fathers Series
COS	*The Context of Scripture*. Edited by William W. Hallo. 3 vols. Leiden: Brill, 1997–2002.
CurBR	*Currents in Biblical Research*
EvQ	*Evangelical Quarterly*
FCB	Feminist Companion to the Bible
GBS	Guides to Biblical Scholarship
GTR	Gender, Theory, and Religion
HSM	Harvard Semitic Monographs

IEJ	*Israel Exploration Journal*
IFT	Introductions in Feminist Theology
ISBL	Indiana Studies in Biblical Literature
IVBS	International Voices in Biblical Studies
JAOS	*Journal of the American Oriental Society*
JBL	*Journal of Biblical Literature*
JFSR	*Journal of Feminist Studies in Religion*
Josephus, *Ant.*	Josephus, *Antiquities of the Jews*
JRAS	*Journal of the Royal Asiatic Society*
JSOT	*Journal for the Study of the Old Testament*
JSOTSup	Journal for the Study of the Old Testament Supplement Series
KTU	*Die keilalphabetischen Texte aus Ugarit*. Edited by Manfried Dietrich, Oswald Loretz, and Joaquín Sanmartín. Münster: Ugarit-Verlag, 2013. 3rd enl. ed. of *KTU: The Cuneiform Alphabetic Texts from Ugarit, Ras Ibn Hani, and Other Places*. Edited by Manfried Dietrich, Oswald Loretz, and Joaquín Sanmartín. Münster: Ugarit-Verlag, 1995.
LCBI	Literary Currents in Biblical Interpretation
OBT	Overtures to Biblical Theology
OTL	Old Testament Library
Proof	*Prooftexts: A Journal of Jewish Literary History*
SB	Sources bibliques
SBL	Society of Biblical Literature
SemeiaSt	Semeia Studies
SemeiaSup	Semeia Supplements
SIDIC	*Journal of the Service internationale de documentation judeo-chrétienne*
SJOT	*Scandinavian Journal of the Old Testament*
SymS	Symposium Series
VT	*Vetus Testamentum*

VTSup	Supplements to Vetus Testamentum
WAW	Writings from the Ancient World
WBC	Word Biblical Commentary
WMANT	Wissenschaftliche Monographien zum Alten und Neuen Testament
ZAW	*Zeitschrift für die alttestamentliche Wissenschaft*

Mishnah, Talmud, and Related Literature

b. B. Bat.	Bava Batra
b. Ber.	Berakot
b. Šabb.	Šabbat
b. Sanh.	Sanhedrin
b. Soṭah	Soṭah
b. Yebam.	Yebamot
Midr. Yal. Lekach Tov	Midrash Yalkut Lekach Tov
Midr. Yal. Shimoni	Midrash Yalkut Shimoni

Contributors

Laura K. Carlson holds a master of divinity from Yale Divinity School and is a doctoral candidate in Hebrew Bible at Yale University. She is writing her dissertation on the relationship between archives and historiography in Ezra–Nehemiah, directed by Carolyn Sharp and Hindy Najman.

Sheila C. DeLuca is a graduate of the Hartford Biblical School in Hartford, Connecticut, and a member of Contemplative Outreach/Centering Prayer groups. She is a medical missionary to Haiti, a Catholic retreat director, and a proud mother of four.

Rev. Rajkumar Boaz Johnson received his PhD from Trinity International University and Trinity International Divinity School. He is professor of Hebrew Bible and theological studies at North Park University, Chicago, and is known for his solidarity with the Dalits (untouchables) in his native India.

Lynn Kaye is an assistant professor at the Ohio State University's Department of Near Eastern Languages and Cultures. Her research focuses on Jewish law, classical rabbinic literature, and philosophies of time.

Rev. Maggie Low has a PhD in Old Testament from Union Theological Seminary in New York and is currently a lecturer in Old Testament at Trinity Theological College, Singapore. She is an ordained Presbyterian minister.

Fr. John Madden is a priest of the Roman Catholic Diocese of Worcester, Massachusetts, and pastor of St. John's Church. His parish models an integrated combination of worship and social justice.

Rev. Surekha Nelava has a PhD in biblical studies from Drew University. She is currently serving as pastor of Harmony Community Lutheran Church and the Global Peace Lutheran Fellowship in Maryland.

Rev. Sarah W. Wiles is the pastor of Bethany Presbyterian Church in Tacoma, Washington, and a graduate of Union Theological Seminary in New York. She is the fourth generation of ministers in her family—the first Presbyterian after three generations of Baptist ministers.

Foreword

"Tell It on the Mountain"—or, "And You Shall Tell Your Daughter [as Well]"

Athalya Brenner-Idan

Universiteit van Amsterdam/Tel Aviv University

What can Wisdom Commentary do to help, and for whom?

The commentary genre has always been privileged in biblical studies. Traditionally acclaimed commentary series, such as the International Critical Commentary, Old Testament and New Testament Library, Hermeneia, Anchor Bible, Eerdmans, and Word—to name but several—enjoy nearly automatic prestige, and the number of women authors who participate in those is relatively small by comparison to their growing number in the scholarly guild. There certainly are some volumes written by women in them, especially in recent decades. At this time, however, this does not reflect the situation on the ground. Further, size matters. In that sense, the sheer size of the Wisdom Commentary is essential. This also represents a considerable investment and the possibility of reaching a wider audience than those already "converted."

Expecting women scholars to deal especially or only with what are considered strictly "female" matters seems unwarranted. According to Audre Lorde, "The master's tools will never dismantle the master's house."[1] But this maxim is not relevant to our case. The point of this commentary is not to destroy but to attain greater participation in the interpretive dialogue about biblical texts. Women scholars may bring additional questions to the readerly agenda as well as fresh angles to existing issues. To assume that their questions are designed only to topple a certain male hegemony is not convincing.

At first I did ask myself: is this commentary series an addition to calm raw nerves, an embellishment to make upholding the old hierarchy palatable? Or is it indeed about becoming the Master? On second and third thoughts, however, I understood that becoming the Master is not what this is about. Knowledge is power. Since Foucault at the very least, this cannot be in dispute. Writing commentaries for biblical texts by feminist women and men for women and for men, of confessional as well as non-confessional convictions, will sabotage (hopefully) the established hierarchy but will not topple it. This is about an attempt to integrate more fully, to introduce another viewpoint, to become. What excites me about the Wisdom Commentary is that it is not offered as just an alternative supplanting or substituting for the dominant discourse.

These commentaries on biblical books will retain nonauthoritative, pluralistic viewpoints. And yes, once again, the weight of a dedicated series, to distinguish from collections of stand-alone volumes, will prove weightier.

That such an approach is especially important in the case of the Hebrew Bible/Old Testament is beyond doubt. Women of Judaism, Christianity, and also Islam have struggled to make it their own for centuries, even more than they have fought for the New Testament and the Qur'an. Every Hebrew Bible/Old Testament volume in this project is evidence that the day has arrived: it is now possible to read *all* the Jewish canonical books as a collection, for a collection they are, with guidance conceived of with the needs of women readers (not only men) as an integral inspiration and part thereof.

In my Jewish tradition, the main motivation for reciting the Haggadah, the ritual text recited yearly on Passover, the festival of liberation from

1. Audre Lorde, "The Master's Tools Will Never Dismantle the Master's House," in *Sister Outsider: Essays and Speeches* (Berkeley, CA: Crossing Press, 1984, 2007), 110–14. First delivered in the Second Sex Conference in New York, 1979.

bondage, is given as "And you shall tell your son" (from Exod 13:8). The knowledge and experience of past generations is thus transferred to the next, for constructing the present and the future. The ancient maxim is, literally, limited to a male audience. This series remolds the maxim into a new inclusive shape, which is of the utmost consequence: "And you shall tell your son" is extended to "And you shall tell your daughter [as well as your son]." Or, if you want, "Tell it on the mountain," for all to hear.

This is what it's all about.

Editor's Introduction to Wisdom Commentary

"She Is a Breath of the Power of God" (Wis 7:25)

Barbara E. Reid, OP

General Editor

Wisdom Commentary is the first series to offer detailed feminist interpretation of every book of the Bible. The fruit of collaborative work by an ecumenical and interreligious team of scholars, the volumes provide serious, scholarly engagement with the whole biblical text, not only those texts that explicitly mention women. The series is intended for clergy, teachers, ministers, and all serious students of the Bible. Designed to be both accessible and informed by the various approaches of biblical scholarship, it pays particular attention to the world in front of the text, that is, how the text is heard and appropriated. At the same time, this series aims to be faithful to the ancient text and its earliest audiences; thus the volumes also explicate the worlds behind the text and within it. While issues of gender are primary in this project, the volumes also address the intersecting issues of power, authority, ethnicity, race, class, and religious belief and practice. The fifty-eight volumes include the books regarded as canonical by Jews (i.e., the Tanakh); Protestants (the "Hebrew Bible" and the New Testament); and Roman Catholic, Anglican, and Eastern Orthodox

Communions (i.e., also including Tobit, Judith, 1 and 2 Maccabees, Wisdom of Solomon, Sirach/Ecclesiasticus, Baruch, including the Letter of Jeremiah, the additions to Esther, and Susanna and Bel and the Dragon in Daniel).

A Symphony of Diverse Voices

Included in the Wisdom Commentary series are voices from scholars of many different religious traditions, of diverse ages, differing sexual identities, and varying cultural, racial, ethnic, and social contexts. Some have been pioneers in feminist biblical interpretation; others are newer contributors from a younger generation. A further distinctive feature of this series is that each volume incorporates voices other than that of the lead author(s). These voices appear alongside the commentary of the lead author(s), in the grayscale inserts. At times, a contributor may offer an alternative interpretation or a critique of the position taken by the lead author(s). At other times, she or he may offer a complementary interpretation from a different cultural context or subject position. Occasionally, portions of previously published material bring in other views. The diverse voices are not intended to be contestants in a debate or a cacophony of discordant notes. The multiple voices reflect that there is no single definitive feminist interpretation of a text. In addition, they show the importance of subject position in the process of interpretation. In this regard, the Wisdom Commentary series takes inspiration from the Talmud and from *The Torah: A Women's Commentary* (ed. Tamara Cohn Eskenazi and Andrea L. Weiss; New York: Women of Reform Judaism, Federation of Temple Sisterhood, 2008), in which many voices, even conflicting ones, are included and not harmonized.

Contributors include biblical scholars, theologians, and readers of Scripture from outside the scholarly and religious guilds. At times, their comments pertain to a particular text. In some instances they address a theme or topic that arises from the text.

Another feature that highlights the collaborative nature of feminist biblical interpretation is that a number of the volumes have two lead authors who have worked in tandem from the inception of the project and whose voices interweave throughout the commentary.

Woman Wisdom

The title, Wisdom Commentary, reflects both the importance to feminists of the figure of Woman Wisdom in the Scriptures and the distinct wisdom that feminist women and men bring to the interpretive process. In the Scriptures, Woman Wisdom appears as "a breath of the power of God, and a pure emanation of the glory of the Almighty" (Wis 7:25), who was present and active in fashioning all that exists (Prov 8:22-31; Wis 8:6). She is a spirit who pervades and penetrates all things (Wis 7:22-23), and she provides guidance and nourishment at her all-inclusive table (Prov 9:1-5). In both postexilic biblical and nonbiblical Jewish sources, Woman Wisdom is often equated with Torah, e.g., Sirach 24:23-34; Baruch 3:9–4:4; 38:2; 46:4-5; 2 Baruch 48:33, 36; 4 Ezra 5:9-10; 13:55; 14:40; 1 Enoch 42.

The New Testament frequently portrays Jesus as Wisdom incarnate. He invites his followers, "take my yoke upon you and learn from me" (Matt 11:29), just as Ben Sira advises, "put your neck under her [Wisdom's] yoke and let your souls receive instruction" (Sir 51:26). Just as Wisdom experiences rejection (Prov 1:23-25; Sir 15:7-8; Wis 10:3; Bar 3:12), so too does Jesus (Mark 8:31; John 1:10-11). Only some accept his invitation to his all-inclusive banquet (Matt 22:1-14; Luke 14:15-24; compare Prov 1:20-21; 9:3-5). Yet, "wisdom is vindicated by her deeds" (Matt 11:19, speaking of Jesus and John the Baptist; in the Lucan parallel at 7:35 they are called "wisdom's children"). There are numerous parallels between what is said of Wisdom and of the *Logos* in the Prologue of the Fourth Gospel (John 1:1-18). These are only a few of many examples. This female embodiment of divine presence and power is an apt image to guide the work of this series.

Feminism

There are many different understandings of the term "feminism." The various meanings, aims, and methods have developed exponentially in recent decades. Feminism is a perspective and a movement that springs from a recognition of inequities toward women, and it advocates for changes in whatever structures prevent full human flourishing. Three waves of feminism in the United States are commonly recognized. The first, arising in the mid-nineteenth century and lasting into the early twentieth, was sparked by women's efforts to be involved in the public sphere and to win the right to vote. In the 1960s and 1970s, the second wave focused on civil rights and equality for women. With the third wave, from the 1980s forward, came global feminism and the emphasis on the contextual nature of interpretation. Now a fourth wave may be emerging, with a stronger emphasis on the intersectionality of women's concerns with those of other marginalized groups and the increased use of the internet as a platform for discussion and activism.[1] As feminism has matured, it has recognized that inequities based on gender are interwoven with power imbalances based on race, class, ethnicity, religion, sexual identity, physical ability, and a host of other social markers.

Feminist Women and Men

Men who choose to identify with and partner with feminist women in the work of deconstructing systems of domination and building structures of equality are rightly regarded as feminists. Some men readily identify with experiences of women who are discriminated against on the basis of sex/gender, having themselves had comparable experiences; others who may not have faced direct discrimination or stereotyping recognize that inequity and problematic characterization still occur, and they seek correction. This series is pleased to include feminist men both as lead authors and as contributing voices.

Feminist Biblical Interpretation

Women interpreting the Bible from the lenses of their own experience is nothing new. Throughout the ages women have recounted the biblical stories, teaching them to their children and others, all the while interpreting them afresh for their time and circumstances.[2] Following is a very brief sketch of select foremothers who laid the groundwork for contemporary feminist biblical interpretation.

One of the earliest known Christian women who challenged patriarchal interpretations of Scripture was a consecrated virgin named Helie, who lived in the second century CE. When she refused to marry, her

1. See Martha Rampton, "Four Waves of Feminism" (October 25, 2015), at http://www.pacificu.edu/about-us/news-events/four-waves-feminism; and Ealasaid Munro, "Feminism: A Fourth Wave?," https://www.psa.ac.uk/insight-plus/feminism-fourth-wave.

2. For fuller treatments of this history, see chap. 7, "One Thousand Years of Feminist Bible Criticism," in Gerda Lerner, *Creation of Feminist Consciousness: From the Middle Ages to Eighteen-Seventy* (New York: Oxford University Press, 1993), 138–66; Susanne Scholz, "From the 'Woman's Bible' to the 'Women's Bible,' The History of Feminist Approaches to the Hebrew Bible," in *Introducing the Women's Hebrew Bible*, IFT 13 (New York: T&T Clark, 2007), 12–32; Marion Ann Taylor and Agnes Choi, eds., *Handbook of Women Biblical Interpreters: A Historical and Biographical Guide* (Grand Rapids: Baker Academic, 2012).

parents brought her before a judge, who quoted to her Paul's admonition, "It is better to marry than to be aflame with passion" (1 Cor 7:9). In response, Helie first acknowledges that this is what Scripture says, but then she retorts, "but not for everyone, that is, not for holy virgins."[3] She is one of the first to question the notion that a text has one meaning that is applicable in all situations.

A Jewish woman who also lived in the second century CE, Beruriah, is said to have had "profound knowledge of biblical exegesis and outstanding intelligence."[4] One story preserved in the Talmud (b. Ber. 10a) tells of how she challenged her husband, Rabbi Meir, when he prayed for the destruction of a sinner. Proffering an alternate interpretation, she argued that Psalm 104:35 advocated praying for the destruction of sin, not the sinner.

In medieval times the first written commentaries on Scripture from a critical feminist point of view emerge. While others may have been produced and passed on orally, they are for the most part lost to us now. Among the earliest preserved feminist writings are those of Hildegard of Bingen (1098–1179), German writer, mystic, and abbess of a Benedictine monastery. She reinterpreted the Genesis narratives in a way that presented women and men as complementary and interdependent. She frequently wrote about feminine aspects of the Divine.[5] Along with other women mystics of the time, such as Julian of Norwich (1342–ca. 1416), she spoke authoritatively from her personal experiences of God's revelation in prayer.

In this era, women were also among the scribes who copied biblical manuscripts. Notable among them is Paula Dei Mansi of Verona, from a distinguished family of Jewish scribes. In 1288, she translated from Hebrew into Italian a collection of Bible commentaries written by her father and added her own explanations.[6]

Another pioneer, Christine de Pizan (1365–ca. 1430), was a French court writer and prolific poet. She used allegory and common sense

3. Madrid, Escorial MS, a II 9, f. 90 v., as cited in Lerner, *Feminist Consciousness*, 140.

4. See Judith R. Baskin, "Women and Post-Biblical Commentary," in *The Torah: A Women's Commentary*, ed. Tamara Cohn Eskenazi and Andrea L. Weiss (New York: Women of Reform Judaism, Federation of Temple Sisterhood, 2008), xlix–lv, at lii.

5. Hildegard of Bingen, *De Operatione Dei*, 1.4.100; PL 197:885bc, as cited in Lerner, *Feminist Consciousness*, 142–43. See also Barbara Newman, *Sister of Wisdom: St. Hildegard's Theology of the Feminine* (Berkeley: University of California Press, 1987).

6. Emily Taitz, Sondra Henry, Cheryl Tallan, eds., *JPS Guide to Jewish Women 600 B.C.E.–1900 C.E.* (Philadelphia: Jewish Publication Society of America, 2003), 110–11.

to subvert misogynist readings of Scripture and celebrated the accomplishments of female biblical figures to argue for women's active roles in building society.[7]

By the seventeenth century, there were women who asserted that the biblical text needs to be understood and interpreted in its historical context. For example, Rachel Speght (1597–ca. 1630), a Calvinist English poet, elaborates on the historical situation in first-century Corinth that prompted Paul to say, "It is well for a man not to touch a woman" (1 Cor 7:1). Her aim was to show that the biblical texts should not be applied in a literal fashion to all times and circumstances. Similarly, Margaret Fell (1614–1702), one of the founders of the Religious Society of Friends (Quakers) in Britain, addressed the Pauline prohibitions against women speaking in church by insisting that they do not have universal validity. Rather, they need to be understood in their historical context, as addressed to a local church in particular time-bound circumstances.[8]

Along with analyzing the historical context of the biblical writings, women in the eighteenth and nineteenth centuries began to attend to misogynistic interpretations based on faulty translations. One of the first to do so was British feminist Mary Astell (1666–1731).[9] In the United States, the Grimké sisters, Sarah (1792–1873) and Angelina (1805–1879), Quaker women from a slaveholding family in South Carolina, learned biblical Greek and Hebrew so that they could interpret the Bible for themselves. They were prompted to do so after men sought to silence them from speaking out against slavery and for women's rights by claiming that the Bible (e.g., 1 Cor 14:34) prevented women from speaking in public.[10] Another prominent abolitionist, Sojourner Truth (ca. 1797–1883), a former slave, quoted the Bible liberally in her speeches[11] and in so doing challenged cultural assumptions and biblical interpretations that undergird gender inequities.

7. See further Taylor and Choi, *Handbook of Women Biblical Interpreters*, 127–32.

8. Her major work, *Women's Speaking Justified, Proved and Allowed by the Scriptures*, published in London in 1667, gave a systematic feminist reading of all biblical texts pertaining to women.

9. Mary Astell, *Some Reflections upon Marriage* (New York: Source Book Press, 1970, reprint of the 1730 edition; earliest edition of this work is 1700), 103–4.

10. See further Sarah Grimké, *Letters on the Equality of the Sexes and the Condition of Woman* (Boston: Isaac Knapp, 1838).

11. See, for example, her most famous speech, "Ain't I a Woman?," delivered in 1851 at the Ohio Women's Rights Convention in Akron, OH; http://www.fordham.edu/halsall/mod/sojtruth-woman.asp.

Another monumental work that emerged in nineteenth-century England was that of Jewish theologian Grace Aguilar (1816–1847), *The Women of Israel*,[12] published in 1845. Aguilar's approach was to make connections between the biblical women and contemporary Jewish women's concerns. She aimed to counter the widespread notion that women were degraded in Jewish law and that only in Christianity were women's dignity and value upheld. Her intent was to help Jewish women find strength and encouragement by seeing the evidence of God's compassionate love in the history of every woman in the Bible. While not a full commentary on the Bible, Aguilar's work stands out for its comprehensive treatment of every female biblical character, including even the most obscure references.[13]

The first person to produce a full-blown feminist commentary on the Bible was Elizabeth Cady Stanton (1815–1902). A leading proponent in the United States for women's right to vote, she found that whenever women tried to make inroads into politics, education, or the work world, the Bible was quoted against them. Along with a team of like-minded women, she produced her own commentary on every text of the Bible that concerned women. Her pioneering two-volume project, *The Woman's Bible*, published in 1895 and 1898, urges women to recognize that texts that degrade women come from the men who wrote the texts, not from God, and to use their common sense to rethink what has been presented to them as sacred.

Nearly a century later, *The Women's Bible Commentary*, edited by Carol Newsom and Sharon Ringe (Louisville: Westminster John Knox, 1992), appeared. This one-volume commentary features North American feminist scholarship on each book of the Protestant canon. Like Cady Stanton's commentary, it does not contain comments on every section of the biblical text but only on those passages deemed relevant to women. It was revised and expanded in 1998 to include the Apocrypha/Deuterocanonical books, and the contributors to this new volume reflect the global face of contemporary feminist scholarship. The revisions made in the third edition, which appeared in 2012, represent the profound advances in feminist biblical scholarship and include newer voices. In both the second and third editions, *The* has been dropped from the title.

12. The full title is *The Women of Israel or Characters and Sketches from the Holy Scriptures and Jewish History Illustrative of the Past History, Present Duty, and Future Destiny of the Hebrew Females, as Based on the Word of God.*

13. See further Eskenazi and Weiss, *The Torah: A Women's Commentary*, xxxviii; Taylor and Choi, *Handbook of Women Biblical Interpreters*, 31–37.

Also appearing at the centennial of Cady Stanton's *The Woman's Bible* were two volumes edited by Elisabeth Schüssler Fiorenza with the assistance of Shelly Matthews. The first, *Searching the Scriptures: A Feminist Introduction* (New York: Crossroad, 1993), charts a comprehensive approach to feminist interpretation from ecumenical, interreligious, and multicultural perspectives. The second volume, published in 1994, provides critical feminist commentary on each book of the New Testament as well as on three books of Jewish Pseudepigrapha and eleven other early Christian writings.

In Europe, similar endeavors have been undertaken, such as the one-volume *Kompendium Feministische Bibelauslegung*, edited by Luise Schottroff and Marie-Theres Wacker (Gütersloh: Gütersloher Verlagshaus, 2007), featuring German feminist biblical interpretation of each book of the Bible, along with apocryphal books, and several extrabiblical writings. This work, now in its third edition, has recently been translated into English.[14] A multivolume project, *The Bible and Women: An Encylopaedia of Exegesis and Cultural History*, edited by Irmtraud Fischer, Adriana Valerio, Mercedes Navarro Puerto, and Christiana de Groot, is currently in production. This project presents a history of the reception of the Bible as embedded in Western cultural history and focuses particularly on gender-relevant biblical themes, biblical female characters, and women recipients of the Bible. The volumes are published in English, Spanish, Italian, and German.[15]

Another groundbreaking work is the collection The Feminist Companion to the Bible Series, edited by Athalya Brenner (Sheffield: Sheffield Academic, 1993–2015), which comprises twenty volumes of commentaries on the Old Testament. The parallel series, Feminist Companion

14. *Feminist Biblical Interpretation: A Compendium of Critical Commentary on the Books of the Bible and Related Literature*, trans. Lisa E. Dahill, Everett R. Kalin, Nancy Lukens, Linda M. Maloney, Barbara Rumscheidt, Martin Rumscheidt, and Tina Steiner (Grand Rapids: Eerdmans, 2012). Another notable collection is the three volumes edited by Susanne Scholz, *Feminist Interpretation of the Hebrew Bible in Retrospect*, Recent Research in Biblical Studies 7, 8, 9 (Sheffield: Sheffield Phoenix, 2013, 2014, 2016).

15. The first volume, on the Torah, appeared in Spanish in 2009, in German and Italian in 2010, and in English in 2011 (Atlanta: SBL Press). Four more volumes are now available: *Feminist Biblical Studies in the Twentieth Century*, ed. Elisabeth Schüssler Fiorenza (2014); *The Writings and Later Wisdom Books*, ed. Christl M. Maier and Nuria Calduch-Benages (2014); *Gospels: Narrative and History*, ed. Mercedes Navarro Puerto and Marinella Perroni; English translation ed. Amy-Jill Levine (2015); and *The High Middle Ages*, ed. Kari Elisabeth Børresen and Adriana Valerio (2015). For further information, see http://www.bibleandwomen.org.

to the New Testament and Early Christian Writings, edited by Amy-Jill Levine with Marianne Blickenstaff and Maria Mayo Robbins (Sheffield: Sheffield Academic, 2001–2009), contains thirteen volumes with one more planned. These two series are not full commentaries on the biblical books but comprise collected essays on discrete biblical texts.

Works by individual feminist biblical scholars in all parts of the world abound, and they are now too numerous to list in this introduction. Feminist biblical interpretation has reached a level of maturity that now makes possible a commentary series on every book of the Bible. In recent decades, women have had greater access to formal theological education, have been able to learn critical analytical tools, have put their own interpretations into writing, and have developed new methods of biblical interpretation. Until recent decades the work of feminist biblical interpreters was largely unknown, both to other women and to their brothers in the synagogue, church, and academy. Feminists now have taken their place in the professional world of biblical scholars, where they build on the work of their foremothers and connect with one another across the globe in ways not previously possible. In a few short decades, feminist biblical criticism has become an integral part of the academy.

Methodologies

Feminist biblical scholars use a variety of methods and often employ a number of them together.[16] In the Wisdom Commentary series, the authors will explain their understanding of feminism and the feminist reading strategies used in their commentary. Each volume treats the biblical text in blocks of material, not an analysis verse by verse. The entire text is considered, not only those passages that feature female characters or that speak specifically about women. When women are not apparent in the narrative, feminist lenses are used to analyze the dynamics in the text between male characters, the models of power, binary ways of thinking, and the dynamics of imperialism. Attention is given to how the whole text functions and how it was and is heard, both in its original context and today. Issues of particular concern to women—e.g., poverty, food, health, the environment, water—come to the fore.

16. See the seventeen essays in Caroline Vander Stichele and Todd Penner, eds., *Her Master's Tools? Feminist and Postcolonial Engagements of Historical-Critical Discourse* (Atlanta: SBL Press, 2005), which show the complementarity of various approaches.

One of the approaches used by early feminists and still popular today is to lift up the overlooked and forgotten stories of women in the Bible. Studies of women in each of the Testaments have been done, and there are also studies on women in particular biblical books.[17] Feminists recognize that the examples of biblical characters can be both empowering and problematic. The point of the feminist enterprise is not to serve as an apologetic for women; it is rather, in part, to recover women's history and literary roles in all their complexity and to learn from that recovery.

Retrieving the submerged history of biblical women is a crucial step for constructing the story of the past so as to lead to liberative possibilities for the present and future. There are, however, some pitfalls to this approach. Sometimes depictions of biblical women have been naïve and romantic. Some commentators exalt the virtues of both biblical and contemporary women and paint women as superior to men. Such reverse discrimination inhibits movement toward equality for all. In addition, some feminists challenge the idea that one can "pluck positive images out of an admittedly androcentric text, separating literary characterizations from the androcentric interests they were created to serve."[18] Still other feminists find these images to have enormous value.

One other danger with seeking the submerged history of women is the tendency for Christian feminists to paint Jesus and even Paul as liberators of women in a way that demonizes Judaism.[19] Wisdom Commentary aims to enhance understanding of Jesus as well as Paul as Jews of their day and to forge solidarity among Jewish and Christian feminists.

17. See, e.g., Alice Bach, ed., *Women in the Hebrew Bible: A Reader* (New York: Routledge, 1998); Tikva Frymer-Kensky, *Reading the Women of the Bible* (New York: Schocken Books, 2002); Carol Meyers, Toni Craven, and Ross S. Kraemer, eds., *Women in Scripture* (Grand Rapids: Eerdmans, 2000); Irene Nowell, *Women in the Old Testament* (Collegeville, MN: Liturgical Press, 1997); Katharine Doob Sakenfeld, *Just Wives? Stories of Power and Survival in the Old Testament and Today* (Louisville: Westminster John Knox, 2003); Mary Ann Getty-Sullivan, *Women in the New Testament* (Collegeville, MN: Liturgical Press, 2001); Bonnie Thurston, *Women in the New Testament: Questions and Commentary*, Companions to the New Testament (New York: Crossroad, 1998).

18. Cheryl Exum, "Second Thoughts about Secondary Characters: Women in Exodus 1.8–2.10," in *A Feminist Companion to Exodus to Deuteronomy*, FCB 6, ed. Athalya Brenner (Sheffield: Sheffield Academic, 1994), 75–97, at 76.

19. See Judith Plaskow, "Anti-Judaism in Feminist Christian Interpretation," in *Searching the Scriptures: A Feminist Introduction*, ed. Elisabeth Schüssler Fiorenza (New York: Crossroad, 1993), 1:117–29; Amy-Jill Levine, "The New Testament and Anti-Judaism," in *The Misunderstood Jew: The Church and the Scandal of the Jewish Jesus* (San Francisco: HarperSanFrancisco, 2006), 87–117.

Feminist scholars who use historical-critical methods analyze the world behind the text; they seek to understand the historical context from which the text emerged and the circumstances of the communities to whom it was addressed. In bringing feminist lenses to this approach, the aim is not to impose modern expectations on ancient cultures but to unmask the ways that ideologically problematic mindsets that produced the ancient texts are still promulgated through the text. Feminist biblical scholars aim not only to deconstruct but also to reclaim and reconstruct biblical history as women's history, in which women were central and active agents in creating religious heritage.[20] A further step is to construct meaning for contemporary women and men in a liberative movement toward transformation of social, political, economic, and religious structures.[21] In recent years, some feminists have embraced the new historicism, which accents the creative role of the interpreter in any construction of history and exposes the power struggles to which the text witnesses.[22]

Literary critics analyze the world of the text: its form, language patterns, and rhetorical function.[23] They do not attempt to separate layers of tradition and redaction but focus on the text holistically, as it is in

20. See, for example, Phyllis A. Bird, *Missing Persons and Mistaken Identities: Women and Gender in Ancient Israel* (Minneapolis: Fortress, 1997); Elisabeth Schüssler Fiorenza, *In Memory of Her: A Feminist Theological Reconstruction of Christian Origins* (New York: Crossroad, 1984); Ross Shepard Kraemer and Mary Rose D'Angelo, eds., *Women and Christian Origins* (New York: Oxford University Press, 1999).

21. See, e.g., Sandra M. Schneiders, *The Revelatory Text: Interpreting the New Testament as Sacred Scripture*, rev. ed. (Collegeville, MN: Liturgical Press, 1999), whose aim is to engage in biblical interpretation not only for intellectual enlightenment but, even more important, for personal and communal transformation. Elisabeth Schüssler Fiorenza (*Wisdom Ways: Introducing Feminist Biblical Interpretation* [Maryknoll, NY: Orbis Books, 2001]) envisions the work of feminist biblical interpretation as a dance of Wisdom that consists of seven steps that interweave in spiral movements toward liberation, the final one being transformative action for change.

22. See Gina Hens-Piazza, *The New Historicism*, GBS, Old Testament Series (Minneapolis: Fortress, 2002).

23. Phyllis Trible was among the first to employ this method with texts from Genesis and Ruth in her groundbreaking book, *God and the Rhetoric of Sexuality*, OBT (Philadelphia: Fortress, 1978). Another pioneer in feminist literary criticism is Mieke Bal (*Lethal Love: Feminist Literary Readings of Biblical Love Stories* [Bloomington: Indiana University Press, 1987]). For surveys of recent developments in literary methods, see Terry Eagleton, *Literary Theory: An Introduction*, 3rd ed. (Minneapolis: University of Minnesota Press, 2008); Janice Capel Anderson and Stephen D. Moore, eds., *Mark and Method: New Approaches in Biblical Studies*, 2nd ed. (Minneapolis: Fortress, 2008).

its present form. They examine how meaning is created in the interaction between the text and its reader in multiple contexts. Within the arena of literary approaches are reader-oriented approaches, narrative, rhetorical, structuralist, post-structuralist, deconstructive, ideological, autobiographical, and performance criticism.[24] Narrative critics study the interrelation among author, text, and audience through investigation of settings, both spatial and temporal; characters; plot; and narrative techniques (e.g., irony, parody, intertextual allusions). Reader-response critics attend to the impact that the text has on the reader or hearer. They recognize that when a text is detrimental toward women there is the choice either to affirm the text or to read against the grain toward a liberative end. Rhetorical criticism analyzes the style of argumentation and attends to how the author is attempting to shape the thinking or actions of the hearer. Structuralist critics analyze the complex patterns of binary oppositions in the text to derive its meaning.[25] Post-structuralist approaches challenge the notion that there are fixed meanings to any biblical text or that there is one universal truth. They engage in close readings of the text and often engage in intertextual analysis.[26] Within this approach is deconstructionist criticism, which views the text as a site of conflict, with competing narratives. The interpreter aims to expose the fault lines and overturn and reconfigure binaries by elevating the underling of a pair and foregrounding it.[27] Feminists also use other postmodern approaches, such as ideological and autobiographical criticism. The former analyzes the system of ideas that underlies the power and

24. See, e.g., J. Cheryl Exum and David J. A. Clines, eds., *The New Literary Criticism and the Hebrew Bible* (Valley Forge, PA: Trinity Press International, 1993); Edgar V. McKnight and Elizabeth Struthers Malbon, eds., *The New Literary Criticism and the New Testament* (Valley Forge, PA: Trinity Press International, 1994).

25. See, e.g., David Jobling, *The Sense of Biblical Narrative: Three Structural Analyses in the Old Testament*, JSOTSup 7 (Sheffield: University of Sheffield, 1978).

26. See, e.g., Stephen D. Moore, *Poststructuralism and the New Testament: Derrida and Foucault at the Foot of the Cross* (Minneapolis: Fortress, 1994); *The Bible in Theory: Critical and Postcritical Essays* (Atlanta: SBL Press, 2010); Yvonne Sherwood, *A Biblical Text and Its Afterlives: The Survival of Jonah in Western Culture* (Cambridge: Cambridge University Press, 2000).

27. David Penchansky, "Deconstruction," in *The Oxford Encyclopedia of Biblical Interpretation*, ed. Steven McKenzie (New York: Oxford University Press, 2013), 196–205. See, for example, Danna Nolan Fewell and David M. Gunn, *Gender, Power, and Promise: The Subject of the Bible's First Story* (Nashville: Abingdon, 1993); David Rutledge, *Reading Marginally: Feminism, Deconstruction and the Bible*, BibInt 21 (Leiden: Brill, 1996).

values concealed in the text as well as that of the interpreter.[28] The latter involves deliberate self-disclosure while reading the text as a critical exegete.[29] Performance criticism attends to how the text was passed on orally, usually in communal settings, and to the verbal and nonverbal interactions between the performer and the audience.[30]

From the beginning, feminists have understood that interpreting the Bible is an act of power. In recent decades, feminist biblical scholars have developed hermeneutical theories of the ethics and politics of biblical interpretation to challenge the claims to value neutrality of most academic biblical scholarship. Feminist biblical scholars have also turned their attention to how some biblical writings were shaped by the power of empire and how this still shapes readers' self-understandings today. They have developed hermeneutical approaches that reveal, critique, and evaluate the interactions depicted in the text against the context of empire, and they consider implications for contemporary contexts.[31] Feminists also analyze the dynamics of colonization and the mentalities of colonized peoples in the exercise of biblical interpretation. As Kwok Pui-lan explains, "A postcolonial feminist interpretation of the Bible needs to investigate the deployment of gender in the narration of identity, the negotiation of power differentials between the colonizers and the colonized, and the reinforcement of patriarchal control over spheres where these elites could exercise control."[32] Methods and models from sociology and cultural anthropology are used by feminists to investigate

28. See Tina Pippin, ed., *Ideological Criticism of Biblical Texts: Semeia* 59 (1992); Terry Eagleton, *Ideology: An Introduction* (London: Verso, 2007).

29. See, e.g., Ingrid Rosa Kitzberger, ed., *Autobiographical Biblical Interpretation: Between Text and Self* (Leiden: Deo, 2002); P. J. W. Schutte, "When *They*, *We*, and the Passive Become *I*—Introducing Autobiographical Biblical Criticism," *HTS Teologiese Studies / Theological Studies* 61 (2005): 401–16.

30. See, e.g., Holly Hearon and Philip Ruge-Jones, eds., *The Bible in Ancient and Modern Media: Story and Performance* (Eugene, OR: Cascade, 2009).

31. E.g., Gale Yee, ed., *Judges and Method: New Approaches in Biblical Studies* (Minneapolis: Fortress, 1995); Warren Carter, *The Gospel of Matthew in Its Roman Imperial Context* (London: T&T Clark, 2005); *The Roman Empire and the New Testament: An Essential Guide* (Nashville: Abingdon, 2006); Elisabeth Schüssler Fiorenza, *The Power of the Word: Scripture and the Rhetoric of Empire* (Minneapolis: Fortress, 2007); Judith E. McKinlay, *Reframing Her: Biblical Women in Postcolonial Focus* (Sheffield: Sheffield Phoenix, 2004).

32. Kwok Pui-lan, *Postcolonial Imagination and Feminist Theology* (Louisville: Westminster John Knox, 2005), 9. See also, Musa W. Dube, *Postcolonial Feminist Interpretation of the Bible* (St. Louis: Chalice, 2000); Cristl M. Maier and Carolyn J. Sharp,

women's everyday lives, their experiences of marriage, childrearing, labor, money, illness, etc.[33]

As feminists have examined the construction of gender from varying cultural perspectives, they have become ever more cognizant that the way gender roles are defined within differing cultures varies radically. As Mary Ann Tolbert observes, "Attempts to isolate some universal role that cross-culturally defines 'woman' have run into contradictory evidence at every turn."[34] Some women have coined new terms to highlight the particularities of their socio-cultural context. Many African American feminists, for example, call themselves *womanists* to draw attention to the double oppression of racism and sexism they experience.[35] Similarly, many US Hispanic feminists speak of themselves as *mujeristas* (*mujer* is Spanish for "woman").[36] Others prefer to be called "Latina feminists."[37] Both groups emphasize that the context for their theologizing is *mestizaje* and *mulatez* (racial and cultural mixture), done *en conjunto* (in community), with *lo cotidiano* (everyday lived experience) of Hispanic women as starting points for theological reflection and the encounter with the divine. Intercultural analysis has become an indispensable tool for working toward justice for women at the global level.[38]

Prophecy and Power: Jeremiah in Feminist and Postcolonial Perspective (London: Bloomsbury, 2013).

33. See, for example, Carol Meyers, *Discovering Eve: Ancient Israelite Women in Context* (New York: Oxford University Press, 1991); Luise Schottroff, *Lydia's Impatient Sisters: A Feminist Social History of Early Christianity*, trans. Barbara and Martin Rumscheidt (Louisville: Westminster John Knox, 1995); Susan Niditch, *"My Brother Esau Is a Hairy Man": Hair and Identity in Ancient Israel* (Oxford: Oxford University Press, 2008).

34. Mary Ann Tolbert, "Social, Sociological, and Anthropological Methods," in *Searching the Scriptures*, 1:255–71, at 265.

35. Alice Walker coined the term (*In Search of Our Mothers' Gardens: Womanist Prose* [New York: Harcourt Brace Jovanovich, 1967, 1983]). See also Katie G. Cannon, "The Emergence of Black Feminist Consciousness," in *Feminist Interpretation of the Bible*, ed. Letty M. Russell (Philadelphia: Westminster, 1985), 30–40; Renita Weems, *Just a Sister Away: A Womanist Vision of Women's Relationships in the Bible* (San Diego: Lura Media, 1988); Nyasha Junior, *An Introduction to Womanist Biblical Interpretation* (Louisville: Westminster John Knox, 2015).

36. Ada María Isasi-Díaz (*Mujerista Theology: A Theology for the Twenty-First Century* [Maryknoll, NY: Orbis Books, 1996]) is credited with coining the term.

37. E.g., María Pilar Aquino, Daisy L. Machado, and Jeanette Rodríguez, eds., *A Reader in Latina Feminist Theology* (Austin: University of Texas Press, 2002).

38. See, e.g., María Pilar Aquino and María José Rosado-Nunes, eds., *Feminist Intercultural Theology: Latina Explorations for a Just World*, Studies in Latino/a Catholicism (Maryknoll, NY: Orbis Books, 2007).

Some feminists are among those who have developed lesbian, gay, bisexual, and transgender (LGBT) interpretation. This approach focuses on issues of sexual identity and uses various reading strategies. Some point out the ways in which categories that emerged in recent centuries are applied anachronistically to biblical texts to make modern-day judgments. Others show how the Bible is silent on contemporary issues about sexual identity. Still others examine same-sex relationships in the Bible by figures such as Ruth and Naomi or David and Jonathan. In recent years, queer theory has emerged; it emphasizes the blurriness of boundaries not just of sexual identity but also of gender roles. Queer critics often focus on texts in which figures transgress what is traditionally considered proper gender behavior.[39]

Feminists also recognize that the struggle for women's equality and dignity is intimately connected with the struggle for respect for Earth and for the whole of the cosmos. Ecofeminists interpret Scripture in ways that highlight the link between human domination of nature and male subjugation of women. They show how anthropocentric ways of interpreting the Bible have overlooked or dismissed Earth and Earth community. They invite readers to identify not only with human characters in the biblical narrative but also with other Earth creatures and domains of nature, especially those that are the object of injustice. Some use creative imagination to retrieve the interests of Earth implicit in the narrative and enable Earth to speak.[40]

Biblical Authority

By the late nineteenth century, some feminists, such as Elizabeth Cady Stanton, began to question openly whether the Bible could continue to be regarded as authoritative for women. They viewed the Bible itself as

39. See, e.g., Bernadette J. Brooten, *Love between Women: Early Christian Responses to Female Homoeroticism* (Chicago and London: University of Chicago Press, 1996); Mary Rose D'Angelo, "Women Partners in the New Testament," *JFSR* 6 (1990): 65–86; Deirdre J. Good, "Reading Strategies for Biblical Passages on Same-Sex Relations," *Theology and Sexuality* 7 (1997): 70–82; Deryn Guest, *When Deborah Met Jael: Lesbian Feminist Hermeneutics* (London: SCM, 2011); Teresa Hornsby and Ken Stone, eds., *Bible Trouble: Queer Readings at the Boundaries of Biblical Scholarship* (Atlanta: SBL Press, 2011).

40. E.g., Norman C. Habel and Peter Trudinger, *Exploring Ecological Hermeneutics*, SymS 46 (Atlanta: SBL Press, 2008); Mary Judith Ress, *Ecofeminism in Latin America*, Women from the Margins (Maryknoll, NY: Orbis Books, 2006).

the source of women's oppression, and some rejected its sacred origin and saving claims. Some decided that the Bible and the religious traditions that enshrine it are too thoroughly saturated with androcentrism and patriarchy to be redeemable.[41]

In the Wisdom Commentary series, questions such as these may be raised, but the aim of this series is not to lead readers to reject the authority of the biblical text. Rather, the aim is to promote better understanding of the contexts from which the text arose and of the rhetorical effects it has on women and men in contemporary contexts. Such understanding can lead to a deepening of faith, with the Bible serving as an aid to bring flourishing of life.

Language for God

Because of the ways in which the term "God" has been used to symbolize the divine in predominantly male, patriarchal, and monarchical modes, feminists have designed new ways of speaking of the divine. Some have called attention to the inadequacy of the term *God* by trying to visually destabilize our ways of thinking and speaking of the divine. Rosemary Radford Ruether proposed *God/ess*, as an unpronounceable term pointing to the unnameable understanding of the divine that transcends patriarchal limitations.[42] Some have followed traditional Jewish practice, writing *G-d*. Elisabeth Schüssler Fiorenza has adopted *G*d*.[43] Others draw on the biblical tradition to mine female and non-gender-specific metaphors and symbols.[44] In Wisdom Commentary, there is not one standard way of expressing the divine; each author will use her or his preferred ways. The one exception is that when the tetragrammaton, YHWH, the name revealed to Moses in Exodus 3:14, is used, it will be without vowels, respecting the Jewish custom of avoiding pronouncing the divine name out of reverence.

41. E.g., Mary Daly, *Beyond God the Father: A Philosophy of Women's Liberation* (Boston: Beacon, 1973).

42. Rosemary Radford Ruether, *Sexism and God-Talk: Toward a Feminist Theology* (Boston: Beacon, 1983).

43. Elisabeth Schüssler Fiorenza, *Jesus: Miriam's Child, Sophia's Prophet; Critical Issues in Feminist Christology* (New York: Continuum, 1994), 191 n. 3.

44. E.g., Sallie McFague, *Models of God: Theology for an Ecological, Nuclear Age* (Philadelphia: Fortress, 1987); Catherine LaCugna, *God for Us: The Trinity and Christian Life* (San Francisco: HarperCollins, 1991); Elizabeth A. Johnson, *She Who Is: The Mystery of God in Feminist Theological Discourse* (New York: Crossroad, 1992). See further Elizabeth A. Johnson, "God," in *Dictionary of Feminist Theologies*, 128–30.

Nomenclature for the Two Testaments

In recent decades, some biblical scholars have begun to call the two Testaments of the Bible by names other than the traditional nomenclature: Old and New Testament. Some regard "Old" as derogatory, implying that it is no longer relevant or that it has been superseded. Consequently, terms like Hebrew Bible, First Testament, and Jewish Scriptures and, correspondingly, Christian Scriptures or Second Testament have come into use. There are a number of difficulties with these designations. The term "Hebrew Bible" does not take into account that parts of the Old Testament are written not in Hebrew but in Aramaic.[45] Moreover, for Roman Catholics and Eastern Orthodox believers, the Old Testament includes books written in Greek—the Deuterocanonical books, considered Apocrypha by Protestants.[46] The term "Jewish Scriptures" is inadequate because these books are also sacred to Christians. Conversely, "Christian Scriptures" is not an accurate designation for the New Testament, since the Old Testament is also part of the Christian Scriptures. Using "First and Second Testament" also has difficulties, in that it can imply a hierarchy and a value judgment.[47] Jews generally use the term Tanakh, an acronym for Torah (Pentateuch), Nevi'im (Prophets), and Ketuvim (Writings).

In Wisdom Commentary, if authors choose to use a designation other than Tanakh, Old Testament, and New Testament, they will explain how they mean the term.

Translation

Modern feminist scholars recognize the complexities connected with biblical translation, as they have delved into questions about philosophy of language, how meanings are produced, and how they are culturally situated. Today it is evident that simply translating into gender-neutral formulations cannot address all the challenges presented by androcentric texts. Efforts at feminist translation must also deal with issues around authority and canonicity.[48]

45. Gen 31:47; Jer 10:11; Ezra 4:7–6:18; 7:12-26; Dan 2:4–7:28.

46. Representing the *via media* between Catholic and reformed, Anglicans generally consider the Apocrypha to be profitable, if not canonical, and utilize select Wisdom texts liturgically.

47. See Levine, *The Misunderstood Jew*, 193–99.

48. Elizabeth Castelli, "*Les Belles Infidèles*/Fidelity or Feminism? The Meanings of Feminist Biblical Translation," in *Searching the Scriptures*, 1:189–204, here 190.

Because of these complexities, the editors of the Wisdom Commentary series have chosen to use an existing translation, the New Revised Standard Version (NRSV), which is provided for easy reference at the top of each page of commentary. The NRSV was produced by a team of ecumenical and interreligious scholars, is a fairly literal translation, and uses inclusive language for human beings. Brief discussions about problematic translations appear in the inserts labeled "Translation Matters." When more detailed discussions are available, these will be indicated in footnotes. In the commentary, wherever Hebrew or Greek words are used, English translation is provided. In cases where a wordplay is involved, transliteration is provided to enable understanding.

Art and Poetry

Artistic expression in poetry, music, sculpture, painting, and various other modes is very important to feminist interpretation. Where possible, art and poetry are included in the print volumes of the series. In a number of instances, these are original works created for this project. Regrettably, copyright and production costs prohibit the inclusion of color photographs and other artistic work. It is our hope that the web version will allow a greater collection of such resources.

Glossary

Because there are a number of excellent readily available resources that provide definitions and concise explanations of terms used in feminist theological and biblical studies, this series will not include a glossary. We refer you to works such as *Dictionary of Feminist Theologies*, edited by Letty M. Russell with J. Shannon Clarkson (Louisville: Westminster John Knox, 1996), and volume 1 of *Searching the Scriptures*, edited by Elisabeth Schüssler Fiorenza with the assistance of Shelly Matthews (New York: Crossroad, 1992). Individual authors in the Wisdom Commentary series will define the way they are using terms that may be unfamiliar.

Bibliography

Because bibliographies are quickly outdated and because the space is limited, only a list of Works Cited is included in the print volumes. A comprehensive bibliography for each volume is posted on a dedicated website and is updated regularly. The link for this volume can be found at wisdomcommentary.org.

A Concluding Word

In just a few short decades, feminist biblical studies has grown exponentially, both in the methods that have been developed and in the number of scholars who have embraced it. We realize that this series is limited and will soon need to be revised and updated. It is our hope that Wisdom Commentary, by making the best of current feminist biblical scholarship available in an accessible format to ministers, preachers, teachers, scholars, and students, will aid all readers in their advancement toward God's vision of dignity, equality, and justice for all.

Acknowledgments

There are a great many people who have made this series possible: first, Peter Dwyer, director of Liturgical Press, and Hans Christoffersen, publisher of the academic market at Liturgical Press, who have believed in this project and have shepherded it since it was conceived in 2008. Editorial consultants Athalya Brenner-Idan and Elisabeth Schüssler Fiorenza have not only been an inspiration with their pioneering work but have encouraged us all along the way with their personal involvement. Volume editors Mary Ann Beavis, Carol J. Dempsey, Amy-Jill Levine, Linda M. Maloney, Ahida Pilarski, Sarah Tanzer, Lauress Wilkins Lawrence, and Seung Ai Yang have lent their extraordinary wisdom to the shaping of the series, have used their extensive networks of relationships to secure authors and contributors, and have worked tirelessly to guide their work to completion. Two others who contributed greatly to the shaping of the project at the outset were Linda M. Day and Mignon Jacobs, as well as Barbara E. Bowe of blessed memory (d. 2010). Editorial and research assistant Susan M. Hickman has provided invaluable support with administrative details and arrangements. I am grateful to Brian Eisenschenk and Christine Henderson who have assisted Susan Hickman with the Wiki. There are countless others at Liturgical Press whose daily work makes the production possible. I am especially thankful to Lauren L. Murphy, Managing Editor, and Justin Howell for their work in copyediting, Colleen Stiller, Production Manager, Stephanie Nix, Production Assistant, and Tara Durheim, Associate Publisher for Academic and Monastic Markets.

Authors' Introduction

A few months ago, while working on this commentary, Alice had dinner at the home of Marianne Flynn, a friend, and told her about our project. She responded enthusiastically that she loved the biblical Ruth because of her compassion. In the course of the conversation Marianne contrasted Ruth's behavior with acting ruthlessly. The exchange led Alice to return home and look up the history of the word "ruth." She found the following:

Contemporary English does not use the noun "ruth." The word may originally derive from the Nordic language; it can be traced back to twelfth-century England where it meant "pity or compassion, sorrow or grief because of the fate of another." The adjective and adverb developed in the fourteenth century; the adjective "ruthful" was used as late as the seventeenth century. Someone who is "ruthless" is, according to the dictionary, "without pity or compassion; cruel; merciless."[1] Much to our surprise, no dictionaries we examined derive the word ruth and its extended usage from the biblical character Ruth.[2]

1. Dictionary.com, adapted from the *Random House Dictionary*, 2015. *The Collins English Dictionary Complete and Unabridged* 2012 digital edition provides a similar definition and includes the word "hard-hearted." Other dictionaries contain similar definitions.

2. These dictionaries include the following: *The New Shorter Oxford English Dictionary*, vol. 2, *N–Z* (Oxford: Clarendon, 1993); *A New English Dictionary on Historical Principles*, vol. 8, collected by the Philosophical Society, ed. James A. H. Murray

Retelling the Story

We begin with a simple retelling of the story. We also recognize, and want our readers to recognize, that our summary is inevitably a slight distortion, but we retell the story so that the reader who is unfamiliar with it can appreciate issues that emerge later in our introduction. Retelling any narrative is an interpretation. A teller includes some details and omits others; the details she omits tend to emphasize those she includes. A teller may paraphrase and select words in her retelling that have multiple meanings and nuances. A teller may use synonyms for words in the "original" text, and that "original" may be, as in the case of the book of Ruth, already a translation. These are caveats as we here, very briefly, retell the story of Ruth.

The book of Ruth recounts the story of a family from Bethlehem in Judah—a mother, father, and two sons—who travel to Moab during a time of famine in their own country. While they are in Moab, the father, Elimelech, dies. The sons, Mahlon and Chilion, marry Ruth and Orpah, Moabite women. Ruth and Orpah are both childless when Mahlon and Chilion die. When Naomi learns that the famine is over in Bethlehem, she (now a childless widow) decides to return home. Ruth and Orpah expect to accompany their mother-in-law to Judah, yet Naomi tries to convince them to remain in their own land, arguing that they have more chances for a better life in their own country. Orpah goes back home to her mother's house, but Ruth chooses to remain with Naomi. Ruth, though a Moabite, pledges loyalty to Naomi—to her land, to her people, and even to her God, YHWH.

When the two women arrive in Bethlehem, women of the town greet them, welcoming Naomi back. Naomi shares with them the blessing and loss of her husband and sons that she understands to be her God's doing. The two women have arrived in Bethlehem during the barley harvest, and Ruth sets out to glean, consistent with a provision available in Israel to widows. She gleans in Boaz's field. When Ruth meets Boaz, he is protective of her. When Ruth learns from Naomi that he is

---

(Oxford: Clarendon, 1910); and *Webster's New Universal Unabridged Dictionary*, 2nd ed. (New York: Simon & Schuster, 1979). Webster includes one entry for both the biblical book and character Ruth and another entry for the noun "ruth" meaning "pity, tenderness." It considers both Ruth and ruth a probable contraction of the Middle English word *ruethe*, which it understands to mean compassion. Of course, it is not credible to derive the name of a biblical book and character that predate the Common Era from Middle English. It is possible that the Middle English word *ruethe* derives from the biblical book and character, but we could find no evidence to that effect.

a close relative and may therefore be a potential source of support for the women, Ruth does as Naomi directs: she goes to the threshing floor and, in an encounter with Boaz (the details of which are ambiguous), Ruth asks him to provide security for her. He readily agrees to redeem her, if a closer relative declines. Boaz then meets Naomi's closer kinsman, and they agree that Boaz may acquire both Naomi's land and her daughter-in-law Ruth. Boaz proceeds to marry Ruth; Ruth bears a son, Obed, thereby becoming the ancestress of Israel's King David.

This summary is a skeleton and cheats the richness of the narrative, as we hope our commentary will show, but its intent is to allow the reader unfamiliar with the story to understand the references and allusions embedded in the remainder of the introduction.

A Feminist Approach

The book of Ruth, as even our short retelling shows, lends itself to feminist commentary. Not only is the title of the book named after a woman who is one of the narrative's major characters, but also women (namely, Naomi and Ruth) and women's interests drive the narrative. Even Orpah, who drops out of the narrative after her decision to remain in Moab in chapter 1, reveals herself to be her own person. Obedient to Naomi's urgings, Orpah deviates from the path Ruth chooses. Each of the women's decisions has significant consequences. Of the four named male characters in the story, three die before the end of chapter 1. Boaz, introduced in chapter 2, carries the story through to its ending.

Feminists who read the story today laud the courage of Naomi and her ability to overcome loss; they praise Ruth's determination, and her willingness to risk the known for the unknown, to claim as her own a foreign land, a foreign people, and even a foreign God. They read the story of women who, in the face of tremendous hardship, are determined to survive. The women depend on each other and, at least through part of the narrative, are not dependent on men. They are women who, just as they have cared for their husbands, care for one another. While no one denies that a culture in which men dominated produced the story, and that elements of that patriarchal culture are evident in the story, still the story provides role models for strong, courageous, caring, and risk-taking women in a more egalitarian culture.

The commentary that follows provides considerably greater detail, highlighting feminist values evident in the story while also acknowledging how the narrative has lent itself to reinforcing patriarchal values.

Jewish and Christian Theology/ies of Ruth, Briefly

Though Judaism is more commonly associated with practice than with theology, if one were to identify a Jewish theology for the book of Ruth, it would center on the Hebrew term חסד (which we will refer to through this commentary in terms of its transliteration *ḥesed*), meaning "loving kindness" or "kindness." God acts with loving kindness toward all of creation, toward all human beings, and, in particular, toward God's chosen people. God calls people to act with loving kindness toward one another. A critical theme and value that permeates Israel's identity and the Ruth narrative is this *ḥesed*, which in the Bible is demonstrated, for example, by God (Gen 24:12, 14; Exod 20:6; 2 Sam 2:6); by Jonathan toward David (1 Sam 20:8) and David toward Jonathan (2 Sam 9:1); and by the narrative's key characters in the book of Ruth. As we progress through our commentary, we will pay close attention to this quality.

Christians do not have a theology of the book of Ruth, per se, although they see the narrative's characters acting with godly virtues, which they try to imitate. In addition to loving kindness, they see generosity and courage and, depending on how they interpret the characters' behaviors, fidelity, self-sacrifice, humility, obedience, and perseverance. These are virtues that Christians associate with following Christ.

The Enigma of Ruth

The character of Ruth may well be every bit as wonderful as the above endorsements and a cursory reading of the text suggest. We know what she does, and what she says, and what others say of her, including the praise she receives. Yet we do not know what she is thinking or what inspires her actions and speech. Perhaps selflessness inspired the childless widow to leave her homeland and her culture and her mother's house in order to travel with her mother-in-law to Naomi's homeland, where she might or might not be welcomed. Her mother-in-law likely was at least a little older than she, and she was also a childless widow. Ruth's accompanying her, lest Naomi have to go alone, could merit praise, especially if the trip were dangerous. But perhaps Ruth thought that she was infertile, given that she had been married for ten years without having produced a child, and that going to Judah with Naomi would avoid the shame her infertility might have brought at home. Perhaps Ruth was infatuated with her mother-in-law and intrigued by the thought of a kind of independence from men. Perhaps the thrill of a new place and a new people called to her adventurous spirit. Perhaps she was not quite so selfless. In other words, there are other ways of reading the character of Ruth and the book of Ruth than as a story that reinforces behaviors that are the stereotype of what every "good" woman should do.[3] The character of Ruth may be every bit as wonderful as tradition suggests, but for different reasons.

The Book of Ruth in Jewish and Christian Worship

Jews read the entire book of Ruth annually, on the festival of Shavuot,[4] the holy day that commemorates the giving of the Torah at Sinai. Its reading is meant to engender heartfelt appreciation of Torah and the practice of *ḥesed,* which always requires struggle and sacrifice. It is also a common text for Modern Orthodox B'not Mitzvah (the Jewish coming-of-age ritual for twelve-year-old young women).

Christians, by contrast, read the book selectively and sparsely. Not on any Sundays and only twice every other year on two weekdays do passages occur in the Roman Catholic Lectionary,[5] and these in the form of intermittent verses: Ruth 1:1, 3-6, 14b-16, 22 (paired with Matt 22:34-40,

3. In a recent feature in the *New York Times* (March 8, 2016), the actress Sarah Paulson discussed her portrayal of the lead prosecuting attorney in the O. J. Simpson murder trial, Marcia Clark (John Koblin, "Sarah Paulson on Playing the Bruising Role of Marcia Clark," http://www.nytimes.com/2016/03/09/business/media/sarah-paulson-on-playing-the-bruising-role-of-marcia-clark.html?_r=0). In the article, Paulson admits to her criticism of Ms. Clark's appearance and demeanor during the trial (Paulson was nineteen years old at the time). Now, as an older woman and the actress chosen to play the part of Ms. Clark, Paulson realizes the arrogance and stupidity of her judgments and describes the media's criticism of Ms. Clark during the O. J. Simpson trial as a "witch trial" of Ms. Clark. Paulson states, "The idea that a woman who was very strong, who wore maybe shorter skirts than people thought was appropriate, had a bad haircut, didn't wear a lot of makeup, looked a little tired because she was raising a 3- and 5-year-old and was going through a divorce and was trying the trial of the century, should be taken to task for her lack of concealer and her bad haircut?" Looking back, Paulson realized that the media was demanding the "stereotypical good woman" when judging Ms. Clark, including a feminine hairstyle and a smile. What the article reveals in relation to Ruth is the ease with which interpreters can make facile, albeit incorrect, judgments of women.

4. Leviticus 23:15-22 describes this harvest festival, often called the festival of weeks, that takes place the day after seven weeks after the offering of first fruits. The festival comes into Greek as Pentecost.

5. The lectionary is a book that contains the biblical readings most mainline Christians officially designate to be read at specific religious services.

Jesus' teaching on the two great commandments)[6] and Ruth 2:1-3, 8-11; 4:13-17 (paired with Matt 23:1-12, Jesus' denunciation of the scribes and Pharisees).[7] Apparently the pairing of the verses from Ruth with the selected passage from Matthew 22 was done because the reading from Ruth depicts the love of God and neighbor of which the gospel speaks. The verses record the family's journey to Moab, the death of Elimelech, the marriages of Chilion and Mahlon, their deaths, and then Ruth's pledge of loyalty to Naomi, including to her land, her people, and her God. The verses from Ruth paired with the passage from Matthew 23 detail the barley harvest, Ruth's gleaning in Boaz's field, Ruth's marriage to Boaz and the birth of their son, the fact that Ruth is worth more to Naomi than seven sons, and the genealogy that links Obed to David. The text provides a strong contrast to the behavior that Jesus is denouncing and, in the likely interpretation of the liturgists, embodies Jesus' teaching that "all who exalt themselves will be humbled, and all who humble themselves will be exalted" (Matt 23:12). While a feminist critique laments the fact that the lectionary relegates these important passages from the book of Ruth to biennial reading and omits entirely other significant passages from Ruth,[8] the pairing of these texts with the Matthean texts does highlight their importance.

Couples often choose Ruth 1:14-16 as a reading for wedding ceremonies.[9] In the text Ruth pledges lifelong loyalty, and even loyalty beyond death, to her mother-in-law Naomi. Read as a covenant of lifelong commitment similar to the one the two persons marrying wish to make to each other, the reading is very appropriate. Some feminists who read the text more literally—Ruth pledging loyalty until death and beyond to another woman—believe the use of the text at a marriage between two heterosexuals distorts the actual text and is an example of how heterosexuality has dominated all relationships.

6. Matthew 22:34-40 is also read on the Thirtieth Sunday in Ordinary Time, Year A.

7. Matthew 23:1-12 is also read on the Thirty-First Sunday in Ordinary Time, Year A.

8. We cannot help but notice and lament the omission of the threshing-floor scene in Ruth 3, which has much to say about loyalty and courage and which could easily be paired with any of many readings central to the New Testament. Another egregious omission from the lectionary readings is the passage in the book of Esther (1:1–2:4) that details another woman's (Queen Vashti) courage in the face of her drunken husband (a text that, unfortunately, would resonate with the experience of many women).

9. The Roman Catholic edition of the lectionary provides a choice of readings for wedding Masses but does not include the Ruth passage.

Cultural Interpretation

While Jewish and Christian and other biblical scholars have interpreted the book of Ruth throughout history, literary and visual artists have also contributed their interpretations of the book and its characters. In his *Divine Comedy* (*Paradiso*, canto 32: Tenth Heaven: The Empyrean), Dante Alighieri (1265–1321) describes Ruth as "the gleaner-made, meek ancestress of David the psalmist"; in John Bunyan's (1628–1688) *Pilgrim's Progress*, Ruth is the model for Christiana's youthful companion Mercy; and in John Milton's (1608–1674) *Paradise Lost*, Ruth is the paradigm for his virtuous young lady.

Visual artists, including those anonymous artists who produced illustrations in early Bible manuscripts, have also depicted characters and scenes from the story of Ruth. One can find depictions of Ruth clinging to Naomi, of Ruth and Boaz, of Naomi nursing Ruth's child as Ruth stands by, and more. Because most of this art is small, painted at the corner of a page, the facial features and emotional qualities are hard to determine. Later, Michelangelo portrayed Ruth as a Madonna figure with Obed in a fresco on an arch in the Sistine Chapel (between 1508 and 1512). Rembrandt's 1650 sketch of "Boaz pouring six measures of barley into Ruth's veil" depicts Ruth leaning gracefully toward Boaz in a manner that communicates her pleasure. Nicolas Poussin's "Ruth Meets Boaz" (1660) depicts Ruth kneeling before Boaz. The characters are small, set in a large landscape with other gleaners and harvesters in the background; still, Ruth is kneeling at Boaz's feet. William Blake's 1795 painting "Ruth and Naomi" portrays Naomi with hands outstretched as if she were saying to Ruth, "I have nothing to offer." Both James Tissot (1896) and Marc Chagall (1960) have paintings titled "Ruth Gleaning." While Tissot's watercolor contrasts Ruth with the other women gleaners (they are working back-to-back, while Ruth stands alone), Chagall captures the heat of the sun under which Ruth was working with bright reds and oranges. Chagall produced a series on Ruth in 1960, including "Ruth, Naomi and Orpah," that depicts the three women working in the field clinging so closely to each other that their bodies look almost inseparable. Also in the series are "Ruth and Boaz Meet," which captures the joy and exuberance of their encounter, and two paintings on the threshing floor. In "Ruth at the Feet of Boaz," Chagall has depicted Ruth's breasts bared but her head is at his feet. In "Boaz Wakens and Sees Ruth at His Feet," Boaz is standing. Both are naked, and the paintings leave open the possibility of an intimate sexual encounter. Philip Hermogenes Calderone's

1920 "Ruth and Naomi" is deeply expressive and worth noting. We will discuss it more at length later in the commentary.

Whether in the form of literary production or artistic expression, Ruth became an ongoing meaningful ingredient in Western culture and lent herself to a wide range of interpretations. What the artist intended to capture in the work and what the viewer or reader sees are to some extent determined by the cultural circumstances in which the work was produced (conformity to or divergence from them). How the reader or viewer engages the work is similarly dependent. The feminist may prefer one or another production because of his or her interpretation of the character of Ruth and how the work of art confirms or challenges that interpretation.

We are aware that men have dominated Western public culture, as the art examples above illustrate. But two women artists are worth noting. The Dutch-French Romantic painter Ary Sheffer produced "Ruth and Naomi" somewhere in the mid-nineteenth century. She captures the moment when Naomi is directing Ruth to return home and Ruth, placing her hand over Naomi's, seemingly declines. While considered sentimental, Sheffer's work captures well the poignancy of the exchange. In 2006, the American artist Sandy Freckleton Gagan produced an oil-on-canvas painting of Ruth and Naomi titled "Whither Thou Goest," which brings the two women together under a shared cape. Each is full of personality, with Naomi having gray hair and a walking stick but also eyes determined and looking outward. Ruth is looking at Naomi with a posture that depicts the seriousness of their situation and of her commitment. The two women are clearly en route together.

A Pleasure, an Opportunity, and a Challenge

Introducing the book of Ruth is a pleasure, an opportunity, and a challenge. It is a pleasure because the book has the distinction of being one of only three books in the Old Testament[10] named after a woman, a woman who is the book's leading character. The other books are Esther and Judith. Esther rises to fame as queen because she is beautiful and more sexually seductive than the other women with whom she competes. (King Ahasuerus had banished the former queen, Vashti, because she refused to obey the directive of her drunken husband to come to his party and display her beauty.) Judith, who is well represented in Renais-

10. As the general introduction suggests, we are using the term "Old Testament" to refer to the books included in the Tanakh and also those books considered by some Christian communities as Deuterocanonical.

sance art, exchanges her widow's clothing for attractive attire, seduces the Assyrian general Holofernes, and cuts off his head, thereby saving not only her own city, Bethulia, but Jerusalem as well. Susanna, whose tale appears in the Greek versions of Daniel, is technically not its own book of the Old Testament, yet she deserves mention. She is known for her beauty and her purity and for rejecting the advances of some lascivious elders, even at the risk of death.

Ruth provides support for her mother-in-law and becomes the great-grandmother of King David. While these narratives may be, in contemporary terms, fiction,[11] like all narratives they communicate cultural values important at the time of their composition—either reinforcing them, resisting them, or demonstrating a complex combination of both—and they continue to do so today. Because these narratives all have women at their center, the values they impart affect women in particular.

Writing a commentary on the book of Ruth for the Wisdom Commentary series is also an opportunity. It is an opportunity for the writers, and ideally for the readers as well, to reflect deeply on the character of Ruth in her own time and in ours. Who she was in her own time is important for who she is and can be for us. Ruth, like all of us, lived in a world of limited choices, yet she broadened those choices. She did not passively accept the status quo, the stereotype, the expected; she chose a future and pursued it. She disobeyed her mother-in-law to remain with her; in traveling west, she risked the known for the unknown; she chose unfamiliarity and insecurity; she worked hard and risked her reputation. And when Ruth did the stereotypical thing that women often do—marry and have a child—it was because she chose to do it. If she could behave thusly in the culture of ancient Israel, surely she provides a role model for what women can do today. The complex character whose life is set in the time of the Judges but whose story may date from centuries later can be interpreted in multiple ways; reading Ruth from our vantage point can, among other things, deepen our compassion, increase our perseverance, and affirm our sexuality.

Although Ruth is the leading character in the narrative, she is not the only character. Women dominate the story: Ruth's mother-in-law Naomi, her sister-in-law Orpah, and the women of the city. Yet Boaz is not to be forgotten; nor should we forget the three men of Bethlehem—Elkanah, Mahlon, and Chilion—whose deaths left three women widows. Some

11. The distinction between "truth" (fact) and "fiction" is a modern one. Sometimes fiction is the best conveyor of truth.

of Ruth's actions, and the decision making that leads to them, take place in response to circumstances beyond her control. Her responses to those circumstances allow the narrative to unfold as it does, and they allow contemporary readers to bring their stories to her story—for comparison and contrast, for insight and inspiration, for challenge and change.

Finally, writing a commentary on the book of Ruth is a challenge. As with all books of the Bible, the book of Ruth has been studied and reflected upon for centuries, from multiple perspectives using multiple methods. While the last fifty or so years have added the insights of more women scholars regarding the text, the contributions of these scholars are as diverse as the women themselves, and they have added to the complexity of the history of interpretation. The challenge in a new feminist commentary is to collect and present what we consider the best of traditional and contemporary scholarship while adding our own voices, the insights to which our study and reflection have led. We have tried to do our best.

The co-authors of this commentary, Mahri and Alice, both believe that Barbara Reid has done an excellent job in presenting, in the general introduction, "methodologies." She has taken the reader on a whirlwind tour from modernity's introduction of objectivity and historical criticism to postmodernity's critique of the possibility of total objectivity, and the introduction of methods that admit that the reader/interpreter's social location or, more precisely, subject position (for we are both products of our context and individuals) matters. We note that some premodern assumptions and methods have resurfaced as a part of postmodernity. Communities infused by faith, the assumption that dominated premodernity, now understand themselves as comprising a distinct social location as well as a distinctive interpretive lens.[12] The plurality of interpretation and the legitimacy of contradiction, which are integral to early rabbinic interpretation, reassert themselves in postmodernity.

Placement of the Book in the Canon

We assume that a presumption of historical truth is the reason behind Christians' placement of the book of Ruth between the books of Judges

12. Sandra M. Schneiders has been a leader among Roman Catholic feminist scholars in arguing for a privileged place for the believing community in postmodern interpretation in *The Revelatory Text: Interpreting the New Testament as Sacred Scripture*, rev. ed. (Collegeville, MN: Liturgical Press, 1999).

and 1 Samuel. The first-century Jewish scholar Josephus similarly places Ruth after the book of Judges (ending with Samson) and before the birth of Samuel in his *Antiquities of the Jews*. The Jewish canon places the book among the Writings (Ketuvim), between the book of Proverbs and the Song of Songs. Ruth, the woman of strength (3:11), resonates with the woman of strength depicted in Proverbs 31:1 and with the independent young woman in the love story of Songs of Songs, who goes after her beloved in the middle of the night (Song 3:1-4; 5:6-7). The book of Ruth is the second of the "Five Megillot" or scrolls in the Writings that include Song of Songs, the book of Ruth, the book of Lamentations, Ecclesiastes, and the book of Esther.

Neither position necessarily accords the book greater or lesser status. However, Rajkumar Boaz Johnson, one of our contributing voices, reflects below, from his context, on the importance of the placement of the book.

The Book of Ruth and the Slums of India

I was reared in one of the slums of New Delhi. The slums are composed of low-caste and outcast peoples' groups who have fled extreme forms of slavery and humiliation in rural India. They are looking for an escape. Women and children—girls and boys—are property of high-caste landowners in rural India, where 80 percent of India lives. These high-caste landowners use and abuse them in whichever way they desire, all in the name of religion. Yet, when these people come to urban areas like Delhi, Mumbai, and Mother Teresa's Calcutta, they find themselves in deeper enslavement to the high-caste lords of the slums. The low-caste and outcast, shudra and atishudra, according to Hindu religion, deserve their lot. They are fulfilling their karma. I made up my mind, from the time I was a child, that when I grew up I was going to do something to change this.

Every year between 10,000 and 20,000 farmers commit suicide in India. Eighty percent of India lives in the rural, agriculture-based economy. Sure, India has experienced economic growth in recent years. But this economic growth has only helped the minority high-caste communities further enslave the majority low-caste and outcast communities—all in the name of religion.

This, in brief, is the background to these comments on the book of Ruth. The story of Ruth and Boaz takes on quite a different meaning when read by a low-caste and outcast person. The story addresses the issues I have raised from two different perspectives, the LXX, Christian Bible canonical perspective and the Hebrew Bible canonical perspective.

The LXX puts the book of Ruth right after the book of Judges. This canonical sequence follows the narrative in Judges 21, where the elders of Israel advise the Benjaminite young men to violently seize the daughters of Shiloh (vs. 21). Judges 21:23 reports that they did indeed "lift up" (נשא) women into what may be termed sexual slavery.

The book of Ruth follows the book of Judges with a description of the attitude of the sons of Elimelech and Naomi toward the women of Moab. Ruth 1:4 reads, "They took [נשא] for themselves Moabite women." In other words, they did precisely the same thing to Moabite women that the Benjaminite young men had done to the daughters of Shiloh, i.e., they raped them. In the NRSV as in most English Bibles, the text reads, "they married Moabite women." However, the Hebrew word is more descriptive of certain groups of women, like the daughters of Shiloh, who were used, "raised" for temple prostitution.

This is indeed a very disturbing picture. Such aggression is commonplace in rural and slum India. High-caste men consider it their right to rape low-caste women, because it is their religious duty to do so. Low-caste women and boys are called *nautch*, dance girls and boys. They belong to castes like the *kanjaris*, prostitutes. Therefore, they are forcibly taken by high-caste men and raped in a religiously oriented and religiously sanctioned act. It seems clear to me that the story of Ruth is addressing this horrible practice and attitude—both then and now.

In the Hebrew canon, the book of Ruth follows the book of Proverbs, where Ruth, like the capable wife/valiant woman of Proverbs 31:10 is described as an אשת חיל (*eshet ḥayil*)—a physically, mentally, spiritually strong woman (Ruth 3:11, 4:11).

Rajkumar Boaz Johnson

History of Interpretation

Premodernity

The biblical book of Ruth is part of both the Jewish and Christian canons of Scripture and has therefore been the subject of interpretation and a participant in the development of culture, especially in the West, throughout history.[13] Jews reflected on the book and tried to determine its purpose. The authors of Ruth Rabbah 2.8 reasoned that the book's purpose was to tell us how great the reward is for those who practice loving kindness.[14] The Midrash Yalkut Lekach Tov asserts that the book is meant to establish the greatness of King David's lineage,[15] whereas the Midrash Yalkut Shimoni states that the book is meant to show that if one does the right thing, one will eventually see success. According to this medieval-period midrash, which likely repeats interpretations from earlier rabbinic texts, many Jewish communities read Ruth on the festival of Shavuot.[16]

Jews consider Ruth the "model of faith, the mother of all converts to Judaism."[17] The rabbis recognized her as a righteous person,[18] but she was also a Moabite. While the narrative of Ruth does not disparage the Moabites, Deuteronomy 23:3-6 forbade the Moabites' admission to the congregation of the Lord.[19] The rabbis needed to reconcile her righteous character and her Moabite identity. They found a way: basing their interpretation on the masculine singular form in the biblical text, מואבי (Moabite, Deut 23:3), only *male* Moabites were forbidden to come

13. Ruth does not appear in the Qur'an and is therefore not the object of Islamic interpretation.

14. *Ruth Rabbah*, trans. L. Rabinowitz, vol. 8 of *Midrash Rabbah*, 2nd ed. (London: Soncino, 1971). Ruth Rabbah is a sixth-century compilation of earlier rabbinic traditions that was first printed as *Midrash Ruth* in 1545 and later became known as Ruth Rabbah when it was printed together with midrashim on the Torah and other scrolls. Midrash (plural midrashim) is a genre devoted to exegesis and analysis of passages in the Tanakh; midrashim span the tannaitic period (pre-200 CE), the amoraic period (c. 400 CE), and into the early Middle Ages and beyond.

15. From the *Zohar Hadash* on the book of Ruth, 31b, cited in Rabbi Yehuda Y. Steinberg, *Harvest of Kindness: Megillas Rus and the Power of Chesed*, 18 (Southfield, MI: Targum Press, Inc., 2010). The Zohar is a library of medieval kabbalistic texts that come from late thirteenth- to early fourteenth-century Spain. The library contains twenty-four documents comprising three separate bibliographic entries: *Zohar Hadash*, *Tiqqune Ha-Zohar*, and the *Zohar* itself. Not surprisingly, early Christian commentary on Ruth agrees with Jewish sources regarding the importance of the book's genealogy of David, since David is the ancestor of Jesus (Matt 1:1-16).

16. See n. 4.

17. Athalya Brenner, *I Am . . .: Biblical Women Tell Their Own Stories* (Minneapolis: Fortress, 2005), 102.

18. Ruth Rab. 2.12.

19. The text explains that the Moabites did not meet the Israelites with food and water on their journey out of Egypt; they also hired Balaam, the prophet, to curse the Israelites.

into the congregation of the Lord. The rabbis thus permitted both the conversion of and marriage to Moabite women.[20]

Another aspect of Ruth's identity that concerned the rabbis was Ruth's beauty. While many contemporary feminists lament the amount of attention given to (and money spent on) women's physical beauty, other times and other cultures have considered the outside (physical appearance) as an expression of the inside (the heart). For whatever reason, the rabbis speculated whether or not Ruth was beautiful and concluded that she was. According to Ruth Rabbah 4.4, Boaz noticed her because she looked much younger than her age: about Naomi's referring to Ruth as daughter, Rabbi Jannai commented: "She was forty years of age and yet you call her daughter? The answer is that she looked like a girl of fourteen."[21] Today, some Orthodox Jewish communities have embraced reading Ruth along with certain other biblical texts as a way to increase women's liturgical participation. Some women host all-women readings, an innovative practice that is encouraged by the Jewish Orthodox Feminist Alliance (JOFA).[22] Historically, men have read the scroll on the afternoon of Shavuot, though some communities have added the practice of having women read the scroll for the congregation.

Early Christian biblical interpretation focused on Jesus, whom Christians believe to be the center of history. For early interpreters of the Christian Bible, the content of the Hebrew Bible/Old Testament was helpful insofar as it shed light on the person of Jesus and the central tenets of the Christian faith. Themes such as creation and the fall (Genesis), the praise of God and petition to God in the Psalms (read a-historically), and the promise of a Messiah received much more attention than the depiction of the giving of the Torah to Moses on Mount Sinai or even the exile. David was of course important because he was the king of Israel, ancestor of the new "King of the Jews." It is not surprising, therefore, that for early Christians (remember that those having close access to the biblical texts were almost, if not exclusively, all men) the book of Ruth derives its importance because of Ruth's identity as the great-grandmother of

20. B. Yebam. 76b–77a, cited in Leila Leah Bronner, *From Eve to Esther: Rabbinic Reconstructions of Biblical Women* (Louisville: Westminster John Knox, 1994), 64.

21. Cited in ibid., 75.

22. See https://www.jofa.org/megillat-ruth-book-club. We are indebted to Lynn Kaye for her insights into contemporary practices of Orthodox women.

David and therefore an ancestor of Jesus. Matthew 1 includes Ruth in the genealogy that traces Jewish history from Abraham to Jesus.[23]

Early Christian interpretation of elements of the book of Ruth and the character of Ruth, like that of most biblical books and characters, did not originally take place in formal commentaries but in comments that were often embedded in sermons or in letters or essays written for other purposes. Hippolytus of Rome (170–236) and Origen (c. 184–253), while saying nothing of Ruth's physical appearance, present her as a role model and an ideal based on her perceived virtues. St. Ambrose (c. 340–397), commenting on the Gospel's extension to all peoples, references Ruth, the foreigner who married a Jew and who is included in Jesus' genealogy. St. Jerome (c. 347–420), writing to someone who had just lost a loved one, praises Ruth for her protection of the bereaved Naomi and identifies her reward as becoming an ancestor of Christ.[24] Isidore of Seville (c. 560–636) identifies Ruth as a "type"[25] of the Gentiles, representing the pagans who converted to Christianity or of the church.[26] Aelred of Rievaulx (1110–1167) uses Boaz's treatment of Ruth as a model of friendship and of how to treat others.[27] Hugh of Saint-Cher (c. 1200–1263) describes the book of Ruth as being a "little story of Christ and the Church, in which

23. Matthew also includes Tamar, Rahab, the wife of Uriah, and Mary in the genealogy. Because both Tamar and Rahab figure in the book of Ruth, we will discuss the inclusion of these women in the Matthean genealogy later.

24. John R. Francke, ed., *Ancient Christian Commentary on Scripture: Old Testament*, vol. 4: *Joshua, Judges, Ruth, 1–2 Samuel* (Downers Grove, IL: InterVarsity Press, 2005), 181–82.

25. Christian exegesis often saw an Old Testament person, object, or event as a type, that is, a prefigurement of some person, object, or event in the New Testament or in the church.

26. Lesley Smith, *Medieval Exegesis in Translation: Commentaries on the Book of Ruth* (Kalamazoo: Western Michigan University, 1996), 8. See also Elena Giannarelli, "Ruth in the Church Fathers," *SIDIC* 23 (1990): 12–15.

27. Aelred writes, "When Boaz observed the poverty of Ruth, the Moabite, he spoke to her as she was gathering ears of corn behind his reapers, consoled her and invited her to the table of his servants, and sparing in kindly fashion her embarrassment, he ordered his reapers to leave ears of corn even purposefully so that she might collect them without shame. In the same way we ought the more adroitly seek out the needs of our friends, anticipate their requests by good service, and observe such demeanor in our giving that the recipient, rather than the giver, appears to be bestowing the favor" (*On Spiritual Friendship*, ed. Marsha L. Dutton, trans. Lawrence C. Braceland, CF 5 [Collegeville, MN: Cistercian Publications, 2010], 119).

the sacraments lie hidden."[28] Finally, "none of Augustine's writings contains any comments on Ruth," perhaps because "Ruth contains no theological problems or doctrinal difficulties; its problems are only the understanding of linguistic queries and Hebrew custom."[29]

While premodern Christian biblical interpreters presumed the literal accuracy of the biblical text, insofar as nothing they knew contradicted it, they understood literal accuracy to be of minor importance.[30] Of considerably greater importance were the text's spiritual purposes. Assuming that God inspired the biblical text and that it contains revelation, early Christians believed that the Bible's primary purpose was to reveal God and to inspire God's people to be faithful to God's teachings.

Modernity

Early rabbinic and early Christian interpretation of biblical texts was dependent on assumptions tied to faith and the sacred character of the Bible as well as the interpreters' own personal and communal social locations in a culture of faith. In contrast, the Enlightenment and modernity deemphasized faith and questioned divine authorship and divine inspiration of the Bible. Consequently, those interested in studying the Bible began to do so while bracketing faith assumptions and commitments. With the ascendancy of reason, scholars began to ask what could factually be known about the world that produced the biblical texts and what the Scriptures meant for that world. History began to increase in importance. Understanding the texts required knowledge of the political,

28. Smith, *Medieval Exegesis in Translation*, 41. We have no record of what Hugh of St. Cher was identifying as the sacraments, but, in accord with the definition of sacrament, we can assume that he was referring to various acts of kindness embedded in the narrative that would make God present.

29. Man Ki Chan, *A Comparative Study of Jewish Commentaries and Patristic Literature on the Book of Ruth* (PhD diss., University of Pretoria, 2010).

30. Early Christian acceptance of the literal accuracy of the biblical texts differs significantly from contemporary fundamentalism insofar as the literal accuracy of the texts was assumed but of relatively little importance to early Christians. Their concerns were spiritual, and their methods of interpretation were often symbolic and allegorical. Contemporary fundamentalists, on the other hand, defend with great commitment the literal accuracy of the biblical texts. For them, God cannot err, and since the Bible is the word of God, everything contained in it must be *factually* true. Fundamentalists differ also from many modern and postmodern Christians who, while continuing to consider the texts inspired and sources of revelation, recognize factual errors in the text, which they associate with the limited knowledge of the texts' human authors.

cultural, and social contexts in which they were produced, that is, *the world behind the texts*. The study of archaeology and the geography of the Ancient Near East rose in importance, as did the study of cognate languages, including Sumerian, Egyptian, Phoenician, Ugaritic, and eventually Eblaite.[31] Histories of Israel became common.[32]

Rather than asking what was going on *in* the book of Ruth, scholarship shifted to what was going on in the world that produced the book of Ruth. The biblical texts became subject to analysis as any ancient document would be—Who wrote them? When? Why? How did their literary form contribute to the accomplishment of their purpose?

At the same time historical scholars came to recognize the instability of the text: the difficulty in determining the earliest manuscripts and the discrepancies among hand-copied texts.[33] Text-critical scholars developed rules to try to determine which readings were more accurate. Moderns came to separate what the ancients believed from what they [the moderns] believed. Ruth was no longer forty, as Rabbi Jannai had said (who could know her age?), nor was she a type of the church, as Isidore of Seville had posited. They assumed that Old Testament texts had primary meanings in their own historical contexts and were not written as predictors of the coming of Christ, nor did they contain details about a Messiah yet to come. The author of Ruth was human, not divine, and therefore, his (or her, or even their) knowledge was limited. Even had Ruth lived when the book said she did, "in the days when the Judges ruled" (1:1), the book could not have been written before the time of David, since David is mentioned in the text. But did Ruth live at all? Perhaps its author *created* the narrative for some political or social purpose, such as to reinforce or challenge existing values or practices. These were modern issues. There is, indeed, an objectivity in who wrote a text, when it was written, and the identification of its literary form, and there is an objectivity in the effort to establish the cultural world that produced the text; to the extent that this information can be known, it can reveal

31. For translations of many ancient Egyptian, Assyrian, and Babylonian texts, see James A. Pritchard, *The Ancient Near East: An Anthology of Texts* (Princeton: Princeton University Press, 2010).

32. Among the standard histories of Israel are Martin Noth's *History of Israel*, 2nd ed. (New York: HarperCollins, 1960); John Bright's *A History of Israel*, 4th ed. (Louisville: Westminster John Knox, 2000), and J. Maxwell Miller's *A History of Ancient Israel and Judah*, 2nd ed. (Louisville: Westminster John Knox, 2006).

33. See, for example, Bruce Metzger and Bart Ehrman's work on the New Testament (*The Text of the New Testament: Its Transmission, Corruption, and Restoration* [New York: Oxford University Press, 2005]).

objectively the text's purpose.[34] Answering modernity's questions and wrestling with its issues led, in the case of the book of Ruth, to several theories about when the narrative was written, why, and by whom.

Dating

Scholars have theorized that Ruth is a folktale that recasts certain incidents in the myth of the Egyptian goddess Isis;[35] others see the story as a Hebraized version of the Eleusinian mysteries in which Naomi and Ruth take the roles of Demeter the goddess of grain and Persephone, her daughter brought to the underworld;[36] still others find in Ruth a story of a sacred prostitute from Moab, who goes to Bethlehem's "sacred high places" (the threshing floor) to be impregnated as a mother-goddess of the Davidic line.[37] The scholars who developed these theories believed that the Israelites adapted one or another of the foreign myths to create a mythological or epic backdrop for the ancestry of David.[38] "Older"[39] scholars who put forth these views, which are for the most part abandoned today, represent a period in historical criticism that sought insight into biblical texts from the literature of surrounding peoples.

While the intent may have been to provide a backdrop for the ancestry of David, these comparisons with deity also served to raise Ruth's stature. Most recently, building on comparative literature, the feminist Susan McCaslin has brought together Naomi and Ruth with Persephone and Demeter in her poem, "Persephone Finds Ruth on the Threshing

34. Dennis J. McCarthy examined the historical and cultural shifts in "God as Prisoner of Our Own Choosing: Critical-Historical Study of the Bible, Why and Wither," in *Historicism and Faith: Proceedings of the Fellowship of Catholic Scholars*, ed. Paul L. Williams (Scranton, PA: Northeast Books, 1980), 17–47.

35. Herman Gunkel, "Ruth," in *Reden und Aufsaetze* (Göttingen: Vandenhoeck & Ruprecht, 1913), 65–92, esp. 90–92; cited in Jack M. Sasson, *Ruth: A New Translation with a Philological Commentary and a Formalist-Folklorist Interpretation* (Baltimore: Johns Hopkins University Press, 1979), 248.

36. Michael C. Astour, *Hellenosemitica: An Ethnic and Cultural Study in West Semitic Impact on Mycenaean Greece* (Leiden: Brill, 1967), 278–79; cited in Sasson, *Ruth*, 248.

37. Sasson and others criticize this line of thinking; see Sasson, *Ruth*, 248; also H. G. May, "Ruth's Visit to the High Place at Bethlehem," *JRAS* (1939): 75–78.

38. Jack M. Sasson, "Ruth," in *The Literary Guide to the Bible*, ed. Robert Alter and Frank Kermode (Cambridge: Harvard University Press, 1987), 320. These theories assume the proximity and interdependence of cultures or of later civilizations borrowing from earlier ones.

39. Ibid.

Floor."[40] McCaslin's poem highlights the "woman to woman" relationship between Naomi and Ruth, Persephone's encouragement of Ruth's seduction of Boaz, and then, assuming sexual intercourse on the threshing floor in Ruth 3, speaks of Jesse and David and "numberless unnamed daughters" who proceed from their union that night.

In attempting to determine when the book of Ruth was written, scholars have examined the Hebrew used in the narrative—its vocabulary and grammatical structures.[41] Answering the question requires that one look for words and phrases contained in the book that appear only in later, exilic (roughly 586–539 BCE) or postexilic (post-539 BCE) Hebrew. If one finds no such vocabulary or grammar, one may credibly date the book sometime in the preexilic period, which could be as early as the tenth century or as late as the seventh century BCE, although there is increased wariness of dating any of the biblical books as early as the tenth century based on the lack of evidence for writing in ancient Israel during the early monarchic period. "Preexilic" has more often come to mean the time after the fall of the northern kingdom of Israel to the Assyrians (722 BCE).[42]

The book of Ruth does contain some linguistic markers that occur only in later biblical Hebrew, most important of which is the presence of four "Aramaisms" (words adopted from Aramaic).[43] The influence of Aramaic on Hebrew became significant during and after the Babylonian exile, and the presence of Aramaisms could therefore support the notion that the book is exilic or postexilic.[44] However, the number of Aramaisms is

40. Susan McCaslin, "Persephone Finds Ruth on the Threshing Floor," *JFSR* 28 (2010): 101–2.

41. For discussions of the question of language in relation to the dating of the book of Ruth, see Edward F. Campbell, *Ruth*, AB 7 (New York: Doubleday, 1975), 23–28; Sasson, *Ruth*, 244–46; and Tamara Eskenazi and Tikva Frymer-Kensky, *The JPS Bible Commentary: Ruth* (Philadelphia: Jewish Publication Society of America, 2011), xvii–xviii.

42. Scholars have reconstructed Israel's history, taking into consideration both the dominance and perseverance of the oral tradition as well as an increased incentive to create a written record after the Assyrian invasion.

43. These four Aramaisms are the following: (1) The *piel* infinitive construct of קום (לקים) in 4:7, denoting "to confirm" or "to fulfill"; (2) the use of שלף and נעל together in 4:7 and 4:8, denoting "remove a sandal"; (3) the rare verb שבר in 1:13 meaning "to hope, wait for"; and (4) the *hitpael* form of the verb עגן in 1:13, meaning "to hinder (oneself), keep (oneself) from" (see also Robert H. Holmstedt, *Ruth: A Handbook on the Hebrew Text* [Waco, TX: Baylor University Press, 2010], 37–39). See also Eskenazi and Frymer-Kensky, *Ruth*, xvii.

44. Amy-Jill Levine suggests that the text is postexilic based on the Aramaisms present ("Ruth," *Women's Bible Commentary*, ed. Carol A. Newsom and Sharon H. Ringe, exp. ed. [Louisville: Westminster John Knox, 1998], 84–90, esp. 85). Levine

quite small, to some even negligible;[45] moreover, the Hebrew influenced by Aramaic may have entered an earlier established text at a later date. As such, the presence of Aramaisms does not "prove" a late dating and may be unreliable as a means of dating a text.[46]

Dating Ruth is not just a matter of language. What was going on in the world behind the text that would have made its production more likely at one time than another? Certain aspects of the text make it "fit" in the preexilic period, while others suggest its composition after the exile. Here, we examine both sides with our distinct voices; Mahri presents the preexilic argument and Alice the postexilic one. Readers may see contradictions in the two arguments presented here, which is the result of two people interpreting the same text differently. It is up to the reader to decide which argument she or he prefers.

The Preexilic Argument

We consider first why numerous scholars (including Mahri) support the possibility of a preexilic dating.[47] When examining the book of Ruth as literature, the story and its style compare well to older, preexilic nar-

---

comments that if the text is postexilic, then it may be written as a reaction against the idea of enforced divorce of foreign wives in Ezra–Nehemiah, "even as it reflects the society's suspicion of foreign wives." In other words, while one could argue that the text reflects an alternative perspective to Ezra–Nehemiah in the postexilic period, the narrative itself is not entirely void of suspicion of foreign women, as demonstrated in the consistent focus on Ruth's Moabite heritage. Levine's comments indicate uncertainty about the date of the book's origin.

45. See the careful discussion in Campbell, *Ruth*, 22–23. Others have argued that some grammatical structures in Ruth are used elsewhere only in late passages, yet this is debatable; nowhere, it seems, does the book employ language, syntax, or grammar that is clearly and inescapably limited to late biblical Hebrew.

46. Holmstedt (*Ruth*, 31) finds it difficult to determine definitively the date of the book of Ruth on its linguistic features, as there are earlier and later linguistic indicators present in the book. He concludes that "the data suggest that the book sits on the relative dating line between books like Gen–Deut, Josh–Kings on the one side and Ezra-Neh, Chronicles, and Qohelet on the other." See also Sasson, who objects to the use of these Aramaisms to date Ruth; he writes that "dating a Hebrew text on literary and linguistic bases will continue to be a most unreliable approach as long as our extrabiblical corpus of Hebrew vocabulary remains as sparse as it is presently" (*Ruth*, 244; also A. Hurvitz, "The Chronological Significance of 'Aramaisms' in Biblical Hebrew," *IEJ* 18 [1968]: 234–40; and Campbell, *Ruth*, 24–25).

47. Arguments for preexilic dating can be found in, among others, Campbell, *Ruth*, 26–27; Sasson, *Ruth*, 250–52; Robert L. Hubbard, *The Book of Ruth* (Grand Rapids: Eerdmans, 1988), 46; and Kirsten Nielsen, *Ruth*, OTL (Louisville: Westminster John Knox, 1997), 28–29.

ratives in Genesis, Judges, and the narrative about David.[48] It is folkloric in nature[49] and recounts the tale of Ruth, Naomi, and Boaz memorably and somewhat oddly, similar to stories such as Ehud in Judges 3:15-29, the "left-handed" Benjaminite who surprises King Eglon on the privy to kill him; Jerubbaal in Judges 7, whose troops YHWH sends home from battle for not lapping up water like dogs; and the tale of young David in 1 Samuel 17, who kills the great Philistine Goliath with a slingshot. It is self-contained and, while it holds many parallels to other biblical stories, the core narrative and its characters (until the genealogy of David in Ruth 4) is independent from other biblical texts and could have been written separately from these stories.

Some of the stories that provide the most striking parallels to the book of Ruth are those that are similarly focused on foreign women and etiologies for foreigners. Lot and his daughters in Genesis 19:30-38 is one such story; the daughters get their father drunk and sleep with him, giving birth to Ammon and Moab, the ancestor of Ruth. The story does not condemn the incest or "rape" of Lot overtly, yet the purpose is an etiology that explains the hostilities between Israel and two of its closest neighbors. The story of Tamar in Genesis 38 is quite positive toward the heroine Tamar, though the absence of any pedigree may suggest she is non-Hebrew; she covers her face and allows her father-in-law Judah to mistake her for a prostitute, thus getting pregnant with his children and giving birth to the line of King David (Tamar and Perez, her son, are part of the genealogy in Ruth 4:12). We will discuss the stories of Lot and his daughters, and Tamar and Judah, throughout this commentary as they relate to the narrative of Ruth.

The narrative also portrays the marriage between a Moabite woman and an Israelite man positively; David descends from their line in the final genealogy in Ruth 4. Regardless of the dating of this final genealogy, the core story and its characters therefore become a source of pride in David's ancestry, giving him pedigree with enough nuance to make his ancestors unusual and memorable in a way that accords more with the style of these older narratives than it does with the Chronicler's pristine story of David.[50] Among the earlier stories of David, Ruth is similar to 1 Samuel 22:3-4, in which the king of Moab offers asylum

48. See also Campbell, *Ruth*, 5.

49. The notion of Ruth as folklore is the backbone of Sasson's *Ruth* study.

50. The postexilic books of Chronicles delete much of what is detrimental to the character and reputation of David as it is depicted in the David story of 2 Samuel, including the stories of Bathsheba (2 Sam 11) and Tamar (2 Sam 13), and David's ordering the census (2 Sam 24).

to David's parents at David's request. There is no polemic in this text, which presents the king of Moab as one of David's allies as he flees from Saul. Similarly, Ruth is not a polemical text. While other biblical texts display hostility toward Moabites (e.g., Deut 23:4-9; Neh 13:1-3), the book of Ruth does not. Yet neither does the book exhibit awareness of some of the postexilic concerns regarding inclusion/exclusion, including Ezra–Nehemiah's concern with genealogical purity, or Third Isaiah's (Isa 55–66) focus on inclusion around worship of YHWH. While Ruth pledges to worship Naomi's YHWH, what primarily defines Ruth is not worship of YHWH but loyalty to Naomi.

One of the main arguments for a postexilic dating is that the book engages with this postexilic debate regarding the inclusion of foreigners (see below for a more careful discussion of this argument). Yet for Mahri and others, it is reductive to assume that the story *must* be written during a later time, simply because it deals in some sense with the inclusion of a foreign woman. There is nothing exclusively postexilic about the narrative that would unarguably point toward this later framework. As shown above, plenty of earlier stories discuss "foreigners" in some sense; Israelites were clearly aware of and interested in people on their periphery early on. Indeed, the self-understanding of Israel is based on the memory of being foreigners in Egypt, and no matter how we date the written Torah, a fundamental and likely deep-rooted principle of Israel was that it treat foreigners well (see Lev 19:33-34). To assume that a biblical text must be postexilic if it focuses on the inclusion of a foreigner therefore draws an invisible and fabricated line between the complexities of preexilic and postexilic realities and considerations.

Not only is the narrative independent of a particular historical time period, but its geography is similarly independent. Elsewhere, the geography of certain texts betrays historical context; for example, texts that depict an expansive landscape that runs far south of Jerusalem and far into the northern territories suggest a later, preexilic context after the political expansions under King Omri (ninth century BCE) yet before the fall of the northern kingdom. Yet the landscape in the book of Ruth is self-contained—the story begins in Moab but is centered in Bethlehem of Judah, so it is clearly Judahite—yet it is unaware of palace, temple, monarchy (with the exception of the final genealogy for David), any kind of religious or political structure aside from the communal language of clans and elders, or even a community centered in Jerusalem, whether pre- or postexilic.

For these reasons, Mahri and other scholars would argue that a substantial core of the book of Ruth could date to the preexilic period, even while the narrative continues to be redacted, reinterpreted, and possibly added to in light of the exile and in the postexilic periods. Biblical texts written in the preexilic period continued to be edited and changed well into the last few centuries BCE, in light of shifting present realities that reinterpret the past. In other words, just because a book is relevant in the postexilic period does not mean that it was authored only then; to assume so is historically impoverishing. The book of Ruth may have been reworked and added to at a later date, while earlier elements remained but took on a different meaning.

The Postexilic Argument

Despite good reasons for dating the book of Ruth to the preexilic period, many scholars (including Alice) date the majority or entirety of the narrative to the period after the exile.[51] Preexilic and postexilic peace would have been understood very differently. According to the postexilic argument, postexilic peace in the Persia Period would come at the price of submission to a foreign power rather than as a consequence of the Israelites' infiltrating and conquering the land that had belonged to the Canaanites. The Persian Empire dominated the Jews politically, and it appointed leaders from Yehud, the name now given to the former southern kingdom of Judah, who would govern the returned exiles and others in the land; the Persians required them to pay tribute, thus weakening an already weak economy. However, the locals in Yehud could control their religious practice (e.g., Ezra 9:9). Returnees from exile and those who had never left the land had an enormous incentive to use religion to reestablish their identity.[52] Sacred time could replace or complement sacred space (the temple). Religious authorities could require of the aliens who lived among them the same practices required of the Israelites themselves (e.g., Ezek 14:7; 47:22-24).

51. See Ziony Zevit, "Dating Ruth: Legal, Linguistic and Historical Observations," *ZAW* 117 (2005): 574–600; also Frederic W. Bush, *Ruth, Esther*, WBC 9 (Dallas: Word Books, 1996), 30; Campbell, *Ruth*, 26–27; and Eskenazi and Frymer-Kensky, *Ruth*, xvi–xix.

52. As a monarchic feast, the Sabbath was linked to the feast celebrating the new moon (e.g., 2 Kgs 4:23; Amos 8:5) and was a feast shared with other ancient Near Eastern peoples. During the exile and after, the Sabbath became a separate institution, a sign of the covenant between Israel and the Lord and lacking a parallel among other peoples (e.g., Ezek 20:20; see also Neh 10:31). See also K. Kohler, "The Sabbath and Festivals in Pre-Exilic and Exilic Times," *JAOS* 37 (1917): 209–23, esp. 211.

Whereas leadership during the monarchy demanded that the Israelites have nothing to do with foreign women who would lead them to worship foreign gods, many of the Israelites living in exile likely married foreign women. Consequently, many of those returning from exile may themselves have been the offspring of sexual unions or marriages with foreign women, or would have taken foreign women as wives (e.g., Ezra 10:18-43). While Persia would have no reason to object if Israelite males married foreign women who worshiped other gods, Israelite religious leaders certainly would. Their creation of a postexilic identity for the people meant a total commitment to YHWH, and the best way to ensure such fidelity was to remove peoples associated with idolatry (e.g., Ezra 9:1-2; Neh 13:23) and forbid intermarriage (e.g., Neh 10:30; 13:25). Purity of bloodlines would also help to guarantee that foreigners would not come to possess ancestral land. According to Ezra–Nehemiah, it became imperative to forbid Israelite men from marrying foreign women and even to rid themselves of the foreign wives they had already taken; it became mandatory that they divorce foreign wives who had come to Israel with their own gods and their own languages, and who were raising their children in their own languages and potentially teaching them allegiance to their gods (see Neh 13:24).

Foreign women thus posed a religious threat, not a political or economic one. The issue became whether or not all foreign wives, simply because they were foreigners, should be rejected even if they committed themselves to Israel's God. That is the historical context in which many scholars situate the book of Ruth and on the basis of which they believe the book to be postexilic. While Ruth is a Moabite, she professes total commitment to YHWH by committing to Naomi; further, she marries her dead husband's next-of-kin to ensure that Naomi's land remains within the family. A subtext of the book of Ruth is that Ruth (that is, foreign women who profess and demonstrate loyalty to the covenant community and their God) should be embraced, not expelled. Those who argue for a postexilic setting understand the book of Ruth as a polemic against Ezra and Nehemiah—to allow foreigners into the congregation of the Lord. The book represents a universalistic trend similar to the exilic prophecy of Deutero-Isaiah[53] and texts such as Isaiah 25:6: "On this mountain the Lord of hosts will make for all peoples a feast of rich food."[54] The Ruth

53. Campbell, *Ruth*, 26–27.
54. Isaiah 24:1–27:12 is dated to the sixth century BCE.

narrative, if produced during the Persian Period, accomplishes several exilic and postexilic goals. It presents a foreign woman who does not lead Yehudites to worship foreign gods (in fact, she comes to worship YHWH); it integrates well the foreigner; and as if that were not enough, it reminds Yehudites that they are heirs of the Davidic promise, thereby ideally igniting aspirations for the reestablishment of David's monarchy.[55]

The book of Ruth is not alone in its defense of foreigners. The narrative of Jonah, also four chapters in length, presents a prophet of YHWH who disobeys divine directives while the hated Assyrians hear and obey the warning Jonah brings them. It is not the insiders, the Jews, but the despised outsiders, the Assyrians (like the Moabite), who take YHWH seriously. Ruth and Jonah both make the case that being foreign is not the problem; being uncommitted to YHWH is. The narrative of Ruth functioned both *to undermine* the prohibition against mixed marriage and also *to protest* the insistence on ethnic purity by Judahite leadership.[56]

Telling or retelling a story in a difficult political and/or religious climate can be very powerful. Vaclav Havel wrote two plays, *The Garden Party* (1963) and *Memorandum* (1965), in Czechoslovakia when it was under Communist rule. Both plays explore the self-delusions and moral compromises that characterize life under a totalitarian government. Seeing the works as dangerous political propaganda, the Soviets banned both. Havel later became the first president of the non-Communist Czech Republic. In the case of Havel's plays, he "harmlessly" confronted citizens with the compromising behaviors of which they were guilty; no

55. Peter H. W. Lau, "Another Postcolonial Reading of the Book of Ruth," in *Reading Ruth in Asia*, ed. Jione Havea and Peter H. W. Lau, IVBS 7 (Atlanta: SBL Press, 2015), 15–34, esp. 33.

56. Jon L. Berquist provides an excellent description of how people behave who are forced to live under foreign rule. The analysis presented above, positing a postexilic dating of Ruth, resonates with his description; what Berquist describes as "imperialization" and the reactions it engenders can apply more broadly to diverse expressions of domination: "Imperialization is a strong and momentous force in human history, but it always breeds resistance. The interaction of imperial and local cultures urges some people to hold more tightly to their traditional ways of life and thought, as well as to the previous pre-imperial autonomy. When imperial intensification creates a new class of local ruling elites, other social segments form as well, through social stratification, and this creates competing interests of different groups. The process of imperialization simultaneously generates the process of resistance. Within a society, this happens in a variety of institutions at once" ("Resistance and Accommodation in the Persian Empire," in *In the Shadow of Empire: Reclaiming the Bible as a History of Faithful Resistance*, ed. Richard A. Horsley (Louisville: Westminster John Knox, 2008), 54.

longer able to deny, they needed to resist. With respect to the book of Ruth, the narrative offers an imaginative scenario that may be countercultural while also encouraging its audience to resist cultural control. By setting the narrative in the "harmless" past, the author diminished the story's true agenda.

At a Catholic college when a mid-level administrator hesitated to admit in a public panel that he was gay, someone suggested that he tell his audience that he was going to tell four short biblical stories, stressing the incorporation of the stories' outsiders—the story of Ruth, the story of Jonah, the story of the Good Samaritan (Luke 10:25-37), and the story of Jesus meeting the Samaritan woman at the well (John 4:1-42)—and then sit down. She urged, "Just tell the stories; if they get it, they get it." Narratives have the power to present difficult content in non- or less-threatening ways. Not all narratives do that, of course, but biblical stories of the outsiders' inclusion told to a Jewish or Christian audience may help that audience recognize contemporary outsiders and become more willing to include them. Isaiah 56:3-8, clearly postexilic, echoes Ruth and Jonah; the verses include both eunuchs and foreigners among God's people, asking only that they keep the Sabbath and not profane it and that they refrain from doing evil.[57]

When all is said and done, however, there are no easy answers. Scholars date the book of Ruth to the long period of the Judean monarchy and to the postexilic (Persian) period, and they view the book as either serving to reinforce traditional values or as serving to resist and reject imposed practices. In the Bible, the treatment of Gentiles varies from book to book, with both positive and negative depictions, and across time periods. Rather than narrow the origin of the story to a confined period of time, we choose to see the themes within the story as reaching across the preexilic/postexilic divide.[58] The theme of inclusion would be pertinent in the late preexilic period as much as in the postexilic period,[59] and Ruth is not a polemical piece that responds narrowly to one option or the other.

57. Isaiah 56:3-7 reads: "Do not let the foreigner joined to the Lord say, 'The Lord will surely separate me from his people.' . . . [T]he foreigners who join themselves to the Lord . . . I will bring to my holy mountain, and make them joyful in my house of prayer; their burnt offerings and their sacrifices will be accepted on my altar; for my house shall be called a house of prayer for all peoples."

58. Campbell, *Ruth*, 27.

59. Katharine Doob Sakenfeld, *Ruth*, Interpretation: A Bible Commentary for Teaching and Preaching (Louisville: Westminster John Knox, 1999), 5.

Authorship and Authority

If we can determine the book of Ruth's author,[60] we will be in a better position to determine the book's date of composition and / or its purpose. For centuries scholars assumed male authorship, just as they assumed male authorship of all other biblical books.

In the case of Ruth, the book contains resemblances to several biblical texts, believed to be authored by men, that detail unusual circumstances surrounding a leader's birth. The matriarchs Sarah, Rebecca, and Rachel all had difficulty conceiving and then produced important sons.[61] There is nothing "miraculous" about the birth of Ruth's son, but her circumstances are also unusual. She is not identified as infertile,[62] yet she was married for ten years without conceiving a child. We can surmise, then, that behind Ruth lay a certain anxiety related to her pregnancy because of many unfruitful engagements in sexual intercourse. Moreover, Ruth was a Moabite; that in itself is not unusual, but it is insofar as she became the mother of important descendants in Israel.

Though the Genesis texts contain narratives about each of the matriarchs, whose maternal activity was essential and even determinative, the women fade in the tradition. God, for example, is identified as being "the God of Abraham," and then of the women's sons, "Isaac and Jacob," rather than the God of Sarah, Rebecca, and Rachel. In a similar way Ruth fades from the narrative after giving birth to Obed, and then the male genealogy takes over to find its climax in the birth of David. The greater importance accorded men after Ruth gives birth suggests, but of course does not prove—there likely were women intent on advancing the role of men in the culture—that a man authored the book of Ruth.

Most recently (the last fifty years or so), scholars have begun to question the book's male authorship and authority.[63] The book of Ruth is different from many other biblical books in that it bears the name of its

60. According to Bava Batra 14b in the Babylonian Talmud, the prophet Samuel was the author of the book of Ruth. See also Eskenazi and Frymer-Kensky, *Ruth*, xvi.

61. This is true also for Hannah in 1 Samuel and, in the New Testament, for Elizabeth, the mother of John the Baptist (Luke 1:24-25, 36-37, 66); Mary is likewise depicted as having unusual circumstances surrounding the conception of Jesus (Luke 1:26-35, 38).

62. A reader might conclude that Ruth's first husband was sterile.

63. See also Campbell, *Ruth*, 22–23; Hubbard, *Book of Ruth*, 24; Adrien J. Bledstein, "Female Companionships," in *A Feminist Companion to Ruth*, ed. Athalya Brenner, FCB 3 (Sheffield: Sheffield Academic, 1993), 116–33; Fokkelien van Dijk-Hemmes, "Ruth: A Product of Women's Culture?," in Brenner, *A Feminist Companion to Ruth*, 134–39.

main character, a woman. Second, it contains more dialogue, an explicit expression of relationship, than any other book in the Old Testament. Third, Naomi, another female character, is also central to the narrative. The narrative depicts one of the two major relationships as that between two women, Ruth and Naomi. But there is more: Naomi is willing to travel, without family, from Moab to Judah alone; another woman is willing to go alone (as the only foreigner) to another land. For the first three of the four chapters of the book, two distinct women are the principal actors. Sounds like a woman could have written the story!

While a hypothesized gender of the author has the potential to influence one's reconstruction of the narrative's date and purpose, like the date and purpose themselves, it lacks certainty. It might also narrow our reading since as soon as we assign a male or female author, we are likely to impose stereotypes. And our stereotype of a female author could easily lead to another distortion, since not all women are alike.[64] On the other hand, it could lead to a greater sense of pride in the accomplishment of our sister(s). Because the weight of our assumption has been on male authorship, imagining female authorship could increase our awareness of other achievements of women of which we are ignorant.[65]

When considering authorship it is also important to keep in mind that the question of women's voices and women's authority in the text is just as important as that of women's authorship.[66] Texts do not have to be written by women to be driven by women's lives, concerns, and traditions. Then, we have to ask ourselves *which* women and *which* concerns these might be. For example, a womanist perspective (a movement based on the marginalization of black women and other minority women's perspectives) might be very different from a white woman's perspective; yet again, there is no singular "white woman's" or "black woman's"

64. Some African American women, for example, describe themselves as "womanist" to distinguish themselves from white, middle-class American feminists. Race, class, sexual orientation, age, and cultural background are only a few of the markers that differentiate among women.

65. History often hides the accomplishments of women, or they remain unnamed. By way of a very small sampling, women inventors include: Margaret A. Wilcox, the car heater (1830); Anna Connelly, the fire escape (1887); Mary Beasely, the life raft (1882); and Letitia Geer, the medical syringe that can be operated with one hand (1899).

66. Fokkelien van Dijk-Hemmes has argued that it is more valuable to search for women's authority in texts rather than "remain imprisoned by a concept of female authorship" (Athalya Brenner and Fokkelien van Dijk-Hemmes, *On Gendering Texts: Female and Male Voices in the Hebrew Bible* [Leiden: Brill, 1993], 108).

perspective. A rich woman's perspective might be very different from a poor woman's perspective (with the same caveat that there is no singular perspective for a "rich" or a "poor" person); and the perspective of a Latina woman raised in a village in Mexico might be very different from a Latina woman raised with all the luxuries of wealth in San Juan, Puerto Rico. When we consider perspective, we must continually break down any of the stereotypes or rigid ideas of what that perspective might be.

The multiplicity of possibilities regarding the world behind the text (the identification of a text's author, the date of its composition, and its purpose)—the major concern of the Modern Period—though disappointing to some, can allow us to explore with greater openness and imagination both the world of the text and the contemporary world in front of the text. Like the ancient rabbis, we believe that the texts are fuller than any one interpretation.

We have provided the above comments that pertain to the book of Ruth and the historical-critical method since historical criticism dominated biblical scholarship for more than two centuries. Many feminist biblical scholars find it useful if incomplete, and they choose to augment the method with other methods that Barbara Reid's introduction references. The commentary that follows will use many methods that we believe provide insights into the particular verses and the appropriation of them in contemporary contexts.

Postmodernity

Postmodernity brought with it the gradual recognition that objectivity is very difficult, if not impossible, to achieve; it challenged the assumption of objectivity that had prevailed in the modern period and responded to it with the counter-assumption that almost everything is conditioned by the interpreter or the interpreting community's perspective. That does not mean that a text's history is not important or that the search for that history is irrelevant. It simply balances a false sense of objectivity by acknowledging the import of perspective.[67]

67. Thomas Kuhn brought this "false sense of objectivity" to attention in the sciences. While the educated layperson is familiar with the idea of "scientific objectivity," he pointed out that forces other than science may control research. Money supports some research while other research is denied funding. The reasons for providing or withholding funding are often political and determined by special or vested interests rather than objectivity. When a scientific theory (e.g., the earth is the center of the

Building on a "sociology of knowledge,"[68] a postmodern perspective recognizes that historical "facts" are hard to determine and that many so-called facts are really only educated guesses or even biased guesses; they are perspectival, and a person's or group's social location may determine the perspective. While there is a fact, the historical fact of the Vietnam War, for example, much that is associated with that war and presented as fact is determined by perspective. To the Vietnamese it is the "American War."[69] Likewise, a famous "history" of the Civil War, *The Blue and the Gray*[70] by Henry Steele Commager, depicts the war using original letters and documents that provide personal details, including some that are sympathetic to the Confederate soldiers. By its selection of "facts" the book achieves a very different understanding of the war than what was traditionally presented in history textbooks, at least those used in the North. For an additional and different example, while it is a fact that more women died of breast cancer than of AIDS, it was a political decision to spend more money on AIDS research, leading most Americans to conclude incorrectly that AIDS was the greater threat to life.[71]

With respect to biblical studies, increased appreciation of perspective pointed scholars back to the historical circumstances that gave rise to historical criticism in the first place; though methodologically studying

---

universe) is shown to be incorrect, other theories associated with it must necessarily shift (*The Structure of Scientific Revolutions*, 50th ann. ed. [Chicago: University of Chicago Press, 2012]).

68. Sociologists recognized, long before "postmodernity" became a buzzword among scholars, that the social location of groups of people affected their interests and concerns. Their studies of "gender, race, and class" (before such categories as age, sexual orientation, and other groups came into purview) showed that people belonging to one or another group tended to hold similar positions. While identifying people as belonging to these groups may lead to the wrongful stereotyping of individuals, it also establishes the reasons for stereotypes. People who grow up in a country that had been colonized, for example, "know" different experiences and tend to read differently from those who "do not know" or who have never had that experience.

69. See also Karen Gottschang Turner with Phan Thanh Hao, *Even the Women Must Fight: Memories of War from North Vietnam* (New York: Wiley & Sons, 1999).

70. Originally published in 1950 and republished in New York by Wings Books/Random House in 1996.

71. In 2006, the statistics went like this: 1.4 million people were diagnosed with cancer, while far fewer people were diagnosed with AIDS. Half of those diagnosed with cancer will die of the disease; AIDS has a higher mortality rate. $4.75 billion was spent on cancer research; $3 billion was spent on AIDS research. AIDS is 99 percent preventable; cancer is not. www.neogaf.com/forum/showthread.php?t=184291.

the world behind the text, it was the world in front of the text that had occasioned the method. A postmodern perspective takes very seriously, methodologically, that we all view reality through a particular lens. Women reading the book of Ruth may focus on, in particular, the depiction of the women characters; readers from drought-stricken areas may focus on the famine that sent Elimelech's family to Moab. Lawyers may be interested in the disposal of Elimelech's property, and the homeless may wonder where Ruth and Naomi found lodging. Postmodernity allows the social location of each of us to matter.

Therefore, a postmodern approach emphasizes *the world in front of the text* by recognizing that, ultimately, it is the reader who constructs meaning. We bring to every experience that we have our own social location; we bring our age, our sex, and our class: the totality of our experiences. However, and this is important, the meaning that we are constructing is *as a reader*; it is not constructed out of nothing or only ourselves; we construct meaning by engaging with a text or texts, and in this case, the book of Ruth and our commentary.[72]

We believe that a good commentary includes insights from premodernity, modernity, and postmodernity, that it takes into consideration *the world behind the text*, *the world of the text*, and *the world in front of the text*. A good commentary also includes insights from *the worlds that received the texts* (the history of interpretation). We also believe that a good commentary is as inclusive as possible, for which reason we welcome the voices that have made an important contribution to the commentary by adding their insights to our own.

72. To be concrete, maybe because I (Alice) am older, I identify with Naomi more than the other characters when I read the text. I particularly like Sandy Freckleton Gagon's depiction in her painting "Whither Thou Goest" of Naomi's gray hair; in the image, Ruth holds Naomi with one arm while holding up a cloth that covers the two women with the other. Naomi looks older, and she exudes strength. And since the only living members of my family (a sister and brother-in-law) have just moved from Pennsylvania, where we grew up, to Florida, where I have never spent much time, I am feeling a little dislocated and am thinking of Naomi in Moab.

I (Mahri) am younger, and I do not identify with Naomi. Perhaps I will someday, perhaps not. Yet neither do I identify with Ruth and her decisions. In fact, I have a strange sense of anger toward her, particularly the notion of a commitment that takes a woman away from family, culture, and her own identity; she becomes known only as the outsider ("Moabite") or as "daughter-in-law" to Naomi. I suppose if I were to relate to any of the characters, it would be Orpah. She is the truly liberated one: liberated from the drama of the narrative and from the reader's probing.

What Constitutes a Feminist Commentary? How Is This Commentary Feminist?

A commentary is not feminist because women have produced it. Those who think that only women are feminists and that men cannot be feminists are fewer in number now than fifty years ago, when women almost never wrote commentaries and when those who wrote commentaries did not attend to women characters. Still, as the general introduction makes clear, that which makes something feminist can differ among feminists. For some, a feminist commentary highlights the women characters, even displacing, to the extent possible, their male counterparts. For example, the God of Abraham, Isaac, and Jacob becomes the God of Sarah, Rebekah, Leah and Rachel, Ruth and Naomi, even Orpah, sidelining Boaz, Obed, and David in the book of Ruth. For others, a feminist commentary deliberately deconstructs traditional interpretation and highlights the significance of seemingly insignificant characters (e.g., awarding the many unnamed women of the Bible greater recognition than is explicit in the biblical texts).[73] For still others, a feminist commentary uses historical criticism—for example, the findings of archaeology—to explain why texts are written as they are (e.g., how plagues or pestilences or drought that threatened a people's future likely led to the protection of pregnant women, and then how that protection in the form of restrictions continued and became normative).[74] Some feminists, using a "hermeneutics of suspicion,"[75] expose and denounce the male-dominated culture that

73. See, for example, the unnamed maidservant in 2 Samuel 17 and the unnamed wise woman in 2 Samuel 20, both of whom help to save the Davidic dynasty. See Alice L. Laffey, "Naming the Unnamed: Toward a Feminist Reconstruction of the Old Testament," a paper presented at the annual meeting of the Society of Biblical Literature, Anaheim, CA, November 23, 1985 (Abstract published in *AAR/SBL Abstracts*, 1985). Not all unnamed biblical characters are insignificant, nor are they all female. Adele Reinhartz, for example, suggests that the "next-of-kin" in the book of Ruth (4:1) remains nameless because it is the relationship rather than the character that is primary. This character delays the narrative's progression rather than forwarding it (*"Why Ask My Name?" Anonymity and Identity in Biblical Narrative* [New York: Oxford University Press, 1998], 20).

74. Carol Meyers, "The Roots of Restriction: Women in Early Israel," *BA* 41 (1978): 91–103.

75. A term first used by Paul Ricoeur and later adopted by Elisabeth Schüssler Fiorenza and others, a "hermeneutics of suspicion" refers to the recognition of the pervasiveness of cultures and texts in which men dominate. In response, many feminists "suspect" the cultures and texts and refuse to take statements or situations at

they consider to permeate all of the biblical texts. Other commentators seek and expose rays of light and hope in the texts, exceptions to what they admit to be a dominantly male-centered culture. Some are more tolerant of the past (i.e., that was then) while others are impatient with the present and demand a different future.

As the general introduction points out, biblical interpretation throughout the Common Era, until the twentieth century, was predominantly a male endeavor, whether Jewish or Christian. Elizabeth Cady Stanton's *The Woman's Bible*, published at the end of the nineteenth century,[76] said loudly and clearly that not all women read the Bible in the same way that men do. For instance, with respect to the book of Ruth, Stanton's commentary identifies Rahab as the mother of Boaz. She therefore interprets Ruth through the gospels (Matt 1:5 states that Salmon is "the father of Boaz by Rahab"), which reveals her Christian lens, yet in doing so she deliberately brings to the fore another biblical woman. And when referring to the friendship between Ruth and Naomi, the commentary notes and highlights that such a relationship is "so unusual."[77]

Each person's priorities will differ based on such factors as sexual orientation, economic situation, culture, and religion; yet culturally conditioned and generally speaking, men's priorities have been different from women's historically.[78] What men might not notice or else ignore, many women might find offensive and wrong or, conversely, see as

---

face value (Schüssler Fiorenza, *In Memory of Her: A Feminist Theological Reconstruction of Christian Origins* [New York: Crossroad, 1994]; and Schüssler Fiorenza, *Bread Not Stone: The Challenge of Feminist Biblical Interpretation*, ann. ed. [Boston: Beacon, 1995]).

76. The Project Gutenberg e-book of *The Woman's Bible* by Elizabeth Cady Stanton (1898). Produced by Carrie Lorenz and John B. Hare. wattpad.com/13271-the-woman%275-bible.

77. In Matt 10:34-39 Jesus declares that he has come to bring a sword to the earth. That sword includes setting a daughter-in-law against her mother-in law (v. 35).

78. Thomas Jefferson and Charles Thompson are both men possessing culturally conditioned priorities. In his *Notes on the State of Virginia*, Jefferson quotes and reinforces a comment by Charles Thompson, then Secretary of Congress, in reference to Ruth and American "Aborigines" women. Referring to Ruth 3:7, Jefferson identifies Aboriginal women as a threat to Christian men because, *like Moabite women who posed a threat to Israelite men*, these women are hypersexualized (*Notes on the State of Virginia*, ed. Frank Shuffelton [New York: Penguin Putnam, 1999], 201). Laura E. Donaldson concludes: "Although cloaked in the rhetoric of Enlightenment gentility, the statements by Thompson and Jefferson nevertheless disseminate a cautionary tale . . . both American Indian and Moabite women exist as agents not only of evil and impurity but also of men's sexual frigidity" (see "The Sign of Orpah: Reading

courageous and well worth comment. While men, for example, might praise Ruth's humility, women reading the same passage might very well resent the circumstances that require Ruth's subservience. In more recent commentaries on Ruth, female scholars have paid more attention to the relationship between Naomi and Ruth, and some have even suggested that the two women are involved sexually.[79]

Even though the book is named after its leading character and that character dominates the narrative, men have praised Ruth for the feminine virtues espoused in the particular male-dominated culture in which the book was being interpreted; writes feminist biblical scholar Leila Leah Bronner, "[Ruth's] qualities as developed in rabbinic interpretation—modesty, obedience, devotion to wifely and maternal duties—are not the qualities sought by feminists. Ruth is not independent, autonomous, and free of male control; she is docile and submissive, and this is why the sages laud and honor her."[80] In a typical nineteenth-century Calvinist sermon delivered by Rev. Charles Spurgeon, Ruth wins praise for her faithfulness.[81]

In the twentieth century, women in the West, aided finally by access to education, began to interpret the biblical texts from feminist perspectives, even if they did not use the term. They saw in the texts what others had failed to see. For example, one commentary praises Ruth for "loving God enough to break the rules."[82] This female author evaluated Ruth's words and actions differently from Rev. Spurgeon. More recently still, the voices of women from that part of the globe considered eastern by western standards, or southern by northern standards, have begun to comment on the biblical texts in light of the particularities of their own

---

Ruth through Native Eyes," in *Ruth and Esther*, FCB 3, 2nd ser., ed. Athalya Brenner [Sheffield: Sheffield Academic, 1999], 130–44, esp. 134).

79. See J. Cheryl Exum, *Plotted, Shot, and Painted: Cultural Representations of Biblical Women*, 2nd rev. ed. (Sheffield: Sheffield Phoenix, 2012), 161–207; also Comea M. Walthall, "Ruth's Relevance to the Same-Sex Marriage Debate," in *Global Perspectives on the Old Testament*, ed. Mark Roncace and Joseph Weaver (Boston: Pearson Education, 2014), 195–96.

80. Bronner, *From Eve to Esther*, 80.

81. E.g., Spurgeon selects five verses from the book of Ruth on which to deliver five sermons: 1:16 and then 2:12, 14, 15, and 16. He names the first "Ruth Deciding for God" and then proceeds to preach about deciding for Christ. In each of the sermons, Spurgeon uses Ruth as a springboard for preaching about faithfulness to Christ and his message (*Spurgeon's Sermons on Ruth* [Apollo, PA: Ichthus Publications, 2014]).

82. Carolyn Custis James, *The Gospel of Ruth: Loving God Enough to Break the Rules* (Grand Rapids: Zondervan, 2011).

cultural experiences. Surekha Nelavala, who is a contributing voice to this commentary, attests that Ruth has been interpreted in traditional Indian culture to reinforce the female qualities and behaviors that men value in women. Preachers have found those qualities in Ruth and hold them up as ideals for women.

Ruth as an Ideal Woman?

The force of the story of Ruth resides in its capacity to provoke both resistance and admiration. Ruth is admired for her faultless female personality that fits perfectly into a patriarchal society. Traditionally, sermons preach that Ruth is likable because she is an ideal woman who stands out as an example while her virtues sustain the patriarchal order. Logically, such sermons suggest that women emulate her in their own families and lives. Why not? Who would not want to be a wife/daughter-in-law like Ruth? In the story, Ruth's personality does not resist most social expectations but contains all of the virtues that a patriarchal society would appreciate in a woman: Ruth is modest, vulnerable, responsible, obedient, committed, charming, and, we assume, young and beautiful.

Surekha Nelavala

Clearly, not all feminists would reject all of the characteristics that Nelavala implies are patriarchal and that reinforce patriarchy. While the assumption of marriage as well as obedience may be troublesome, for example, being vulnerable and responsible and committed may not be. Nelavala is nevertheless rightly addressing how Ruth has been used in male-dominated societies to encourage qualities and circumstances that can make women submissive. In many African contexts, interpretations of the story of Ruth also confirm the common opinion that marriage offers the only possible meaningful life for women.[83]

Although traditional interpreters of the book of Ruth have used the book and its character Ruth to affirm traditional cultural values, the book of Ruth, more easily than many other biblical books, can be read holistically as feminist and produce feminist commentary. Composed in a patriarchal era (no matter when it was written!), it can be read as,

83. Madipoane Masenya, "Ruth," in *The Global Bible Commentary*, ed. Daniel Patte (Nashville: Abingdon, 2004), 86–91, esp. 90. While we acknowledge that not all African countries and cultures are alike in this respect, we take our lead here from Masenya.

in many ways, challenging and transcending patriarchy. We hope to accomplish that goal.

The book of Ruth tells a story, but there is much that it does not say. We do not know why Elimelech, and apparently only Elimelech, in response to a famine, took his family to Moab. We do not know how difficult it was for Elimelech and his sons to settle in Moab. We do not know when Ruth and Orpah, two Moabite women, became the wives of Mahlon and Chilion, Elimelech's sons. We do not know if Ruth and/or Orpah were pretty according to the standards of beauty in Moab or the ancient Near East in general, or if they had large dowries. Other, unanswerable questions concerning Ruth and Orpah include the following: Was their marrying Israelite men a boon? Did they fear remaining unmarried, or married to men less desirable than the Israelite men they married? Did Ruth and Orpah like each other? What were their ages with respect to each other and with respect to Naomi? Was it safe for Orpah to return home alone when she left Naomi and Ruth in chapter 1?

The reason for bringing these unknowns to the fore—for asking these questions or for lamenting the lack of information and answers—is the bearing these unknowns could have on our understanding of the characters. What it cost Naomi to travel to Moab and what it cost Ruth and Orpah to marry Israelite men surely say something about the degree of the women's strength and fortitude. Their beauty and their dowries, or the lack thereof, could contribute to the likelihood of Ruth and Orpah having Moabite suitors and to their level of self-confidence. The relationship of the two Moabite women to each other has a lot to say about competition or collaboration, issues that are significant in current feminist discourse. Many women reading their story today might wonder about Orpah's safety as she returned home alone, insofar as they, concerned about their own physical safety, wonder to what extent they can identify with her in this regard. These are certainly not the only questions that the text does not answer, but at least some contemporary feminists would be interested in pondering such unknowns.

Other questions similarly remain unanswered. We do not know if the Judahite family could, or did, buy land in Moab; if they did, we do not know whether Naomi sold that land or abandoned it. If they did have land, perhaps they acquired it through Orpah's or Ruth's family, which might explain marriage to one or both of these women. If they did not have access to land, we do not know how the family members supported themselves while living away from Judah. Once Naomi and Ruth returned alone and Ruth went to work in the fields (chap. 2), we do not know how common it was for women to be molested when they were working outside the city in the fields,[84] or how Boaz could be so sure (if he was) that the next-of-kin would be unwilling to redeem Ruth (chap. 4). Are any of these unknowns important to the reader? If not, perhaps the reader will not think to ask them. If they are, then why doesn't the narrative provide the information?

The first part of this set of unknowns comes to mind because economics dominate women's and men's lives today. One's economic situation, that is, one's class, matters, even as one's race, one's gender, one's age, and similar categories matter. It is possible that the narrative's author was deliberate in not providing the economic answers so that all classes could identify with the characters, thinking that they were "like us." But it does make a difference, at least today, whether or not you can afford to buy land, or whether you can afford to walk away from it. The extent of Naomi and Ruth's economic desperation, once they were in Judah, is ambiguous. Naomi does own land so she is not yet economically desperate; on the other hand, Ruth does glean in the fields so she shares the plight of the widow and the poor. The ambiguity may be more contemporary than we realize. No one—then or now—can eat land. Economic decisions are always value decisions. Women, who with their children comprise the largest percentage of the world's poor, must make choices: rent or food; food or medicine; money invested in this child or that one. Knowing the range of choices Ruth and the other characters in the book had (or did not have) helps us better to understand them and identify (or not) with them. As feminists we care about the plight of women, our sisters Ruth and Naomi and Orpah, and the plight of our contemporary sisters whose struggles and courage and perseverance strengthen us.

Adele Berlin explains unanswered questions in the narrative as the way in which the text "selectively represents" the information that it conveys to the reader; acknowledging "selective representation" may help us to accept unanswered questions that the text provokes.[85] Thinking

84. Genesis 34 records the possible rape (the Hebrew is vague) of Jacob's daughter Dinah; the sexual encounter took place when she had gone "out to visit the women of the region" (v. 1). Though the circumstances are different, the recorded incident (if it is rape, that is) is either a cautionary tale (don't go outside acceptable confines lest something bad happen to you) or an actual account of what has happened when women travel outside obviously protected areas.

85. Adele Berlin, *Poetics and Interpretation of Biblical Narrative*, ed. David M. Gunn, BLS 9 (Sheffield: Almond Press, 1983), 99–100.

about these questions will never provide definitive answers, but it may help make the characters in the narrative more real, deepen our empathy for them, or help us better identify with one or another of them.

Already twelve years ago Kathleen O'Connor[86] presented a paper at the Catholic Biblical Association's annual meeting in which she merely changed the name of Job to Johanna (and made other necessary gender changes). By doing so she completely changed the reading experience of the narrative for the readers in the task force who were mostly women and who began to "connect" differently with the book's main character. They, like Job, had suffered. Though none of them, to our knowledge, had lost a child, they felt, vicariously, not only the pain of a parent who has lost a child but also the pain of a mother who has borne the child that she has lost. Since most of the Bible's main characters are men, O'Connor's choice of Job was logical; she chose a narrative with relatively few characters and a fairly straightforward theme. To our knowledge, no one has changed the genders of the characters in the book of Ruth. Doing so would be counterproductive, at least for women. There are already so many male characters with whom men can identify, and women don't need more. O'Connor geared her feminist strategy toward helping women better recognize themselves in the Bible's male characters.

A couple of years later, Athalya Brenner, in *I Am . . .: Biblical Women Tell Their Own Stories*,[87] went beyond O'Connor's efforts; she used her imagination to say what the text does not say and to make the characters better known to their readers. According to Brenner, Ruth declares herself an intellectual and claims that contemporary feminists are right to connect her with the Torah, traditionally the intellectual domain of Jewish males. While interpreters of the biblical book debate whether Ruth, a Moabite, knew the levirate law,[88] Brenner allows her readers to believe that she did. The information that Brenner presents may not be factually accurate, but many of the details reported in the biblical narrative may not be historical either; what Brenner has done by adding details that are not in the biblical text is to provide female characters, in this case Ruth, with more of a voice and personality than the biblical text itself does. Brenner's version of Ruth wants to give Ruth a voice and allow her to set the record straight: "There is no compelling textual reason to

86. See Kathleen O'Connor's *Lamentations and the Tears of the World* (Maryknoll, NY: Orbis Books, 2002), and *Jeremiah: Pain and Promise* (Minneapolis: Fortress, 2012).

87. See n. 18 above.

88. The levirate law (Deut 25:5) requires an Israelite man to marry the childless widow of his brother.

think I was beautiful or sexy; there is no compelling reason to think that Boaz was old or older; if he calls me 'daughter' (Ruth 2 and 3), this is an expression of his social superiority over me more than anything else."[89]

Musa W. Dube, in "The Unpublished Letters of Orpah to Ruth,"[90] has done something similar to Brenner. Using her imagination, she has created a dialogue between Ruth and Orpah that is absent from the biblical text. Our commentary does not go as far as O'Connor or Brenner or Dube. It does, however, intermittently provide a few more imaginative questions like those we have posed earlier that the biblical text does not answer. We do this for a motive similar to the other women's: to stimulate your imaginations and to help you enter as fully as possible into the biblical text. If our questions are helpful to you, by all means, use them. If they are not, nothing is lost by our offering them.

What we are really asking is that you, our readers, make the book of Ruth your own. Join in conversation; have a voice. Read our commentary and learn about the worlds behind, in, and in front of the text, but also be conscious of the fullness of meaning that can only be found by your engaging with the story and its characters in a way that is open. For some readers, that openness may lead to new ideas, a greater appreciation of the narrative, and new insights into its wisdom. For others, in addition to those goals, it may lead to an encounter with God.

A Global Perspective

One of the goals of this commentary series is to incorporate biblical scholarship that scholars from continents other than North America and Europe have produced. If postmodernity recognizes the importance of social location in all interpretation, then not only must the interpretation of Judaism and Christianity's foundational texts take place all over the world but, to the extent that is possible, it should be shared all over the world. North American and European biblical interpretation has traveled to South America, to Australia, to Africa, and to Asia more often than South American, Australian, African, and Asian biblical interpretation has made its way to Europe and North America. There are several reasons for this, including Western assumptions of superiority, greater opportunities for wealth and education distributed more broadly among the people in the West, the colonization of peoples by the West, and so forth. This assumption

89. Brenner, *I Am*, 105.

90. In Brenner, *Ruth and Esther*, 145–50.

of Western superiority and its accompanying denigration of other peoples is, we believe, as Catholic Christians and as people who accept the UN Declaration of Human Rights, fundamentally wrong. In fact, we believe that we have much to learn from one another, that diversity and difference are to be sought and valued rather than feared. Though we have seen an increased desire for isolationist policies and a resurgence of nationalism recently, as well as attempts to legitimate religious prejudice, we do, in fact, live in a global society. None of us can deny, whether we like it or not, that we are politically, economically, and religiously interconnected.

We, therefore, have tried to include contributions of biblical scholars from as many other parts of the world as possible with respect to the book of Ruth. Yet this goal has proven to be difficult to accomplish; for example, Mahri tried to enlist two women in the Dominican Republic (where she served in the Peace Corps) to share their experiences with Ruth, yet the combination of near-to-impossible phone communication, lack of e-mail or internet, and the women's concerns with their writing abilities made the endeavor unsuccessful. We therefore recognize that even the attempt to bring in "Contributing Voices" makes certain assumptions about those voices and their privilege, including education and access to communication. We therefore admit that a good percentage of our Contributing Voices come from within the United States; we have tried to make those voices as diverse in age, sex, religion, cultural heritage, and experience as possible.

When researching recent scholarship on the book of Ruth, we found many books and articles written in the East (e.g., Asia) or in the South (e.g., Africa) by scholars whose country or people had been colonized. Many of these scholars, and Westerners who themselves or whose ancestors had lived in former colonies, acknowledge that their experience or their cultural memory of colonization affects the lens through which they view biblical texts. Having been subject to political, economic, social, and cultural controls as well as religious proselytizing by a foreign, or at least dominating, power, they read the biblical texts with an eye to how the authors of the biblical texts may have been resisting the influences of controlling foreign powers in their own time or how the texts seem to have served the interests of those powers.[91]

91. Musa W. Dube, Judith E. McKinley, and Kwok Pui-lan, among others, combine both feminist and postcolonial perspectives. See, for example, Musa W. Dube, *Postcolonial Feminist Interpretation of the Bible* (St. Louis: Chalice, 2000); Judith E. McKinley, *Reframing Her: Biblical Women in Postcolonial Focus* (Sheffield: Sheffield Phoenix, 2004), and Kwok Pui-lan, *Postcolonial Imagination and Feminist Theology* (Louisville: Westminster John Knox, 2005).

According to Peter Lau, "A postcolonial hermeneutic is one of resistance, used to rail against all forms of hegemonic power, including political, social, economic, and ideological." He continues that when "applied to biblical texts a postcolonial hermeneutic can highlight and undermine abuses of power."[92] We would argue that other experiences of oppression (e.g., gender, racial, religious, economic) provide a similar lens that affects one's reading and interpretation of the texts. But given the "history" of the peoples of the ancient Near East that the Tanakh relates, and given that most, though not all, interpreters of the Bible have been males from the West who do not claim colonized origins, we want to listen closely to this and other perspectives that have been almost always absent from biblical interpretation. Postcolonialism, then, when applied to biblical studies, focuses on the role of empires (e.g., Assyrian, Babylonian, Persian but also British, American, Russian, French, and Japanese) and reactions to them in the composition and reception of the biblical texts.

Kwok Pui-lan, currently William F. Cole Professor of Theology and Spirituality at the Episcopal Divinity School in Cambridge, Massachusetts, recognizes that the Bible came to Asia as the Scripture of the Christian missionaries and as part of Western colonization; as such, it sought to civilize and to save the people of Asia. She writes, "During the missionary era, Christian proclamation was essentially a one-way traffic: Christian missions presumed that they possessed the truths necessary for salvation and the people [of Asia] were treated as missiological objects, passive recipients of such [truths]."[93]

Many scholars who work from a postcolonial perspective focus on the world in front of the text (their world that has been subject to colonization)[94] and then the world of the text (determining how the text

92. Lau, "Another Postcolonial Reading of the Book of Ruth," 15.

93. "Postcolonialism, Feminism and Biblical Interpretation," in *Scripture, Community and Mission: Essays in Honor of D. Preman Niles*, ed. Philip L. Wikeri (Hong Kong: Christian Council of Asia; London: Council of World Missions, 2002), 261–76, esp. 261; quoted in Havea and Lau, "Reading Ruth Again, in Asia," in Havea and Lau, *Reading Ruth in Asia*, 12.

94. E.g., R. S. Sugirtharajah and Fernando F. Segovia, who both prioritize the world in front of the text: see Sugirtharajah, "Biblical Studies after the Empire: From a Colonial to a Postcolonial Mode of Interpretation," in *The Postcolonial Bible*, ed. R. S. Sugirtharajah (Sheffield: Sheffield Academic, 1998); additionally, the essays in *Teaching the Bible: The Discourses and Pedagogy of Biblical Theology*, ed. Fernando F. Segovia and Mary Ann Tolbert (Maryknoll, NY: Orbis Books, 1998) emphasize contemporary social locations and concerns.

itself aligns with their experience).[95] They tend to focus on, in particular, biblical books they consider to be exilic or postexilic. Many of these postcolonial scholars have chosen to interpret the book of Ruth according to this exilic or postexilic paradigm.[96] They have determined, though they may not do so explicitly, that the book of Ruth is a product of the Persian Period; they then assume cultural imperialism toward the returned exiles to Judah, and the Jews'[97] determination not to be obliterated but to resist cultural control.[98] While Persian control in their own land may have been better than exile in Babylonia (e.g., Isa 44:24-28), the returned exiles were still subject to a foreign power, and Judahites in leadership positions may have required the common people to conform, at least in certain respects, to behaviors that coincided with their compromising agendas (e.g., taxation). Colonized peoples, who have experienced both foreign domination and excessive influence from collaborators among their own leadership, look for traces of such behavior in the biblical texts.[99]

95. E.g., Lau, who insists that the world of the text is an essential aspect of interpretation for postcolonial readings ("Another Postcolonial Reading of the Book of Ruth," 16). He does not imply the text's literal accuracy in any premodern sense, but neither is he privileging the world in front of the text (as many postmoderns do) at the expense of the text itself.

96. E.g., Lau, "Another Postcolonial Reading of the Book of Ruth," 30–33; Sin Lung-Tong, "The Key to Successful Migration? Rereading Ruth's Confession through the Lens of Bhabha's Mimicry," in Havea and Lau, *Reading Ruth in Asia*, 35–46, esp. 43–46; Yan Lin, "'Who Is More to You than Seven Sons': A Cross Textual Reading Between the Book of Ruth and a Pair of Peacocks to the Southeast Fly," in Havea and Lau, *Reading Ruth in Asia*, 47–55; Roi Nu, "A Reinterpretation of Levirate Marriage in Ruth 4:1-12 for Kachin Society," in Havea and Lau, *Reading Ruth in Asia*, 57–72; R. S. Wafula, *Biblical Representations of Moab: A Kenyan Postcolonial Reading* (New York: Lang, 2014), esp. 7.

97. The biblical authors writing after the exile tend to speak not of "Israelites" but of "Judeans" and then "Jews." After the exile monotheism becomes normative, and the religious and liturgical traditions develop enough to be securely labeled as Judaism (e.g., Neh 8 and the importance of the read scroll), a tradition that is connected specifically to the people of Judah.

98. See Naveen Rao, who dates Ruth to the time of Ezra–Nehemiah and posits that the book critiques Persian-sponsored oppression of marginal communities among the returned exiles, especially widowed women. Rao sees Ruth as unsettling the order that she joins, thus making the established society "more open to differences and otherness" (Rao, "The Book of Ruth as a Clandestine Scripture to Sabotage Persian Colonial Agenda: A Paradigm for a Liberative Dalit Scripture," *Bangalore Theological Forum* 41 [2009]: 114–34; cited in Havea and Lau, "Reading Ruth Again, in Asia," 11–12).

99. Alice was amazed when, close to forty years ago, her Roman landlady referred to the increased wearing of jeans by female Italian teenagers as "American imperialism." From Alice's perspective, the young women were not forced to wear

But scholars from colonized nations do not limit their focus and critiques to empire. In 1988, Chandra Talpade Mohanty[100] rightly criticized the Western feminist inclination to universalize the category "woman" as if all women, anywhere and at any time, faced the same traditions, structures, and histories of gender oppression. Indeed, she recognized and rejected the Western feminist tendency to generalize about women in developing countries—for example, they are all poor or they are all uneducated—and thus erase the differences among women in terms of race, class, ethnicity, religion, or national identity. Because of her, and women (and men) like her,[101] postcolonial feminist theory has significantly contributed to a growing understanding of gender dynamics in the context of other forms of oppression.

With respect to the book of Ruth, postcolonial interpretation is sensitive to border crossings and migration, phenomena that many colonial peoples have experienced.[102] Naomi journeyed to Moab, occasioned by necessity, and then journeyed back to Judah. The Moabite Orpah married a man of Judah and then was willing to journey to the homeland of her widowed mother-in-law. Ruth also married a man of Judah; she journeyed with Naomi from her homeland to Naomi's. Ruth made a life for herself in Judah and then married another Judahite; finally, Ruth converted to the religion of Judah. These experiences of crossing from one

---

jeans. From Signora Salvi's perspective, because America was so dominant in the world, cultural and economic pressures caused Italians to adopt American ways. While this is not an example of colonization, it does speak of foreign influence by an economically more powerful country and the compliance, willing or not, by Italian manufacturers and retailers.

100. Chandra Talpade Mohanty, "Under Western Eyes: Feminist Scholarship and Colonial Discourses," *Feminist Review* 30 (1988), 60–88.

101. Not much earlier, Alice Walker's *The Color Purple* (Chicago: Houghton Mifflin Harcourt, 1985) and Sherley Anne Williams's *Dessa Rose* (New York: HarperCollins, 1986) were published. These American novels, each in its own way, clearly demonstrated that the lives of white women and African American women are not shaped by the same traditions, structures, histories, and types of gender oppression (see Renita Weems, *Just a Sister Away* [San Diego: LuraMedia, 1988]).

102. For example, see Yani Yoo, "Ruth as a Marriage Migrant," in *Global Perspectives on the Old Testament*, ed. Mark Roncace and Joseph Weaver (Boston: Pearson, 2014), 193–95; Jione Havea, David J. Neville, and Elaine M. Wainwright, eds., *Bible, Borders, Belonging(s): Engaging Readings from Oceania*, SemeiaSt 75 (Atlanta: SBL Press, 2014); Hisako Kinukawa, ed., *Migration and Diaspora: Exegetical Voices of Women in Northeast Asian Countries*, IVBS 6 (Atlanta: SBL Press, 2014).

place to another, of taking on new customs and culture, or not belonging to one land or people are experiences common to many colonized peoples and aspects of the book of Ruth with which they identify.

Further, a postcolonial perspective identifies with Naomi and Ruth's agency and strength as well as Ruth's hybridity. Their circumstances may require them to take unusual initiatives and to adopt demanding behaviors (e.g., Ruth and Naomi's traveling together to Judah and Ruth's efforts to provide for herself and her mother-in-law), and they may experience themselves as having a combined identity of more than one nation and culture. Many Cubans, for example, learned Spanish in their homes, and then learned Russian in school, and then English, and then a country outside Cuba became their adopted homeland. They are their past but they are different from that past in their present. Ruth remains a Moabite even as she bears the ancestor of David, the future king of Israel. Finally, from a postcolonial perspective, Ruth's mixed marriage, as a Moabite to the Judahites—to Mahlon and especially Boaz—presents an alternative to those who would seek ethnic purity as a way to construct Judah's postexilic identity; it resists that form of cultural control even as it validates colonized peoples.

In order to enhance our understanding and appreciation of the book of Ruth as fully as possible, we have drawn on colleagues from around the world and included their insights, by way of both contributing voices and footnoted material.

Translating Ruth and the Woman of Proverbs 31:10

I have done much work on the Bible translation of an amazing Indian woman, Pandita Ramabai. She was born in 1858 and died in 1922, just about the time Gandhi was coming into India. She was a self-taught woman, who became the professor of Sanskrit at the oldest university in India. She came from a high-caste family but decided to marry a low-caste person in Calcutta. Sadly, her husband died, and during this period of grief, she became a follower of Jesus. As a very young widow, she returned back to her hometown, Pune, and engaged in a huge amount of work for the good of low-caste and outcast girls. She rescued girls from religious and secular prostitution centers. She rescued girls from the practice of *sati*, a ritual in which girls are forced to jump into the funeral pyres of their dead husbands. She pleaded with people not to kill their infant girls but instead to give them to her. Soon she had hundreds of girls in her home called *Mukti Sadan*, the house of salvation. She began teaching them the Bible. However, when she read the Bible in the local language called Marathi, she realized that much of the language in the Marathi Bible was very demeaning to the low-caste and outcast girls she had rescued. The term for God was the word used for the high-caste deity, who was responsible for the enslavement of low-caste and outcast girls. The term for heaven was the place where only the highest caste Hindus go. There they are given many low-caste women as a trophy for their karma on earth. Ramabai saw all this as an injustice to the women of India. So, in the face of much opposition from the high-caste leadership of the Bible Society of India, she took on the task of translating the whole Bible into the language of the low-caste and outcast peoples' groups of India. She had gained the knowledge of Hebrew, Aramaic, and Greek and painstakingly translated each verse of the Bible. The translation was completed in 1922, just before she died.

The Indian Bible translations generally describe the woman of Proverbs 31:10 as a humble, coy, silent wife. Ramabai described her as a spiritually, mentally, and physically just person.

This was Ramabai's solution to the violence and enslavement of girls in India. It seems clear to me that the Hebrew canonical sequence in which Ruth follows Proverbs also offers a just solution to the problem of violence against women in global societies—ancient as well as modern.[103]

Rajkumar Boaz Johnson

Traditional, Feminist, Global?

"The reader's task is to determine whether the book affirms Ruth or ultimately erases her, whether she serves as a moral exemplar or as a warning against sexually forward Gentile women."[104] Obviously the book of Ruth can be read in several ways.[105] Ruth is the heroine who

103. See Rajkumar Boaz Johnson, "Pandita Ramabai's Translation and Use of Proverbs 31," in Roncace and Weaver, *Global Perspectives on the Old Testament*, 168–69.

104. Levine, "Ruth," 85.

105. In defending her "reading against the grain," Gale Yee notes what we hope this introduction has suggested, that the ambiguity of the text creates an openness to multiple very diverse interpretations ("'She Stood in Tears amid the Alien Corn': Ruth, the Perpetual Foreigner and Model Minority," in *They Were All Together in One Place? Toward Minority Biblical Criticism*, ed. Randall C. Bailey, Tat-Siong Benny Liew,

shows extraordinary kindness (*ḥesed*) toward her mother-in-law, to the degree that she leaves her own country and culture, willingly embraces Israelite identity, claims YHWH as her God, and marries Boaz. Or Ruth is the Moabite who takes advantage of an opportunity to see a new, and hopefully better, world. Ruth functions in the book to establish the ancestry of David, Israel's greatest king. Or Ruth is a heroine who models resistance to genealogical purity and the controls of Persian rule. Ruth and Naomi may be as close as sisters or as distant as Naomi's lack of expressed appreciation for her daughter-in-law might suggest. What is the "takeaway"? Should contemporary women and men seek to be like Ruth, showing loyalty, love, and loving kindness? Should they do so by conforming to their culture's expectations or by challenging them? It is important to recognize and understand why not all readers, including all women—and for good reason—will read the story in the same way.

About the Authors

While we have speculated about the authorship of the book of Ruth, we wish now to tell you a little about ourselves, this commentary's authors. Each of us has a voice that feminism allows us to use. I (Alice Laffey) am the older scholar, finishing my career at the College of the Holy Cross. I have a doctorate in Sacred Scripture (SSD) from the Pontifical Biblical Institute in Rome.

My training was predominantly in historical criticism, the world behind the text. At the time I began graduate school I was a Sister of Mercy. I wanted to study Scripture and my superior believed that the best place to do so was Europe, not because America lacked outstanding biblical scholars but because the quality of American graduate programs, as she understood them, was more dependent on particular faculty than on an established curriculum. I was sent to Rome, to the Pontifical Biblical Institute. As a Roman Catholic enrolled in a Jesuit school, I assumed that the Scriptures were inspired and contained revelation, and so I was also very much interested in, and educated to, the world of the text, what

and Fernando F. Segovia, SemeiaSt 57 [Atlanta: SBL Press, 2009], 119–40, esp. 127). Yee claims solidarity with other scholars whose work challenges traditional interpretations, including Robert Maldonado, Laura Donaldson, Kwok Pui-lan, Francisco García-Treto, Angela Wai Ching Wong, as well as Danna Nolan Fewell and David M. Gunn, Amy-Jill Levine, Tod Linafelt, and Timothy K. Beal.

Alonso Schökel spoke of as *The Inspired Word.*[106] I was already a feminist, having participated with Elisabeth Schüssler Fiorenza and Rosemary Radford Reuther, among others, in the Women's Ordination Conference.[107] But studying in an almost exclusively male, clerical atmosphere can quickly make one more radical. I began to notice the myriad ways the Roman Catholic Church discriminates against women. I began to ask a lot of questions having to do with why things are the way they are and why things can't be different; for example, not only why women are excluded from ordination but also why they are excluded from all significant decision-making roles of the Church. It's fair to say that I began to question all assumptions, and I pretty much still do.[108] But we live in history, and I ended up doing my doctoral dissertation on 2 Samuel 7 (David's monarchy), closer to my director's area of expertise, rather than my intellectual interest, the rape of Tamar (2 Sam 13). Had my male director, Dennis J. McCarthy, SJ, not been a feminist, I probably would not have survived.

Shortly after coming to Holy Cross in 1981 I began to teach a seminar on "Women in the Bible," and a few years later I changed its title to "Women and/in the Bible." Unfortunately, my first book,[109] prompted by my wonderful white affluent Catholic students, gave only a very small nod to the race and class and other particularities of biblical women. I provided the names of the kings' wives, as the biblical texts do, most of whom say and do nothing except bear the next king, but I ignored the unnamed women, many of whom act courageously (e.g., those who helped to save the Davidic dynasty, a "servant-girl" [2 Sam 17] and a

106. *The Inspired Word: Scripture in the Light of Language and Literature* (New York: Herder and Herder, 1965).

107. An organization begun in 1975 and comprised of women and men who seek the ordination of women to a new kind of priestly ministry in the Roman Catholic Church.

108. One of the assumptions that has always haunted me has to do with money and status. Why are money and status important? When is enough enough? Why do I need to become a full professor? Can I be a professor unless I am genuinely a student? Why should Americans presume that America should be number one in the world? Why isn't it better to have long lunches with wine, like the Italians do, than to divinize efficiency? Why is something "exclusive" good, when my goal is to be inclusive? Who came up with the term "political correctness"? To what extent do political correctness and humanistic values overlap? How can Christians follow Jesus who became human and took the form of a servant (Phil 2:5-8), while spending our lives climbing ladders? The list of assumptions and questions goes on and on.

109. *An Introduction to the Old Testament: A Feminist Perspective* (Philadelphia: Fortress, 1988).

"wise woman" [2 Sam 20]). By doing so, I reinforced the discrimination that accompanies class. And I had no excuse. Before going to Rome in 1973, I had taught at an inner-city girls' high school, at the time of the assassination of Martin Luther King Jr., where race and class were always on the front burner. But I didn't connect the dots. Within two months of my book's publication I knew that it was simplistic and wrong. But at the time (1988), there were not a lot of monographs focusing on Old Testament women and feminist issues. Somewhat to my embarrassment the book is still in print.[110]

But patriarchy and hierarchy are about the distribution of power. I have continued throughout my career to learn about the distribution of power and how cultures legitimate domination. I gravitated toward reader-response criticism[111] so that I could introduce in my work, up front, the limiting lens through which I was working. I was interested in power and therefore wanted to explore texts where the seemingly powerless or less powerful do great things. I must confess I didn't work on Ruth early on because its power relations are less overt and I didn't appreciate them. I studied, for example, the role of the ass in the story of Balaam (Num 22–24), the pet in Nathan's parable to David (2 Sam 12), Queen Vashti's courage in disobeying the king (Esth 1:1–2:4), and the six women who save the Davidic dynasty (Michal, 1 Sam 19; Abigail, 1 Sam 25; an unnamed maidservant, 2 Sam 17; an unnamed wise woman, 2 Sam 20; Jehosheba and an unnamed nurse, 2 Kgs 11).

I am a heterosexual female, happily single, born and living in the first world, the United States; I am white, upper middle class, educated, and deeply committed to faith in God as a more or less practicing Catholic. This lens colors everything I see and touch, including the biblical text.

110. Some of my other feminist work includes: "Feminist Biblical Studies as a Discipline and the Responsibilities of a Catholic Feminist Biblical Scholar," in *Themes in Feminist Theology for the New Millennium (IV)*, ed. Gaile Pohlhaus (Villanova, PA: Villanova University Press, 2006), 25–52; "The Influence of Feminism on Christianity," in *Daughters of Abraham*, ed. Yvonne Yazbeck Haddad and John L. Esposito (Gainesville: University Press of Florida Press, 2001); "A Liberation Perspective: Patriarchy, Monarchy and Economics in the Deuteronomistic History," in *Pluralism and Oppression: Theology in World Perspective*, ed. Paul Knitter, The 1988 Annual Publication of the College Theology Society, vol. 34 (Washington, DC: University Press of America, 1991), 221–35.

111. This method pays attention to the reader's role in creating the meaning and experience of a literary work; the reader completes the meaning of the literary work through interpretation.

Fully aware that a tenured academic is secure and privileged, I have tried to choose nonconventional routes. I have tried to uncover biblical characters and biblical texts that are or present society's underdogs and yet emerge as society's heroes.

The power of domination is often subtle, and although I tried to become aware of its tyranny, I spent most of my life unaware of the power I/we exert over the natural world and the abuse in which I am complicit. The cultural norms of patriarchy and hierarchy and my culture's and Church's complacency with inequality (e.g., the "given" of women receiving unequal pay for equal work; the all-too-common expectation that wives, even though also working full time outside the home, bear greater responsibility than their husbands for work in the domestic sphere, including parenting; the continued exclusion of women from significant ecclesial leadership roles) caused me to reflect on our relationship with the natural world and my/our deliberate and unwitting participation in that abuse. I was coming to this insight just about the time that the news media began to make us aware of the environmental crisis and at the time when increasing numbers of my students were becoming vegetarians. I began to use historical criticism to try to imagine the ancients' relationship to nature. Egypt's ten plagues became ecological imbalance. Whereas the ancients knew their dependence—at least the agrarians among them—I am often blinded by affluence. Living in the first world I will eat—even if there is a drought or a flood "somewhere else." And so I have tried to become more aware.[112] The book of Ruth begins with a famine in Judah.

And that's about where I am now, struggling with a global feminism that includes postcolonialism and a global environmentalism, and interpreting the biblical texts in ways that promote equality and difference. Because these texts are Scripture for me, they have been a primary influence in shaping my identity and guiding my thought and action.

And I (Mahri Leonard-Fleckman) am the younger scholar, just beginning my career at the University of Scranton and now at Providence College, both Catholic schools.

Like Alice, I am privileged: white, upper middle class, from the United States, etc. I come from a mixed Jewish-Protestant background; my sister

112. See, for example, my books *Appreciating God's Creation through Scripture* (New York: Paulist, 1997); *The Pentateuch: A Liberation-Critical Reading* (Minneapolis: Fortress, 1999).

and I were raised in a secular home but were steeped in religion, thanks to strong extended family. My sister was more naturally drawn to the mix of Presbyterian and Evangelical Christianity on our mother's side, while I was drawn to the Conservative and Reform Judaism on our father's side. From an early age I understood "subjectivity": the lens of my southern, first-generation Jewish grandmother was worlds apart from that of my conservative Protestant grandfather. I grew up with a sensibility toward interreligious and intercultural "dialogue" (more often tension!) and adeptness at straddling worlds without fully belonging to either. As I grew up, I was hungry to learn and to understand people; I became a bookworm, a lover of languages, literature, history, and culture.

After college, I served in the Peace Corps in the Dominican Republic. While there, I was attracted to the spirituality around me, particularly in the older women who were my friends and mentors. Their religious identities were infused with the local culture and the difficulties of their daily lives. I had never read the Bible, and after putting out a plea to relatives, I soon received two: the Tanakh (in English) and the NIV Study Bible. I read the texts as literature and as cultural documents (which was my college training, after all) and as revelation. I remember waking up early in the morning and spending hours poring over the texts by the light of a lantern. I found the Bible to be deeply consoling. Looking back, I don't think that I had a clear understanding of how the Tanakh and the Christian Old Testament were distinct at that point, nor did I realize that in turning toward the tradition of the people around me I was somehow turning away from Judaism.

I began to attend the local Catholic church, where chickens ran across the floor, a priest presided once a month (if that), and women ran the services. I loved climbing the hills to attend *horas santas*, where women crowded into tiny homes and prayed the rosary together. Simultaneously, I became friends with a Canadian family living in Santiago, about two hours from the village where I lived. They ran a nondenominational, English-speaking house church for expatriates, and I began to travel in some weekends to attend church. Eventually, I was baptized in the ocean. Despite the fact that I was again straddling cultural and religious worlds, at that point, I somehow believed there was one "Christianity."

My future plans took an abrupt turn, and after finishing my service, I left for Union Theological Seminary in New York with the goal of becoming a pastor. My first shock was in realizing that there were many, many "Christianities," each of which had a distinct identity from the others, and that I had to choose one. After a while, I wandered into the

Spanish service of a local Catholic church and felt like I had come home. The second shock was that I became Roman Catholic, after quitting and rejoining the RCIA[113] program three times (I don't know who was more shocked, I or my women friends, who have since become pastors and Episcopal priests).

Yet the more that I became immersed in Christianity, the more I ached for the Jewish world of my family. I found some solace in studying the Tanakh and Jewish-Christian relations and in taking classes in conjunction with the Jewish Theological Seminary (JTS) across the street. After receiving my master of divinity, I began doctoral work in the Department of Hebrew and Judaic Studies at New York University, where I was rigorously trained in traditional, critical tools of biblical analysis and ancient Near Eastern studies. My dissertation was on the political development of the House of David in the context of literary history and in relation to early first-millennium Aramaean polities.[114] While working on my doctorate, I also fell in love with and married a man who is Buddhist, which has added another rich dimension to interreligious dialogue (and tension!).

Only a few years out of NYU, I am a young scholar who seeks integration, in scholarship as much as in life. My feminism is about justice and about the voice and dignity of all people, all life. It is rooted in the understanding of what it means to straddle worlds without ever fully feeling at home. As a feminist biblical scholar, I am drawn first and foremost to the worlds within and behind the text. In studying ancient languages, culture, literature, and history, I find keys that unlock these worlds to me and that help me understand the people I encounter there. I care about the integrity of the voices within the text, both heard and unheard, and about trying to bridge those voices to our own. Two years ago at the University of Scranton, I taught a course called "Sexuality and Gender in the Old Testament." The support for and reactions to this course were overwhelmingly positive from both students and colleagues. I found that the best way to teach was simply to sink into the text and the stories and to allow students the freedom to encounter the ancient world and tell *me* what issues emerged for them. I hope that my work in this project allows readers the same freedom.

113. RCIA: the Rite of Christian Initiation for Adults, a yearlong conversion program into the Roman Catholic Church.

114. Mahri Leonard-Fleckman, *The House of David: Between Political Formation and Literary Revision* (Minneapolis: Fortress, 2016).

Collaboration

Mahri and Alice met in the fall of 2014, not too long after Mahri had completed her PhD and moved with her husband to Worcester. Mahri came highly recommended to Alice by several mutual colleagues, so Alice invited Mahri to lunch. At the end of the meal or shortly thereafter we agreed to work together on the Ruth commentary. We wished to model cooperation rather than competition. It is fair to say that it has been a rewarding experience for both of us. Trained differently, and in different eras of biblical studies, we have tried to work through our different emphases and write together a feminist commentary that is integrated and cohesive. With excellent suggestions from our editor, Amy-Jill Levine, University Professor of New Testament and Jewish Studies at Vanderbilt University, with whom we were also able to work collaboratively, we have sought to diminish our differences without losing our individual voices. Alice began the introduction, providing its skeleton, but it has had many wise suggestions and much good editing from Mahri. Alice is also primarily responsible for the commentary provided in chapters 1 and 4, while Mahri has been the primary author of the commentary for chapters 2 and 3. Though Mahri "lived" in Worcester, while we were writing the commentary she was teaching in Pennsylvania, so we thank the people behind our internet services for making our communication efficient—if not always the face-to-face meetings that we would have preferred.

While the two of us have co-authored this volume, we are dependent on the knowledge and insights of others. We have "given credit where credit is due" to the extent that we could in the footnotes. The interaction we have had with those monographs and articles has greatly enhanced our work. We have also asked other voices to contribute their insights into the text and to add to our interpretations in the body of this commentary. They join in the conversation with us. We did not predetermine criteria on the basis of which we would invite contributors. We invited our friends or people whom we admired, people whom we thought would make interesting and diverse contributions. In a few cases we invited "strangers," known to us only through their writing. We are grateful for their contributions.

In reading this commentary you will notice that the authors and contributing voices do not all agree, and that is as it should be. While each segment of the book—our introduction and each of the four chapters—has been written and edited by both of us, we emphasize different methods and often, as a consequence, depend on different sources. We have therefore chosen to identify the parts of the commentary where each of us has had the greater influence.

We have also edited the work of some of our contributing authors, but those contributors agreed that we could do so. We have not diluted or changed the thrust of their contributions, but sometimes we have shortened them or tried to sharpen their focus. The greatest violence we have done to their contributions has been to take a coherent whole and present it as segments. Sometimes we have responded to their contribution. It is our hope that you, our readers, also contribute your insights. All of our voices are needed to contribute to everyone's better understanding if this commentary is to be truly feminist. Neither of us, nor any one of us alone, has all the perspectives or all the answers or all the insights. We need each other.

Acknowledgments

A French proverb wisely says, "Gratitude is the memory of the heart." As we complete this manuscript we are filled with many happy memories, including memories of Barbara Reid who conceived of the project, Amy-Jill Levine who became our volume editor, and the many people at Liturgical Press who worked with us to bring the project to completion, including Colleen Stiller, Lauren L. Murphy, and Tara Durheim, as well as nameless (to us) copyeditors, designers, and proofreaders. We also want to thank Kellyann Falkenberg Wolfe, who developed the indices. Alice is particularly grateful to Hans Christoffersen, who "gave her another chance" with Ruth after she had returned the contract for the Hosea volume, and to Mahri for her unending patience and editing, including the tedious and thankless tasks of conforming footnotes to appropriate style and changing transliterations into Hebrew characters. Mahri is grateful to Alice for including her in the project and for her example of wisdom and humility throughout. In addition to those who supported the project directly, we have and have had many people in our lives who provided and continue to provide daily support in myriad ways; they too have helped to bring the volume to completion. Mahri singles out her spouse, Judson Brewer; Alice singles out her rescue dog, Maggie. Both of us have deep-felt gratitude to family and many friends. Finally, we also thank the early authors and editors of the book of Ruth and those, throughout history, who have shared their insights about the book and have provided us with learning and joy.

Ruth 1

Finding Alternatives

Introducing the Characters: Setting and Situation (1:1-5)

Verse 1 provides the timing of the story, its setting, its circumstances, and its initial action. And yet the sentence is generic. For example, the timing is not precise. It covers potentially a span of more than two hundred years, from about 1250 to 1050 BCE. "The days when the judges ruled" can suggest a time of rest (peace)—at least, according to the biblical text—under the leadership of Othniel (Judg 3:11), Ehud (Judg 3:30), Deborah (Judg 5:31), and Gideon (Judg 8:28). And yet those judges were also military leaders who delivered the Israelites from peoples who were oppressing them. When the judges died, according to the text, Israel again lapsed into apostasy, and peace and autonomy were replaced by foreign rule. The text does not name a specific judge who was ruling; it provides only an indefinite time frame; judges usually ruled at this time, but if no judge were ruling, there may have been less peace. In fact, the book of Judges suggests that the period of the judges was unstable, marked by intermittent peace but also by warfare among the land's various inhabitants.

While Judges 4 and 5 depict two women, Deborah and Jael, who are involved in the conflict with King Jabin of Hazor, we can conclude that many other women suffered from the consequences of political instability

Ruth 1:1-5

[1]In the days when the judges ruled, there was a famine in the land, and a certain man of Bethlehem in Judah went to live in the country of Moab, he and his wife and two sons. [2]The name of the man was Elimelech and the name of his wife Naomi, and the names of his two sons were Mahlon and Chilion; they were Ephrathites from Bethlehem in Judah. They went into the country of Moab and remained there. [3]But Elimelech, the husband of Naomi, died, and she was left with her two sons. [4]These took Moabite wives; the name of the one was Orpah and the name of the other Ruth. When they had lived there about ten years, [5]both Mahlon and Chilion also died, so that the woman was left without her two sons and her husband.

and fighting. Men could rape and abuse women without personal consequences (Judg 19:25); the Benjaminites, almost wiped out by the other tribes because of their complicity in the rape, need to repopulate. Although the deaths of the Benjaminite women are not mentioned, the text presupposes this loss: the men of the tribe received four hundred young virgins of Jabesh-gilead as wives (with these women having no say; Judg 21:14), and they abducted the young female dancers of Shiloh to make them wives also (Judg 21:21-23). From what the texts do say, one can infer what life must have been like for many women in the days when "there was no king in Israel" (Judg 17:6; 18:1; 19:1).

Many other Old Testament texts are set in a time of famine (e.g., Gen 12:10; 26:1; 41:30, 54; 2 Sam 21:1; 1 Kgs 18:2; 2 Kgs 4:38).[1] But it is difficult to determine whether each of the references to famine, including this one, is historical or simply a literary technique to provide a setting and introduce new action. Perhaps the original audience for the story of Ruth would have been able to pinpoint the timing more precisely, given the notice that it was a time of famine.[2] The topography of Israel, particu-

1. According to William Grebe, there are eighty-four references to "famine" in the Old Testament (*Meal, Metaphor, and More: Food in the Old Testament* [honors thesis, College of the Holy Cross, 2011]). Whether these references are to historical famines or to famines that are literary fictions, the number of references collectively gives an impression of the topography of Israel as dry land.

2. Keil (1807–1888) and Franz Delitzsch (1813–1890), while acknowledging that the time of famine cannot be determined with certainty, connect it with the devastation of the land by the Midianites (Judg 6) (*Commentary on the Old Testament*, vol. 2: *Joshua, Judges, Ruth, 1–2 Samuel* [Grand Rapids: Eerdmans, 1978], 470). Jack M. Sasson believes the text suggests a widespread famine beyond Bethlehem. He notes that the

larly in the south where Judah is located, is dry land. There is more sun than rain. Without adequate irrigation, poor harvests and subsequent famine were frequent. Warfare makes agriculture volatile,[3] and even during those times when there is peace, agriculture is subject to forces that people cannot control. Even to this day farmers are "the ultimate gamblers." They can do everything within their power to secure a good harvest—choose fertile land, fertilize it, plow well, plant good seed, weed, destroy pests—yet sunshine and rain, over which they have no control, determine the yield.

While there is more than one cause of famine—dearth of water, flooding, pests, political turmoil, war—the human cost is always great. And in a religiously oriented world, when bad things happen, it is natural to ask for more than a scientific explanation. Why is YHWH letting this happen? Has YHWH caused it? Is it YHWH's punishment for wrongdoing? What wrongdoing? The text's original audience could not help but ask what YHWH's role was in this suffering, and yet the text does not explain or indicate how the original audience would have answered these questions. Nor does it suggest that the people *did* anything with their answers: repented, fasted, prayed, apostatized. One family we know of chose to move. The question remains open: how did they, and how do we, react to famine?

There is also the question of whether the famine mentioned in Ruth was real. According to Madipoane Masenya, "No famines are associated with this period."[4] She does not provide evidence for this assertion and, because of the uncertainty of the time during which the narrative is set (the period of the judges extends over two hundred years), her assertion is doubtful. Still, if she is right, the famine functions as the excuse to move the narrative forward. Whether the famine is historical or literary, in other Old Testament narratives that identify famine as the reason to leave one place for another (e.g., Abraham in Gen 12:10-20 and Isaac in Gen 26:1-11), the married men make their wives available to foreigners; here, in contrast, the men travel and then take foreign wives.

---

book of Judges does not record any famines, but he assumes their occurrence over the period that lasted for generations (*Ruth: A New Translation with a Philological Commentary and a Formalist-Folklorist Interpretation* [Baltimore: Johns Hopkins University Press, 1979], 15).

3. See the connection between sword and famine in Isa 51:19; Jer 5:12; 14:12, 15-16.

4. Madipoane Masenya, "Ruth," in *The Global Bible Commentary*, ed. Daniel Patte (Nashville: Abingdon, 2004), 86–91, esp. 87.

Famines and the Vulnerable

The context of the story of Ruth is crucial to note from the perspective of places like India. Ruth 1:1 begins with a famine. Famines are times when the most vulnerable people, mainly women and children, become more vulnerable at the hands of the high-caste people. In times like that they immigrate to places where they can find food. Usually, people move from very dry rural areas to the cities. In the cities they become more vulnerable to high-caste people. However, some seek to become the middlemen between the high-caste people and the low-caste people. In this case they become more dangerous than the high-caste people. In the book of Ruth, this is evident in how the sons of Elimelech treat Moabite women. They "lift up," נשא, the two women into religiously oriented sexual slavery. (See the commentary on Ruth 1:4.)

In places like Delhi, a city far removed from the cult of religious prostitution, one encounters this phenomenon all the time. An awfully sad example is the 2012 gang rape of a low-caste girl on a bus in New Delhi. The story is depicted in the documentary titled *India's Daughter*, a BBC production, directed by Leslee Udwin. The young woman who was gang-raped came from a family that was trying to escape the injustices and pain of their low-caste village. She was a medical student. She was dating a high-caste young man, who knew he could not marry her. The people who gang-raped her were low-caste men, who also had tried to escape their problems in low-caste villages. Yet, they wanted to teach her a lesson by horribly raping her and leaving her for dead in the streets of Delhi. Several months after this tragedy, the documentary sadly shows a group of unrepentant men, who are on death row for their crimes but who were clear in their minds that they had done the right thing.

Several leaders, including Prime Minister Manmohan Singh, decried this attitude and called for a change in the moral fiber of India.

Rajkumar Boaz Johnson

Just as verse 1 does not name the judge, it does not name the man of Bethlehem in Judah who went to Moab. The only particulars it does provide are Bethlehem of Judah, the origin of the man, and Moab, his destination. The places are specific, suggesting their importance to what follows. Bethlehem, בית לחם, ironically meaning "house of bread,"[5] apparently has no bread; that is why the man is leaving his home. Moab, his

5. Richard R. Losch describes Bethlehem as originally dedicated to the Chaldean god of fertility, Lachmo (*The Uttermost Part of the Earth: A Guide to the Bible* [Grand Rapids: Eerdmans, 2005], 51).

destination, apparently has food. The travel will not be temporary, such as for reasons of trade. Land takes time to recover from famine. The man will live in Moab, which seems to be a more desirable place for him to live at this time than in Bethlehem. There is no indication of his emotions with respect to this move. The statements are factual: there is a famine; he moves. But the man does not go alone. His wife and two sons accompany him. Again, the verse makes statements about what happened, says something vague about when, and says something specific about why.

The reader may wonder if this was the only family affected by the famine. Since nothing is said about the extent of the famine and its effect on other Bethlehemites, one may conclude that the narrative itself is not historical but that the author had other reasons for creating it. If this was the only family to leave in the face of famine, the author may intend their action to express a lack of faith that YHWH would provide. But the author may have other motives as well. Again, we do not know the names of the man's family members, only that they too went to live in Moab.[6] Verse 1 sets the stage for a generic story (no names are everyone's names; a famine is any obstacle or tragedy); a generic story allows its audience, then and now, to identify.

Verse 2 specifies the general statements of verse 1. We are provided with the names of the family members.[7] Fifty years ago, Christian children in the West were most often named after a relative—a parent, a grandparent—or their middle name was the last name of their mother. That tradition has declined, at least in the United States.[8] In ancient Israel, a person's

6. Jeanette Mathews refers to Elimelech and his family as either refugees or exiles. While she recognizes a semantic difference between the two terms (those fleeing and those either having fled or been taken away), she argues that both result from removal from one's home country in response to adverse circumstances within it. In this case, famine forces the emigration ("Deuteronomy 30: Faithfulness in the Refugee Camps of Moab, Babylonia, and Beyond," in *Bible, Borders, Belonging(s): Engaging Readings from Oceania*, ed. Jione Havea, David J. Neville, and Elaine M. Wainwright, SemeiaSt 75 [Atlanta: SBL Press, 2014], 157–70).

7. These are not common biblical names. In fact, these names—Elimelech, Naomi, Mahlon, and Chilion—occur only in the book of Ruth. This is not, however, a rare phenomenon. There are no other characters in the Bible named after the patriarchs, Abraham, Isaac, Jacob (unless we count the several men in the New Testament named "James," which in Greek is the same name as "Jacob"), etc., and there are many characters named only once, in genealogies, about whom we know nothing other than their place in an ancestral line.

8. When Alice was in Peru many years ago, she met two twin boys, Elton and John; they were named, together, after a famous English musician. The lay administrator of the parish where she stayed, who was a bit older than the twins, was named Elvis.

name also held significance. It often referred to the person's character or destiny: for example, Abraham, meaning "ancestor of a multitude of nations" (Gen 17:5);[9] and Benjamin, meaning "son of the right hand" (Gen 35:18).[10] Names were also chosen to express some aspect of the nation's situation. For example, Shear-jashub is one of Isaiah's sons, and his name means "a remnant shall return" (Isa 7:3); although the parent of Emmanuel is ambiguous, his name means "God is with us" (Isa 7:14).

Elimelech in Hebrew (אלימלך) means "my God [אלי, transliterated *elî*] is king [מלך, *melek*]," or "to whom God is king";[11] Elimelech's name reinforces that the narrative takes place "in the time of the judges" when "there was no king in Israel" (Judg 17:6; 18:1; 19:1; 21:25). Perhaps Elimelech's name is meant deliberately to recall the period of the judges, before the monarchy. Gideon, for example, fresh from his victory over the Midianites, tells the people, "I will not rule over you, and my son will not rule over you; the LORD will rule over you" (Judg 8:23). According to 1 Samuel 8:7, during the time of the judges YHWH was king. When the people ask Samuel for a king, YHWH replies, "They have not rejected you, but they have rejected me from being king over them." Elimelech's name represents fidelity to YHWH.

Whereas the book of Ruth begins during the time of the judges with a man of Judah whose name means "my God is king," the narrative ends with a genealogy, the climax of which is David (4:17, 22), the future king of Israel. The book spans the transition to monarchy even as Samuel, the last of the judges and the anointer of Saul and David, spans the transition to monarchy. Elimelech may represent the old guard, whose very own daughter-in-law issues in the new era. There is irony in the fact that the

---

Apparently their parents chose names of people whose work they admired—famous, successful men from the first world—for their sons. When Alice asked Rajkumar Boaz Johnson to contribute to our commentary she realized that in thirty-five years of teaching at a Christian school she had never taught a Boaz. When she asked Boaz if he knew anyone else by that name, he said he had met a couple of men in Israel with the name.

9. While the NRSV translates "ancestor" in Gen 17:5, the Hebrew is אב, "father," a word consistent both with Abraham's sex and with the patriarchal culture in which the text was produced.

10. Rachel, dying in childbirth, named the child Ben-oni, meaning "son of my sorrow," whereas Jacob called the child "son of the right hand." Rachel may have chosen the name because of her impending death; Jacob may have used a name that expressed his closeness to the son because of his love for Rachel. While we cannot determine the characters' motivations in naming the child, we can note that the names had significance to them.

11. See Keil and Delitzsch, *Commentary*, 472. They attest that these are "genuine Hebrew names."

man for whom God is king dies outside his homeland, the very land over which the king will rule.

Naomi (נעמי) means "pleasant" or "the gracious,"[12] "winsome" or "my lovely one."[13] Like the name Elimelech, Naomi's name implies good. Yet whereas Elimelech's name connects him with YHWH, Naomi's refers to her beauty or temperament (sweetly or innocently charming) in a way that reinforces, at least for the contemporary reader, female stereotypes. (Recall that the rabbis later speculated on Ruth's beauty.) Although subtle, these names work to reinforce patriarchy, indicating appropriate roles for this woman and man.

The names of the two sons, by contrast, sound foreboding or even sinister: Maḥlon (מחלון) means "weakly"[14] or "weakening and pining,"[15] and Chilion (כליון) means "pining"[16] or "blot out and perish."[17] Language describes reality (the two young men's deaths), but language also creates reality. Naming that has negative implications can produce disastrous consequences in the same way that any negative reinforcement can.

Verse 2 repeats that the family is from Bethlehem of Judah and adds that they were Ephrathites. The author may be repeating him- or herself because the story was originally told orally, and repetition serves memory; yet the author may also be deliberately reinforcing an inconsistency. Something is not quite right if there is a famine in the "house of bread." The author may be subtly foreshadowing the tragic deaths that follow. In addition, the author may be foreshadowing the narrative's ending, Judah's genealogy through David (4:17, 22). The Old Testament attests to the term "Ephrathite" five times, yet only in Ruth 1:2 and 1 Samuel 17:12[18] is the term translated as such; elsewhere, the term is translated "Ephraimite."[19] The term "Ephrath/Ephrathah" is connected

12. Ibid.

13. Jack M. Sasson, "Ruth," in *The Literary Guide to the Bible*, ed. Robert Alter and Frank Kermode (Cambridge, MA: Harvard University Press, 1987), 322.

14. Keil and Delitzsch, *Commentary*, 472; Jennifer Koosed says that Mahlon means "Sickness" (see *Gleaning Ruth: A Biblical Heroine and Her Afterlives*, Studies on Personalities of the Old Testament [Columbia: University of South Carolina Press, 2011], 36).

15. Sasson, "Ruth," 322.

16. Keil and Delitzsch, *Commentary*, 472.

17. Sasson, "Ruth," 321; according to Koosed, Chilion means "The End" (*Gleaning Ruth*, 36).

18. In the NRSV, 1 Sam 17:12 reads: "Now David was the son of an Ephrathite of Bethlehem in Judah, named Jesse, who had eight sons."

19. In addition to Ruth 1:2 and 1 Sam 17:12, the gentilic name "Ephrathite" (אפרתי) is attested in the following texts, all of which appear as "Ephraimite" in the English

to Bethlehem in biblical tradition; for example, the prophet Micah (eighth century BCE) addresses Bethlehem of Ephrathah, "one of the little clans of Judah," and declares that a person would come forth from Bethlehem of Ephrathah who would "rule in Israel, [and] whose origin was from of old" (5:2).[20] Later interpreters associated this prediction with David, while Christians identify Bethlehem as the birthplace of Jesus (Matt 2:1; Luke 2:4), who is said to descend from the line of David.[21] Together, Ephrathah and Bethlehem in Ruth 1:1-2, along with the repetition of Bethlehem, intensify the contrast between fertility and famine.

The famine takes Elimelech and his family to Moab. Genesis 19:30-37 tells the story of Moab's origin, the son of Lot's daughter. According to this passage, Lot and his daughters leave the city of Sodom, which YHWH destroys because of its evildoing. Believing that YHWH has destroyed the entire human race and that there is no one left with whom to have children, the women make their father drunk, have sexual intercourse with him, and produce two sons by incest, Ben-ammi (Ammon) and Moab (see also the discussion on Lot and his daughters in the in-

---

translations (e.g., NRSV, JPS, NABRE): 1 Sam 1:1, which describes Elkanah, Hannah's husband and Samuel's father, as an "Ephrathite"; Judg 12:5, which discusses the fugitives from Ephraim across the Jordan as from "Ephraim" and as "Ephrathites"; and 1 Kgs 11:26, in which Jeroboam is called an "Ephrathite." In an argument that is creative yet inconclusive based on the evidence, Sara Japhet argues that "Ephrath" and "Ephrathite" identify people from Ephraim who eventually settle in the towns of Judah, including Bethlehem; eventually, Bethlehem and Ephrath/ah became synonymous ("Was David a Judahite or an Ephraimite? Light from the Genealogies," in *Let Us Go Up to Zion: Essays in Honour of H. G. M. Williamson on the Occasion of His Sixty-Fifth Birthday*, ed. Iaian Provan and Mark Boda, VTSup 153 [Leiden: Brill, 2012], 297–306; see also Nadav Na'aman, "Ephraim, Ephrath and the Settlement in the Judean Hill Country," *Zion* 49 [1984], 325–31 [in Hebrew]).

20. Mic 5:2 = 5:1 in the Masoretic Text. Ephrathah also occurs in Ps 132:6 and in Ruth 4:11, while Ephrath occurs in Gen 35:16, 19 and 48:7 as a synonym for Bethlehem, and in 1 Chr 2:19, 24, 50; and 4:4, in genealogies of Judah. Losch identifies Ephrathah as a "small village near the city eventually absorbed into Bethlehem" (*The Uttermost Part of the Earth*, 51). According to Keil and Delitzsch, Ephrathah is an old name for Bethlehem and means "sprung from Bethlehem" (*Commentary*, 472). If sprung from Bethlehem, then, like Bethlehem, it is also a fertile place ("a house of bread").

21. Luke 2:4 reads: "Joseph also went from the town of Nazareth in Galilee to Judea, to the city of David called Bethlehem, because he was descended from the house and family of David." Raymond E. Brown, among others, points to the discrepancies between the infancy accounts in Matthew and Luke, emphasizing not their historical inaccuracy but their theological relevance. The gospel texts connect Bethlehem as both David's and Jesus' birthplace (*The Birth of the Messiah: A Commentary on the Infancy Narratives in the Gospels of Matthew and Luke* [New York: Doubleday, 1977]).

troduction and at Ruth 3:6-9). The narrative does not overtly condemn the women's behavior or, importantly, the sons that they produce, yet as stated in the introduction, it does perhaps explain the hostilities between Israel and its neighbors.[22] Israel intermittently experienced hostile relations with Moab (e.g., Num 22–25; 1 Sam 14:47; 2 Sam 8:2; 2 Kgs 3:4-27; Isa 15–16; Jer 48; Ezek 25:8-11; Amos 2:1-3; Ezra 9:1; and Neh 13:1), and during the time of the judges, at least according to Judges 3:12-30 and 10:6,[23] Moab was an enemy of Judah.

According to Deuteronomy 23:3-4, the animosity between Israel and Moab derived from the Moabites' lack of hospitality when the Israelites left Egypt. The text reads: "No Ammonite or Moabite shall be admitted to the assembly of the Lord. Even to the tenth generation, none of their descendants shall be admitted to the assembly of the Lord, because they did not meet you with food and water on your journey out of Egypt, and because they hired against you Balaam son of Beor, from Pethor of Mesopotamia, to curse you." Numbers 22–25, considered older than Deuteronomy, records the narrative regarding the king of Moab trying, unsuccessfully, to get the prophet Balaam to curse the Israelites. According to Numbers 25:1-2, Israelite men had sexual relations with Moabite women and joined the Moabites in offering sacrifices to their gods.[24] In the Ruth narrative, although an Israelite man has sexual relations with a Moabite woman, there is no proselytism on Ruth's part. Her own religion is never mentioned and, in fact, she comes to choose Naomi's God. Nor is there any indication in the Ruth narrative that the Moabites were inhospitable to Elimelech's family. In the passages in Numbers and Deuteronomy, it is the Moabites' behavior—their lack of hospitality and their idolatry—that warrants condemnation, not their ethnicity.[25]

22. There are resonances between this story of Moab's origins and the story of Ruth (e.g., Elimelech and his family leaving a land that could no longer support them, Ruth's difficulty in producing a child with her first husband).

23. See also Peter H. W. Lau, "Another Postcolonial Reading of the Book of Ruth," in *Reading Ruth in Asia*, ed. Jione Havea and Peter H. W. Lau, IVBS 7 (Atlanta: SBL Press, 2015), 21.

24. Numbers 25:1-2 reads: "While Israel was staying in Shittim, the people began to have sexual relations with the people of Moab. These invited the people to the sacrifices of their gods, and the people ate and bowed down to their gods."

25. Irmtraud Fischer interprets Ruth's Moabite identity as a reversal of Deut 23:3-4 by employing the *halakhah*, "If the reason no longer applies, the prohibition is no longer justified." In other words, in this instance, the Moabite woman is not luring anyone into idolatry (which is the reason for the prohibition), and therefore it

Judah, in some periods more than others, experienced amenable relations with Moab. For the purposes of the Ruth narrative, the author may have chosen Moab as the destination of Elimelech and his family simply because the country is located just east of Judah and borders the Jordan River (see Deut 1:5), or because Moab was likely fertile, possessing arable land that was able to grow food. There is a certain irony here, or a reversal, because the very place that refused the Israelites food and water on their journey out of Egypt now provides food and water for this family from Bethlehem, the house of bread. But those explanations do not seem sufficient in themselves. The author refers to Moab and identifies Ruth as a Moabite repeatedly throughout the narrative.

While the following subtle connections of the Ruth story with Moab's origin may not be the reason Ruth is identified as a Moabite, still the resonances help to suggest that the author deliberately intended to identify Ruth as a Moabite. Just as Lot and his family left Sodom because it was destroyed and could no longer support them, Elimelech and his family left Bethlehem because, in a state of famine, it could no longer support them. Just as Lot's wife looked back to her homeland, Naomi actually went back. We note that just as Lot, Abraham's nephew, impregnated the mother of Moab (the Moabites), Boaz, the Israelite, impregnated Ruth, the Moabite who would become the ancestor of Israel's King David.

In recent years much has been written about border crossings and the plight of refugees. Even as we write this commentary, there is support for closing the southern border of the United States to undocumented people coming from south of the border; there are refugees pouring into Europe and Australia from war-torn Syria. Each situation is different, but there is suffering and heartache in each. Many readers of the book of Ruth can readily identify with the "man of Bethlehem in Judah" who, along with his wife and two sons, leaves his own country in order to survive.

Many people who leave their homes seek refuge in a land that is culturally and politically foreign to them because they cannot survive, politically and/or economically, in their own land; they are desperate.

is unjustified to reject her. See B. Rosh Hashana 31b, cited in "The Book of Ruth: A 'Feminist' Commentary to the Torah?," in *Ruth and Esther*, FCB 3, 2nd ser., ed. Athalya Brenner (Sheffield: Sheffield Academic, 1999), 24–49, esp. 36. Reading from the perspective of Korean multiculturalism, Yoon Kyung Lee defends the foreigner and resists attributing to them derogatory and unjustified stereotypes ("Postexilic Jewish Experience and Korean Multiculturalism," in *Migration and Diaspora: Exegetical Voices of Women in Northeast Asian Countries*, ed. Hisako Kinukawa, IVBS 6 [Atlanta: SBL Press, 2014], 3–18, esp. 5).

Today there are more than sixty-five million people rightly identified as refugees and internally displaced persons.[26] They read this verse with an existential knowing.[27]

The man who traveled to Moab is unnamed in verse 1, as are his wife and two sons. Yet even there he stands out. He takes a risk different from the risk taken by those who stayed; he leaves his home and homeland in order to avoid the consequences of the famine. He leaves during the time that insufficient food is produced in the land to feed those who depend on it. The narrative would have us believe that only one family responded to the famine by leaving the unproductive land. Perhaps this man and his family were the only Judahites who went to Moab. The departure may be an act of trust in the God who is Elimelech's king, or the act may lack trust: since YHWH is not providing food, Elimelech must take matters into his own hands. One thing is certain, having YHWH as king will not put food on the table.

Elimelech, the man whose name alludes to his God as king, will not be the center of the story's action, though his death in Moab (v. 3) proves a catalyst for the actions of others. They act and carry the narrative forward. What the reader does not as yet know is that not only does this man die but his sons die also; these deaths open the door to Elimelech's wife Naomi becoming a major character who carries on the action of the narrative. With three men gone, a woman (and women) emerges.

A Reflection on Famine

Hunger drives us to enter into a new philosophy and a new, wider boundary as our search leads us on a "sojourn" of satiety. Here, the search becomes twofold; one leading to the other, with satiety being redefined for those who suffer from extreme lack. If one is hungering for food, then God moves them to God's abundance. If one is suffering from thirst, our God directs them to God's well. Where there is God, there is no want, and so the sojourn to

26. Data provided by the United Nations High Commission on Refugees and quoted in CNN online, updated June 20, 2016.

27. The Women's Refugee Commission is currently the only international organization dedicated solely to protecting refugee women's rights to sexual and reproductive health care, freedom from gender-based violence, and economic and social empowerment. See Hisako Kinukawa, ed., *Migration and Diaspora: Exegetical Voices of Women in Northeast Asian Countries*, IVBS 6 (Atlanta: SBL Press, 2014).

satisfaction is accomplished in God.

"They went into the country of Moab and remained there" (Ruth 1:2).

"A certain man from Bethlehem in Judah" takes his family on a sojourn of hope that delivers them to a land that God has not afflicted famine upon. Why? Why is one famine exchanged for another? Why bring this family to gain barley only to suffer a famine of heart, the loss of husband and sons? The answer is found in the three women who, despite strife and deaths, find courage in faith, loyalty to tradition, and unreserved love.

Sheila Clare DeLuca

The final sentence of verse 2 repeats information already known—they went to Moab—but then the verse adds, "they remained there." This last clause may suggest any of at least three scenarios: that the famine lasted a long time in Judah; that famines in Judah occurred repeatedly but not regularly (so that the people could plan); or simply that the family chose to remain in Moab even after the famine had ended. The statement might give further credence to the assumption that Moab was simply more fertile than Judah, that its inhabitants were less likely to suffer famine, and therefore that they were more likely not only to survive but to thrive there.

The statement itself, "and they remained there," gives rise to a multitude of questions. Having left Bethlehem during hard times, would their return be resented by those who had remained in the land and "toughed it out"? Did they hesitate to return to Judah because of Mahlon's and Chilion's Moabite wives? Did the Moabite wives encourage them to stay in Moab, so that the wives could be near their own fathers and mothers? Did Naomi feel guilty for leaving her homeland in the first place and thus was she hesitant to return "during the good times," when the famine was over? These are questions without answers, but we can speculate.

Verse 3 announces the death of Elimelech. He was Naomi's husband, and his passing left her with two sons. The narrator tells the story from Naomi's point of view. It is her husband, her sons, her losses, and eventually it is her daughters-in-law, her return to Bethlehem, her people, her relatives, and her land that she is selling.[28]

28. Carolyn Custis James, *The Gospel of Ruth: Loving God Enough to Break the Rules* (Grand Rapids: Zondervan, 2011), 27. The narrative does not capture Ruth's or Orpah's perspective where Naomi is their "mother-in-law."

Though it is not always the case, the death of a husband in any patriarchal culture can leave his widow vulnerable, if not materially, then socially. We do not know the details of Naomi's situation—she may have felt free of a husband whom she resented, who had forced her to leave her homeland. Though the narratives in Genesis do not detail the deaths of husbands before wives (Abraham buries Sarah [Gen 23:19] and Jacob buries both Rachel [Gen 35:19; 48:7] and Leah [Gen 49:31]), Deuteronomy and many of the prophetic books mandate that the Israelites provide for and protect the widow (e.g., Deut 10:18; 24:19-21; 27:19; Isa 1:17; Jer 7:6; 22:3; Zech 7:10; Mal 3:5)[29] as well as the alien and "orphan."[30] Just as a young unmarried woman's physical well-being and social standing in a patriarchal culture derive from her father, even if in seemingly "emancipated" cultures,[31] the death of a woman's husband may deprive the widow of the physical well-being and social standing that her husband had provided. One theory held by a few scholars who date the book of Ruth to the postexilic period suggests that the book "may have been canonized precisely because it overturns" the Israelite prejudice against women who share Ruth's profile: "Foreign women [in this case, a Moabite]. Poor. Childless. Widows. Single."[32] While this indictment of postexilic Yehudites may seem harsh, it is consistent with the notion that the introduction of any term[33] or ideal may be occasioned by that

29. Our commentary often draws on other biblical texts to elucidate a particular verse in the book of Ruth. This technique is referred to as intertextuality. In premodernity, the technique was used extensively because little consideration was given to the relative dating of texts; all texts were the "word of God." Modernity, in its effort to situate texts historically, would not use a later text to elucidate an earlier text. Postmodernity has returned to using this technique more liberally.

30. While the translation of יתום in the NRSV is "orphan," the Hebrew actually refers to a child lacking a father; the fatherless do not necessarily lack both father and mother but they are considered orphans in the ancient Israelite culture. Their physical security (survival) is threatened, as is their social standing, because they lack a father.

31. In US culture, until very recently, a father walked his daughter down the aisle at her wedding, and the new bride replaced her surname, which was her father's, with the surname of her new husband.

32. Athalya Brenner, *I Am . . .: Biblical Women Tell Their Own Stories* (Minneapolis: Fortress, 2005), 102.

33. According to Lothar Perlitt, the Hebrew term ברית, "covenant," entered into Israel's vocabulary late, when the covenant relationship could not be taken for granted. What formerly had been presumed had to be made intentional (*Bundestheologie im Alten Testament*, WMANT 36 [Neukirchen-Vluyn, DE: Neukirchener Verlag, 1969]). If one considers this theory to be prejudiced against ancient Israel, it is no different than to suggest an American prejudice, for example, in the desire of many people in

behavior or practice not being observed or followed to the extent that it should be.

Fortunately for Naomi, she was not childless; she had sons. They were expected not only to provide for and protect the widow, their mother, but also to carry on the family line by fathering sons themselves. As long as they did so, the family line would not be lost. Responsibility for Naomi's well-being had been transferred from her father to her husband at the time of her marriage; now, having lost her husband, she would find that responsibility for her well-being would transfer to her sons, and her well-being included their potential to bear sons. They would provide for her—or so was likely her expectation. (The Israelites' responsibility to protect the resident alien does not come to the fore until later in the story.)

The narrative suggests that Naomi's two sons accepted their new roles. They must not only provide for their mother but also try to beget sons to continue the genealogical line. They may have had other reasons for marriage, to be sure, but begetting sons was undoubtedly one of them. Living in Moab, they took Moabite wives.[34] As Rajkumar Boaz Johnson's comments above suggest, supported by the Hebrew verb נשא, which literally means "to lift, carry," the translation "took" suggests that the coming together of the men from Judah with the Moabite women was more an act of force than an act of "marriage." Not only does the text hark back to the episode in Judges 21:15-25 (the Benjaminites taking the daughters of Shiloh), which also uses the Hebrew verb נשא (v. 23), but it lacks the more commonly used verb לקח, "to take," thus providing a contrast to the Hebrew expression denoting Boaz's marrying Ruth (לקח) in 4:13. Both Jione Havea[35] and Wil Gafney[36] read verse 23 as "rape marriage." In Havea's

the United States to build a wall to keep out southern neighbors. In fact, the American prejudice is worse, since we have not learned from history.

34. Other foreign wives are attested in the Old Testament. While Brenner (*I Am . . .*, 107), provides a generous list of foreign female partners for Israelite males, listed here are those who are both clearly identified as wives and not identified with any forms of wrongdoing: Joseph's wife Asenath, daughter of Potiphera and priest of On, mother of Ephraim and Manasseh (Gen 41:50-52); Moses' wife Zipporah, the Midianite (Exod 2:21); David's wife Maacah, the daughter of the king of Geshur and the mother of Absalom (2 Sam 3:3); Rehoboam's mother Naamah, an Ammonite (1 Kgs 14:21, 31); and Solomon's Egyptian wife (1 Kgs 3:1).

35. Havea, "Stirring Naomi: Another Gleaning at the Edges of Ruth 1," in Havea and Lau, *Reading Ruth in Asia*, 111–24, esp. 121.

36. Wil Gafney, "Ruth," in *The Africana Bible*, ed. Hugh R. Page Jr. (Minneapolis: Fortress, 2010), 249–54, esp. 250. She translates v. 4: "They abducted for themselves Moabite women" (p. 251).

contemporary context, this rape marriage takes place on the Polynesian island of Tonga.[37] According to Gafney, "The experience of abduction-marriage and forcible pregnancy is not unimaginable to contemporary Africana readers. In some parts of Eastern and Central Africa, women are still abducted and raped into marriage."[38] Gafney points out that the verb נשא occurs five times in the Hebrew Bible with women as objects. Besides Judges 21:23 and Ruth 1:4, the verb occurs in Ezra 10:44 and 2 Chronicles 13:21; 24:3.[39] An examination of these verses strengthens their case. Ezra 10:44, the last verse of the book, reads: "All these had *married* [so the NRSV; the Hebrew is נשא] foreign women, and they sent them away with their children." Not only are the marriages to foreign women, but their husbands are comfortable sending them away. In 2 Chronicles 13:21, after reporting on Abijah's military victories, the passage continues, "Abijah grew strong. He *took* [נשא] fourteen wives, and became the father of twenty-two sons and sixteen daughters."[40] In 2 Chronicles 24:3 the priest "Jehoiada *got* [נשא] two wives for him [Joash], and he became the father of sons and daughters." Tod Linafelt focuses on the "taking women motif" as a sign of male power. He argues for the direct literary connection between the men who take women and their related acquisition or loss of political power.[41] Collectively, these verses represent the execution of patriarchal cultures with respect to at least some marriages—not always by violence but in atypical ways that men determine. If Johnson's, Havea's, and Gafney's reading of נשא is correct, by verse 4 both Ruth and Orpah have already been through a lot.[42] Yet they will reveal themselves as survivors.

37. Havea, "Stirring Naomi," 121.

38. Gafney, "Ruth," 251.

39. Ibid., 250.

40. The Hebrew plural נשים means "women" and, contextually, can be translated "wives." Here, despite the NRSV, "women" may be the more accurate translation.

41. Tod Linafelt, "Taking Women in Samuel: Readers/Responses/Responsibility," in *Reading Between Texts: Intertextuality and the Hebrew Bible*, ed. Danna Nolan Fewell, LCBI (Louisville: Westminster John Knox, 1992), 99–113, cited in April D. Westbrook, *'And He Will Take Your Daughters . . .': Woman Story and the Ethical Evaluation of Monarchy in the David Narrative* (New York: Bloomsbury T & T Clark, 2015), 27.

42. In 2006, the UN Secretary General's in-depth study on all forms of violence against women stated: "Marital rape may be prosecuted in at least 104 States. Of these, 32 have made marital rape a specific criminal offence, while the remaining 72 do not exempt marital rape from general rape provisions. . . . Marital rape is not a prosecutable offence in at least 53 countries. Four countries criminalize marital rape only when the spouses are judicially separated. Four countries are considering legislation that would allow marital rape to be prosecuted" (p. 113). In 2011, the UN Women report *Progress of the World's Women: In Pursuit of Justice* stated: "By April

The two wives are specified by their names, Orpah and Ruth.[43] Orpah means either "Nape (of the neck)"[44] or it can mean "Scented" or "Cloudy."[45] It is uncommon in American culture to name a child Orpah, but that was the intent of Oprah Winfrey's (the television personality and cultural icon) Aunt Ida when naming her niece. Oprah's name was written correctly on the birth certificate, Orpah Gail Winfrey, but since it was more difficult to pronounce than Oprah, the letters were gradually reversed.[46] The name Ruth is related to a Semitic root meaning "to be soaked, irrigated."[47] Ruth provides in abundance the water that supports life and growth.

Mahlon and Chilion are now to provide both for their mother Naomi and for their respective wives. This does not mean that Naomi and Ruth and Orpah did not work but rather that the responsibility for providing for the family lay with the males. We know from Ruth 2:8 that women did farm and participate in gathering the harvest. The land, however, was, for the most part, the property of the males (e.g., the land that had belonged to Zelophehad [Num 36] and the distribution of the land among the tribes [Josh 13–21]). We do not know whether Mahlon and Chilion owned land in Moab, if they worked another's land (whoever owned the land could control what was grown on it and owned the produce), or whether Mahlon and Chilion even earned their living in Moab by farming. It is possible that they became traders, wove textiles, crafted pottery, or made their living in another way.

Mahlon and Chilion no doubt hope, though it is not said explicitly, that they will father sons. We do not know whether Ruth and Orpah

---

2011, at least 52 States had explicitly outlawed marital rape in their criminal code" (page 17). Gafney brings the issue closer to home. She writes, "According to Molly Egan and Jason Wood's 1999 Lehigh University report, *The Abolition of Marital Rape Exemption*, in the United States spousal rape was criminalized by only seventeen out of fifty states in 1996" ("Ruth," 252).

43. Sasson ("Ruth," 322) notes that it is common in Hebrew narrative (as here) for a major character's name (i.e., Ruth's) to be written after the name of a lesser character (Orpah).

44. Koosed explains that the idea expressed by this name, "the nape of the neck," is that Orpah's character is embodied in her turning away from Naomi and Ruth. All that was seen was the nape of her neck as she returned to her mother's house (*Gleaning Ruth*, 36). See also Sasson, *Ruth*, 20.

45. Sasson, *Ruth*, 20.

46. Thanks are due to Joseph Flynn for this information. See Oprah Winfrey interview at Academy of Achievement, January 21, 1991; https://en.wikipedia.org/wiki/OprahWinfrey.

47. Sasson, "Ruth," 322.

hoped for the same. The two young men live there "about ten years." The number ten signifies completion, so at the end of a designated time, something will happen.[48] Perhaps the "about" (כ) allows for "approximate completion," the time they spent in Moab with their parents as well as the time they spent with their wives. Verse 4 is not clear, because of what precedes and what follows, whether the "about ten" refers to the entire time the family spent in Moab or the approximate number of years the sons lived in Moab after their father's death or the number of years they were married.[49] The number ten may also suggest that a very long time elapsed during which the marriage produced no children.

Marrying a Husband's Household

Ruth's story, representing a feminine ideal[50] that reaps appropriate blessings in reward, is frequently retold in Indian and Western culture to affirm how Ruth's obedience, humility, responsibility, and hardworking nature result in her becoming a truly blessed woman.

In the Indian interpretive tradition of the story, Ruth stands out as a woman, not because of her achievements and accomplishments as a person, but rather because of how dutiful she was as a wife married into her husband's household.

But does Ruth have any importance in the story independent of that role? What makes Ruth fit into the perception of an "ideal woman" as she appears in the interpretive traditions, especially in India? Additionally, what is at stake with the depiction and interpretation of Ruth as an ideal woman? What is the status of Ruth in her story beyond

48. In Gen 16:3 Abram and Sarai had lived ten years in Canaan without Sarai becoming pregnant; it is then that Sarai gives Hagar to Abram. In Gen 18:32, ten is the number on account of whom YHWH will not destroy Sodom; in Gen 32:15 Jacob sends ten male donkeys to appease Esau; both Deut 4:13 and 10:4 refer to the ten words/commandments that YHWH gives the people.

49. Sasson, *Ruth*, 21.

50. According to Leila Leah Bronner (*From Eve to Esther: Rabbinic Reconstructions of Biblical Women* [Louisville: Westminster John Knox, 1994], 80), "The qualities Ruth displays in the biblical narrative itself, and even more, her qualities as developed in rabbinic interpretation—modesty, obedience, devotion to wifely and maternal duties"—are the qualities, especially modesty, with which the rabbis construct "the feminine ideal." (While we may think that uncovering Boaz's "feet" in chapter 3, for example, is hardly a modest act, it was an act of obedience.) In contrast, feminists seek independence, autonomy, and freedom from male control.

the applause she receives? Responding to these questions from an Indian feminist standpoint, the interpretive lens that I use comes from my sociological observation and analysis of what arguably makes a woman "ideal," especially in the Indian context, and how Ruth so often receives this particular status. I bring here a critical and feminist voice that might read the text differently in the Indian context, mainly because of the cultural milieu that features similarities and resonates with the text.

To introduce one aspect of the image of an ideal woman in the Indian context, I recollect an incident that continues to bother me, though I am also aware that it might earn a woman applause as a likable if not "ideal" woman. Since I serve as a pastor, an Indian family living in the United States of America asked me to conduct a family prayer meeting for the anniversary of their mother's death. During the memorial service, I requested that family and friends share an experience or a memory of their mother, whom they considered a blessed and adored woman. Those present shared how younger women in their community looked up to her as a beloved aunt, someone who was perennially patient and soft-spoken. Most of the positive comments were couched in terms of her obedience and humility as a wife, her patience as a mother, and her skill and hospitality as a member of her church and community.

No one shared anything about her personal life or her passions. When I intentionally asked what she liked doing for pleasure, most people shared that she loved to cook. They determined that her daily chore was her passion. In other words, the mother had strived all of her life to fit into the image of an ideal woman at the cost of self-negation, or, perhaps, she had internalized her duties to be her passion and completely lost her innermost self in the process. No one was able to share any memory as to what made the mother particularly happy, how she refreshed herself, where she found her energy or any creative spark. Her duties toward her family and community left little space for self beyond the necessary routine of self-care. The story of this mother is typical of many mothers, especially in traditional Indian culture; they also share multiple similarities with Ruth. However, the rhetoric in the Indian mother's story, as well as the questions I raise about the story of Ruth, proclaim that there is something wrong with this picture.

Surekha Nelavala

The climax of verse 5 is Naomi's bereft state. She has lost all of the family members with whom she came to Moab; she is alone. Elimelech has died; almost ten years have passed; now Mahlon and Chilion also have died. Perhaps the "about" in verse 4 refers to the fact that one son died only slightly before the other, with the time between their deaths not being long. Whatever the reason for the "about," Naomi's sons are both dead and she is left alone, without the males in her family.

Whether Naomi is an older widow or a younger widow, she has endured much. She left familiarity (her home, her culture, the women of Bethlehem, etc.) and now she has lost her husband and sons. Loss, and the suffering that most often accompanies it, can be an occasion to challenge[51] or even reject the workings of YHWH or, as Job also did, to remain faithful[52] and acknowledge mystery beyond human understanding.[53] Naomi does not reject YHWH, as the following verses make clear.

The NRSV ends the first paragraph of the narrative here, with the assertion that Naomi has lost her husband and sons. The situations and actions recounted so far are few but significant. In fact, everything that will happen in the rest of this chapter and the following three chapters is dependent on the narrative's first five verses. We have learned that there was a famine in Judah; the family—Elimelech, Naomi, Mahlon, and Chilion—moved to Moab; Naomi's husband Elimelech died; Naomi's sons Mahlon and Chilion married; about ten years passed; Naomi's sons Mahlon and Chilion died. Naomi is alone.

Did Elimelech die from old age? What caused Mahlon's and Chilion's "untimely" deaths? Was it sickness? In ancient Israel long life was considered a blessing from the Lord (e.g., 1 Kgs 3:10). God's blessings consisted in health translated into a long life, prosperity during that life (1 Kgs 3:10), and progeny who would continue one's life after death (e.g., Deut 28:4). While both famine (e.g., 2 Sam 24:10-13) and early death (e.g., 1 Sam 1:27-32; 2 Sam 6:3-7) might be interpreted as punishment for unfaithfulness, the biblical texts do not always make those connections, and they are not made here. Job, like Naomi, suffers three major losses.

51. E.g., Numbers 11:14-15; 1 Kings 19:3-4; Jeremiah 20:14; Jonah 4:3, and Job 3:11.

52. Job 1:21: "the LORD gave, and the LORD has taken away; blessed be the name of the LORD." For a modern example, Mother Teresa's private letters, published posthumously, revealed her struggle with the loss of the felt presence of God for much of her later life (*Come Be My Light: The Private Writings of the Saint of Calcutta*, ed. Brian Kolodiejchuk [New York: Image Books, 2009]).

53. Esp. Job 42:1-6.

Naomi suffers the deaths of her husband and of each of her two sons. Job suffers the loss of prosperity, the loss of his children, and the loss of his health. According to the narrative, Job's sufferings occur because God allows them to happen. Here, they simply happen, although several verses later Naomi tells the women of Bethlehem that "the Almighty has dealt bitterly with me" (1:20). Naomi, like Job, does not "curse YHWH."

Yet it does seem reasonable to contrast Naomi's longevity with that of her family members, which sends us back to consider her sons' names. Mahlon means "Weakly" and Chilion means "Blot Out and Perish."[54] Who gave the men these names? What was the author implying by following the death of "my God is king" with the deaths of his sons? The family line had ended. YHWH's kingship will give way to David's monarchy (4:17, 22). The three men die, while Naomi alone endures.

The Power of Hospitality and Welcome

Should Elimelech be indicted for taking his family to Moab? After all, Deuteronomy 23:3-4 states that "No Ammonite or Moabite shall be admitted to the assembly of the Lord. Even to the tenth generation, none of the descendants shall be admitted to the assembly of the Lord, because they did not meet you with food and water on your journey out of Egypt, and because they hired against you Balaam son of Beor, from Pethor of Mesopotamia, to curse you." Some think that the deaths of Elimelech and his sons are the consequences of this infraction.

But if one looks more closely at the Deuteronomic text, it prohibits Moabites from being admitted to the assembly of the Lord but says nothing about going to stay with them in their land. And the response of the Moabites to Elimelech's family is a complete reversal of what their ancestors did: instead of withholding food and water, they allowed this Israelite family to find refuge from famine on their land; instead of cursing them through Balaam, they blessed them through Ruth and Orpah. Little wonder that Naomi entreats YHWH to show kindness to her two daughters-in-law according to what they have done for her. Hospitality has reversed the ancient hatred.

Ruth is, after all, a book that is a reversal of results: from

54. We do not know if Naomi named her sons—women often did the naming (see Ruth 4:17). Rachel, for example, dies at the time of the birth of her second son, naming him Ben-oni ("son of my sorrow"; Gen 35:18).

emptiness to fullness and from barrenness to fertility. It is also a reversal of relationships: from aliens to allies and from attackers to supporters. The change was brought about not by politicians or priests but simply by individuals who recognized a common humanity and shared a basic need for survival. This was a change brought about especially by women who extended empathy for one another's suffering and sought what was best for the other. In other words, it was *ḥesed*, that familial steadfast love, which made the difference.

In Singapore, there is a growing discomfort with migrant workers who overwhelm the infrastructure of our city-state. But occasional acts of kindness break the xenophobia. For example, there was a group of Indian migrant workers who risked their own safety by spontaneously climbing up a high-rise apartment building to rescue a toddler hanging from a balcony. This does not imply that all foreigners are safe; that would be too naïve an assumption. There are foreigners who still attack people whether as acts of terrorism or acts of violence against women. But Christians are called to walk a tightrope between wisdom and welcome. This means that we do not prejudge people by their ethnicity or race but leave room for relationships and ethics to make a difference. This is how Ruth, a Moabite, was admitted into the genealogy of the Davidic kings, which led ultimately, to the Christ.

Maggie Low

Coping with Tragedy, Decisions, and Actions (1:6-14)

Usually a new paragraph begins in English with a named subject, i.e., "Naomi." In verse 6, although Naomi's name does not appear, the narrative's author emphasizes her female identity. "She" is both incorporated into the verb translated as "started" (קום), or more literally "rose up," and also appears as a personal pronoun (היא). There is only one female character, Naomi, who has, so far in the narrative, been the subject of action, so there is no danger of confusing the referent. The text is not explicit either about her destination of "return" (שוב) or the people whom the Lord has considered, but just as "she" is Naomi, the reader fills in the specifics of Naomi's return to Bethlehem of Judah and Israel, to whom the people of Bethlehem of Judah belong, as the identity of the people the Lord has considered. The verse succeeds in being both specific (Naomi, Bethlehem, and Israel) and also generic (she, return, his people), thus

Ruth 1:6-14

[6]Then she started to return with
her daughters-in-law from the coun-
try of Moab, for she had heard in the
country of Moab that the LORD had
considered his people and given them
food. [7]So she set out from the place
where she had been living, she and
her two daughters-in-law, and they
went on their way to go back to the
land of Judah. [8]But Naomi said to her
two daughters-in-law, "Go back each
of you to your mother's house. May
the LORD deal kindly with you, as you
have dealt with the dead and with me.
[9]The LORD grant that you may find se-
curity, each of you in the house of
your husband." Then she kissed them,
and they wept aloud. [10]They said to

allowing the reader to engage in this story and to imagine different places and different peoples.

The word "return" occurs twelve times in chapter 1 (1:6, 7, 8, 10, 11, 12, 15 [twice], 16, 21, 22 [twice]). While most of these occurrences have to do with physical location, the verb can be used more broadly to designate relationships.[55] The term is also used as a literary technique, here and in other books. For example, in the book of Jeremiah, שׁוב is used quite frequently to depict, in addition to geographical movement, the following: (1) turning away from YHWH, (2) turning to idols, (3) turning away from idols, and (4) turning back to YHWH. While many other verbs can and are used to articulate the people of Israel's relationship to geography and to YHWH, the repetition of שׁוב, both here and in Jeremiah, is deliberate. Naomi turned away from Judah toward Moab and is now turning away from Moab toward Judah; Ruth is turning away from Moab toward Judah, but she is also turning toward Naomi.

That the Lord has "given them food" associates agricultural renewal, the right balance of water and sun, with the Lord's blessing. Since the famine, the reason for going to Moab in the first place, has now ended, the possibility of returning home to Judah where food is available becomes attractive. It is, after all, Naomi's homeland, and the Bethlehemites with whom she traveled to Moab—her husband and sons—are no longer her companions in a foreign land. If she has reason to stay in Moab, it is not the reason that brought her there.

55. In v. 15 Naomi tells Ruth that Orpah has "gone back to her people and to her gods"; while the geographic location is Moab, the returning involves relationship, affiliation, and loyalty. In v. 16 Ruth pleads with Naomi not to press her "to turn back from following" her; again, the implication is relational as much as it is geographic.

her, "No, we will return with you to your people." [11]But Naomi said, "Turn back, my daughters, why will you go with me? Do I still have sons in my womb that they may become your husbands? [12]Turn back, my daughters, go your way, for I am too old to have a husband. Even if I thought there was hope for me, even if I should have a husband tonight and bear sons, [13]would you then wait until they were grown? Would you then refrain from marrying? No, my daughters, it has been far more bitter for me than for you, because the hand of the LORD has turned against me." [14]Then they wept aloud again. Orpah kissed her mother-in-law, but Ruth clung to her.

This is the first time YHWH enters explicitly into the text. YHWH "has considered his people" and then satisfied their need with food. The narrator tells us that this is what Naomi had heard. Whether it was the small size and geographical proximity of Israel and Moab that facilitated communication between them, or perhaps international trade, Naomi learned that her homeland was again producing food. Maybe it was Moab's changed economic situation that made her aware that Judah's famine was over. Fewer foods, though insufficient amounts, needed to be imported to Judah from Moab, making more food available in Moab and lowering prices there; maybe Israel was achieving greater status among the nations and exerting a little more influence now that the country was in a less depressed state. Whatever the reason, news spread and reached Naomi: her homeland had food.

The expression, "the LORD had considered [פקד] his people" (v. 6) is an articulation of Naomi's faith. Perhaps there were others who believed in the Lord in Moab, perhaps other Judahites who also had come to Moab to escape the famine and now credited the Lord with providing food in their homeland. We should not ignore the phrase "his people." The narrator assures us that Naomi believes that YHWH is the God of her people, the Israelites. We may rightly conclude that those who believed in YHWH, including Naomi, attributed renewed food in Israel to YHWH's "visiting" or "considering" them, as the NRSV translates: "The LORD had considered his people." Elsewhere, the NRSV translates פקד, with YHWH as the subject, as: "had given heed to" (Exod 4:31); "dealt with" (Gen 21:1); and "took note of" (1 Sam 2:21). Each translation contains a slightly different nuance. In each case YHWH *visits* either his people (Ruth 1:6 and Exod 4:31) or a woman who has had trouble conceiving (Sarah in Gen 21:1 and Hannah in 1 Sam 2:21). None of these passages blames YHWH for causing the original problem (famine, bondage, and difficulty in conceiving, respectively), but the narrators understand YHWH's involvement to provide the remedy.[56]

Verse 6 portrays Naomi's two daughters-in-law[57] traveling back with her to Israel. They had "belonged" to Mahlon and Chilion, and as the men's widows, they continued their connection to the men's family, attached to their mother-in-law. The sons themselves, who were never distinguished by which woman they had married, Orpah or Ruth, diminish further in importance. The narrator does not tie the dead men's identities to their wives, or the widows' identities to their dead husbands, but rather the identities of the two women to their common mother-in-law. It is a family of women.

Hardship provides the background for the actions of these women. The hardship—the loss of husbands and all male family members, and providing for themselves and each other without the men—becomes an opportunity and a challenge. The end of famine in her homeland provides Naomi with hope and possibility; she is going home with her family, two other women, to the place where the famine has ended. But just as going home means saying goodbye, traveling, and taking a risk with the unknown, so being at home will require working to become self-supportive. YHWH may have "considered his people and given them food," but the women must actively cooperate with this gift of YHWH.

Naomi's daughters-in-law are sisters-in-law. Both are Moabites; both had married Israelite men. Yet we know almost nothing of their families or their families' economic circumstances. Further, we do not know how well they knew each other and whether or not they liked each other. The narrator simply records that the two women traveled from Moab together with Naomi. In due course, we learn that both women have "mothers' houses" (v. 8).

Verse 6 begins the journey to Judah. Because the Lord has visited the people and because there is now food, Naomi sets out to go back (שוב) to Judah. Naomi had gone from Judah to Moab; now she returns from

56. Contra Lau, who suggests that if God visits Israel and ends the famine, then God also allowed the famine. He notes that many biblical texts represent famine as a punishment for Israel's disobedience (e.g., Lev 26:19-29; Deut 28:23-24, 38-42; 2 Sam 21:1-14; 1 Kgs 17:1; 18:1-2). See "Another Postcolonial Reading of the Book of Ruth," 21.

57. Koosed notes that the Hebrew word כלה can mean both "daughter-in-law" and "bride." The two English words have very different meanings, but the Hebrew word brings together a legal relationship and the "love, affection, joy and hope" that occasioned it (*Gleaning Ruth*, 35).

Moab to Judah. Verse 6 repeats "Moab" twice for emphasis. The repetition recalls what Moab has meant. This place has been a place of refuge in providing food and doting daughters-in-law for this Bethlehemite family, which is an alternative perspective for any negative reputation Moab has in the Bible. Elsewhere, the Moabites are the result of incest (Gen 19); they refuse to show hospitality to the Israelites (Deut 23:3-4); and their women encourage the Israelite men to practice idolatry (Num 25:1-2). Yet not here; Naomi departs from Moab with two Moabite daughters-in-law accompanying her, emigrating from the place that had supported her family.

Naomi had gone from Judah during a famine; now she returns there when the people have food. But Naomi had gone with her husband and two sons; now she is en route to return as a widow, with two widowed daughters-in-law. "She" is the subject of action. While verse 6 presents Moab both as the place where Naomi was when she heard about food in Judah and as the starting place of her return, here the text becomes more localized but also indefinite: Naomi set out "from the place where she had been living" (literally, "the place which she was there"). It is not identified as her "home" (בית) where she was the center of family life; with no husband or sons to animate the living space, the text suggests a space where she simply existed, despite the fact that her daughters-in-law were likely with her.[58] We know that Naomi will return to Bethlehem in Judah, a particular city that was home in her home country, yet we never know where she lived in the country of Moab. Moab is therefore a vague place, which perhaps represents the perspective of the Judahite author(s) of Ruth, who was an outsider to this foreign country.[59]

58. As recently as thirty-five years ago, it was unacceptable for a young, middle-class, Italian woman to live alone. Her family expected her to live with them, to enter a convent, or to marry and live with her husband. Young women who had graduated school, who were not ready to marry, and who were offered jobs in the cities were desperate to find living situations in the cities that would be acceptable to their parents. Alice, during the years when she lived in Rome (1973–1981), encountered several of these young women who asked, almost begged, her to allow them to live with her or who sought the contact information of other American women living in the city who might be disposed to allow them to share living space. They were desperate to find another woman or women with whom they could live.

59. For many who do not know the United States, New York equals the United States. They do not particularize to other cities or recognize the differences among cities. Only when one begins to belong does it become important to differentiate. When Mahri lived in the Dominican Republic, many times people would ask her, "Which part of New York are you from?"

Only in the latter half of verse 7 are the daughters-in-law subjects who act. They go, leaving the place where they too had been living, to accompany Naomi back to Judah. She goes (fem. sing.), and they accompany her; whereas she is returning, they are going. While they go with her, they may or may not be choosing to go. We do not know. Social expectation—their identification with their mother-in-law since their husbands and even their father-in-law are dead, and they have no sons—may require them to remain with and support Naomi no matter where she is, whether that be in Moab or back in Judah. Or, going with Naomi may be the deliberate choice of the two women. What we do know from the text is this: they go. So far the narrator has been the only speaker, describing all the events and activities that have taken place.

But while the narrator has told us that the three women have begun to return to Judah, the return does not take place before a meaningful conversation occurs among them. Each of the women speaks; Naomi tries to persuade her daughters-in-law to return to their homes; the women disagree and mount opposition to Naomi's point of view; Naomi persists. Eventually she is able to change the mind of one of the daughters-in-law, but Ruth will not give in. She is determined to stay with her mother-in-law and accompany her back to Judah.

The plot now moves forward mostly through dialogue, which accounts for fifty-five of the eighty-five verses of the book, the highest ratio of dialogue to narrative in any of the biblical books. This technique makes the scenes intimate[60] and immediate. Rather than being told what a person is thinking or saying or doing by a third party, the reader or hearer experiences the person's own thoughts directly. There is no "middleman." The technique has the potential to increase the engagement of the reader or hearer, which it does here effectively. While it may be too constrictive to say that identity is "dialogically formed" or that people define themselves "in dialogue with, and sometimes in struggle against," the things that others see in them,[61] speech—and engagement with another speaker—have

60. Sasson, "Ruth," 320.

61. Amy Kalmanofsky, *Dangerous Sisters of the Hebrew Bible* (Minneapolis: Fortress, 2014), 159, quotes and confirms Eunny P. Lee who says that "identity is dialogically formed" ("Ruth, the Moabite: Identity, Kinship, and Otherness," in *Engaging the Bible in a Gendered World: An Introduction to Feminist Biblical Interpretation in Honor of Katharine Doob Sakenfeld*, ed. Linda Day and Carolyn Pressler [Louisville: Westminster John Knox, 2006], 98–101, esp. 93).

the potential to be self-revelatory.[62] Dialogue, in contrast to narration, provides not only the information that the character wishes to communicate but also the precise words that the character uses to covey that information (terse or expansive, vague or detailed, repetitive, etc.). We get to know characters by how they speak as well as by what they say. While an omniscient narrator can say things beyond what a character knows, the omniscient narrator is then providing results rather than progress.

Up to this point, the narrator has described settings, circumstances, and events. Verse 8 contains the first words spoken in the narrative, woman to women. A named subject, Naomi, speaks and dominates the conversation. She speaks directly to her two companions and begins by giving a directive. She tells each of the women to return (שׁוב) to her mother's house.[63] Whereas Naomi will return to Judah, her two daughters-in-law are to return to their mothers' homes, which we can assume are in Moab. The reference to a mother's house is relatively rare in the biblical texts (e.g., Gen 24:28; Songs 3:4; 8:2) in comparison to the much more common "father's house" of patriarchal culture (e.g., Gen 38:11; Deut 22:21). Yet Naomi has been the head of the household since her sons' deaths, and because Ruth and Orpah were with her, she was the head of a household of three. As Naomi demonstrates, women could and did manage households. The phrase may then be the natural choice of a woman, Naomi, who has been independent of men since the deaths of her husband and sons. In other words, she is projecting her own experience on her daughters-in-law, encouraging them to return to a house headed by their own mothers. Perhaps Ruth's and Orpah's fathers (and brothers, if they had them) had also died, and their mothers would be heading up the houses in which they lived. Naomi is encouraging the return of these women to their mothers. There are no Moabite males in this part of the story.

When the phrase "mother's house" occurs elsewhere, it is in the context of sexuality and marriage.[64] Abraham's servant seeks a wife for Isaac.

62. One may also use speech to hide or to be deceptive.

63. As Sasson points out, this verse provides "a powerful indication that levirate marriage is not at stake in this story" ("Ruth," 323). Levirate marriage involved a brother marrying the widow of his brother who died childless. Naomi has no other sons. The redeeming of property, however, extends to close relatives beyond a brother. The latter part of the narrative conflates the two customs.

64. Amy-Jill Levine, "Ruth," *Women's Bible Commentary*, ed. Carol A. Newsom and Sharon H. Ringe, exp. ed. (Louisville: Westminster John Knox, 1998), 84–90, at 86. She also notes that some ancient translations of the Hebrew replace "mother" with "father."

He meets a girl (Rebekah) at a well, and, after the encounter, the girl runs and tells "her mother's house" (Gen 24:28) about the encounter. The girl had a brother, Laban, who "ran out to the man, to the spring" (v. 29). Laban was clearly within his mother's household, which suggests that women were heads of households in which adult males resided. The narrative continues, and Rebekah becomes Isaac's wife.

Within the love poems of Song of Songs, the woman proclaims, "I held him, and would not let him go until I brought him into my *mother's house*, and into the chamber of her who conceived me" (Song 3:4). Later, in Song 8:1, the woman wishes that the man were like a brother who had also nursed at her mother's breast. That would allow her to kiss him outside without anyone thinking badly of her. Song 8:2 continues, "I would lead you and bring you into my *mother's house*, and into the chamber of the one who bore me." The verses are very sexually suggestive. The author of Ruth 1:8 may have wanted the text's original audience to understand that Naomi was sending the women back to their mothers' houses from where marriage and conception could be possible.

Naomi tells the women to return, each to her mother's house. If they were sisters, it was because they shared the same father; yet they clearly did not share the same mother. It is possible that Naomi was, by her directive, deliberately trying to separate the women from each other. She may have preferred one daughter-in-law to the other, or disliked them both, or knew details of the relationship between the two women; any of these scenarios would make separation advantageous. Naomi's words do not provide us with enough clues to make a determination. In Moab, Naomi had been an anchor between the two women, their connection to each other after their husbands' deaths. Other biblical texts provide the reader with competition between sisters who become co-wives (e.g., Gen 30:14-16) and competition between other wives (e.g., 1 Sam 1:6), but none provides clues to a relationship between sisters-in-law.

Naomi then prays for the women. She asks YHWH to deal kindly (עשה חסד) with them, seeking from the Lord the same kindness or *ḥesed* that these two women, her daughters-in-law, had extended to her sons and to her. Before they have a chance to respond to her directive not to accompany her to Judah, Naomi calls on YHWH on their behalf. Her faith is apparent. YHWH is known for showing loving kindness (e.g., 1 Sam 20:14; 2 Sam 2:6; Jer 9:23; Ps 33:5) and Naomi asks YHWH to show it to her daughters-in-law.

Ḥesed, the kindness expressed by YHWH and by various characters at different points during the narrative, is one of the central themes of this short story. Defined by the major lexicon of biblical Hebrew as "goodness, kindness," the term is further nuanced by the passages in which it occurs. With respect to YHWH it is often grouped with other divine attributes, e.g., fidelity (see Gen 24:27; Ps 25:10; 40:11-12). *Ḥesed* is shown in YHWH's redemption from enemies and troubles (e.g., Gen 19:19; 39:21; Exod 15:13) or from sin (e.g., Ps 25:7; 51:2); it is abundant, everlasting, and good (e.g., Num 14:18; Jer 33:11; Ps 69:17). With respect to human beings, it may mean mercy and, rarely, affection, piety, or even lovely appearance (e.g., Prov 20:28; Jer 2:2; Isa 40:6).[65] *Ḥesed* in Ruth 1:9 embodies "an important ingredient of covenant relationship; [it] is more than the loyalty which one expects if he stands in covenant with another person—it is that extra which both establishes and sustains covenant. It is more than ordinary human loyalty; it imitates the divine initiative which comes without being deserved."[66] *Ḥesed* is a summary of Israel's godly and best posture—extending far beyond the book of Ruth to Israel's other literature and to its history in general.[67]

Loving kindness is godly and is thus admired in the people who behave kindly to others. The prophet Micah proclaims: "He has told you, O mortal, what is good; and what does the LORD require of you" and then directs the people to "love kindness" (Mic 6:8). Ruth[68] and Orpah had shown loving kindness; Saul had shown kindness to the Kenites (1 Sam 15:6); David asks Jonathan to show him loving kindness (1 Sam 20:8);[69] and David later deals kindly with Mephibosheth (2 Sam 9:1), to whom he wishes to show "the kindness of God" (v. 3).[70] Ruth and Orpah are Moabites; their treatment in attitude and deeds toward Naomi and her

65. Francis Brown, S. R. Driver, and C. A. Briggs, *Hebrew and English Lexicon of the Old Testament* (Oxford: Oxford University Press, 1972), 338–39.

66. Edward F. Campbell, *Ruth*, AB 7 (New York: Doubleday, 1975), 81.

67. See, for example, Bronner, *From Eve to Esther*, 62–63; Leila Leah Bronner, "A Thematic Approach to Ruth in Rabbinic Literature," in *A Feminist Companion to Ruth*, ed. Athalya Brenner, FCB 3 (Sheffield: Sheffield Academic, 1993), 146–69, esp. 147–48; Yehuda Y. Steinberg, *Harvest of Kindness: Megillas Rus and the Power of Chesed* (Southfield, MI: Targum Press, Inc., 2010), 18.

68. Lau argues that it is Ruth's *ḥesed*, her adoption of Israel's most central virtue, that attracts Boaz to her ("Another Postcolonial Reading of the Book of Ruth," 23).

69. David explicitly connects Jonathan's *ḥesed* to the sacred covenant into which the two men have entered.

70. David shows Mephibosheth kindness for the sake of David's friend and Mephibosheth's father, Jonathan. Politics (restoring Saul's property to his grandson) may be as much the reason for his kindness as godliness.

family prompts Naomi's prayer affirming that YHWH's *ḥesed* is available both beyond the borders of Israel[71] and to non-Israelites.

Here the prayer asks God to deal kindly with Orpah and Ruth as they have done with the dead and with Naomi. We do not know the content of this kindness. The words embody attitudes and behaviors that we can only imagine. It may not have been easy to marry foreigners, even if they resided in one's homeland; they may not have had a choice. The women may have owned property and may have jeopardized its remaining with their tribe or clan by marrying outside their families or countrymen.[72] Their husbands may have been sick before they died and in need of physical care. Their husbands may have been unable to have an erection, to provide physical pleasure, and/or to impregnate the women. While the biblical texts often speak of "barren" women, for whom God opens their wombs, they never speak of men who are unable to impregnate. The women may have been very respectful of the dead, not immediately returning to their countrymen in the hopes of gaining new husbands. Ruth and Orpah may simply have been loving wives, providing warmth and support for their husbands, loving the men to whom Naomi had given life, her beloved sons.

Naomi tells us that the women had also dealt kindly with her. Naomi may be referring to how they treated her as a mother-in-law, with filial respect. In the American culture there are many "mother-in-law" jokes. They presume a previously close relationship between mother and son and now the introduction of another woman who can never meet a mother's expectations for her son. Mother-in-law jokes negatively stereotype both the mother and the son; the problem is always the mother's, and the jokes are a form of "mother-shaming." In contrast, Naomi is

71. Lau, "Another Postcolonial Reading of the Book of Ruth," 28, suggests a comparison with Ps 36:8: "How precious is your steadfast love, O God! All people may take refuge in the shadow of your wings."

72. Israelite law required Zelophehad's daughters to marry within the tribe of their father's clan so that the land would remain within the tribe (Num 36:5-9). There is no evidence, however, that Moabite women would lose their right to own property (we presume they had such a right) if they married outside their tribe or clan. Inscriptions from ancient Egypt and Babylonia attest to women's right to own property, but nothing is said about what would happen to it if they were to marry a foreigner (see Schafik Allam, "Women as Owners of Immovables in Pharaonic Egypt," 123–35, and Amelie Kuhrt, "Non-Royal Women in the Late Babylonian Period: A Survey," 215–39, both in *Women's Earliest Records: From Ancient Egypt and Western Asia*, ed. Barbara S. Lesko, BJS 166 [Atlanta: Scholars Press, 1989]).

complimenting the women *par excellence*, comparing the kindness she wants her YHWH to show the women to the kindness they have shown her. She may be referring to the particular sensitivity they exhibited at the time of her husband's death. The three women may have drawn closer as they shared the grief and loss associated with the deaths of their husbands. Naomi does not detail the particulars, but she tells the women, and the readers, that she had experienced their kindness and was grateful for it. She asks YHWH to repay them with like kindness.

Orpah and Ruth's dealing kindly with Naomi recalls Rahab's dealing kindly with the Israelite spies (Josh 2) and their dealing kindly with her after she helps the Israelites invade Canaan, the land that "the Lord will give" the Israelites (Josh 6). Rahab is protecting the spies with the goal of protecting her own household and her life. She, like Ruth and Orpah, is a foreign woman who treats the Israelite men with *ḥesed*. Rahab is also one of four women (in addition to Ruth) named in Matthew's genealogy.

When Naomi praises the women for their kindness "to the dead and to her," she aligns herself with the dead. By not distinguishing different expressions of kindness, she subtly hints at her experience of her changed status, which is later manifested when she renames herself: "Pleasant" becomes "Bitter" (1:20). And while Naomi prays to YHWH for the well-being of her daughters-in-law, she omits any mention of YHWH's kindness to the dead and to her. She has not rejected YHWH but neither does she claim to have experienced divine *ḥesed* herself.

Verse 9 continues Naomi's prayer. Her petition specifies an expression of the Lord's kindness to her daughters-in-law. She wishes for them security and husbands. The Hebrew word for security (מנוחה) relates the husband's household to a place of material security.[73] Naomi identifies security with the house of a husband. While Jeremy Schipper proposes that Naomi expects the women to return with her, and that the house referred to in verse 9 is the house of their dead husbands in Judah—the Hebrew can be read that way[74]—the text is usually interpreted as referring to the women's returning to Moab with the hope of gaining new husbands. After all, in verse 8, Naomi has told the women to return to their mothers' houses. Although the Hebrew can refer to the men's house in Judah, as Schipper posits, Naomi would be more likely to think of the

73. Jeremy Schipper, *Ruth: A New Translation with Introduction and Commentary*, AYBRL 7D (New Haven: Yale University Press, 2016), 93.

74. Ibid.

house in Judah as Elimelech's house or her house rather than the house of the women's dead husbands.

This last point raises the question of levirate marriage, which stipulates that if a man dies childless, his brother is to marry the widow and conceive a child with her for his deceased brother, so that the dead man's name and line would not be blotted out in Israel. If there is no brother, however, the Torah (Deut 25:5-10) does not state who would be further next-of-kin, in contrast to laws regarding the right to purchase property from family in order to keep land within the family (Lev 25:23-34). (On the question and possible amalgamation of levirate marriage and redemption in Ruth, see also the discussion at 2:18b-23.) Naomi's sending her two daughters-in-law back to their mothers' houses in Moab would suggest that there is no extension of levirate marriage, no likelihood of the women finding Israelite husbands in Judah. If, however, the text has the two women returning with Naomi, Naomi may have hoped for a generous application of the levirate law on the women's (and her sons') behalf.

Many commentators, as we indicated in the introduction, place the composition of the book of Ruth in the Persian Period. Some of these scholars, born and raised in colonized countries, think about the biblical texts in ways that Western scholars had not originally considered. Many of these scholars see similarities between their experiences as colonized people or as descendants of colonized people and details found in the book of Ruth. Jon Berquist, not himself from a colonized country but an expert on postcolonial criticism, has described the behaviors of people who are forced to live under imperial power. He concludes that imperialization always breeds resistance. Some people, he says, hold more tightly to the traditional ways of life and thought of their country's previous pre-imperial autonomy. Others become part of a new group of local ruling elites. In response to the local ruling class, social segments form and create competing interests. He concludes that resistance always develops—in a variety of institutions at once.[75] Looking for this resistance in Ruth, he (and other postcolonial scholars) suggests that it is found in

75. Jon L. Berquist, "Resistance and Accommodation in the Persian Empire," in *In the Shadow of Empire: Reclaiming the Bible as a History of Faithful Resistance*, ed. Richard A. Horsley (Louisville: Westminster John Knox, 2008), 54. While a country need not have been colonized to experience local ruling classes and resistance, such experience is more likely to dominate consciousness in a country where the power and control are held by a foreign power.

a more generous application of the levirate law, extending it beyond a brother, since there are no more brothers, to a next-of-kin.[76]

Naomi continues her prayer for the young women, adding another more specific request. She cannot control the future; still, although it is not possible for the women to have husbands through her, it is possible that they could marry again. She prays that YHWH will provide them with the well-being that comes from having a(nother) husband. The text lacks any mention of what Naomi can do to facilitate the women finding other husbands. Rather, the prayer calls on YHWH to accomplish what Naomi is unable to do. This is more likely to happen, from her perspective, if the women remain in their own country. That is why they must go back (שׁוב), each to her mother's house. Naomi does not let the women, or us, know if she fears that the Moabite women will experience prejudice in Judah, which would be a deterrent to marrying Judahite men, or if she simply wants the women to enjoy the comfort of living in their own culture, among their own people (a comfort of which Naomi herself was deprived for many years).

Naomi links the security she wishes upon her daughters-in-law to marriage. Not all women would agree with Naomi's perspective, as Surekha Nelavala, one of our contributing voices, attests.[77] But cultures

76. In addition to a more generous application of the law, Berquist also argues that resistance can be found in Naomi's prayer, which complements "official" prayer and implies an increased application of prayer that extends to the common people. Berquist's argument does not imply that prayer has ever been limited to officialdom (including during the monarchic period) but rather that ordinary people participate more fully in unofficial religious activities after the exile. There are many causes of change and adaptation: some have a specific purpose and others occur, less purposefully, within a larger culture of change. Postcolonial commentators associate the two examples provided here—a broad application of the levirate law and a broad application of prayer—and identify them as acts of resistance because they resonate with their own experience, changes that put the common people in control. Not everyone will see these behaviors as acts of resistance because not everyone shares the same experience.

As a counter voice, it should be added that Mahri finds Berquist's proposal highly untenable and would argue that there is no clear data to support the notion that common people prayed more after the exile than before. She notes also that the common people (however one qualifies that phrase) need to be distinguished from the scribal culture in charge of writing, copying, editing, and redacting biblical texts.

77. For example, Elaine W. F. Goh disagrees with Naomi's perspective in "An Intertextual Reading of Ruth and Proverbs 31:10-31, with a Chinese Woman's Perspective," in Havea and Lau, *Reading Ruth in Asia*, 73–87, esp. 86. Goh makes the point that Boaz describes Ruth as a woman of strength or אשת חיל (3:11) while Ruth is still

differ, and the ability of individual women to resist cultural expectations also differs. In wanting the best for her daughters-in-law, the *ḥesed* for which she asks YHWH, Naomi is reluctant to risk what she perceives to be in the women's best interest, the material security that she assumes comes with a husband. It would appear that Ruth and Orpah do not share their mother-in-law's priorities.

The emotions of the three women are intense. Naomi kisses them, and they respond with tears. Weeping accompanies kissing in other Old Testament texts, but the same person is the subject of both actions, and the person(s) who initiates the kissing is male (Jacob kissed Rachel and wept [Gen 29:11]; Joseph kissed Jacob and wept [Gen 50:1]) or the actions are reciprocal (David and Jonathan kiss each other and weep [1 Sam 20:41]). In only three other passages in the entire Old Testament is a woman the subject doing the kissing, and always the person being kissed is a male (Prov 7:13; Song 2:1; 8:1; see also Luke 7:36-50, in which a woman kisses Jesus' feet and bathes them with her tears). In this poignant verse Naomi is sending the women away; her kiss suggests how much it is costing her to do so. Yet her desire for their well-being is stronger than her desire for them to remain with her. Ruth and Orpah's tears suggest how much the women appreciate Naomi's generosity, or how much it will cost them to leave Naomi, or that neither choice—to stay or to go—is easy, or simply how much they love her.[78]

The short verse 10 states only the women's response to Naomi's directive; they are insistent[79] that they will return (שׁוב) with Naomi to her people. The two women say nothing about the consequences of the

---

unmarried (in contrast to the woman of strength who is married in Prov 31). The phrase, when used of an unmarried woman, opens the possibility of an unmarried "business woman, teacher, financial planner, manager, property supervisor, and the like" being a woman of strength. Marriage is not essential to the designation. Masenya further asserts: "In many African contexts, we need to resist readings of this story that simply find in it a confirmation of the common opinion that marriage offers the only possible meaningful life for women" ("Ruth," 90). Both articles deal with the authors' respective cultures (in Asia and Africa) and the cultural expectation for women of marriage and family.

78. In the New Testament Paul exhorts the members of respective communities to "greet one another with a holy kiss" (e.g., Rom 16:16; 1 Cor 16:20; 2 Cor 13:12); it is with a kiss that Judas betrays Jesus (e.g., Matt 26:49; Mark 14:45).

79. Schipper, *Ruth*, 94, translates כִּי as "certainly," whereas the NRSV translates the Hebrew as "No." "Certainly" is more polite and respectful, reinforcing what the women had originally pledged; "no," on the other hand, is stronger, expressing a repudiation of Naomi's intent that the women leave her.

decision—whether accompanying Naomi will or will not benefit Naomi or themselves. Naomi has told them to remain in Moab, and she has provided a reason; they have rejected her instruction, period. The reader is privileged to hear the women's conversation but is not quite sure what is behind it, why Naomi and her daughters-in-law say what they do.

Naomi speaks again in verse 11, this time filling in the reason for her directive. Whereas she wants each one of them to find security in the house of a husband (v. 9), she cannot be the source of that security and those husbands. We do not know if the women want the security that Naomi thinks the house of a husband will provide, or if they think the way to achieve that security and husband is by staying in Moab, or even if the two sisters-in-law agree. We are getting Naomi's version of the situation. Her version assumes the provisions of the levirate law (Deut 25:5-10), according to which the women would be expected to marry their dead husbands' brothers. But their dead husbands do not have living brothers. Naomi relates in detail the fact that she is too old to bear more sons and that, even if she could, too much time would need to elapse before they were old enough to be acceptable marriage partners. We do not know how old Naomi is, but she tells us that she is too old to have children so we conclude that she is menopausal. For a woman like Naomi, for whom children are so important, menopause can mean not only infertility but also inability and loss; old can translate into shrunken or useless and incompetent. Though Ruth is still fertile, she gives us no indication that her identity is dependent on children; it is thus fair to assume that menopause might not be an inevitable source of sadness for her.

This is Naomi's perspective, but we do not know if it is a perspective shared by her daughters-in-law. We do not know if the two women even want to marry—whether Moabite or Israelite men—nor do we know if they would want to, even if they could, bear the expected sons for their dead husbands. Naomi is basing her advice about what she thinks will have the best chance of giving the women a future that she is sure is in their best interests.

Naomi insists that they return (שוב), this time turning back from their journey to Bethlehem, and go on their way[80] toward Moab. She asks the

80. In v. 7, הלך בדרך, "to go on the way," occurs; here only הלך, "to go," occurs, though the full meaning is clear. In v. 8 "deal kindly" has a similar construction. The first time the phrase, translated into English as "deal kindly," occurs, the Hebrew is עשה חסד, literally "to make/do loving kindness"; the second time only עשה, "to do,"

women two questions. First, why should they go with her? Naomi sees no benefit to their accompanying her to Judah. The second question, somewhat predicated on the first, asks, rhetorically, whether she still has sons in her womb. From Naomi's perspective, that is the only situation that would justify the Moabite women's travel with her back to Judah. Since she can provide no way for the levirate law to be fulfilled, they may as well remain in their own country. Again, we have only Naomi's point of view. The women may have other reasons for wanting to accompany Naomi to Judah. These Naomi either doesn't know or doesn't address.

In verse 11, Naomi no longer addresses the two women as daughters-in-law but as daughters, a term Boaz later uses for Ruth (2:8; 3:10-11).[81] From the narrative context, we can understand the word as shorthand for "daughters-in-law," as a term Naomi chooses because she did not have daughters of her own, as an assertion of Naomi's changed relationship with the women since they no longer have her sons as husbands, or simply as an expression of endearment. Their common plight may have brought the women closer together. Whatever Naomi's reason for the use of that vocative, it shifts her relationship with the women.

A third time (v. 12) Naomi repeats her directive that the two women turn back (see vv. 8, 11), and a third time Naomi asserts that she is not capable of helping them to fulfill the levirate law (implied in v. 9 and expressed in v. 11 and here). Whereas in verse 11 she asks, "Do I still have sons in my womb?" in verse 12 she answers her own question: she is too old to have a husband. She then proceeds to set conditions and ask another question: (1) even if there were hope for her, (2) if she should have a husband that very night, and (3) if she should bear sons, would the women wait for those sons to be grown (vv. 12-13)? For Naomi, the future for her two daughters-in-law is all about having sons for their dead husbands. Since that is impossible, there is no reason for them to return to Judah with her. Her final question, presupposing that she could have sons that very night, is whether they would refrain from marrying, with the implication of their waiting until her sons were of marriageable age. Again, Naomi is presupposing a scenario in which Ruth and Orpah go to Judah based on the premise that they would bear sons for their dead husbands—an intention that we are not told the Moabite women share.

---

occurs, but the full meaning is clear. In fact, the shortened form, "go," intensifies the desired action.

81. Boaz's designation of Ruth as "daughter" may indicate a difference in age and/or social status. See chapters 2–3.

Naomi continues speaking. She tells "her daughters" that her own plight is greater than theirs. She has lost not only a husband but also two sons. The line of Naomi's Israelite family has been cut off. For the second time, she references YHWH. Whereas in verse 8 she prayed that YHWH would deal kindly with her daughters-in-law, here she tells those same women that the hand, that is, the power, of YHWH has gone out against her. Her bitterness (מר, see 1:20) is so much greater than theirs, not just because of the familial losses but also because of the actions of her YHWH. He has allowed/caused her suffering.

The text does not make explicit anything the people of Israel did that would prompt the land's famine, or anything Elimelech and his family more particularly did to deserve their suffering, though Naomi clearly sees her losses as related to YHWH. While YHWH is the source of everything, Naomi does not name the hardship as punishment for sin. Like Job, she does not connect the actions of YHWH with blessing or curse for specific human behavior: "The Lord gave, and the Lord has taken away." YHWH deserves to be blessed no matter what is sent (Job 1:21-22).[82]

Orpah and Ruth reply not with words but with tears. Whatever their feelings about their own situations, they feel Naomi's pain. Naomi's losses are so great that whether they stay with her or go, it will make no difference. She has lost husband and sons, she has lost the possibility of the continuation of the family line, and she has lost the support of her YHWH. The women's tears speak to these tragedies.

Up to this point in the narrative, the daughters-in-law have not distinguished themselves. Naomi has addressed both of them, and both of them have replied. Only at the end of verse 14 do the women become individuals. Orpah kisses her mother-in-law, a gesture made by Naomi (v. 9) that led to the daughters-in-law's protestation that they would not leave her. Ruth clings (דבק) to her mother-in-law.[83] The verb "cling" as used here signifies "the closest physical position a woman takes to another in the scriptures."[84] The same verb occurs in Genesis 2:24: "Therefore a man leaves his father and his mother and clings to his wife, and they become one flesh." The verb implies close physical

82. Later in the book of Job, Job attributes to YHWH his misfortune but he does not see that misfortune as just punishment for his behavior, that is, his sin.

83. Koosed comments, "Ruth is the disobedient one while Orpah obeys Naomi's wishes" (*Gleaning Ruth*, 37).

84. Levine, "Ruth," 86.

contact, especially in conjunction with verses 16-17.[85] The verb is missing from the LXX, which translates the end of verse 14 as "Orpah returned to her people,[86] but Ruth followed her."[87]

Solidarity in Suffering

In the story of Ruth, like so many low-caste and outcast women in India, Ruth makes the courageous decision to leave her familiar environs to go to Bethlehem with Naomi. It is a poignant story of two women who have seen a lot of pain and bitterness. In the story of Ruth, two women from different parts of the world stick together, because they have the existential experience of bitterness in common with each other.

Rajkumar Boaz Johnson

Pledging Solidarity: Strength and Acceptance (1:15-18)

Verse 15 opens the third paragraph in the NRSV translation yet, here again, the subject is unnamed: "she" says. The "she," Naomi, from whose perspective the story is being told, now speaks directly to Ruth and thus differentiates between her daughters-in-law. Or, they have differentiated themselves. While Orpah returns to (שׁוב) her people, her culture, and her gods, Ruth remains with her mother-in-law despite Naomi's protestations. Naomi repeats again her directive that Ruth too should return (שׁוב) to her people and her gods; she should do what her sister-in-law is doing.

The name Orpah appears only twice in the narrative, in verses 2 and 14. This latter reference mentions her twice, both times as "sister-in-law." She has served her literary purpose by setting up a counterpart to Ruth. While Ruth insists on remaining with Naomi, Orpah goes back to her people and her gods. Later Jewish tradition[88] identifies Orpah as the

85. J. Cheryl Exum, *Plotted, Shot, and Painted: Cultural Representations of Biblical Women*, 2nd rev. ed. (Sheffield: Sheffield Phoenix, 2012), 161–207.

86. Laura Donaldson argues that Orpah, not Ruth, is the book's central character. She is a hero because she chooses her own religion, culture, and people in the face of a power that seeks to eliminate them ("The Sign of Orpah: Reading Ruth through Native Eyes," in *Vernacular Hermeneutics*, ed. R. S. Sujirtharajah [Sheffield: Sheffield Academic, 1999], 209–36).

87. The LXX does not provide an explanation for the changed verb. The change itself suggests that the translator(s) wished to eliminate any possibility that readers might understand the text physically and/or sexually.

88. Ruth Rab. 2.20.

Ruth 1:15-18

15So she said, "See, your sister-in-law has gone back to her people and to her gods; return after your sister-in law." 16But Ruth said,

"Do not press me to leave you
or to turn back from following
you!
Where you go, I will go;
where you lodge, I will lodge;
your people shall be my people,
and your God my God.
17Where you die, I will die—
there will I be buried.
May the LORD do thus and so
to me,
and more as well,
if even death parts me from you!"

18When Naomi saw that she was determined to go with her, she said no more to her.

mother of Goliath, an enemy of Israel and the main adversary of Ruth's descendent, David (1 Sam 17), and thus creates an exaggerated opposition between the two women.[89]

In verse 14, Naomi tells Ruth for a fourth time to return (שוב), this time to follow her sister-in-law. The repetition of שוב, implying return to Judah as well as return to Moab, distinguishes the travel even as it emphasizes the movement.

Ruth's reply is neither a statement of disagreement nor a rational argument designed to counter Naomi's points. It is more a respectful request: "Please do not insist that I leave you." Ruth has listened to Naomi's argument; she resisted; she clung; now she entreats. She asks Naomi not to insist that she leave her and turn back (שוב) from following her.

In verse 16, שוב is not about returning from Bethlehem or to Bethlehem, to Moab or from Moab, it is about "turning back" from a relationship. Ruth is asking Naomi to allow her to continue to follow her. The verb therefore shifts in meaning from a place to a person, to a relationship that Ruth wishes to continue. She does not want to say goodbye. This relationship is more important to Ruth than anything or anyone else. To go and be with Naomi is more important than to remain in or return to her own land, people, culture, and gods.

89. Bronner, *From Eve to Esther*, 69; Brenner, *I Am . . .*, 111. The reason or reasons for this tradition history are unclear. It would appear that the rabbis demonize Orpah in order to divinize Ruth. Ruth is the daughter-in-law who chooses YHWH, whereas Orpah returns to her people's gods. Ruth is also the ancestor of the great King David; by making Orpah the mother of the Philistine leader Goliath whom David kills, the rabbis extend the contrast between the two women. Ruth and David are winners; Orpah and Goliath are losers.

The pledge that follows, on Ruth's lips, contains more words than Ruth has spoken previously. She declares her love and fidelity to Naomi but claims as her own what marks Naomi's identity: the place to which Naomi will go, whatever place; the place where Naomi will take up residence, whatever place; the people to whom Naomi belongs; the YHWH who is Naomi's YHWH;[90] even the place where Naomi will die, Ruth claims for herself.

Though Naomi did not state that she wants to die in her own land, among her own people, and with her God, the reader can assume as much. Naomi is leaving the place where her husband and sons are likely buried;[91] she will not be buried with them, and she will not be there to care for their graves. And so Ruth takes the initiative by affirming that she will die and be buried "where" (in the land) Naomi will die.

Athalya Brenner suggests that Ruth may not have chosen to go with Naomi primarily out of love and devotion but rather that self-interest could have influenced her decision.[92] Motivations are always complex. Ruth may have wanted to go with Naomi, but Ruth may also have sought the adventure that travel and a new land and people would provide. She may also have heard good things about Judah. In fact, going to Judah would have allowed her to leave behind everything she disliked about her own situation in Moab. In addition to wanting to be with and support Naomi, these may be reasons that Ruth wanted to accompany her mother-in-law.

Still, Ruth's profession of loyalty is extraordinary. She seeks the closest possible relationship with Naomi. Her pledge of loving fidelity resembles a declaration of premarital love and loyalty, which is why it has been incorporated into both Jewish and Christian wedding ceremonies. Ruth's loyalty also has resonances with the story of Abraham, for her decision to leave her native country parallels the journey Abraham undertook (Gen 12:1-9). Abraham left his homeland, Ur, just as Ruth left her homeland, Moab, each with a barren, older woman (Sarah and Naomi, respectively). Abraham was responding to the call of God, whereas Ruth was following Naomi.

The copious occurrences of שוב in the book of Jeremiah, like the copious occurrence in the book of Ruth, play on the object toward which or away from which the characters turn. In Jeremiah the object is either YHWH

90. As Koosed notes, only here does Ruth use the personal name of the Israelite god (*Gleaning Ruth*, 51).

91. Moab is also the place where Moses was buried (Deut 34:5-6). The verses evoke another reason why Moab is ambiguous, sometimes an adversary and sometimes, like here, neutral if not beneficial.

92. Brenner, *I Am . . .*, 102–4.

or idols. In the book of Ruth, while the object is often a place, it is also Naomi, the person toward whom Ruth wishes to turn.

These data cumulatively raise a question. What exactly was the relationship that Ruth and Naomi shared, or that Ruth wished for them? The evidence is not conclusive, but neither is it neutral. Are the women physically attracted to each other? Scholars analyzing the same evidence find themselves on both sides of that question based on the verb דבק. J. Cheryl Exum[93] and Comea M. Walthall,[94] for example, lean in the direction of sexual attraction between the two women, while Amy Kalmanofsky[95] and Surekha Nelavala[96] read a nonphysical sisterhood. Exum augments her thesis with an analysis of a painting titled "Ruth and Naomi."[97] The visual exchange between the two women and their embrace suggest physical attraction.

Another consideration is a comparison between Ruth's profession to Naomi and the relationship between David and Jonathan. In the latter case, the writer states that Jonathan swears to protect David: "the Lord do so to Jonathan, and more also, if . . ." (1 Sam 20:13). Jonathan asks from David "the faithful love [*ḥesed*] of the Lord" (v. 14). Further, the narrator records that "Jonathan made a covenant with David, because he loved him as his own soul" (1 Sam 18:3). Jonathan made David swear by his love for him, "for he loved him as he loved his own life" (1 Sam 20:17). Jonathan's love for David was such that he, much to the anger of Saul, his father (1 Sam 20:30-31), would hand over to him the kingship (1 Sam 18:4). Later, David laments Jonathan's death, saying, "greatly beloved were you to me; your love to me was wonderful, passing the love of women" (2 Sam 1:26). David and Jonathan's relationship, which can similarly be interpreted as sexual,[98] resonates with this passage

93. Exum, *Plotted, Shot, and Painted*, 161–207.

94. Comea M. Walthall, "Ruth's Relevance to the Same-Sex Marriage Debate," in *Global Perspectives on the Old Testament*, edited by Mark Roncace and Joseph Weaver (Boston: Pearson Education, 2014), 195–96.

95. Kalmanofsky, *Dangerous Sisters*, 158.

96. Surekha Nelavala, "Patriarchy, a Threat to Human Bonding: Reading the Story of Ruth in the Light of Marriage and Family Structures in India," in Havea and Lau, *Reading Ruth in Asia*, 89–98.

97. The painting is by Philip Hermogenes Calderon (1833–1898). It is now exhibited in the Walker Art Gallery in Liverpool, England.

98. See, for example, Susan Ackerman's *When Heroes Love: The Ambiguity of Eros in the Stories of Gilgamesh and David*, GTR (New York: Columbia University Press, 2005), 165–99. Ackerman compares the David/Jonathan relationship to the Gilgamesh/Enkido relationship and hints of Jonathan's taking the woman/wife role.

from Ruth. Ruth has shown to Naomi the *ḥesed* that Jonathan asks from YHWH for David. In both passages the characters swear an oath. Ruth says, already claiming Naomi's YHWH, "May the LORD do thus and so to me, and more as well, if even death parts me from you."

While the swearing of other oaths takes place in 1–2 Samuel and 1–2 Kings, most characters, like Ruth, swear only one oath: e.g., Eli to Samuel (1 Sam 3:17), Saul to Jonathan (1 Sam 14:14), Solomon about Adonijah (1 Kgs 2:23), and the king of Israel about Elisha (2 Kgs 6:31). Only David swears three oaths: about Nabal (1 Sam 25:22), about not eating (2 Sam 3:35), and about making Amasa leader (2 Sam 19:13). The only other woman in the entire Old Testament who swears an oath, besides Ruth, is Jezebel, Ahab's queen, and she does so, not by YHWH, but by her gods; rather than an oath toward the well-being of another, she swears that Elijah will meet the same fate as the prophets he has killed (1 Kgs 19:2). And so Ruth's oath is unique. She is the only woman who swears an oath for good.

Ruth's expression of loyalty toward Naomi possesses similarities to political treaties or contracts, between two people unrelated by blood, which are found in the historical books, including 1 Kings 22:4 and 2 Kings 3:7. In 1 Kings 22:4, the king of Israel asks the king of Judah if he will follow him to war, and the king of Judah replies, "I am as you are; my people are your people, my horses are your horses." Similarly, in 2 Kings 3:7, the king of Israel requests cooperation from the king of Judah, and the king of Judah replies, "I will; I am with you, my people are your people, my horses are your horses." But there is more in Ruth's oath than one finds in the political treaties. According to Smith,[99] Ruth's words establish "a family relationship with Naomi that transcends the death of the male who had connected them, and in fact this relationship represents a family tie closer than that expressed by the formal status of formal in-laws."

Considering the *ḥesed* and oath in both the Jonathan-David narrative and the Ruth-Naomi narrative as well as the similarity in language between Ruth's profession of loyalty and the political treaties, it is possible to see Ruth's declaration as implying a covenant, that is, a solemn agreement between the parties.[100] Ruth's covenant with Naomi is thus creating a family relationship closer even than that of in-law, as Smith posits, and it suggests that Ruth is leaving behind not only her land, her people, and their gods but even "her mother's house" (v. 8). Adam is to

99. Mark S. Smith, "Your People Shall Be My People: Family and Covenant in Ruth 1:16-17," *CBQ* 69 (2007): 242–58; here 247 and 255.

100. Covenants are often cut between God and humans, in which case the power differential makes them somewhat one-sided. Nevertheless, a covenant is binding and lasting.

leave his father and his mother and "cleave" (the same word that Ruth uses in 1:14) to the woman, and they become one flesh; in like manner, the relationship between Naomi and Ruth is intimate and covenantal.

Ruth's oath is unique in the Bible not only because, as a woman, she swears by YHWH but also because she swears as a woman concerning another woman. Ruth pledges that death will not separate the two women. To return to Judah, Naomi foregoes being buried with her husband and sons. To accompany Naomi to Judah, Ruth foregoes being buried in her own land. Ruth offers Naomi the consolation that she will not die or be buried alone.

One does not contradict another's oath; the oath stands. This oath signaled the depth of Ruth's determination to accompany Naomi to Judah. Though she does not respond in words to Ruth's expression of intimate solidarity, neither does Naomi make any further effort to try to persuade Ruth to return to her people.

What the narrative's author intended—to depict a lesbian relationship, to suggest its likelihood or possibility, or to depict only the intense commitment of a devoted daughter-in-law—is open to each reader's interpretation.[101]

The Song of Ruth

Ruth's voice rises from her heart as she finds words that cast no doubt on her convictions to which she held tightly. Convictions that were her identity she now shared with Naomi. For Ruth, there was no other land, there was no other mother, there was no other people, and there was no other God. Her heart had been won over, and a life apart from any of it would simply not be livable.

So, before her mother and her God Ruth declares her own creed. She exults in her realized conversion with a voice clear and strong. Ruth tells Naomi, what you have, I will have, what you love, I shall love, and I will never, ever, be apart from you unto death. Her prayer extends through her mother and penetrates the heart of God, as if the sentiments that she spoke were the same God had for her. "Entreat me not to leave you."

Sheila Clare DeLuca

101. Because of the relationship that develops between Ruth and Boaz in chapters 2 and 3, it is possible that Ruth could be genuinely sexually attracted to both Naomi and Boaz. Koosed refers to Celine Duncan who, speaking from her own experience, reads the book of Ruth as a "bisexual midrash" ("The Book of Ruth: On Boundaries, Love and Truth," in *Take Back the Word: A Queer Reading of the Bible*, ed. Robert E. Goss and Mona West [Cleveland: Pilgrim Press, 2000], 92–102; cited in Koosed, *Gleaning Ruth*, 55).

God as a Daughter-in-Law

Naomi's loss is staggering. She loses her home and then her spouse and then her sons as well. She loses her past, her present, and her future. The one who started life pleasant receives a bitter lot of suffering, trauma, and loss. Her loss is staggering, and yet it is not inconceivable. Our communities are full of such pain.

Naomi makes up her mind to return to the place of her birth, destitute and alone as she may be. She sends away the last of her family in Moab. But one daughter won't go. Ruth pleads and even insists that she will stay with Naomi. Her pledge of loyalty and loving kindness was of such a simple eloquence that we use her words even today in weddings. And Naomi was silent.

We can see her, old, weary, lips set in a firm, thin line as she listens to Ruth's declaration of steadfast love, love that is not unlike God's love for us. She doesn't respond with gratitude or relief. She doesn't embrace Ruth. "When Naomi saw that she was determined to go with her, she said no more to her" (1:18). That must have been a long walk back to Bethlehem.

Faced with steadfast love, she is simply silent. Perhaps she is too weary for hope. Maybe she is too lost in pain to summon a response. Even if she is secretly thankful she's no longer alone, it seems to be beyond her ability to acknowledge the gift she is given.

It is tempting to criticize her silence. Surely Naomi should have been grateful. Surely she should have been amazed by Ruth's love. Surely her bitterness should have melted away. But she is not grateful or amazed. She does not melt. She holds her silence. And rightly so.

Notice, the story doesn't criticize Naomi's silence. It just holds it. Ruth seems to as well. In this, surely she does better than Job's friends (Job 2:11-13; 4:1-2; 8:1-2; 11:1-3).

Like the prophetic image of Rachel, Naomi refuses all consolation, for her children are no more (Jer 31:15; Matt 2:18). Naomi's silence is faithful. She doesn't turn Ruth away. She allows her to come along, and they trudge on to Bethlehem together. And, the story tells us, over time Ruth brings Naomi out of bitterness and barrenness into a new future of grandchildren and hope.

Faith's testimony is that this is how God comes to us. As Ruth came to Naomi, persistently bearing new life in the face of death, so God comes to us. When we are empty and bitterness fills our mouths, God steals in quietly as a daughter-in-law who will not abandon us. And even if we are too lost to grab on and say thank you, if the most we can do is stay silent and not push this new hope away, God still comes and says, "Do not press me to leave you or to turn back from following you! Where you go, I will go; where you lodge, I will lodge."

Sarah Wiles

God as a Widow

The contribution by Sarah Wiles on p. 44 is very helpful. In it she refers to God as a "daughter-in-law." Of this Mahri commented, "I love it." Me too. Perhaps we can see God from the other side as well. Perhaps God is a widow who has lost both her husband and her two sons. Perhaps God comes to us in vulnerability, in poverty.

Here at St. John's we offer a free meal to the community each weekday morning. We serve an average of over three hundred meals per day in our recently renovated, spacious, and beautiful St. Francis Xavier Center. This ministry has received much attention from the larger community. There have been many stories in the newspapers, on TV, and throughout social media. We are told, "You are doing God's work." Maybe, maybe not. On some days I think that we are. On other days, I am quite sure that we are not. What is certain is that the guests who humble themselves to attend the meal are doing God's work. Every day.

Why does Ruth remain with Naomi? We certainly cannot question or judge Orpah's decision to return to her mother's house. It was what Naomi had requested. There would be, it seemed, only bitterness if she stayed. Then why does Ruth remain? Certainly, the maternal love and care that Naomi had extended to her in the past was a factor. And yet there is something more. Since she has not yet experienced this "something," Ruth does not yet understand it herself. However, Naomi's vulnerability, her poverty, inspire in Ruth the hope that there is more than bitterness ahead.

There is much to be admired in a daughter-in-law displaying such loyalty. The depth of Ruth's concern and the humility of her action on behalf of Naomi is, indeed, God-like. Her care is rewarded. Through Ruth's relationship with Boaz, her hopes—and Naomi's—are fulfilled.

Our two vans travel through the city each day and glean the food necessary to serve our guests. Markets and restaurants, college dining halls and individual families do not scold or rebuke but generously help and encourage. In turn, the vulnerable and poor arrive each day so that we might experience, by little and by little, that it is not bitterness but blessing which awaits us all.

John Madden

"Returning" for the First Time: Homeland and Hardship (1:19-21)

Once the decision is made, the two women travel to Bethlehem. Here, as in verses 1 and 2, Bethlehem is repeated. In the earlier verses, it was the place from which the family departed, and here it is the place to which the family returns. The members of the family have changed, except for Naomi, who remains constant. The arrival of the two women causes some commotion in town.[102] But only the women in the town approach Naomi with their question; only the women enter into potential dialogue and relationship. Traveling alone, without the accompaniment of the men with whom Naomi departed, raised a question for the women: Is this the woman who we think she is? In other words, is this the wife of Elimelech? In addition, we know that time has passed, but we do not know the extent to which Naomi's appearance has changed. Regardless, she is not with the people who would make recognizing her easier. She comes without the familiar but with a stranger.

In American culture today, a woman accustomed to socializing with her husband who then attends social gatherings alone is suspected of being either divorced or widowed; in either case, the woman presents herself alone and is received differently. For some women, the experience resembles Naomi's (bitterness/sadness); for others it signals liberation and independence. Whatever the woman's experience, those who welcome her also have a new experience. The woman may look and act differently, and on several levels she may be difficult to recognize.

As often happens when someone has been away for a long time, people sort of recognize but are not quite sure. Their question, "Is this Naomi?" may be prompted by her appearance, older but possessing the same facial features, for example, or it could be occasioned by the fact that few Bethlehemites, especially women, left for such a long time (at least "about ten years" in v. 4) and then returned. But if the older woman was Naomi, then where was the rest of her family and who was this younger woman with her? Where was she from and why had she come? The women's question is not directed especially toward Naomi. It does not ask, "Are you Naomi?" They seem to be asking each other. Whether the women of the town posed their question to each other or to Naomi, she heard it and replied: Is this Naomi? No.

102. Sasson ("Ruth," 322) points out the personification of the clause "Bethlehem hums" or, as the NRSV translates, "the whole town is stirred."

Ruth 1:19-21

[19]So the two of them went on until they came to Bethlehem. When they came to Bethlehem, the whole town was stirred because of them; and the women said, "Is this Naomi?" [20]She said to them,
"Call me no longer Naomi,
call me Mara,
for the Almighty has dealt
bitterly with me.
[21]I went away full,
but the LORD has brought me
back empty;
why call me Naomi
when the LORD has dealt
harshly with me,
and the Almighty has brought
calamity upon me?"

That name, according to Naomi, no longer applies. More appropriately, she is "Bitter."

Naomi expresses the reason for her changed name. She does not speak of what has happened—the death of her husband and her two sons—as if bad things happen to good people. She says that the Almighty has dealt bitterly with her. Her God, YHWH, clearly controls what she cannot control: life and death. This second part of verse 20 brings together YHWH, how one copes, and bitterness. Up to this point YHWH's name has explicitly entered the narrative three other times: Naomi had heard that "the LORD had considered his people and given them food" (v. 6); Naomi had prayed that, "the LORD [would] deal kindly" with her daughters-in-law (v. 8), and Naomi had admitted to her daughters-in-law that it was "far more bitter" for her than for them because "the hand of the LORD has turned against me" (v. 13). Now, YHWH becomes "The Almighty," שדי, not the name of the particular YHWH of Israel, but a more generic name for God. In contrast to the "kindness" that Naomi had asked YHWH to do for her daughters-in-law, Naomi reports that "The Almighty" had dealt bitterly with her. In naming herself "Mara," that is, "Bitter," she wishes her name to reflect her situation.

Again, not blaming YHWH but nevertheless seeing God's hand/ power (יד) in what had transpired,[103] Naomi describes the situation as she sees it: she had gone away full but YHWH had brought her back empty. The subjects of the two clauses differ. Naomi says that she, agent

103. The Hebrew Bible uses a relatively small vocabulary that allows each noun, verb, adjective, and adverb to have multiple meanings, a large semantic field. The Hebrew term יד can mean both "hand" and "power"; while English speakers would not use the words interchangeably, we can see a connection. Hands are a strong source of power.

and initiator, was the subject of the action of going away (and she did so full); she then says that YHWH was the subject that caused her to return empty. We might say that Naomi went away from an empty land, a land lacking food, and returned when it was full. After all, there had been a famine and now the famine was over. But Naomi is not talking about food; she is talking about loss. The reader does not know where Ruth is during this conversation, whether or not she hears Naomi speak of her emptiness while disregarding Ruth's presence. Naomi is focused on her husband and sons and associates YHWH with their deaths.

Moreover, what has happened to Naomi, YHWH has allowed to happen or has even caused. YHWH has "turned against her" (v. 13) and "dealt bitterly" with her (v. 20); YHWH has "returned her empty" and "dealt harshly" and "brought calamity" (v. 21). Again, like Job, Naomi recognizes her suffering but she does not reject YHWH because of it.

For Naomi, "empty" and "full" are words that connote family. She was full in that she had a husband and sons when she left Bethlehem, even though her stomach was empty. When she returns to Bethlehem, her stomach is full—she has eaten in Moab, and her homeland to which she has returned has food—but she identifies herself as empty because she no longer has a husband and sons. The cultural and social world in which Naomi thrives is family; she thinks she is deprived of them and therefore can never be satisfied.

"Call Me Mara"

I love Mara. I love her because she is me; she is a part of mine and any soul in love with God. I connect to her as a woman, a mother, and a daughter. I understood her confusion that came from the exhaustion of her soul to understand her sorrow but, even greater, her failure to grasp her God's wisdom as she declares the numerous "afflictions" she has received at God's hand.

Life brings us difficult periods where we strive to make it tolerable by gleaning any amount of goodness or good reasoning so that we can still feel loved by God. This is the place most difficult to acknowledge for the faithful; where we feel neglected, rejected, or forgotten by the One who matters most to us. While this is different within human relationships, it is altogether disheartening with God, because we've known God's mercy and kindness on a deeply personal level. So this loss of relationship we feel, while based on our human needs and experiences, brings the faithful to a crossroads: one made by God.

Sheila Clare DeLuca

Naomi's theology is incomplete. She focuses on her losses but fails to see Ruth as a blessing. While the men have died and are buried in Moab, Ruth has accompanied Naomi to Bethlehem and professed that even death will not separate them. Naomi's request that the women call her "Bitter" does not do justice to her situation. Naomi is incapable of seeing the complexity of her situation. It was not all good at the beginning in Bethlehem; yes, she had her husband and sons, but they also had a famine. Now everything is not all bad: she has lost her husband and sons but she has food (which she also had in Moab), and, more important, she has Ruth. While she identifies as Mara, she has not lost all aspects of Naomi. Naomi associates her losses with YHWH but fails to associate Ruth with YHWH. Naomi assumes no personal responsibility for the deaths of her husband and sons—bad things happen to good people—but neither does she credit Ruth (and YHWH) for the good she possesses.

Naomi also repeats: "The Almighty" has dealt harshly (literally "afflicted") with me; the Almighty has brought calamity (literally "evil")[104] on me.[105] In between those two assertions is the statement that YHWH has brought her back empty. If the narrative's first life were in oral storytelling, repetition would increase the chances of the audience hearing and understanding what had been said. Naomi says that YHWH brought her back empty, but that is not true. She may well believe that YHWH allowed the men in her family to die, for which reason she feels empty, but she subsumes everything under YHWH—YHWH has done this—when in fact she is the one who chose to return to Bethlehem. There is no indication that her return is other than her own desire. Yet Naomi's sense of her own agency diminishes.

Ruth's arrival in Bethlehem goes unnoticed. No one asks her name. For Ruth, this was a new city in a foreign land. She herself was not returning; she had come. She had left the comfort of familiar for the discomfort of the unfamiliar. And whereas Naomi had left her homeland with her family—her husband and sons—for food at a time of famine, Ruth had left her homeland, which had food, to travel to a foreign land, to be with what was left of the family into which she had married.

The women do not notice her. The exchange takes place between them and Naomi as if Ruth were invisible. And Naomi's comment to the women contributes to this lack of recognition. Naomi is self-absorbed

104. The terms contrast with *ḥesed.*

105. Lau reads the latter texts in connection with Job where the power of "the Almighty" also extends beyond Israel. See Lau, "Another Postcolonial Reading of the Book of Ruth," 27.

and still identified with the men of her family. She ignores the woman who has professed total commitment to her. How must Ruth feel? What is Ruth learning, through this exchange, about Israel's YHWH?

One thing she is learning is that there is a group of women who frequent the city's entrance and speak their minds. They are the ones who take interest in these newly arrived women to their city—or at least take interest in Naomi. But they say nothing to Ruth and, like Naomi, treat her as though she is invisible. And Ruth, so explicit in her speech to Naomi, remains silent as well. She does not correct her mother-in-law; she does not speak to the women of the town (indeed, we never hear her speak to a woman other than Naomi). Is she concerned that the women of Bethlehem see her as a foreigner, a *Moabite*? Does she think that she will need to prove herself by actions rather than words? Is her silence a form of respect for Naomi, or does she hope for an introduction (one must have been made at some point, for, as we will see, the people of Bethlehem do know who she is)? What does the foreign woman say? What can, what should, she say? Or is her wiser move to remain silent, at least at the beginning?

The Power of Honest Lament

Naomi is often criticized for her lament in which she blames God for her calamity. Is not there bread now in Bethlehem? Is not Ruth her daughter-in-law still with her? But there is no rebuke for her bitterness—not from the town, or the women, or the narrator. Though she questions God, she still acknowledges the sovereignty of God, and therein is faith—raw, honest faith that dares to hold God to who God is. She does not understand what God is doing but she knows that Shaddai (translated as "Almighty") is not a God of emptiness but a God of fertility. That is the context in which the divine name is used in the patriarchal narratives:

"May God Almighty [El Shaddai] bless you and make you fruitful and numerous, that you may become a company of peoples" (Gen 28:3).

"God said to him, 'I am God Almighty [El Shaddai]: be fruitful and multiply; a nation and a company of nations shall come from you, and kings shall spring from you" (Gen 35:11).

"[T]he Almighty [El Shaddai] who will bless you with blessings of heaven above, blessings of the deep that lies beneath, blessings of the breasts and of the womb" (Gen 49:25).

And so none could answer Naomi because such disproportionate suffering is a mystery, and like Job's friends in their initial silence, it is better just to empathize than to criticize. One is allowed to give vent to laments like the psalmists. In the Psalter there are laments that contain confessions and also those that are protestations of innocence. Naomi certainly makes no confession but instead questions God's inscrutable intentions. Although she is not addressing God directly in prayer, neither does anyone else in this book. God is referred to in the third person throughout the narrative, keeping the focus on human actions. Can we not say that Naomi's lament provokes or at least sets the stage for God to act and to vindicate God's own name?

It was because Hannah poured out her tears to God in 1 Samuel 1 that she received the son she asked for, and that son changed the course of Israelite history. It was because Job's wife challenged him to bless/curse God that he opened his mouth and cursed the day of his birth and that eventually led to his whirlwind encounter with the Creator. And so, Naomi's lament is eventually answered with the fullness of a royal genealogy that goes beyond her anticipation. The outpouring of an honest and bold woman avails much.

Maggie Low

Ending and Beginning: Bethlehem and Barley (1:22)

The final verse of the chapter summarizes the situation. Naomi returned (שׁוב), and Ruth, the Moabite,[106] her daughter-in-law, returned (שׁוב) with her, from the country of Moab. The author is doing here with the verb שׁוב what the author has done elsewhere to imply relationship (see v. 15). The return is not only a physical return for Naomi but also a heartfelt one. Naomi's returning to her home and people (v. 16) now includes Ruth. Naomi returns to YHWH's sphere of blessing.[107]

Ruth, the Moabite, has departed the country of Moab. Still, the narrator continues to refer to Ruth as a Moabite (1:22; 2:1, 6, and 21) and so reinforces her status as an "other." In chapter 4 Boaz uses the designation (4:5 and 10), suggesting than an element of her foreignness remains, even after her integration into Israelite society. Ruth is familiar but she is also foreign. From a postcolonial perspective, she is neither Israelite

106. The biblical text identifies Ruth as a Moabite in 1:22; 2:2, 6, 21; 4:5 and 10.

107. Lau, "Another Postcolonial Reading of the Book of Ruth," 22.

Ruth 1:22

22So Naomi returned together with Ruth the Moabite, her daughter-in-law, who came back with her from the country of Moab. They came to Bethlehem at the beginning of the barley harvest.

nor Moabite, but she possesses elements of both.[108] Much study has been done on the relationship of identity to location, in general and with respect to Ruth. Both André LaCocque and Angela Wong see Ruth's role, as a Moabite in Israel, as subversive of efforts to re-create an ethnically pure people among the returned exiles. Wong argues that ethnic minorities "are needed for the vibrancy of a dominant culture."[109]

The land that YHWH had promised to Abraham (Gen 12:1; 15:18; 17:8) is described as "the land which the LORD your God will give/has given you" (e.g., Num 14:23; Deut 1:21; 10:11; 11:9), a land flowing with milk and honey (e.g., Exod 3:8, 17; 13:5).[110] The phrase expresses the blessing of YHWH. During and after the Babylonian exile (587 BCE), the land continued to be a source of identity and well-being. Naomi's decision to return to Bethlehem is consistent with the value that Israelites allotted to the land.

In contrast to what has preceded, verse 22 picks up on verse 19: the destination of the two women was Bethlehem. The chapter ends as it began, with a reference to time. Whereas verse 1 speaks of "the time of the judges," verse 22 speaks of the time of the barley harvest. Whereas verse 1 covers hundreds of years, verse 22 is specific to a certain time of year. Whereas Naomi had left Bethlehem during a famine (v. 1), she

108. Ibid., 25.

109. Wai Ching Wong, "Identity and Hybridity: Ruth in the Genealogy of Jesus: Matthew 1:1-17; Ruth 1–4," *Theologies and Cultures* 6 (2009): 98–109, esp. 102, cited in Havea and Lau, "Reading Ruth Again, in Asia," in *Reading Ruth in Asia*, 6. Wong utilizes the work of Anne Pattel-Gray to explain how indigenous Australians derive their identity through their spiritual connection to the land on which they live (see *Through Aboriginal Eyes: The Cry from the Wilderness* [Geneva: WCC Publications, 1991]).

110. In ancient Egypt, honey was buried with the pharaoh; in Babylonia it was seen as a gift of the god Astarte; in both cultures, like milk, it represents sexuality, fertility, and well-being. See Jonathan Cohen's article "Why Milk and Honey" (www.uhmc.sunysb.edu/surgery/m&h.html).

returned because she had learned there was food in Bethlehem (v. 6); she returned at the beginning of the barley harvest, that is, in early April.[111]

Those of us living in cities and distant from agricultural nuance might easily substitute wheat or grain for barley in this verse and think nothing of it. But ancient Israel had a very different understanding of barley and its harvesting. Barley was used for fodder as well as human food. According to 2 Kings 7:1, its value was half that of wheat during Ben-hadad's siege of Samaria; barley was the last nourishment that could be obtained in a famine or in times of economic distress. Compared to wheat, barley contains little gluten, the protein basis of the grain that allows the flour to rise. Barley bread therefore did not rise nicely, was coarse, and was harder to chew and digest. Still, barley lay between the ancient Israelites and hunger.[112]

Furthermore, barley determined whether an adjustment was needed in the ancient Israelites' calendar. Because the Israelites held to a lunar calendar,[113] in order to have the holidays coincide with the agricultural year an additional month was sometimes needed at the beginning of spring.[114] Messengers from the city went out to the barley fields to see if the barley was at a stage where it could be ripe for the harvest in time for Passover, the feast of the barley harvest (Deut 16:1-12). If the barley were not sufficiently mature, the priests would add another month to

111. Considering the importance of the availability of food for survival in ancient Israel, and in the ancient Near East in general, not as much work has been done on the subject as might be expected. See Athalya Brenner and J. W. van Henten, eds., *Food and Drink in the Biblical Worlds* (Atlanta: SBL Press, 1999); Nathan MacDonald, *Not Bread Alone: The Uses of Food in the Old Testament* (New York: Oxford University Press, 2008); Jean Soler, "The Semiotics of Food in the Bible," in *Food and Culture: A Reader*, ed. Carole Counihan and Penny Van Esterik, 2nd ed. (New York: Routledge, 2008), 57–66; and Koosed, *Gleaning Ruth*.

112. Miriam Feinberg Vamosh, *Food at the Time of the Bible* (Herzlia, Israel: Palphot Ltd, n.d.), 22.

113. The Hebrew lunar calendar contained twelve months of thirty days, yet the actual lunar cycle is only about 29½ days, which results in a year of only 354½ days. Keeping the lunar calendar coordinated with the seasons of the year required adding a thirteenth month seven out of every nineteen years. This additional month was added to the end of the year following the last month, Adar, and was simply called Second Adar. See Dennis Batcher, "Hebrew Calendar of the Old Testament" (www.crivoice.org/calendar.html).

114. Our first evidence of calendrical calculation in Israel is the Paleo-Hebrew Gezer Agricultural Calendar, dated to about the time of Solomon (ninth century BCE).

the calendar. Barley came to symbolize spring.[115] Spring and harvest, associated with new life and fullness of food, bodes well for the returnees to Bethlehem.[116]

115. Vamosh connects two terms: אבב, "freshness, fresh green, spring" (Aramaic), and אביב, fresh young ears of barley (Exod 9:31) or the month of exodus and Passover (Exod 13:4), to state that the ripened barley was known as *abib* or *aviv*, the modern Hebrew word for "spring" (*Food at the Time*, 24–25).

116. While barley was a staple food, associated with spring and new life, biblical texts sometimes also associate it with death: Ben-hadad's right-hand man dies because he refuses to believe Elisha's prophecy of the people's return to prosperity (2 Kgs 7), and the death of Judith's husband (Jdt 8:2) becomes the catalyst for Judith's role in preventing the surrender of her people. Death associated with barley and the barley harvest suggests that something is wrong, but it also portends restoration.

Ruth 2

Gleaning

Ruth's "Luck" and Boaz's Field (2:1-3)

This next scene opens with Naomi and Boaz, yet it revolves around Ruth. The narrative line in verse 1 builds from the description of Boaz to his name: he is a "kinsman" or relative (מידע or מודע; see "Translation Matters" below) of Naomi through her husband. Naomi is separated from Boaz in the placement of their names as bookends to the verse; they will be similarly separated in the distance between the town and fields in which much of the action will take place.[1] The two never meet, a fact that emphasizes Ruth's importance as main character and mediator between Boaz and Naomi throughout the narrative.

While the opening of chapter 2 mirrors that of chapter 1 in its male focus (Boaz in 2:1; the "man of Bethlehem in Judah" in 1:1),[2] this is not to say that the first person mentioned is most important.[3] Boaz is the

1. See Tod Linafelt and Timothy K. Beal, *Ruth and Esther*, Berit Olam (Collegeville, MN: Liturgical Press, 1999), 24–25.

2. Ibid., 24.

3. Contra K. Lawson Younger, who proposes that the book is written by a man, based (in part) on the opening paragraph in chapter 1 and the concluding episode and genealogy that represent male authorship and what he calls "traditional male perspectives" (*Judges, Ruth*, NIV Application Commentary [Grand Rapids: Zondervan, 2002], 389). Yet Younger's view itself reflects a traditional male perspective and does not take seriously the women's concerns that direct the body of the narrative.

Ruth 2:1-3

2:1Now Naomi had a kinsman on her
husband's side, a prominent rich man,
of the family of Elimelech, whose name
was Boaz. 2And Ruth the Moabite said
to Naomi, "Let me go to the field and
glean among the ears of grain, be-
hind someone in whose sight I may
find favor." She said to her, "Go, my
daughter." 3So she went. She came
and gleaned in the field behind the
reapers. As it happened, she came to
the part of the field belonging to Boaz,
who was of the family of Elimelech.

object, not the subject, of the verse. The focus soon shifts to Ruth, whose character dominates the subsequent scenes, from the town to the fields and back. Naomi remains in the town and, so far as we know, the household (from this point until the end of chapter 4, she interacts with Ruth alone), whereas the scenes with Boaz take place on the threshing floor and in the fields. It is Ruth who mediates between the two and moves the narrative forward. The placement of Boaz in the first line defines him as the object and goal of Ruth and Naomi's action.

This opening verse emphasizes the relationship among Boaz, Naomi, and Elimelech by stating that Boaz is "kinsman" to Naomi as well as part of the "family" of Elimelech. The Hebrew word translated as "kinsman" is vague; Boaz could be an acquaintance or a blood relative. Yet the text simultaneously describes Boaz as part of the "family" or משפחה of Elimelech, a word that designates either the immediate family or a larger, extended web of kinship.[4] Distant as the relationship may be,

4. Jack M. Sasson provides a careful overview of the Hebrew משפחה, "family" (*Ruth: A New Translation with a Philological Commentary and a Formalist-Folklorist Interpretation* [Baltimore: Johns Hopkins University Press, 1979], 40); see also Tamara Eskenazi and Tikva Frymer-Kensky, *The JPS Bible Commentary: Ruth* (Philadelphia: Jewish Publication Society of America, 2011), 28. Younger explains that the "family" or משפחה was a broader association of "fathers' houses" or patrilineal lines (*Judges, Ruth*, 440). Carol Meyers suggest that the משפחה functioned as an association of families that helped to maintain peace and protection in times of economic or personal hardships; see "'Women of the Neighborhood' (Ruth 4.17): Informal Female Networks in Ancient Israel," in *Ruth and Esther*, FCB 3, 2nd ser., ed. Athalya Brenner (Sheffield: Sheffield Academic, 1999), 110–27, esp. 117. In his recent commentary on Ruth, Jeremy Schipper focuses on the household organization to understand the relationships among the different characters. Schipper defines the משפחה as a clan that could consist of as many as several extended families that could live and die on the same land (Jeremy Schipper, *Ruth: A New Translation with Introduction and Commentary*, AYBRL 7D [New Haven: Yale University Press, 2016], 44–49).

however, Boaz is somehow related to Elimelech. We will never know the exact parameters of this relationship,[5] though in chapters 3–4, Boaz will divulge to Ruth that there is a closer relation to Naomi than himself.

TRANSLATION MATTERS

The relationship between Naomi and Boaz cannot be determined solely by the word מידע (NRSV "kinsman"), an obscure participial form from the root ידע, "to know."[6] The term could refer to a blood relative or simply someone who is known. The same term appears in 3:2, where the meaning is equally obscure. The word elsewhere in the Bible is translated in the NRSV as "acquaintance" (Ps 31:11), "familiar friend" (Ps 55:13), "close friend" (2 Kgs 10:11; Job 19:14), or "companion" (Ps 88:8, 18). In both 1:2 and 3:2, the Targum (the Aramaic translation of the Hebrew Bible in the first few centuries CE) utilizes the same root in a rare verbal form (אשתמודע), while the Greek is γνώριμος, which translates as "acquaintance," "friend," or someone "well known." These varying translations emphasize the ambiguity of Boaz's relationship to Elimelech and Naomi that will continue throughout the narrative. Based on the connected term "family" (משפחה) in verse 1, Boaz is likely a familial relation rather than a "friend" to Elimelech's family.

Verse 1 subsequently describes Boaz as a "prominent rich man," a translation that perhaps overemphasizes the idea that Boaz is wealthy. The literal translation is that Boaz is a man "mighty" (גבור) of "strength" (חיל), an expression that is used to describe primarily military men[7] and secondarily men of social standing or wealth. Boaz will later refer to Ruth by the feminine equivalent, an אשת חיל or woman of "strength"

5. On this, see Eskenazi and Frymer-Kensky, *Ruth*, 27.

6. For longer discussions of the expression מידע, מודע, and "kinsman," see Paul Joüon, *Ruth: Commentaire Philologique et Exégétique* (Rome: Pontifical Biblical Institute, 1924), 46; Edward F. Campbell, *Ruth*, AB 7 (New York: Doubleday, 1975), 88–90; and Sasson, *Ruth*, 39. Campbell translates the term "covenant-brother," while Sasson suggests "acquaintance." Nielsen prefers "relative" (Kirsten Nielsen, *Ruth*, OTL [Louisville: Westminster John Knox, 1997], 53).

7. Other examples of men referred to as "mighty of strength" include Jephthah (Judg 11:1), David (1 Sam 16:18), Saul (1 Sam 9:1), and Jeroboam (1 Kgs 11:28), all of whom are military commanders and early leaders of Israel. Saul, David, and Jeroboam are also kings. Boaz is the only man in the Bible defined as a "mighty man" who is not also identified as a military leader of sorts, which suggests that he is nonetheless a leader in the community.

(see the discussion at 3:11). So far as we know, Ruth is not rich; the parallel between Boaz and Ruth therefore supports the notion that Boaz is a man of strength or virtue, not merely of wealth. The name Boaz may come from the Hebrew בו עוז, "in him is strength,"[8] and "Boaz" is also the name of one of the two pillars in the entrance to Solomon's temple (1 Kgs 7:21; 2 Chr 3:17). These varying descriptions portray Boaz as a symbolic "pillar,"[9] someone who supports or builds up the community,[10] as well as a possible source of support for the women in terms of marriage, economic stability, and progeny.[11]

Verse 1 sets up the expectation for hope; Naomi has a family relation, however distant. The focus then shifts to Naomi and Ruth "the Moabite." The two women are somewhere in town, and they appear to be alone. The women from the previous scene are nowhere in view. An indefinite, though likely short, amount of time has elapsed since Ruth and Naomi's arrival—the two women arrived in the beginning of the barley harvest, and Ruth now seeks to glean in that harvest. Their immediate need for sustenance suggests that Ruth would not have waited long to find a solution, unless the women of Bethlehem who greeted them in 1:19-20 had cared for them. Whether they are lodging with others or in their own home, the two women appear to be settled.

While verse 1 stresses the family connection between Naomi and Boaz, verse 2 again stresses the nonfamilial, "other" status of Ruth as it did at the end of chapter 1.[12] Yet it is this foreign woman from Moab who seeks to provide food for herself and her Israelite mother-in-law, an idea that contradicts Deuteronomy's admonitions against admitting Moabites (who did not meet the Israelites with food and water on their journey out of Egypt) into the community.[13] Not only will Ruth provide food for Naomi, but Boaz will later provide for Ruth, against the warning in Deuteronomy 23:6: "You shall never promote [the Moabites'] welfare or their prosperity as long as you live." While the relationship

8. See Sasson, *Ruth*, 40–42; also Campbell, *Ruth*, 90–91; *contra* Keil and Delitzsch, who reject this derivation of Boaz's name (*Commentary on the Old Testament*, vol. 2: *Joshua, Judges, Ruth, 1–2 Samuel* [Grand Rapids: Eerdmans, 1978], 477).

9. As a play on the notion of Boaz as a literal "pillar," Danna Nolan Fewell and David M. Gunn refer to him as a "pillar of the community" (*Compromising Redemption: Relating Characters in the Book of Ruth* [Eugene, OR: Wipf & Stock, 1990], 83).

10. See Linafelt and Beal, *Ruth and Esther*, 25.

11. Alice L. Laffey, *Ruth* (New York: Paulist, forthcoming), 12.

12. See Adele Berlin, *Poetics and Interpretation of Biblical Narrative*, ed. David M. Gunn, BLS 9 (Sheffield: Almond Press, 1983), 88.

13. See the introduction above on Deuteronomy 23:4-7.

among Ruth, Naomi, and Boaz could serve to correct or challenge Deuteronomy's admonitions,[14] the narrative demonstrates little awareness of Deuteronomy and could have been written independently of these admonitions. Other biblical texts demonstrate a similar lack of awareness of these negative perceptions of the Moabites, such as 1 Samuel 22:3-4, which describes Moab as a place of safety for David's family when he is fleeing from Saul.[15] Nowhere does the book of Ruth engage the admonitions in Deuteronomy directly, nor is there any judgment in the book specifically against Ruth "the Moabite" or Moabites in general. Rather, any intertextual tension comes from the readers, from the placement of the book in the canon that contains Deuteronomy, and from the history of interpretation; Ruth Rabbah seeks to reconcile Deuteronomy's position with the book of Ruth by stating that the admonitions against inclusion into the community apply only to men (see the introduction),[16] or by describing Ruth as a convert into the community (see Lynn Kaye's contribution at 2:12).[17]

From the book of Ruth alone, the remarkable fact is not that Ruth is a Moabite admitted into the Israelite community but rather that she, the foreign woman, is the one most concerned with Naomi's immediate welfare. There is a similar ironic note in the beginning of chapter 1, in which the Moabites accept Judahite refugees escaping famine from the very place associated with an abundance of food (Bethlehem). The introduction of Ruth the Moabite in 2:2 is similarly ironic. Her name is juxtaposed both with Boaz, who is introduced as Naomi's *family* in verse 1, and with the women or people of Bethlehem in 1:19-20. Yet it is she, the foreigner, who offers help to Naomi.

According to the prescriptions for gleaning (Lev 19:9-10; 23:22; and Deut 24:19-22), the edges of the fields are not to be harvested, and the "gleanings" (that which remains after the first pass) should be left for

14. See Eskenazi and Frymer-Kensky, *Ruth*, xxii.

15. First Samuel 22:3-4 reads, "David went from there to Mizpeh of Moab. He said to the king of Moab, 'Please let my father and mother come to you, until I know what God will do for me.' He left them with the king of Moab, and they stayed with him all the time that David was in the stronghold."

16. Also Ruth Rab. 4.6.

17. Also Ruth Rab. 2.22-24; 3.5. My (Mahri's) argument in this paragraph is one that supports a possible earlier dating of the book of Ruth and reveals the author's perspective; in the introduction and certain statements in chapters 1 and 4, Alice leans toward a later dating. In that case, the book of Ruth stresses inclusion in contrast to Deuteronomy's admonitions and those of Ezra–Nehemiah. These two views are alternative possibilities.

the foreigner or alien (גר) and the poor. The Torah repeatedly emphasizes the concern for the resident alien or foreigner, and it demonstrates not only a commitment to the foreigner's welfare but a pledge to "love" the foreigners residing in the community: "The alien who resides with you shall be to you as the citizen among you; you shall love the alien as yourself, for you were aliens in the land of Egypt" (Lev 19:34; see also Deut 10:19). In chapter 1, Alice discusses the plight of refugees and the current debate about border crossing; in our current context, we would do well to remember these Torah laws, in which the welfare of the foreigner is inseparable from the idea of loving the other as one's very self.

Ruth is aware of the tradition of gleaning, which implies either that Naomi told her of the tradition, or that the tradition was shared by Israel's neighbors.[18] Yet her request to glean may not be made on the basis of legislation for the foreigner and the resident alien. Jeremy Schipper points out that Ruth never self-identifies as a foreigner and that her marriage into an Israelite family would make her both foreign and family (in other words, what he refers to as a "foreign kinswoman") based on the household structure.[19] The gleaning system could be described as an ancient system of welfare, yet a form of welfare that ensured both work and food and therefore acknowledged the dignity in providing for oneself. It also gave everyone in the community the same right to the same grain, unlike the modern welfare system, which provides enough money for people to buy the cheaper, and often far less healthy, options at the grocery store.[20]

18. See the Egyptian *Instruction of Amenemope* 26.9, trans. Miriam Lichtheim (*COS* 1:121), ca. 1300–1075 BCE, which includes admonitions against bothering widows gleaning in fields not their own. Thank you to Mark S. Smith for alerting us to this example.

19. Schipper, *Ruth*, 115.

20. According to *The Washington Post*, cuts in the Supplemental Nutrition Assistance Program (SNAP, formerly known as Food Stamps) reduced the maximum benefit for a family of four from $668/month to $632/month, a cut that equates to roughly sixteen meals a month for a family of three (Brad Plumer, "Food Stamps Will Get Cut by $5 Billion this Week—and More Cuts Could Follow," *The Washington Post* [October 28, 2013], https://www.washingtonpost.com/news/wonk/wp/2013/10/28/food-stamps-will-get-cut-by-5-billion-this-week-and-more-cuts-could-follow/). However, the Special Supplement Nutrition Program for Women, Infants and Children (WIC), which provides increased nutrition and access to health care for pregnant women, breastfeeding women, and children under five years of age, is a more effective program (see Sheila Avruch and Alicia Puente Cackley, "Savings Achieved by Giving WIC Benefits to Women Prenatally," *Public Health Records* 110 [1995]: 27–34).

Ruth takes the initiative either by requesting permission or stating her intention to glean behind someone with whom she might find favor. The expression the NRSV translates as "let me go [now]" (אלכה נא), could be read as an act of deference: "I would like to go," or even "please let me go," though it could be read equally as a declaration of intent: "I am going now."[21] Ruth's statement embodies both initiative and determination,[22] while the particular phrasing also emphasizes the same respect toward Naomi as she had demonstrated in the request "Please do not insist that I leave you" in 1:16.[23]

Ruth's desire is twofold: first, to glean for food and, more important, to glean behind someone who might grant her "favor" or "grace" (חן).[24] In the Bible, the notion of "favor" often applies to two people of unequal

21. One could read the particle נא as either (1) a request for permission, i.e., "please" (see Paul Joüon, *A Grammar of Biblical Hebrew*, trans. and rev. T. Muraoka, SB 14/I-II [Rome: Pontifical Biblical Institute, 1996], par. 114d); or (2) as a declaration, identifying the statement as a logical consequence of the previous statement or the general situation, i.e., "now" (see Thomas O. Lambdin, *Introduction to Biblical Hebrew* [New York: Scribner's Sons, 1971], 170–71).

22. I (Mahri) follow many scholars who interpret Ruth's request as one of initiative and determination. For example, Ilona Rashkow describes Ruth as initiating the situation by effectively saying, "Look, it's a good idea if . . ." ("Ruth: The Discourse of Power and the Power of Discourse," in *A Feminist Companion to Ruth*, ed. Athalya Brenner, FCB 3 [Sheffield: Sheffield Academic, 1993], 26–41, esp. 33). See also Phyllis Trible, *God and the Rhetoric of Sexuality* (Philadelphia: Fortress, 1978), 175; Adrien J. Bledstein, "Female Companionships: If the Book of Ruth Were Written by a Woman . . . ," in Brenner, *A Feminist Companion to Ruth*, 116–33, esp. 122; and Sarojini Nadar, who argues that Ruth's initiative proves that she is "strong-willed, determined, daring, resourceful, and innovative" ("A South African Indian Womanist Reading," in *Other Ways of Reading: African Women and the Bible*, ed. Musa W. Dube [Atlanta: SBL Press, 2001], 159–75, esp. 167).

23. On Ruth's respect toward Naomi, see Eskenazi and Frymer-Kensky, *Ruth*, 28. Esther Fuchs views Ruth as submissive to Naomi and as one who obeys rather than initiates: "Status and Role of Female Heroines in the Biblical Narrative," *The Mankind Quarterly* 23 (1982): 149–60, esp. 157. This view is unsupported by the text, which describes Ruth's initiative, and sometimes disobedience, to Naomi throughout chapters 1–3.

24. According to Younger and Linafelt, Ruth is seeking permission from the landowner to glean, either because this was a custom in Israel (Younger, *Judges, Ruth*, 440) or because Ruth was not aware of the rights of gleaners (Linafelt and Beal, *Ruth and Esther*, 26). Yet Ruth emphasizes that the favor she seeks, the permission to glean, is from the one behind whom she gleans, not from the landowner. Moreover, this reading oversimplifies the open-ended nature of Ruth's statement (the point is that we do not know what kind of "favor" she will seek) and obviates her agency.

social standing, in which a subordinate (often, though not always, a man) seeks or is granted "favor" from another man in a position of authority.[25] Similarly, Ruth seeks "favor" from someone to whom she is subordinate, the one "behind" whom she will glean. Yet Ruth's statement is purposefully indefinite as to what kind of "favor" she will seek. As a foreign widow gleaning, Ruth could be seeking "favor" in the idea of simple kindness. She will indeed find kindness from Boaz. Yet she could also be seeking sexual "favor." The Targum saw this sexual possibility and sought to erase it by changing the Hebrew "favor" to "mercy," רחמים, and so excluding the possibility of desire. Boaz will indeed be attracted to Ruth, though the nature of this attraction remains similarly undefined. In chapters 2 and 3, Boaz infers that his attraction to Ruth derives from her acts of loyalty. Yet in chapter 3, it will seem that Ruth's power also comes through her sexual marketability, which will eventually grant her and Naomi safety through union with Boaz. Regardless of the nature of Boaz's attraction, Ruth demonstrates the reality, ancient and contemporary, that a woman's sexual desirability can be an aspect of her power (as well as a hindrance), even if she is equally commendable for such traits as intelligence, character, or loyalty.

Later in chapter 2, Ruth will find favor with Boaz, partly due to her initiative or engineering of events (Ruth repeats her desire to "find favor" with Boaz in 2:10 and 13). That Boaz has already been set up as a potential helper for the women in 2:1 heightens the expectation that he is the one who will show favor to Ruth; possibly, Naomi and Ruth are already aware of Boaz and are singling him out for Ruth's advances in 2:1-2.[26] Yet later Naomi will exhibit surprise that Ruth happened to glean in Boaz's field (2:19-20); only then will she tell Ruth about this redeemer-kinsman (see the discussion at 2:19-20). There is no indication at the beginning of chapter 2 that Ruth is aware of Boaz. This awareness is for the reader alone, and perhaps for Naomi, who nonetheless has given no clues of Boaz's existence.

25. For example, Saul has "favor" for David in 1 Samuel 16:22; YHWH has "favor" for Noah in Genesis 6:81; and the priest Eli has "favor" for Hannah in 1 Samuel 1:18. Esther also finds "favor" with the king (Esth 2:15, 17; 5:2, 8; 7:3; and 8:5); in this case, the king's "favor" relates to Esther's physical beauty.

26. Sasson argues that both women are already singling out Boaz, based on the notion that "finding favor" in one's sight often has a specific, known individual as its object (*Ruth*, 38–39). Readers may be aware that Boaz is the man who will show Ruth favor in 2:10 and 13, yet for Ruth, any man may be the one to show favor.

Naomi's silence regarding Boaz is perplexing, and it adds to the overall picture of the physical separation between the two. Perhaps, Naomi's pain and suffering (coupled with ten years in Moab and the fact that Boaz is a distant relation) made her momentarily forget about this man or consider him too distant a relation to be of help. She may have been waiting for Boaz, or the closer relation mentioned in chapter 3, to act according to the customs of society.[27] Or, perhaps Naomi did not think well of Boaz. They never meet or speak in the narrative, and during the famine they chose different paths, one remaining in Judah and the other departing. Naomi's proposed plan in chapter 3 sets Ruth up to seduce Boaz rather than simply to ask for his care. She does not demonstrate trust that Boaz will commit selflessly to the women's welfare.

Naomi acknowledges Ruth's request to glean by telling her to "go, my daughter." Naomi also refers to Ruth as "my daughter" in 1:11, 12, and 13. The juxtaposition of this familial expression with the identification of Ruth "the Moabite" emphasizes Ruth's identity as both foreigner and family. This dual identity strengthens a point made in chapter 1: Ruth the foreigner performs a great act of loyalty or *ḥesed* in leaving her home and clinging to Naomi. Boaz will also refer to Ruth as "daughter," which clarifies that Boaz and Naomi are of the same, older generation than Ruth. In chapter 1, Naomi used the language of "daughter" while beseeching Ruth to leave her, and Ruth refused. Now, Naomi repeats "daughter" when Ruth will leave her to go into the fields, yet this time with Naomi's permission.

It is Ruth who takes the active role in chapter 2. Although Naomi's silence in this chapter can be seen as a display of extreme selfishness and even resentment toward her daughter-in-law,[28] this is too critical a

27. Trible proposes that Naomi's silence is the result of being overpowered by emptiness, paralyzed by her situation, or perhaps conforming to the custom of waiting for the man to initiate action (*God and the Rhetoric of Sexuality*, 179). We do not know what prompts Naomi's silence, and we are left to interpret into the text based on our own lives and experiences.

28. Danna Nolan Fewell and David M. Gunn take a negative view of Naomi in "'A Son Is Born to Naomi!': Literary Allusions and Interpretation in the Book of Ruth," *JSOT* 40 (1988): 99–108. Yet Sasson rightly notes that as readers, we are, "perhaps too critically, puzzled by Naomi's failure to participate in the gleanings if her situation was as dire as some commentators are wont to believe" (*Ruth*, 42). There may be a stereotype at play among those who want Naomi and Ruth's situation to be so "dire," to use Sasson's language, namely, that two women surviving alone (i.e., without men) in ancient Israel can only do so with great difficulty.

stance to take toward a woman who is immersed in grief (see 1:20-21)[29] and who responds to Ruth's query not with anger or animosity but with the intimate, or at least familial, "my daughter." Why Naomi does not accompany Ruth to the fields is also left unexplained—she was able to walk from Moab to Judah, so she is clearly able-bodied. Naomi has not instructed Ruth to go to the fields; she has merely acquiesced to Ruth's desire. Yet someone must provide. Ruth places the burden of care for herself and for Naomi on her own shoulders, which reveals an underlying expectation (self-inflicted or otherwise) that it is the younger woman who will do the work. In a contemporary setting, this same expectation may or may not hold true. North America, for example, has coined the term "sandwich generation" for those of middle and perhaps even retirement age who find themselves caring for elderly parents as well as their grown children (and sometimes grandchildren). Ruth herself could be understood to be part of this "sandwich generation," as she will later produce a grandchild for Naomi and therefore care for the generations above and below her.

Chapter 1 introduced a scene of death, focused on the loss of Elimelech and his sons. Chapter 2 begins to restore a balance between death and life, based on Ruth's initiative and the anticipatory hope in Boaz.[30] Yet there is also an undercurrent of isolation to this scene, which is highlighted by the fact that Ruth and Naomi are alone, with no community in view. The text also leaves out the possible desperation underlying the need to glean, in which the women's survival is precarious.[31] In the case of Ruth and Naomi, while the townspeople may have helped them upon their arrival in Bethlehem (they do have a place to live), Ruth's need to

29. On Naomi's grief and the movement from bitterness to joy, see Katharine Doob Sakenfeld, *Ruth*, Interpretation: A Bible Commentary for Teaching and Preaching (Louisville: Westminster John Knox, 1999), 48; Trible, *God and the Rhetoric of Sexuality*, esp. 166, 174–75; also D. F. Rauber, "Literary Values in the Bible: The Book of Ruth," *JBL* 89 (1970): 27–37, esp. 29.

30. Trible writes that the women are "creatures of life" in chapter 2, juxtaposed with the men as creatures of death in chapter 1 (*God and the Rhetoric of Sexuality*, 175). See also Sakenfeld, *Ruth*, 37, on the "anticipatory delight" at the events about to unfold.

31. Jennifer Koosed equates Ruth's gleaning to a contemporary setting of day-to-day living, in which people will dig through trash cans and the local dump in order to survive, which she refers to as the "dirty desperation of poverty" (*Gleaning Ruth: A Biblical Heroine and Her Afterlives*, Studies on Personalities of the Old Testament [Columbia: University of South Carolina Press, 2011], 72). Yet the ancient, legal system of gleaning does not equate with the indignity of modern poverty.

glean implies that the women have no economic security. In chapter 4, a fuller picture will emerge when Boaz discusses Elimelech's land that Naomi sells, and it will seem that (perhaps) Naomi and Ruth have not been so destitute in chapters 2–3 after all. If this is the case, then Ruth may be gleaning precisely to catch the eye of a landowner rather than out of economic necessity. Yet from chapter 2 alone, the women's economic situation is unclear.

The themes of food and gleaning, so crucial to the story, are also intimately linked to gender and sexuality.[32] A cycle is at play—Ruth must work in order to eat, and she must eat in order to sustain her body and her health, in order to work. As a woman, however, Ruth's health is also essential to maintaining her fertility, which is the ultimate hope for the two women (at least according to Naomi in chap. 1). In addition, gleaning itself implies not only survival but also the ability to recognize that which is dropped or left behind as procreative. Jennifer Koosed has explored contemporary gleaning and finds the common impulse "to pick through, pick up, and assemble anew" in a variety of urban and rural settings. Despite Koosed's creative analogue, the two systems are different. The ancient system of gleaning is legally mandated for those without resources; there is nothing legally mandated, and therefore socially sanctioned, about garbage picking. For Ruth, gleaning becomes many things: the means to survival and a dignified way of providing for her and her mother-in-law, as well as a way of sustaining her own body and the hope of creating something new. When Ruth "finds favor" with Boaz later on in the chapter, it is this very relationship that marks the creation of something new and life-giving that comes from Ruth's gleaning. Boaz himself may function as something that Ruth "gleans" for her own purposes.

Ruth takes the first steps to ensure her and Naomi's survival.[33] In a description that hastens the movement between town and fields, Ruth goes, comes, and gleans in the fields behind the reapers. By chance (מקרה), she comes to the field that Boaz owns. The expression "as it happened" contains two forms of the Hebrew root קרה, "to befall/to happen," which strengthens the idea of an astonishing accident, chance,

32. Ibid., x.

33. On Ruth as the one who takes initiative and provides, see Athalya Brenner, "Naomi and Ruth: Further Reflections," in Brenner, *A Feminist Companion to Ruth*, 140–44; also Trible, *God and the Rhetoric of Sexuality*, 175–76, 184, 187, 195–96.

or fate; literally, the Hebrew says: "and it chanced by chance."[34] Here, as elsewhere in the Bible, the Hebrew expression of accident or fate points to human "chance" rather than divine initiative. The term מקרה is most commonly attested in the book of Ecclesiastes in reference to human existence and fate, which is impersonal and indifferent to one's virtue or merit (2:14-15; 3:19; 9:2-3). In 1 Samuel, it is used similarly to depict chance occurrence; first, when the Philistines return the ark to Israel and attempt to discern whether it was God who had inflicted punishment on the people or whether it had been done "by chance" (1 Sam 6:1-9); and second, when David misses a festival meal, and Saul considers it an "accident" (1 Sam 20:26).

In the case of Ruth's "chancing" upon Boaz's field, many scholars propose that there is little distinction between divine initiative and what might be considered "luck"; where luck occurs, God is acting behind the scenes or in the shadows.[35] Yet Tod Linafelt argues convincingly that the logic for seeing divine providence in 2:3 is both circular and faulty, resting on the erroneous supposition that the Bible attributes all such occurrences to providence, when in fact it contains diverse and theologically challenging notions of how God acts in the world.[36] Divine initiative in 2:3 can therefore only be inferred, which is exactly how a "real life" (modern) understanding of the divine works. What one views as chance, another views as divine initiative. This chance encounter may also strengthen the idea that Ruth was not deliberately seeking Boaz, nor has Naomi revealed his existence to her daughter-in-law.

The Moabite Girl Who Returned with Naomi (2:4-7)

Sooner or later, Boaz arrives from Bethlehem, which is likely close walking distance from the fields.[37] The expression הנה, "just then," which could also be translated "presently," can express surprise or wonder in

34. See Younger's translation, "and her chance chanced" (*Judges, Ruth*, 441).

35. Trible writes that "within human luck is divine intentionality" (*God and the Rhetoric of Sexuality*, 176). Similarly, Sakenfeld explains that "luck" is the place within which God acts (*Ruth*, 40). See also Nielsen, *Ruth*, 55; Eunny P. Lee, "Women's Doings in Ruth: A Feminist Biblical Theology of Providence," *JFSR* (forthcoming): 1–7; Robert L. Hubbard, *The Book of Ruth* (Grand Rapids: Eerdmans, 1988), 141; Campbell, *Ruth*, 112.

36. Linafelt and Beal, *Ruth and Esther*, 27–28.

37. Schipper, *Ruth*, 128.

Ruth 2:4-7

[4]Just then Boaz came from Beth-
lehem. He said to the reapers, "The
LORD be with you!" They answered,
"The LORD bless you!" [5]Then Boaz
said to his servant who was in charge
of the reapers, "To whom does this
young woman belong?" [6]The servant
who was in charge of the reapers an-
swered, "She is the Moabite who came
back with Naomi from the country of
Moab. [7]She said, 'Please, let me glean
and gather among the sheaves behind
the reapers.' So she came, and she
has been on her feet from early this
morning until now, without resting even
for a moment."

the suddenness of information conveyed to the reader, rather than accurate chronological movement.[38] Verse 7 explains that Ruth has been in the fields long enough for her to stand out in some way, yet any other information between Ruth's arrival (v. 3) and Boaz's arrival (v. 4) is left out of the story. The time must be early enough for additional work before the midday meal, as demonstrated in verse 14. The absence of chronological information, like the absence of information between the end of chapter 1 and the beginning of chapter 2, is an example of the "selective representation" discussed in our introduction.[39] The narrator selects which pieces of information to pass along to the reader, information that fills in the past in a nonlinear fashion.[40] Simultaneously, the reader recognizes that not everything in the narrative is represented in full or even in part.

From a feminist lens, "selective representation" is important throughout the book of Ruth in that it leaves space to interpret what is silent or excluded, such as the characters' motivations. As in the introduction, readers may put forward a list of questions to fill in through their own experiences and subjectivity. Feminist readers will look, in particular,

38. Berlin, *Poetics and Interpretation*, 92–93. Campbell regards Boaz's arrival as "just the right thing" that occurs, "with little or no lapse of time, and with a distinct hint of wonder" (*Ruth*, 93). He imagines that Boaz arrives not long after Ruth, though long enough for the overseer to have formed a positive impression of her. Sasson translates the expression as "just then" (*Ruth*, 38). Linafelt describes the term as a "dramatic development" in the plot, rather than a temporal clause to indicate that Boaz had arrived right on Ruth's heel (Linafelt and Beal, *Ruth and Esther*, 29).

39. Berlin, *Poetics and Interpretation*, 99–100.

40. Berlin refers to nonlinear information as "dischronologized" in *Poetics and Interpretation*, 96–97.

for the voices that are silenced, controlled, or dominated in some way. It is also up to the reader to discern whether the information presented by the characters in the narrative is to be trusted, in much the same way as we would with personal information given to us in daily life. More conservative biblical readers may balk at the idea that the text presents untrustworthy information, yet part of the beauty of the narrative is that it presents the characters realistically, which includes the fact that people, even characters in the Bible, naturally filter reality through their subjective lenses.

When Boaz arrives at his field, he greets his workers respectfully, in the name of YHWH, and they respond in kind. The greeting and response could be confirmation of divine presence,[41] or of Boaz's genuine interest in his workers.[42] They could also be clichés, with little meaning behind a generic "hello" and subsequent "how are you?" (the latter of which, in colloquial US English, has become so overused as to function now as a statement rather than a request for additional information).

The introduction to Boaz invites the reader to ponder the nature of this man. We gain little information about Boaz throughout the story—we never know what underlies his kindness toward Ruth, beyond a few exclamations of her loyalty in chapters 2 and 3. Depending on how we read the text, we may view Boaz as generous and kind, someone who acts from pure intentions for the well-being of others. Or, we could be wary of Boaz, a man who represents privilege—he is a man with both wealth and power, as demonstrated by his authority in his fields. Similar to our decisions about Ruth and Naomi, how we interpret Boaz's character will depend on our experiences as readers, our decisions regarding the social location and intentions of the author(s), and the ways in which we make meaning from the text. The interaction between Boaz and his reapers in 2:4 could be as emblematic of self-interest and a sense of entitlement as it is a respectful, or simply banal, greeting.

Boaz's elite status (he is a landowner with servants) as well as the expectations that come with that status are juxtaposed to Ruth's poverty and socially precarious state. While we might expect this status differential to place Boaz in a fixed position of power over Ruth, the power dynamics turn out to be quite fluid. As we will see, Ruth influences Boaz and displays a remarkable amount of agency, while Boaz embraces

41. See Hubbard, *Book of Ruth*, 144; Sakenfeld, *Ruth*, 40.

42. See Nielsen, *Ruth*, 57; Campbell, *Ruth*, 112; Eskenazi and Frymer-Kensky, *Ruth*, 31.

her proposals and treats Ruth with respect. As the story unfolds, the relationship between Boaz and Ruth presents us with opportunities for nuancing our understanding of the relationship among class, gender, and power, in particular the ways in which someone with limited social standing (Ruth) can nonetheless drive the narrative and influence those with greater privilege (Boaz).

As soon as Boaz arrives, he notices Ruth. Although we might expect Boaz to be concerned primarily with the harvest and the laborers in general, the first and only question he asks his servant is about Ruth, the נערה, "young girl." The word נערה often refers to a young woman, though not necessarily a virgin; included in the list are Rebekah (Gen 24:14, 16), Dinah (Gen 34:3), the "concubine" (Judg 19:3), Abishag the Shunammite (1 Kgs 1:3), and Esther (Esth 2:4). The term can also refer to attendants or servants, including the young women who work for Boaz (Ruth 2:8, 22, 23; 3:2) and for Abigail in 1 Sam 25:42.[43] The Targum similarly refers to Ruth as a "young woman," ריבא, while the Greek uses distinct terms for Ruth; she is a νεᾶνις, "young woman" (2:5), or παῖς, "child" (2:6), in contrast to κοράσιον, "girl/young woman" used for the female workers in Boaz's field (2:8, etc.). In the Hebrew, Boaz's "servant" in 2:5 is himself called a נער, "young man," and the servant's response to Boaz refers to Ruth as the נערה (see also 4:12).

The term "young woman" contrasts with the more intimate language of "my daughter" in verse 8, the NRSV's translation "worthy woman" (literally a "woman of strength") in 3:11, and Boaz's later reference to Ruth as a "woman" (אשה) (see the discussion at 4:10 and 13).[44] Here, the description of Ruth as a "young woman" is part of a cluster of repeated references to the "young women" or "young men" who work for Boaz (vv. 8-9). The difference between Boaz's age and that of the "youth" emphasizes not only relative age but also relative power: that which is older is synonymous with power and authority, while that which is younger is synonymous with subordination to that authority. Yet gender also intrudes into this paradigm; the "older" woman, such as Naomi, may be typed as more vulnerable than a man of the same age, Boaz.

Ruth's age is a mystery (as are the ages of Boaz and Naomi). We know that Ruth was married for ten years in Moab before her husband died, so her youthfulness compared to Boaz is less an objective reality as it is

43. See also the servants or attendants of Pharaoh's wife (Exod 2:5) and of Wisdom (Prov 9:3).

44. On this, see Berlin, *Poetics and Interpretation*, 89.

a relative indicator of Boaz's age. Later, Boaz commends Ruth for not going after young men (3:10), which suggests that the "young men" are closer to her own age than he is. Campbell calculates that Ruth would be somewhere between twenty-five and thirty, while Naomi and Boaz would be in their forties. It does seem that everyone working on Boaz's field is quite young, with the exception of Boaz, whom Campbell goes so far as to label a "senior citizen."[45] The Midrash even states that Boaz is eighty years old, based on his calling Ruth "my daughter" and the notion that Ruth was as old as forty when she came to Bethlehem (see the discussion in the introduction).[46] The term "young woman" may simply reflect the relative age between Boaz and Ruth; it may also connote a woman of marriageable age and situation.[47] Yet to a reader who knows Ruth's story, it may sound infantilizing: this is a woman who was married for ten years, widowed, left her family of origin of her own volition, and has now ventured into the fields independently of Naomi to support herself and her mother-in-law in a very precarious economic situation. Even today, people address mature women by such expressions as "young lady" or "sweetie"; while they may be trying to be friendly and perhaps even complimentary, these types of addresses can sound similarly infantilizing. In the case of Ruth, she may look young and of marriageable age, but she is not a child.

The age difference between Boaz and Ruth poses no challenge in imagining a possible sexual relationship between the two characters. J. Cheryl Exum argues that, according to the "heterosexist double standard" by which older men are sexually attractive yet older women are not,[48] the potential age difference between Boaz and Ruth fulfills a stereotype and fantasy by which an older man ends up with a younger woman. Though Boaz's concern for Ruth could be viewed as paternal, there is no problem crossing the line between paternal and sexual interest. In fact, the paternal and the sexual are overlapping boundaries in the narrative, which evokes the story of Lot and his daughters (see the discussion at 3:6-9 and at 1:2), the result of which is Ruth's Moabite ancestry.

45. Campbell, *Ruth*, 109. J. Cheryl Exum counters the "senior citizen" comment with, "What ever happened to 'middle-age?' " (*Plotted, Shot, and Painted: Cultural Representations of Biblical Women*, 2nd rev.ed. [Sheffield: Sheffield Phoenix, 2012], 178).

46. Ruth Rab. 4.4 and 6.2.

47. See Linafelt and Beal, *Ruth and Esther*, 30–31.

48. See Exum, *Plotted, Shot, and Painted*, 178 (176–81).

When Boaz asks his servant to whom Ruth belongs, the literal question in Hebrew is: "To whom is that young woman?" The question, which is rare in the Bible, is elsewhere directed to servants by people in positions of power (Gen 32:18; 1 Sam 30:13).[49] Sasson prefers a softer translation ("Where does this young woman fit in?") that he argues refers to Ruth's ancestry or family.[50] The formulation of the question indicates either a dependent or interdependent relationship.[51] The question also likely reflects the patriarchal culture: Boaz could be asking whether Ruth is married or engaged based on the man or patriarchal line to whom she belongs. In 2 Samuel 11, when David inquires after Bathsheba, he receives an answer based on the patriarchal line: she is "Bathsheba daughter of Eliam, the wife of Uriah the Hittite" (2 Sam 11:3). The identification of a woman with a patriarchal line is not so different from contemporary societies, in which it is still generally assumed that a woman takes her husband's last name when she marries.[52]

However, there is another option in interpreting Boaz's question. Sasson's translation opens the space for a familial response that could engage the matriarchal line as well as the patriarchal. When Naomi told Ruth and Orpah to return home, her wording was that each return to her "mother's house" (1:8). In a few verses, Boaz will again reference Ruth's mother when he states that she has left "father and mother and your native land" (2:11). Therefore, when Boaz asks, "to whom is that young woman," he could be referring not only to a possible husband but to her family in a broad sense, mother as well as father. Practically, this is the only way for Boaz to identify Ruth; her identity is wrapped

49. Nielsen, *Ruth*, 57; Linafelt and Beal, *Ruth and Esther*, 30.

50. Sasson, *Ruth*, 46–47. See also Eskenazi and Frymer-Kensky, *Ruth*, 32. Sakenfeld (*Ruth*, 41) similarly perceives the question to be about family connections, though specifically in terms of patriarchy (i.e., Ruth's husband, son, or father).

51. Trible (*God and the Rhetoric of Sexuality*, 176) and Levine ("Ruth," *Women's Bible Commentary*, ed. Carol A. Newsom and Sharon H. Ringe, exp. ed. [Louisville: Westminster John Knox, 1998], 84–90) argue that the statement reflects dependence on or belonging to a man. Contra Campbell, who proposes that the question probes Ruth's circumstances rather than her status as "belonging" to another person (*Ruth*, 95).

52. For example, my (Mahri's) mother hyphenated her last name when she married, from Leonard to Leonard-Fleckman. It was an uncommon choice at the time (1970s), and she experienced constant frustration when people, including family, would refuse to acknowledge the "Leonard" still in her name. I did not truly understand her frustration until I began to have similar experiences when I married (in 2013) and, like many women of my generation, did not take my husband's last name. Societal expectations are slow to change.

up in the identity of the family. The genealogy at the end of chapter 4 will again emphasize this point, yet there the opening matriarchal focus will shift to a very patriarchal one.

The servant cannot identify Ruth based on the category of family: her husband is dead, her father-in-law is dead, and he does not know her father's or mother's name (indeed, neither do we). He therefore answers the question indirectly by emphasizing that she is the "Moabite"[53] who came back with Naomi from Moab. Without stating Ruth's name (Boaz has not asked who *she* is), the servant identifies Ruth based on her Moabite heritage, which supports Sasson's proposal that Boaz has requested information primarily about Ruth's ancestry. The servant also connects Ruth to Naomi, her mother-in-law. Moreover, the servant doubles the reference to Moab: she is a Moabite, and she "came back" (שׁוב) with Naomi, which is strange language for someone who has arrived in Israel for the first time. The servant therefore returns us to the language of chapter 1, in which both Orpah and Ruth are consistently told to "go back" or return (שׁוב) to their land, while they state their desire to "return" (שׁוב) with their mother-in-law (see the discussion at 1:6-8, 10-12, 15-16, 22). The same expression is used later to describe Naomi as one who has "come back from the fields of Moab" (4:3). Although the servant labels Ruth the "Moabite," he simultaneously perceives her as someone who has permanently left Moab in order to "return" to Judah with her family, Naomi.

Koosed argues that the servant's response treats Ruth as if she were a "stray dog" returned with Naomi, unbidden and unwanted.[54] According to Koosed, the servant betrays intense dislike for Ruth based primarily on his own negative stereotypes of Moabites and even his "revulsion" at Ruth's poverty.[55] Yet the text need not support this conclusion. There is no judgment in the servant's statement; he merely states the reality of

53. While the Hebrew does not contain the definite article, the Septuagint and Syriac translations do. Ruth is "the Moabite" in those texts.

54. Koosed, *Gleaning Ruth*, 73. See also Jonathan Grossman, " 'Gleaning Among the Ears'—'Gathering Among the Sheaves': Characterizing the Image of the Supervising Boy (Ruth 2)," *JBL* 126 (2007): 703–16. Grossman proposes that the servant has strong reservations about Ruth's Moabite status, and her behavior in the fields, and that his response in vv. 6-7 contrasts with Boaz's generosity and kindness in the subsequent verses.

55. Koosed, *Gleaning Ruth*, 74–75. Koosed cites Grossman, who proposes that the primary reason for the servant's distaste for Ruth is his hatred of Moabites ("Gleaning Among the Ears," 711).

Ruth's identity. Moreover, Israel's gleaning rights were for the resident alien, and likely the servant would have been accustomed to "strangers" arriving to glean. Although this would not necessarily prevent revulsion or dislike, we also do not know whether the servant himself is a resident alien; we know nothing about his background. In fact, we know less about him than we know about Ruth. The text is not particularly interested in the "servant" class, or the "lower classes" per se. The servant's added response in describing Ruth as returning with Naomi could even be interpreted as one of admiration at Ruth's devotion.[56] Boaz's positive reaction to Ruth in verses 8-9 suggests that the servant's tone is, if not positive, at least neutral.

The servant continues by explaining what Ruth had requested: to "glean" and "gather" "among" (using the preposition ב, translated often as "in" or "at") the sheaves. The task of gleaning takes place behind, not among, the sheaves; gleaners gather up single stalks that have fallen during the harvest. If the servant is accurately reporting earlier dialogue (it is otherwise unrecorded), then Ruth has perhaps requested something beyond her rights—to gather among the standing sheaves, or among those that were already bundled.[57] The issue is further complicated by verses 15-16, in which Boaz grants Ruth this very privilege, to glean among the standing sheaves. Frederic Bush goes so far as to state that it "stresses credulity to the breaking point" that Ruth would make such a request unless it were granted to her by the owner of the field.[58] One explanation is that Ruth merely uses the wrong prepositions in Hebrew (her primary language is Moabite), or that she knows the Israelite practice only generally. Yet elsewhere, Ruth plays with Hebrew, including lending double meaning to a single Hebrew root (see 2:10); her proficiency in Hebrew is therefore not in question. More likely, the issue is our English translation of the preposition ב, which more simply translates as "in" or "at" rather than "among." In verses 2-3 and 7, the preposition is paired with the language of gleaning "behind" someone. When Boaz grants Ruth the rights to glean "among," the Hebrew is not ב, but rather בין "between." Likely, Ruth has merely requested to glean within her rights.

56. See Hubbard, *Book of Ruth*, 152.

57. See Joüon, *Ruth*, 49; Frederic W. Bush, *Ruth, Esther*, WBC 9 (Dallas: Word Books, 1996), 114; Grossman, "Gleaning Among the Ears," 703–5; and Koosed, *Gleaning Ruth*, 74–75.

58. Bush, *Ruth*, 114.

TRANSLATION MATTERS

In the NRSV, the end of verse 7 is translated as "without resting even for a moment." The more literal translation is that Ruth "has rested in [or returned to] the house very little." There are multiple problems in translating this phrase. First, it is unclear whether the verb שבתה (NRSV "resting") at the end of verse 7 comes from the root שבת, "to rest"; ישב, "to sit/dwell"; or שוב, "to return." In addition, the NRSV skips the Hebrew term בית, "house," at the end of the verse. Sasson has proposed that Ruth has been "standing," waiting for Boaz since morning, spending "little time at home."[59] Tamara Eskenazi and Tikva Frymer-Kensky argue that the primary sense is that Ruth has been working hard all day.[60] Edward Campbell simply refuses to translate the second half of verse 7,[61] while Linafelt offers an incomprehensible translation: "She came and stood from then the morning and until now; this is her sitting the house a few."[62] Katharine Doob Sakenfeld notes that the particular translation is not essential for the reader's understanding of what continues to unfold in the story,[63] yet this is the only verse that may suggest that Ruth and Naomi reside in a house.

Boaz sees a stranger and is curious. We do not know whether he finds her attractive, and even the notion of "attraction" need not be synonymous with physical beauty or sexual attraction alone. The narrative makes no comment about Ruth's physical appearance, which contrasts with descriptions of other biblical women as physically beautiful as well as sexually desirable.[64] The ambiguity around Ruth's physical ap-

59. Sasson, *Ruth*, 38.

60. Eskenazi and Frymer-Kensky, *Ruth*, 33. They propose that the "house" is a "hut" or lean-to on the fields in which workers can rest. Therefore, they translate the verse as Ruth "has rested but little in the hut." See also Nielsen, who takes the same ultimate sense from the line but translates that Ruth has "only sat down for a moment in there" (*Ruth*, 56).

61. Campbell, *Ruth*, 86.

62. Linafelt and Beal, *Ruth and Esther*, 32.

63. Sakenfeld, *Ruth*, 41–42.

64. In Genesis, all of the matriarchs are described physically; three are beautiful (Sarah in 12:11; Rebekah in 24:16; Rachel in 29:17), while Leah is described in terms of her "lovely" or "weak" eyes, depending on the translator's rendering (Gen 29:17). Of the Genesis women, the scribes are unconcerned with describing the physical appearance of the slaves who give birth to sons of Abraham and Jacob (Hagar being the most notable), as well as Dinah in Genesis 34 and Tamar in Genesis 38. Other biblical women labeled in terms of their beauty are Abigail (1 Sam 25), Bathsheba (2 Sam 11), Tamar (2 Sam 13), and Esther. In the Apocrypha, the book of Judith is named for its heroine who is "beautiful in appearance" and "very lovely to behold" (Jdt 8:7). Male characters can also be described as physically attractive, with or without the sexual desirability,

pearance is similar to that of biblical heroines such as Tamar in Genesis 38, who drives the plot through initiative and cunning that necessitates Judah's sexual desire but not necessarily her physical beauty (see also the discussion at 3:3 and 4:12). Breaking stereotypes of biblical heroines, Elizabeth Cady Stanton was careful to argue *against* Ruth's beauty, stating that hard work in the fields had "withered her" and that Boaz prized Ruth for her virtues, her "great moral qualities of head and heart."[65] Traditional Jewish sources, including the Midrash and Rashi, attribute Boaz's attention to Ruth's modesty and obedience.[66]

Although there is no reason to think anything of Ruth's physical appearance, Boaz notices her instantly. The text supports multiple interpretations for why: perhaps Ruth was easily noticed because she was a stranger in a small community,[67] or she stood out as hardworking and focused.[68] Yet attraction in a general sense, and perhaps sexual desirability, likely plays a role.[69] The Midrash states that Ruth was forty years old but looked like a girl of fourteen and that "whoever saw her was sexually excited."[70] Moreover, it may have been Ruth's intention to attract Boaz

---

depending on how one reads into the text (e.g., Saul in 1 Sam 9:2 and David in 1 Sam 16:12). Joseph's beauty clearly attracts the attention of Potiphar's wife in Genesis 39.

65. Elizabeth Cady Stanton, *The Woman's Bible* (Seattle: Coalition Task Force on Women and Religious, 1981), 41.

66. For example, Ruth Rab. 4.6 describes Ruth as a modest dresser who was careful to lower her body when gleaning rather than bending over; Rashi, following the Talmud, states that she was less greedy and more modest than the other women in the fields (see b. Sabb. 113b; Eskenazi and Frymer-Kensky, *Ruth*, 32; also Hillel I. Millgram, *Four Biblical Heroines and the Case for Female Authorship: An Analysis of the Women of Ruth, Esther and Genesis 38* [Jefferson, NC: McFarland & Company, 2008], 45; and Leila Leah Bronner, *From Eve to Esther: Rabbinic Reconstructions of Biblical Women*, 64 [Louisville: Westminster John Knox, 1994], 72–73).

67. Trible, *God and the Rhetoric of Sexuality*, 176; Nielsen, *Ruth*, 57; Sakenfeld, *Ruth*, 41.

68. Berlin, *Poetics and Interpretation*, 86; also Eskenazi and Frymer-Kensky, *Ruth*, 33. Campbell pushes the limits of the text too far: he states that Ruth had been "standing" all day without working, awaiting Boaz's arrival to grant her special request to both "glean" and "gather." This would account for his immediate notice of Ruth, if she were merely standing aside from the gleaning (Campbell, *Ruth*, 96; also Sasson, *Ruth*, 47–48). Rashkow suggests that Ruth's unusual request to gather *and* glean was what sparked Boaz's interest ("Ruth: The Discourse of Power," 34). Yet Boaz notices Ruth before he hears anything about what she has requested.

69. Fewell and Gunn understand Boaz's interest in Ruth to be mainly sexual, which does not require physical beauty (*Compromising Redemption*, 40–44).

70. Ruth Rab. 4.4. Beattie translates the same statement from R. Johanan as "everyone who saw her ejaculated semen" (Derek R. G. Beattie, *Jewish Exegesis of the Book of Ruth* [Sheffield: Sheffield Academic, 1977], 191). In this interpretation, R. Johanan

(or perhaps any man) from the moment that she told Naomi her goal to "find favor" with someone in the field.[71]

Ruth and Boaz Engage in Conversation (2:8-13)

Following the exchange between Boaz and his servant, Boaz and Ruth speak for the first time (vv. 8-13). Boaz's interest goes beyond inquiring about Ruth; now, he speaks to her directly in the first of two dialogues between the pair (the second takes place on the threshing floor in chapter 3). Boaz initiates both dialogues, and both are concerned with Ruth's well-being (and implicitly Boaz's, as well) rather than Naomi's.[72] In each case, Ruth further directs or manipulates the conversation, and in both cases, Boaz presents himself as Ruth's enthusiastic protector.[73]

Boaz begins the conversation by referring to Ruth as "my daughter," language that reflects his relative age as well as paternal care and plausible attraction. The language is reminiscent of the daughters of Lot in Genesis 19, who have sex with (or rape) their drunken father and later give birth to Ben-ammi (Ammon) and Moab (see also the discussion at Ruth 3:6-9). In calling Ruth "my daughter," he also aligns himself with Naomi and offers Ruth protection; at the end of the chapter, Naomi will demonstrate concern for Ruth in a similar way.[74] Phyllis Trible has observed that Boaz acts as a "male counterpart" to Naomi;[75] while Boaz and Naomi never meet, Ruth moves between their respective domains in the narrative, from the town to the fields.

The conversation is then beautifully constructed to build slowly upon the information it presents to the reader. In verses 8-9, Boaz issues in-

---

connects the word for chance, מקרה (when Ruth "chances" upon the field), to loss of semen, קרי, to suggest that Ruth is unusually beautiful. As discussed in greater detail in the introduction, the church fathers, including Hippolytus of Rome (170–236) and Origen (ca. 184–253), say nothing of Ruth's physical appearance; rather, they spiritualize Ruth based on her perceived virtues. She becomes a typology of the Church (*typus Ecclesiae*) or a "type of the gentiles" (*typus gentium*), who represents the pagans who are converted to Christianity (see the discussion on the church fathers and Ruth in Elena Giannarelli, "Ruth in the Church Fathers," *SIDIC* 23 [1990]: 12–15).

71. Jon L. Berquist argues that Ruth's intention to seduce Boaz is apparent as early as chapter 2 and builds into chapter 3 ("Role Differentiation in the Book of Ruth," *JSOT* 57 [1993]: 23–37). The text does not necessarily support such a reading.

72. See Eskenazi and Frymer-Kensky, *Ruth*, 33.

73. See Nielsen, *Ruth*, 57.

74. See Trible, *God and the Rhetoric of Sexuality*, 176; Campbell, *Ruth*, 110; and Linafelt and Beal, *Ruth and Esther*, 34.

75. Trible, *God and the Rhetoric of Sexuality*, 176.

Ruth 2:8-13

[8]Then Boaz said to Ruth, "Now listen, my daughter, do not go to glean in another field or leave this one, but keep close to my young women. [9]Keep your eyes on the field that is being reaped, and follow behind them. I have ordered the young men not to bother you. If you get thirsty, go to the vessels and drink from what the young men have drawn." [10]Then she fell prostrate, with her face to the ground, and said to him, "Why have I found favor in your sight, that you should take notice of me, when I am a foreigner?" [11]But Boaz answered her, "All that you have done for your mother-in-law since the death of your husband has been fully told me, and how you left your father and mother and your native land and came to a people that you did not know before. [12]May the LORD reward you for your deeds, and may you have a full reward from the LORD, the God of Israel, under whose wings you have come for refuge!" [13]Then she said, "May I continue to find favor in your sight, my lord, for you have comforted me and spoken kindly to your servant, even though I am not one of your servants."

structions on how Ruth is to glean in his field and not any other. Boaz seeks to restrict her movements and reduce the risk of male competition by keeping her within his own field or close to him.[76] He slowly narrows the space that Ruth is to inhabit with four imperatives: do not go into another field, do not leave my field, keep close to my young women, and follow behind the reapers.

When Boaz instructs Ruth to "keep close" to his young women (v. 8), the Hebrew verb is to "cling" (דבק). Ruth had also "clung" to Naomi in 1:14 (see the discussion there). The notion of "clinging" can refer to sexual intimacy or to the establishment of a new family, as in Genesis 2:24, when a man "clings" to his wife, and Genesis 34:3, when Shechem "clings" to Dinah. Here, the word denotes less intense physical contact; Ruth is told to "cling" or stay close to the other women who are gleaning in the field lest she run the risk of being molested. Eskenazi and Frymer-Kensky propose that Boaz has moved Ruth closer into the Judahite circle and into his household by having her join his "young women,"[77] though she becomes more than one of these young women when he calls her "my daughter."

Boaz continues to instruct Ruth to keep her eyes on the field being reaped and to follow after the reapers (v. 9). He has ordered the young men not to "bother" Ruth. The Hebrew term נגע has a variety of meanings,

76. Fewell and Gunn, *Compromising Redemption*, 42, 84–85; also Levine, "Ruth," 87.

77. Eskenazi and Frymer-Kensky, *Ruth*, 34.

including to "touch" and "strike," and implies the possibility of sexual attack or unwanted attention.[78] The issue of being "bothered" while gleaning is not unique to ancient Israel, as demonstrated in the Egyptian *Instruction of Amenemope*, which advises its audience not to "pounce on a widow when you find her in the field."[79] In the case of Ruth, nothing has thus far suggested that she is in danger in the fields. Boaz's seeming concern may reflect a desire to keep her close or protect her from unwanted attention, no matter the reality of the danger.

Sasson views Boaz's statements to Ruth in verses 8-9 as embodying the "correct" behavior expected of a man of substance. Boaz has done little more for Ruth than what would be required of him by the customs of gleaning.[80] To what extent Boaz would have demonstrated the same interest or care for any gleaner is impossible to know.[81] Yet what goes beyond this correct behavior is the instruction that Ruth should share the water that the "young men" have drawn from the well. Robert Alter describes this instruction as alluding to a literary convention or "type scene" in biblical narrative, in which encounters at wells lead to betrothals.[82] In these scenes, a young man or his surrogate arrives in a foreign land, encounters a girl or נערה at a well, someone draws water, the girl rushes home to spread news of the stranger's arrival, often there is a meal, and marriage ensues.[83] These encounters include the story of Abraham's servant and Rebekah (Gen 24:10-61), Jacob and Rachel (Gen 29:1-20), and Moses and the Midianite priest's seven daughters (Exod 2:15-21). In the New Testament, Jesus meets the Samaritan (foreign) woman at the well (John 4) and they discuss marriage. Alter proposes

78. Nielsen proposes that Boaz fears that Ruth will be sexually attacked (*Ruth*, 58); also Linafelt and Beal, *Ruth and Esther*, 34–35. Sakenfeld suggests that a foreigner would be more likely to be victimized than an Israelite (*Ruth*, 43). Contra Sasson, who views Boaz's warnings and use of language as harmless (*Ruth*, 50).

79. *Instruction of Amenemope* 26.9 (*COS* 1:121).

80. Sasson, *Ruth*, 49.

81. See Sakenfeld, *Ruth*, 43.

82. Prior to Alter, Robert C. Culley discussed the repetition of the well motif as evidence of oral transmission in biblical narrative (*Studies in the Structure of Hebrew Narrative*, SemeiaSup 62 [Philadelphia: Fortress, 1976], 41–43).

83. Robert Alter, *The Art of Biblical Narrative*, rev. ed. (New York: Basic Books, 2011), 60–69; also Levine, "Ruth," 87; Linafelt and Beal, *Ruth and Esther*, 35; and Eskenazi and Frymer-Kensky, *Ruth*, 35. See also Esther Fuchs's discussion of the power dynamics at work in these type scenes, in which there is a gradual diminishment of the woman's role and an increased emphasis on the man ("Structure and Patriarchal Functions in the Biblical Betrothal Type-Scene," in *Women in the Hebrew Bible: A Reader*, ed. Alice Bach [New York: Routledge, 1999], 45–51).

that the story of Ruth is a transformation of the type scene, rotated "180 degrees on the axes of gender and geography."[84] The hero is a woman, the foreign soil is Judah, and Ruth is called a נערה, as if she were unmarried rather than a young widow.

Through this transformation of the betrothal scene, Ruth is adopted into the line of Genesis matriarchs, yet she also fulfills the role of the man according to Alter's literary pattern. She is to drink from the water that the young men (not Boaz) offer her at the well, which changes the pattern and introduces the question of whether Ruth will end up with one of the young men rather than with Boaz. Moreover, the language of springs and wells is sexually coded, and the notion of "drinking" from the well recalls such texts as Proverbs 5:15, which reminds the (male) listener that marital sexual pleasure is better than that of adultery ("drink water from your own cistern, flowing water from your own well"). Here, Ruth is told to drink water from the young men's well, again reversing the imagery. The scene could also be a sign of future marriage to Boaz, or it could be designed to create tension between Ruth and the young men, on the one hand, and the older Boaz, on the other. This tension vanishes in chapter 3, when Boaz praises Ruth for going after him rather than "young men" (3:10).

Ruth's response to Boaz in verses 10 and 13 is both clever and ambiguous.[85] Rather than say a mere "thank-you," Ruth responds in such a way as to assure the conversation continues.[86] She falls, bows before him, and asks why he has shown her "favor," חן. She thus fulfills her own desire to find "favor" in someone's eyes (v. 2). While the verb for "bowing" or worshiping (שחה) is common, it is exaggerated with the expression of "falling" (נפל) prostrate, or, more literally, "upon her face." There are many examples of this pairing of verbs in Samuel–Kings, often before the king;[87] in 1 Samuel 25:23, Abigail similarly falls down (נפל) and bows or worships (שחה) before David. Like Abigail before David, Ruth's actions demonstrate an overstated humility before Boaz.

84. Alter, *Art of Biblical Narrative*, 70.

85. Carolyn J. Sharp describes Ruth as acting with "extraordinary subtlety" in this scene ("Feminist Queries for Ruth and Joshua," *JSOT* 28 [2014]: 229–52, esp. 243); also Linafelt and Beal, *Ruth and Esther*, 35–36.

86. Nielsen, *Ruth*, 58; Linafelt and Beal, *Ruth and Esther*, 36; Eskenazi and Frymer-Kensky, *Ruth*, 36.

87. Examples include David before Jonathan (1 Sam 20:41); Abigail before David (1 Sam 25:23); and the woman of Tekoa before David (2 Sam 14:4). On the relationship between David and Jonathan and the love they profess for each other, see chapter 1 and the discussion on love in 4:13-17.

Ruth also plays with the root נכר, which translates "to recognize, disguise, or treat as foreign," by using it twice in one question. Ruth asks Boaz why he has noticed her (נכר) or singled her out, a "foreigner" or, more literally, "foreign woman" (נכריה). Elsewhere in the Bible, the feminine form of "foreigner" tends to have negative connotations, in particular, the "foreign woman" in Proverbs 2:16; 5:20; 7:5, translated by the NRSV as a "loose" woman or an "adulteress."[88] Ruth will play the role of the dangerous woman on the threshing floor in chapter 3, although there too she subverts the pattern, as we will see.

Boaz then tells Ruth that he has been told of all she has done for her mother-in-law, thus admitting that he knew of Ruth and Naomi's arrival in Bethlehem. Why he had not reached out to them prior to Ruth's appearance in his field goes unstated; perhaps Ruth simply moved more quickly than he by showing up in the fields right after their arrival. If there were any neglect on his part, this is not indicated by the text. Boaz does not apologize, nor does Ruth suggest that Boaz had shirked his responsibilities. In addition, Boaz's previous knowledge of Ruth intimates that he may have already guessed Ruth's identity when he requested information from his servant. Though the servant did not acknowledge Ruth's familial connection to Naomi (v. 6), Boaz does. His actions are reminiscent of David's in 2 Samuel 11 when he sees Bathsheba from his rooftop and "inquires" about her; the Hebrew is ambiguous enough that he could either be asking for Bathsheba's identity or merely confirming what he already knew (2 Sam 11:2-3). As is the case with Ruth, Bathsheba's motives can only be guessed; unlike David's illicit affair with Bathsheba and subsequent murder of Uriah, however, the relationship between Boaz and Ruth is restrained and appropriate, and both characters are esteemed for their virtue.

While the servant spoke of Judah as the place of arrival or return, Boaz reorients the reader by referring to Judah as the foreign place and Moab the native one. He sees from Ruth's perspective; she is no longer the stranger but rather the one who left father and mother and native

88. See Eskenazi and Frymer-Kensky, *Ruth*, 36–37. The Hebrew in Proverbs is more open to interpretation—the "foreign" woman is that which is "foreign" to the young man; in other words, she is foreign to him in that she is married or belongs to another man. Although the NRSV takes liberties in interpreting the language as "loose" or "adulteress," from a contemporary perspective the Hebrew is equally problematic in the notion that a woman "belongs" to another man. The text itself is quite negative in its descriptions of this woman; she is portrayed as the opposite of wisdom, and her ways lead to "death" and to Sheol (5:5-6).

land to come to a place she did not know. This is the second reference to Ruth's mother (see the discussion at 2:5-6). The expressions "native land" and "people" describe the identity of persons when viewed by outsiders,[89] though here, it is Boaz who views his own people (and himself) as if from the outside. His concern for Ruth presents him as someone who has compassion for Ruth's situation and understanding for the other, perhaps from his own self-awareness of Israel as a stranger and sojourner.[90] By the end of the narrative Boaz will give Ruth legal status, as it were, through marriage and through progeny.

While Ruth does not need actual immigration papers in order to stay in ancient Israel, Boaz's patronage could help her obtain the economic security that she and Naomi (who is not a foreigner!) desperately need. The notion of finding security through Boaz again takes us back to the question of what it means to "find favor" in verse 2 and whether Ruth's desire to glean is about more than simply obtaining food. From a contemporary perspective, many citizens of the United States mistrust foreigners (women and men) who marry United States citizens, based on the perception that their primary purpose is to obtain a green card (permanent US residency). As a result, visa interviews can be similar to interrogations, in which officials test couples for their sincerity. As part of my (Mahri's) Peace Corps training in the Dominican Republic, I was taught to mistrust the intentions of Dominican locals; I was told that their goal was to marry North Americans in order to get to the United States. This warning had varied effects among the volunteers. Later on, volunteer friends who married Dominicans went through the "interrogation" proceedings for their partners' travel and residency visas.

Boaz's emphasis in verse 11 is on Ruth's loyalty to Naomi.[91] Boaz then calls on YHWH to reward Ruth for this "deed" (NRSV "deeds") of loyalty to her mother-in-law[92] and for seeking refuge under YHWH's

89. Eskenazi and Frymer-Kensky, *Ruth*, 38.

90. Trible, *God and the Rhetoric of Sexuality*, 177. The commandment to treat the stranger well is at the heart of the Pentateuch, e.g., Deut 10:19, "You shall also love the stranger, for you were strangers in the land of Egypt"; Exod 22:21, "You shall not wrong or oppress a resident alien, for you were aliens in the land of Egypt"; Exod 23:9, "You shall not oppress a resident alien; you know the heart of an alien, for you were aliens in the land of Egypt."

91. The Targum adds that Ruth has become a proselyte, and that from her will come forth "kings and prophets" because of the kindness that she showed to her mother-in-law (2:11).

92. On the meaning of "your deed," see Campbell, *Ruth*, 99–100; also Eskenazi and Frymer-Kensky, *Ruth*, 38.

"wing," כנף. The imagery of God's protective wing alludes to Psalm 91:4: "he will cover you with his pinions, and under his wings you will find refuge."[93] The language also alludes to 3:9, in which Ruth tells Boaz to spread his "wing" over her. Considering that the narrative is so focused on human actions, the connection between YHWH and Boaz is intentional. While some consider Boaz to deflect attention from himself by drawing YHWH into the matter,[94] the narrative is equating Boaz with YHWH insofar as it concerns Ruth's protection. There is also a sexual undercurrent to the entire conversation, particularly in the Hebrew כנף, which can also connote "genitals."[95] Ruth later, pointedly, tells Boaz that it is his כנף under which she will find refuge (see the conversation at 3:9). The power dynamics imply that Boaz, in YHWH's role, is the one in power. Yet in the threshing floor scene to come, Ruth will be the one driving the narrative and actions.

Finding Refuge under the "Wings" of the God of Israel

Boaz's praise of Ruth for sheltering or finding refuge under the "wings" of the God of Israel (Ruth 2:12), gives the rabbis of late antiquity their language for conversion to Judaism. From the sixteenth century on, we have references to Ashkenazic Jews from Northern and Eastern Europe reading the book of Ruth on Shavuot, the Feast of Weeks. The theme of finding "refuge" under God's wings, understood as conversion to Judaism and acceptance of the covenant with God, is one reason why Ruth is associated with Shavuot. Though in the Bible Shavuot is an agricultural pilgrimage festival, the rabbis associate it with the anniversary of the revelation of law at Mount Sinai. On Shavuot, Jews mark the anniversary of Israel entering a covenant with their God by reading the story of Ruth's personal journey to find refuge "under God's wings."

This rabbinic connection between Ruth and the Sinaitic covenant is not only thematic. It also has textual resonances in the Pentateuch. The image of wings appears in Exodus 19:4-5,

93. Sakenfeld, *Ruth*, 45; also Campbell, *Ruth*, 100. As Nielsen observes, Boaz's reply to Ruth constitutes the climax to the entire chapter (*Ruth*, 59).

94. See Linafelt and Beal, *Ruth and Esther*, 36. André LaCocque claims that Boaz demonstrates only a "surface piety" in his response to Ruth, by attempting to deflect responsibility to YHWH (*Ruth, A Continental Commentary*, trans. K. C. Hanson [Minneapolis: Fortress, 2004], 72–73).

95. Levine, "Ruth," 87 (see Deut 22:30).

in a preamble to Israel before the revelation of law at Mount Sinai. From the mountain, God tells Moses to say, "You have seen what I did to the Egyptians, and how I bore you on eagles' wings and brought you to myself. Now therefore, if you obey my voice and keep my covenant, you shall be my treasured possession out of all the peoples. Indeed, the whole earth is mine." The wings in this quotation are not God's own but a poetic expression of the power, alacrity, and care with which the Israelites left bondage. Directly connected with the eagles' wings is God's expectation of obedience to his laws promulgated at Sinai.

The notion of finding refuge under God's wings (Ruth 2:12) appears again in Ruth 3:9, when Ruth visits Boaz at night and asks him to "spread your cloak [=wings] over your servant." Eleventh-century commentator Rashi interprets "spread your cloak" as Ruth asking Boaz to marry her. Rashi's interpretation is likely more than contextual. In Ezekiel 16:8, God is described as "spreading a cloak" over Israel as an act of commitment, in which marriage is metaphor for covenant. This passage is the only other verse where God "spreads his wings" over someone. Based on the cloak/wings that refer to God (2:12) and to a human protector, Boaz (3:9), Ruth joins Israel through her commitment to Naomi, her people, and her God and then solidifies her place in Israelite society through marriage to Boaz. Her story provides a counterbalance to the other rabbinic example of conversion, Jethro (Moses' father-in-law), who is understood to have "converted" in response to reports of awesome miracles in Egypt. Reading and preaching about Ruth as an example for Jews to follow in their acceptance of God's covenant on Shavuot may serve to magnify the significance of human relationships in keeping the covenant with God. Following the rabbinic principle, "all Israel stand as guarantors for one another," Jewish law emphasizes interpersonal obligations as Divine service and that each Jew's actions enhance or detract from the welfare of the whole. Rabbinic Judaism conceives commitment to the community as constitutive of being Jewish. The first thing a prospective convert is told, according to Jewish legal codes, is about the tenuous existence of Jews in the diaspora, not the tenets of faith or lists of rules. As a prayer from the Sabbath liturgy avers, "All those who faithfully engage with the needs of the community, the Holy Blessed One will pay their wages."

Lynn Kaye

Based on Boaz's statement of Ruth's loyalty in verses 11-12, Trible has famously connected Ruth's journey to the call of Abraham.[96] According to Trible, Ruth is a foreigner like Abraham, who is called to break from her previous identity in order to receive a promise for the future. Unlike Abraham, however, Ruth's initiative is entirely her own. God did not call or bless her; she called herself, even against Naomi's will, knowing that her decision may well signal the "death" of her former identity and her line should she not remarry. In verses 11-12, she receives a blessing not from God but from Boaz. Not only has Ruth broken with family, land, and religion, but she has also "reversed sexual allegiance" in committing to an older woman in a world in which life depends on men.[97] Trible's Abraham paradigm can be extended to include Rebekah and Jacob, who leave mother and father and travel to a land that is foreign to them.[98] Whereas Abraham in Genesis follows the call of God, and Jacob listens to his father, Ruth and Rebekah answer for themselves. Rebekah's family blesses her as she departs from their home (Gen 24:60); here in 2:11-12, someone finally praises Ruth for her actions.

Although Boaz's reply in verses 11-12 does not necessitate another response, Ruth continues to speak in the same exaggerated manner as in verse 10. She again stresses the notion of finding "favor" in the eyes of her "lord." She states that Boaz has "spoken kindly to her," or, more literally, has "spoken to her heart." The expression generally connotes comfort, yet it can also imply courtship.[99] Ruth identifies herself twice as Boaz's

96. Trible, *God and the Rhetoric of Sexuality*, 177. Alter states that the connection between Abraham and Ruth makes her a "matriarch by adoption" (*Art of Biblical Narrative*, 71). See also Sasson, *Ruth*, 52; Linafelt and Beal, *Ruth and Esther*, 36; Tikva Frymer-Kensky, *Reading the Women of the Bible: A New Interpretation of Their Stories* (New York: Schocken Books, 2002), 244; and Millgram, *Four Biblical Heroines*, 49. Millgram overemphasizes the Abraham connection, viewing the effect of Ruth's faith as "so extraordinary" to Boaz "that he has no words adequate to express his wonder."

97. Trible argues that Ruth's decision surpasses Abraham's leap of faith; indeed, "there is no more radical decision in all the memories of Israel" (*God and the Rhetoric of Sexuality*, 173).

98. See Irmtraud Fischer, "The Book of Ruth: A 'Feminist' Commentary to the Torah?," in *Ruth and Esther*, FCB 3, 2nd ser., ed. Athalya Brenner (Sheffield: Sheffield Academic, 1999), 24–49, at 43. For a reversal of the Rebekah connection, see Frymer-Kensky, who compares Boaz (not Ruth!) to Rebekah (*Reading the Women of the Bible*, 244). Like Rebekah, Boaz was the "providential one" in three key ways: he came from Elimelech's family, he was mindful of God, and he treated Ruth with kindness.

99. On the various nuances of "speak to the heart," see Eskenazi and Frymer-Kensky, *Ruth*, 39. Expressions of courtship include Gen 34:3, in which Shechem had intercourse with (and possibly raped) Dinah and now wishes to marry her; and Hos

"servant," or, more harshly, "slave" (שפחה). The NRSV (and JPS) use the less provocative translation of "servant," rather than "slave," the latter of which recalls literal slavery and inhumane relationships between slave and slave owner. The same language is used for Hagar (e.g., Gen 16:2, 3) and for Zilpah and Bilhah, the servants/slaves of Leah and Rachel (Gen 29:24, 29) who also become wives or concubines of Jacob (Gen 30:4, 9). In a brilliant maneuver, Ruth stresses that she is not even of the status of a slave, yet in utilizing the terminology she nonetheless characterizes herself according to this status in order to overstate her subservience to Boaz.

In 3:9, Ruth will again refer to herself as Boaz's "servant" using a different Hebrew term, אמה. The word can mean either "servant" or "slave," and again it characterizes both Hagar (e.g., Gen 21:10, 12) and Bilhah (Gen 30:3). In a variety of situations, אמה also denotes a woman who can be taken as a concubine or wife (e.g., Judg 9:18; 19:19; 1 Sam 25:41; as well as Gen 21:10, 12). The distinction between the two Hebrew words for "servant" or "slave" is subtle, and in the case of Ruth so subtle that the words appear to be identical;[100] both terms are therefore translated as "servant" in the NRSV. In her self-designations, Ruth subtly manipulates Boaz and slowly progresses to shift her identity from a "foreigner" (2:10), to a slave (2:13), and, finally, to a servant or, possibly, a concubine or wife (3:9).[101] Abigail behaves similarly when addressing David in 1 Samuel 25:41; like Ruth, she bows down to the ground and refers to herself as David's "servant" (אמה) who is but a "slave" (שפחה). Abigail is similar to Ruth in other ways; she is a widow who influences the actions of a man of higher social standing (David). Through the use of eloquent language and exaggerated deference, she uses her status in the social hierarchy in order to achieve what she desires.

Ruth's responses to Boaz in verses 10 and 13 have been interpreted as acts of humility and deference,[102] gratitude,[103] and even timidity.[104] While Ruth may be humble, she is certainly not timid, as demonstrated by her

2:16 and Isa 40:1-2, in which God or his messenger speaks to the heart of Israel or Jerusalem, as would a husband.

100. See Campbell, *Ruth*, 123.

101. Berlin, *Poetics and Interpretation*, 88.

102. See Campbell, *Ruth*, 111.

103. Nielsen states that Ruth expresses "surprise and gratitude" at Boaz's generosity (*Ruth*, 58); Eskenazi and Frymer-Kensky view Ruth's actions as gestures of humility and thankfulness because of the unexpected privileges that Boaz has granted her (*Ruth*, 36; also Frymer-Kensky, *Reading the Women of the Bible*, 244).

104. Sakenfeld claims that Ruth acts almost timidly by demonstrating a deferential demeanor toward Boaz (*Ruth*, 45).

exaggerated actions, embellished speech, and her second, unnecessary response to Boaz (v. 13). Moreover, Ruth's actions and speech contain initiative and daring,[105] and they are a source of power that she uses to draw Boaz into her life. In her artful use of language, Ruth flatters Boaz while placing herself into his care. She reminds him subtly that if the divine plays any role in rewarding or protecting her, it will be done entirely through human hands.[106] Koosed has argued that Ruth is mocking Boaz through actions that are so extreme as to border on self-humiliation and denigration, yet self-abasement is not the same as mockery.[107] There is no evidence that she "mocks" or makes fun of Boaz, who has already demonstrated overwhelming kindness toward her. Rather, her response ensures continued kindness and ongoing protection. As Ilona Rashkow proposes, Ruth's power is made manifest through the discourse that she constructs.[108]

Boaz is also a strong character in the scene. Some have interpreted his actions as mere reactions to Ruth's resourcefulness,[109] yet Boaz acts with generosity and care before Ruth speaks to him (vv. 8-9). Koosed argues that Boaz has not granted Ruth special permission beyond the normal expectations and that she does not need his benevolence in order to glean.[110] However, it is unlikely that every gleaner would attract such attention; in verses 8-9 alone, Boaz granted Ruth more than the simple rights of gleaning. Trible has proposed that Boaz has "patriarchal power" and "authority" within the story, while Ruth controls the plot.[111] Ruth certainly has control in the narrative, but Boaz also has agency. He treats Ruth with care and respect (and perhaps a little lust), but he, too, makes choices in his actions and responses that show respect for Ruth.

The Conversation Continues (2:14-18a)

The scene continues from Ruth's final comment to Boaz in verse 13 and the meal described in verse 14. Boaz tells Ruth to draw near from where she is resting or working and to eat the bread, dipping it into the

105. Trible, *God and the Rhetoric of Sexuality*, 177–78.

106. See also LaCocque, *Ruth, A Continental Commentary*, 72–73.

107. Koosed, *Gleaning Ruth*, 76.

108. Rashkow, "Ruth: The Discourse of Power," 35–36.

109. Trible, *God and the Rhetoric of Sexuality*, 177–78.

110. Koosed writes, "It is no virtue to allow the homeless to eat out of your trash; it is no virtue to let the poor pick up after your harvesters" (*Gleaning Ruth*, 76). Koosed's statement convicts those who believe they are "giving" when they are simply throwing out. Yet in the case of Boaz, she overstates, as discussed above.

111. Trible, *God and the Rhetoric of Sexuality*, 177–78.

Ruth 2:14-18a

14At mealtime Boaz said to her, "Come here, and eat some of this bread, and dip your morsel in the sour wine." So she sat beside the reapers, and he heaped up for her some parched grain. She ate until she was satisfied, and she had some left over. 15When she got up to glean, Boaz instructed his young men, "Let her glean even among the standing sheaves, and do not reproach her. 16You must also pull out some handfuls for her from the bundles, and leave them for her to glean, and do not rebuke her."

17So she gleaned in the field until evening. Then she beat out what she had gleaned, and it was about an ephah of barley. 18aShe picked it up and came into the town.

vinegar or "sour wine" (חמץ). The use of imperatives commands and invites; Boaz asserts his authority by assuming that Ruth will obey him. Ruth sits down beside or "to the side" of the reapers and not necessarily within the group. Boaz heaps up or "holds out" a generous amount of parched grain, which was a common, staple food. Ruth is given plenty of food—she eats to satisfaction and there are leftovers. Three successive verbs rhythmically accentuate this abundance in Hebrew: ותאכל ותשבע ותתר (transliterated: *wattōʾkal wattiśbaʿ wattōtar*); "she ate, she was satisfied, and there remained (leftovers)." The repetition of the words stresses Boaz's generosity[112] as well as her efficiency. There is no conversation over the meal; Ruth merely eats to satisfaction. Yet the language of eating to satisfaction emphasizes the abundance, and it sets up a contrast to the famine in chapter 1. Moab had provided food for Elimelech and his family when there was a famine in Bethlehem; now Bethlehem provides food for Ruth in the midst of her (and Naomi's) emptiness coming out of Moab. Ruth has eaten enough not merely to survive but to be full and to anticipate the "leftovers" that she will bring to Naomi in 2:18. In other occurrences of the phrase "to eat until satisfied," it is God who is the provider; here, it is Boaz.[113]

After the meal, Boaz instructs his young men not only to allow Ruth to glean "among" the sheaves (see the discussion at 2:7) but to allow her to pull out sheaves from the bundled grain without "reproaching" (literally "humiliating," כלם) or "rebuking" her. In so doing, Boaz separates Ruth from his workers and grants her special privileges, which could

112. See Sasson, *Ruth*, 56.

113. Linafelt and Beal, *Ruth and Esther*, 39. Examples in which God is the provider include Deut 6:11; 8:10, 12; 11:15; 14:29; 31:20; Joel 2:26; Ps 78:29; 2 Chr 31:10.

potentially make Ruth more susceptible to the reproach of others who would envy her position. This isolation between Ruth and the other workers perhaps accounts for Boaz's admonitions not to reproach or rebuke her. It also makes Ruth appear more vulnerable and less capable of caring for herself without Boaz as her male protector.

At the end of the day, Ruth beats out an ephah of barley. Although not precisely delineated anywhere in the Bible, the amount could be as much as five times the amount that Ruth and Naomi would have needed for the day.[114] The abundance of Boaz's generosity and Ruth's hard work culminates in this final line, as Ruth leaves the field and carries home an overabundant, perhaps unrealistic, amount of grain. According to Campbell, "We are not called upon to add to her [Ruth's] list of virtues that she was as strong as an ox."[115] Yet why not? Despite Boaz's protection, there is nothing to prevent us from viewing Ruth as a physically strong woman. From a feminist perspective, being strong, physically or otherwise, in no way detracts from a woman's appeal. These final lines anticipate the end of chapter 3, in which Ruth will again carry home an overabundance of grain; there, the quantity is great enough to be absurd. While the grain in chapter 3 will be a gift from Boaz, here it is the result of Ruth's hard work. She has therefore become the provider or breadwinner for Naomi, and she has also successfully acquired Boaz's favor.

Mother-in-Law and Daughter-in-Law (2:18b-23)

These verses represent a narrative shift[116] toward a greater emphasis on the familial relationship between Ruth and Naomi. Once Naomi sees how much Ruth has gleaned, and that her daughter-in-law has provided for her, she rarely classifies Ruth again as a foreigner. Naomi's first look, however, is to the grain and the impressive amount of material gain, rather than to the woman who has been working all day. Ruth has therefore proven herself through her hard work more than through her first act of loyalty in traveling with Naomi from Moab. Perhaps the older woman is finally realizing that Ruth's presence will not be a burden. The first word in verse 18b is "mother-in-law," חמות, and four of six attesta-

114. Eskenazi and Frymer-Kensky, *Ruth*, 42. Campbell proposes that the load would have amounted to twenty-nine pounds at the minimum, forty-seven pounds at the most (*Ruth*, 104).

115. Campbell, *Ruth*, 104.

116. Sakenfeld, *Ruth*, 47.

Ruth 2:18b-23

18b [A]nd her mother-in-law saw
how much she had gleaned. Then
she took out and gave her what was
left over after she herself had been
satisfied. 19 Her mother-in-law said to
her, "Where did you glean today? And
where have you worked? Blessed be
the man who took notice of you." So
she told her mother-in-law with whom
she had worked, and said, "The name
of the man with whom I worked today
is Boaz." 20 Then Naomi said to her
daughter-in-law, "Blessed be he by the
LORD, whose kindness has not forsaken
the living or the dead!" Naomi also said
to her, "The man is a relative of ours,
one of our nearest kin." 21 Then Ruth
the Moabite said, "He even said to me,
'Stay close by my servants, until they
have finished all my harvest.'" 22 Naomi
said to Ruth, her daughter-in-law, "It is
better, my daughter, that you go out
with his young women, otherwise you
might be bothered in another field."
23 So she stayed close to the young
women of Boaz, gleaning until the end
of the barley and wheat harvests; and
she lived with her mother-in-law.

tions of the expression are within verses 18b-23. Each verse contains at least one reference to "mother-in-law" or "daughter-in-law," minus the one outlying "Ruth the Moabite" (v. 21). This new emphasis on Ruth and Naomi as family is further demonstrated by Naomi's inclusion of Ruth in the statement that Boaz is a relative "of ours" in verse 20.

The shifting descriptors for Ruth—Ruth the Moabite, Ruth the daughter-in-law—are a reminder that identity is porous. Although the narrative never identifies Ruth by her family of origin, there is a constant and fluctuating emphasis on her sex, ethnicity, and family relations: Ruth the Moabite, foreigner, non-Israelite; Ruth the widow; or Ruth the woman. Ruth is always identified in relation to others—the daughter-in-law to Naomi, the servant (and eventually wife) to Boaz, or the foreigner/Moabite to both. The only self-descriptors that Ruth uses are in relation to Boaz, namely, foreigner, slave, and servant. We too are often defined in relation to others and by others' perceptions. Betty Friedan once wrote, "The Feminine Mystique permits, even encourages, women to ignore the question of their identity. The mystique says they can answer the question 'Who am I?' by saying 'Tom's wife . . . Mary's mother.'"[117] Ruth is a reminder that all of us, men and women alike, can face a "terrifying

117. Betty Friedan, *The Feminine Mystique* (New York: W. W. Norton, 1963; repr. 1997), 126.

blank"[118] when asked to ponder our true identity. Ruth may view herself according to the various labels given to her by others, yet she also uses them as part of her own power and engineering of events.

The movement from the fields to the home is direct; the succession of verbs states that Ruth carries the grain directly home to her mother-in-law, brings it out, and gives to Naomi what remained from her lunch (literally: "from her abundance").[119] We never see Naomi eat; rather, the older woman begins to ask her questions. Verse 19 is filled with suspense, drawn out by the repetitiveness of Naomi's two questions and Ruth's response. Naomi asks Ruth where she had gleaned as well as where she had worked, and she offers a blessing for whoever took notice of Ruth (see v. 9).[120] Ruth's response is similarly repetitive; she states the same verb from Naomi's second question twice (עשה, "to work/to do").[121] Trible notes that the conversation builds on incongruities: Ruth knows Boaz as the man in whose fields she gleaned; meanwhile, Naomi does not know in whose fields Ruth gleaned, yet she knows Boaz.[122] Moreover, we do not know what Naomi has been doing all day while Ruth was away; she remains entirely disconnected from the scene in the fields.

When Ruth finally states Boaz's name, Naomi breaks into a second blessing. At the end of chapter 1, Naomi mourns her relationship with the God of Israel. Now, she turns to praise. Her language of blessing

118. Ibid.

119. Ruth shares the remains of the meal, not the unprocessed grain. Sasson translates this sentence, "Her mother-in-law saw how much she had gleaned when Ruth brought out the leftovers from her full meal in order to give them to her" (*Ruth*, 57). Eskenazi and Frymer-Kensky suggest that Ruth eats her fill of the leftovers before giving the rest to Naomi (*Ruth*, 42). Yet the Hebrew states that Ruth merely takes out and gives to Naomi "from her abundance," without stating that she eats any herself. Rather than eat again, it appears that Ruth merely gives the remains from her earlier meal to her mother-in-law.

120. The root נכר, "to recognize," in this blessing in v. 19 relates back to Ruth's question to Boaz in v. 10: "Why have I found favor in your sight, that you should take notice [נכר] of me, when I am a foreigner [נכריה]?" See Sasson, *Ruth*, 58–59; LaCocque, *Ruth*, 77; Nielsen, *Ruth*, 63; Linafelt and Beal, *Ruth and Esther*, 41; Eskenazi and Frymer-Kensky, *Ruth*, 43. Regarding the repetitive nature of Naomi's questions, Fewell and Gunn imagine that the sight of grain "sets her eyes bulging and prompts the demand to know where Ruth has been working" (*Compromising Redemption*, 77).

121. Campbell notes that Ruth's response is "redundant in the extreme" and so prefers the LXX, which cleans up the redundancies to read: "And Ruth told her mother-in-law where she had worked and said . . ." (Campbell, *Ruth*, 106).

122. Trible, *God and the Rhetoric of Sexuality*, 179.

contains genuine ambiguity as to whether Boaz or YHWH is the one "whose *ḥesed* has not forsaken the living or the dead," and her blessing reminds us of the connection between YHWH and Boaz in the previous dialogue.[123] The narrator leaves the subject ambiguous on purpose, as part of the sustained indistinctness between divine and human action in the story.[124] It is equally ambiguous as to whom Naomi is referencing as "living" and "dead." Ruth was the living recipient of Boaz's *ḥesed* in the fields, so perhaps she is the "living" of Naomi's blessing, including or excluding Naomi. Naomi's dead husband and sons could count as the "dead" who remain at the forefront of Naomi's memory, yet Naomi may be referring to herself as dead, in keeping with her anguish at the end of chapter 1 and her stillness in the beginning of chapter 2. In terms of agency and voice, she now comes back to life.

Finally, Naomi discloses the relationship between Boaz and her family. She tells Ruth that Boaz is "a relative of ours" (literally: "someone near to us"), "one of our nearest kin." This is the first attestation in Ruth of the גאל, the "nearest kin" or "redeemer," which will become the most consistent description of Boaz's relationship to Naomi (and Ruth) in chapters 3–4. The גאל refers to the duty of a male relative to redeem or maintain property within the family, as well as to prevent a family

123. See the previous chapters on the importance of *ḥesed* in the book of Ruth. For the relationship between divine and human *ḥesed*, see also Nelson Glueck, *Hesed in the Bible*, trans. Alfred Gottschalk (Cincinnati: Hebrew Union College, 1967); and Katharine Doob Sakenfeld, *The Meaning of Hesed in the Hebrew Bible: A New Inquiry*, HSM 17 (Missoula, MT: Scholars Press, 1978). Commentators who favor YHWH as the antecedent of the action include Campbell, *Ruth*, 106; Sakenfeld, *The Meaning of Hesed*, 103–7; Frymer-Kensky, *Reading the Women of the Bible*, 246; and Eskenazi and Frymer-Kensky, *Ruth*, 43–44. Sakenfeld cites Gen 24:27, in which Abraham's steward offers a similar blessing of YHWH in relation to Rebekah's hospitality. Frymer-Kensky proposes that both attestations, in Gen 24:27 and Ruth 2:20, are variations of formulaic blessings to YHWH.

Others favor Boaz as the antecedent of the action: see Glueck, *Hesed in the Bible*, 41–42; Basil Rebera, "Yahweh or Boaz? Ruth 2:20 Reconsidered," *BT* 36 (1985): 317–27; Hubbard, *Book of Ruth*, 186; Michael E. W. Thompson, "New Life Amid the Alien Corn: The Book of Ruth," *EvQ* 65 (1993): 197–210, esp. 205; Bush, *Ruth, Esther*, 134–37; Koosed, *Gleaning Ruth*, 82–83.

124. See especially Sasson, *Ruth*, 60; C. John Collins, "Ambiguity and Theology in Ruth: Ruth 1:21 and 2:20," *Presbyterion* 19 (1993): 97–102; Sakenfeld, *Ruth*, 47–48. Eskenazi and Frymer-Kensky draw attention to the play on words between Boaz and the Hebrew "forsake" (עזב; *ʿazab*) to strengthen the notion that Boaz acts as God's agent (Eskenazi and Frymer-Kensky, *Ruth*, 44). Collins proposes that the author intends us to ask, "YHWH or Boaz?" and answer "yes."

member from falling into slavery, according to the laws of redemption in Leviticus 25:25-55 and 27:9-33.[125] Outside of the Torah, the process of land redemption is seen when Jeremiah buys the field of his cousin Hanamel in accordance with the responsibility or "right of redemption" to retain the family's inheritance (Jer 32:6-25). On the divine level, God is Israel's redeemer (Isa 44:23; Ps 103:4). The redeemer must embody the principles of righteousness and support for those within the broad circle of the family who are less fortunate.

In the Bible, the redeemer is not necessarily a blood relative but rather one who "acts" as a kinsperson or plays the part of the kinsperson to redeem land or a family line. In the case of Boaz, the blood relationship between Boaz and Elimelech will be further clarified in 3:12 when Boaz acknowledges that although he is a redeemer, there is another redeemer "closer" in relation. The word גאל is then used throughout chapters 3 and 4 in reference to Boaz and the unnamed other גאל who is even "closer" to the women.

What makes the laws of redemption sticky in the book of Ruth is that we have yet to hear of land to be redeemed (more on this in chaps. 3–4). Moreover, Naomi's preoccupation in chapter 1 is not with land redemption but rather with the security of her daughters-in-law through marriage. The narrative therefore amalgamates the role of redemption with the second legal institution of levirate marriage discussed earlier; this institution protects a widow and the line of her dead husband through sexual union between the dead husband's brother and the widow to produce a child (Deut 25:5-10).[126] Genesis 38 describes the levirate marriage gone wrong when Tamar's first brother-in-law dies and her father-in-law, Judah, refuses his youngest son to her. She therefore tricks Judah into sexual intercourse and becomes pregnant; Judah subsequently calls her righteous when he realizes her deceit was born from his refusal to allow his third son to marry her (see also the discussion in chap. 4, which reinforces the connection to Tamar through the genealogy that includes her son Perez). Chapter 1 further discusses the question of levirate marriage in 1:11-13 when Naomi tells Ruth and Orpah that she has no more sons to provide for them.

It is difficult to know where the parameters lie between the responsibilities of land redemption and of "redeeming" the widow. Boaz is not

125. See Levine, "Ruth," 87; Linafelt and Beal, *Ruth and Esther*, 42.

126. Eskenazi and Frymer-Kensky, *Ruth*, xxxii–xxxviii, 44. See also Bronner, *From Eve to Esther*, 77–79.

Elimelech's brother or son, so if this is a levirate situation, it is an odd one. In 4:3-9, Boaz refers to the regulations of redemption that deal with the preservation of a share of property for impoverished landowners (see Lev 25:23-34; also Jer 32:8-15), and chapter 4 details the transaction of land along with the woman (Ruth). The relationship between the laws and the narrative is therefore hopelessly entangled.[127] We do not know all the parameters of the law, and the text could be either deliberately antiquating what happened "back then" or demonstrating expansion from the laws.

In the book of Ruth, the two practices of redeeming the land and the levirate are harmonized and applied to a specific situation. According to Campbell, these two laws have the same underlying principle: to preserve and care for the family; the narrative therefore creates a natural link between levirate marriage and the principles of redemption.[128] Levirate marriage ensured the widow's economic support as much as it perpetuated the name of the dead man. It can therefore be likened to an ancient form of social security. However, it also depended on a woman's body and used her body as if it were property. The laws speak only of the man's refusal to enact his levirate duty, not of the woman's. The question of whether or not levirate marriage was good for the woman likely depended on the situation and context.

Ruth then explains to Naomi how Boaz had taken a special interest in her.[129] She relays the information incorrectly when she recounts Boaz's statement about "clinging" to his "young men" or male workers, when in fact Boaz had told her to "cling" to his "young women" workers (2:8). The reference to "young men" could refer to all the reapers, male and female, yet the most plausible situation is that she has lied to Naomi, as she will do again in chapter 3. She does not tell Naomi about either the meal or Boaz's special attention and protection. By purposefully self-aligning with the men who work in the fields,[130] Ruth may be testing Naomi, to see if Naomi has a similar concern as Boaz for Ruth's safety.[131] Ruth therefore

127. Campbell proposes that the difference between law and the book of Ruth demonstrates the distinction between law and how it was carried out in different situations, in this case in the narrative of Ruth (*Ruth*, 134).

128. Ibid., 137; also Fischer, "The Book of Ruth," 40–41.

129. See Campbell, *Ruth*, 107; also Trible, *God and the Rhetoric of Sexuality*, 180.

130. Eskenazi and Frymer-Kensky, *Ruth*, 45. See also Nielsen, who states that Ruth is "choosing" to stay with the men over the women (*Ruth*, 64).

131. Fewell and Gunn, *Compromising Redemption*, 98.

discloses and alters slightly only the most salient points for Naomi's benefit, and she leaves out either what she wants to remain her own secret, or what she might consider to be superfluous information.

Naomi then gives Ruth advice, even if it seems that she should have offered this advice at the beginning of the chapter. She switches the gender to remind Ruth to "cling" to the *female* workers. She warns her not to go out into other fields, lest she be "bothered" (פגע). Naomi's caution contains a different verb from Boaz's admonitions to his workers against scolding or rebuking Ruth (vv. 15-16). The Hebrew פגע that Naomi uses has much stronger and more violent connotations than Boaz's language, including translations such as to "strike down" or "attack violently."[132] Nowhere in the Bible does the word imply sexual assault. Naomi's word choice reflects concern over Ruth's well-being in the fields, and perhaps a stronger concern than Boaz's of potential dangers.

In these verses, Naomi acts in ways the reader may have wished her to act at the beginning of the chapter: demonstrating concern for Ruth in the fields and informing her of their connection to Boaz. The same question sparked in verse 1 continues to engage us here: did Naomi deliberately allow Ruth to be put in danger, and if so, why? What sparks Naomi's sudden concern for Ruth is her return from the fields with grain and the subsequent discussion of Boaz. Perhaps the possibilities evoked by Ruth's return help Naomi wake up from her grief or return to life, as hinted at in her statement of the *ḥesed* that "has not forsaken the living or the dead." Or, Naomi is beginning to realize that Ruth is an asset rather than a burden, based on the information and material help that resulted from her day's work. As discussed earlier with Boaz's character, how we interpret Naomi's silence in verse 1 and subsequent concern for Ruth in verses 20-22 depends on how we judge her character throughout.

It is Naomi's daughter-in-law who initiates action in chapter 2. She does not wait for something or someone to provide for her; if she had, we do not know how long that wait would have been. Rather, she relies on her own resourcefulness and daring. When she returns to her mother-in-law with grain and information about Boaz, Naomi then shifts from grief to action. For Naomi, Boaz is the answer to their problems, and this belief will cause her to propose a daring plan for Ruth at the beginning of chapter 3. Meanwhile, Ruth's focus at the end of chapter 2 remains,

132. Campbell, *Ruth*, 108. For more violent uses of the word, see Judg 15:12; 1 Sam 22:17-18; 2 Sam 1:15; Isa 64:4. The same root is used in 1:16 when Ruth says to Naomi, "Do not press me [פגע] to leave you."

as it was at the beginning of the chapter, rooted in her self-reliance, her desire to provide for Naomi, and perhaps even her goal to prod Naomi into action.

The chapter ends as it began. Ruth moves from town to fields, sticking close to the young women and gleaning or reaping in Boaz's fields until the end of the barley and wheat harvests. Historically, the barley harvest would be June/July, and the total duration of the barley and wheat harvest would have lasted seven weeks (Deut 16:9-12). According to Ruth Rabbah 5.11, the barley and wheat harvests end in August. We are told that Ruth "lived" with her mother-in-law, which reinforces their relationship. The verb does not necessarily imply that the two have a home; ישב is ambiguous and can mean that they dwelt in their own home or squatted elsewhere. Whereas Ruth had the first word in the chapter, Naomi has the last, as she did in chapter 1. She will also have the first word in chapter 3. We are left pondering the question of how Boaz and Ruth will be reunited. This is answered in the following chapter.

Ruth 3

Searching for Rest

Naomi's Plan (3:1-5)

According to the final verses in the previous scene, chapter 3 begins sometime after the conclusion of the barley and wheat harvests. The end of the harvest season means that Naomi and Ruth have lost their access to reaping and must find another means of livelihood. The question of what any poor person does at the end of the harvest season is left unanswered in the narrative, as is the discussion of any further job prospects for Ruth or Naomi. We also do not know whether Naomi had been working all along, and we need not assume her to have been sedentary. Although the narrative provides no information, we might imagine her to have performed such tasks as textile work, tending children, cleaning, or baking. The momentum continues from the end of chapter 2 and the revelation of Boaz as a potential redeemer for the women.

Whereas Ruth initiates speech and action in chapter 2, here the initiator is Naomi. Her voice continues from 2:22 in the same tone of concern for her daughter-in-law. She tells Ruth that she must find her "security" or, more literally, "rest." The same Hebrew root, נוח, appears in 1:9, where Naomi expresses concern that each of her daughters-in-law

Ruth 3:1-5

[3:1]Naomi her mother-in-law said to
her, "My daughter, I need to seek some
security for you, so that it may be well
with you. [2]Now here is our kinsman
Boaz, with whose young women you
have been working. See, he is winnow-
ing barley tonight at the threshing floor.
[3]Now wash and anoint yourself, and put
on your best clothes and go down to the
threshing floor; but do not make yourself
known to the man until he has finished
eating and drinking. [4]When he lies down,
observe the place where he lies; then, go
and uncover his feet and lie down; and
he will tell you what to do." [5]She said to
her, "All that you tell me I will do."

finds "security" (מנוחה) "in the house of your husband."[1] Although the root is often translated as security, and in 1:9 it is clearly connected to marriage, here the context is more vague. The broader implications of נוח are rest, peace, or protection. The name Noah (נח) derives from this term; he (through the divine promise) provides security from the flood for those in his ark. Noah may also remind us of the later threshing-floor scene in chapter 3: Ruth's uncovering of Boaz's "feet" or genitalia after Boaz had been drinking can be a reminder of how Ham, the son of Noah, saw his father's "nakedness" (ערוה) after Noah passed out from consuming wine (Gen 9:21-22).

Elsewhere in the Bible, the root נוח is related to physical rest or even peace, and it is most commonly attributed to YHWH. YHWH gives rest to the soul in Psalm 116:7 ("Return, O my soul, to your rest, for the Lord has dealt bountifully with you") and "rest" from pain, turmoil, and hard service under foreign rule (Isa 14:3). YHWH also gives "rest" to the people following the ceasing of work on the Sabbath (Exod 23:12; Deut 5:14).[2] In addition, the root נוח is connected to the land of Israel, a place of safe haven (מנוחה) in which YHWH will grant the people rest (נוח) and safety (Deut 12:9-10). We do not hear Ruth's opinion here, and Naomi's optimism in

1. While the NRSV translates the Hebrew in 1:9 and 3:1 as "security," the JPS translates the Hebrew as "security" in 1:9 and as "home" in 3:1. The Greek ἀνάπαυσιν in the LXX similarly translates as "rest" in 3:1 and 1:9. See the discussion at 1:9; also Jeremy Schipper, *Ruth: A New Translation with Introduction and Commentary*, AYBRL 7D [New Haven: Yale University Press, 2016], 93.

2. Genesis 2:3 translates God's rest literally as שבת (root *šābat*, which leads to Shabbat or the Sabbath), the ceasing of activity. The laws of Exod 23:12, however, command the human to cease activity (שבת) on the seventh day, so that the animals may "rest" (נוח). The notion of "rest" as something granted by the other is therefore distinct from the active ceasing of activity.

finding Ruth "rest" or security in her homeland may not correspond to Ruth's own sense of security as a foreigner residing in the land.

The book of Ruth is the only biblical text to equate the idea of a woman's rest to marriage or male protection.[3] Although this is not the only perspective in the book of Ruth, Naomi's concern for Ruth's rest is a driving force behind the events on the threshing floor in chapter 3. The plan that Naomi proposes therefore stems not from any idea of romance between Ruth and Boaz but from a survival instinct.[4] Surekha Nelavala has compared Naomi's perspective to a traditional, patriarchal view in which men are understood to be providers and women dependents; in some traditional households, including that of ancient Israel, women come into the household of their husband to live within the patriarchal line (this is not the case in Gen 2:24, however, which states that a man leaves his parents and "clings," דבק, to his wife).[5] Yet this is not only a traditional view; a similar perspective can be found in contemporary ideas that a woman, in particular, is at rest or complete only when married or in a relationship. For example, the popular song "Waiting for You," by Isobel Anderson, begins by stating, "I need a man who can take care of me, and make me feel safe and happy."[6] Of course, this is not the only contemporary perspective; multiple songs espouse the view that women are better off independent from men.[7]

Yet a cursory reading of the book of Ruth may foster the perspective that a woman is incomplete on her own. If we do not read into the gaps and examine the characters critically, we could easily conclude that the whole point of the book is to make Ruth a wife and mother (or that the whole point is the genealogy that leads to David). For example, John

3. Robert L. Hubbard describes this "rest" as "settling down," or as a "permanent home" for Ruth (*The Book of Ruth* [Grand Rapids: Eerdmans, 1988], 198).

4. Katharine Doob Sakenfeld calls this a "theology of survival" (*Ruth*, Interpretation: A Bible Commentary for Teaching and Preaching [Louisville: Westminster John Knox, 1999], 87), though it is unclear what is theological about it.

5. Surekha Nelavala, "Patriarchy, a Threat to Human Bonding: Reading the Story of Ruth in the Light of Marriage and Family Structures in India," in *Reading Ruth in Asia*, ed. Jione Havea and Peter H. W. Lau, IVBS 7 (Atlanta: SBL Press, 2015), 92. As a counter-balance to the assumed patriarchal line in ancient Israel, see Cynthia B. Chapman, *The House of the Mother: The Social Roles of Maternal Kin in Biblical Hebrew Narrative and Poetry*, AYBRL (New Haven: Yale Univerisity Press, 2017). Chapman's book came out while this commentary was in press.

6. From the album "In My Garden" (2013).

7. E.g., the Pussycat Dolls, "I Don't Need a Man," in *PCD* (Pussycat Dolls, 2005); and Destiny's Child, "Independent Woman, Pt. 1 and 2," in *Survivor* (Sony, 2001).

Piper, a well-known conservative pastor (Calvinist Baptist), refers to Ruth as "God's Ideal Woman" because of her commitment to Naomi, and he explains the entire movement of the story as God's "glory" that comes to fruition only when God gives Ruth a husband and a child. This "glory," marriage and children, proves that Ruth's life is the "life of the godly."[8] However, any perspective assuming that a woman will only feel "safe" and "happy" when she is married, or that marriage and children are the culmination of a woman's life, is limited at best and highly problematic at worst. Should a woman marry and/or have children because she is socially coerced into following particular gender roles, rather than live in accordance with what she finds most fulfilling, she could have an unhappy life indeed.

This perspective of a "rest" that comes only through male protection is not the book's only perspective. Up to this point, Ruth has seemed indifferent to the idea of marriage or male security,[9] and whether or not she desires such a relationship is unaddressed in the narrative. Indeed, Ruth's own initiative and determination through chapter 3 demonstrate that she can be an equal provider or source of rest for her mother-in-law. The end of the book supports this reality, when the women of the town tell Naomi that Ruth is worth more to her than "seven sons" (see the discussion at 4:15).

In contrast to other biblical stories, particularly in Genesis, Naomi's concern for Ruth's rest or security lacks any explicit concern for bearing children.[10] In Genesis, God's promise to Abraham and Sarah to "make of them a great nation" depends on the perpetuation of the line. The concern for progeny is then central to the Sarah-Hagar story (Gen 16, 21), to Rebekah's infertility (Gen 25), and to the saga of Leah, Rachel, Zilpah, Bilhah, and Jacob (Gen 30). Ruth's story bears greater resemblance to the story of Tamar and her father-in-law Judah in Genesis 38, in which the goal of progeny is understated. We do not know what drives Tamar's actions—perhaps she *is* driven by the desire to have children,

8. See John Piper's online series on Ruth: http://www.desiringgod.org/messages/by-series/ruth-sweet-bitter-providence.

9. See the discussion in Sarojini Nadar, "A South African Indian Womanist Reading," in *Other Ways of Reading: African Women and the Bible*, ed. Musa W. Dube (Atlanta: SBL Press, 2001), 159–75, at 168.

10. See Amy-Jill Levine, who states that, for Naomi, "marriage and sons are the only sources of a woman's security and value" ("Ruth," *Women's Bible Commentary*, ed. Carol A. Newsom and Sharon H. Ringe, exp. ed. [Louisville: Westminster John Knox, 1998], 84–90, at 86).

though she could equally be driven by the desire to protect her rights, by vengeance, or even by the desire to kill her father-in-law. Yet like Ruth, Tamar protects her own welfare by soliciting the male protagonist and, in the end, Judah calls her more "righteous" than he (Gen 38:26). Much like the ending of the book of Ruth, sons arrive at the end of Tamar's story, almost as an afterthought. The genealogy at the end of Ruth begins with Perez, Tamar's son (see the discussion at 4:18-22). Yet the end of the book of Ruth is already foreshadowed by Naomi's grief in chapter 1, when she states that her age prohibits her from bearing additional children (1:11-13).

Naomi's focus on Ruth's "rest" leads directly into mention of Boaz. At the end of chapter 2 Naomi revealed to Ruth that Boaz was a relative or redeemer (גאל); now, Naomi refers to Boaz as a kinsman or relative, מודע (see "Translation Matters" on p. 57). Without telling Ruth what this relationship is or what it will mean, Naomi issues a series of commands to her daughter-in-law. According to Naomi (and we never know the source of her information), Boaz will be "winnowing barley" (separating grain from the chaff) on the threshing floor that night. Naomi's description of Boaz eating, drinking, and staying out all night suggests that his actions are linked to harvest festivities. In preparation for her meeting with Boaz, Ruth is to bathe, anoint herself (i.e., put on perfume), and put on her best garments, conveyed by the Hebrew word שמלה, "cloak." The description of Ruth's preparations recalls marriage rituals in Ezekiel 16:8-10, in which God metaphorically spreads the edge of his wing over Jerusalem, then bathes, anoints, and clothes her in preparation for marriage (see the discussion at 3:9). The connection with Ezekiel implies that Ruth is preparing herself physically in some way, perhaps for marriage or perhaps merely for seduction.

The emphasis on Ruth's physical preparations recollects other stories of female heroines who use clothing as a primary weapon for guile, seduction, and, in some cases, even destruction of the enemy. In Genesis 38, Tamar's veil becomes the means of hiding her identity and tricking her father-in-law into thinking she is a prostitute. In Esther 2:9-12, women of the king's harem, including Esther, are prepared for twelve months with treatments of myrrh and perfumes before visiting the king. In the book of Judith, the protagonist prepares herself to meet the army commander Holofernes by bathing, anointing, and dressing in her finest clothes and jewelry (Jdt 10:3-4). There is little distinction between the descriptions of Judith's preparations for seduction and for battle. Judith uses Holofernes's desire for her to get him drunk enough to pass out, and subsequently she cuts off his head (Jdt 12:16–13:10). Similarly, the story of Jael describes in two different texts the mothering (Judg 4) or seduction (Judg 5) of the unassuming army commander Sisera. Though Jael's guile does not have to do with physical dress, she tricks him into trusting her and drives a tent peg through his temple to kill him while he lies sleeping (Judg 4:21-22) or is perhaps awake eating (Judg 5:25-27). Outside of the Bible, in the Ugaritic "Tale of Aqhat" from ancient Syria, Pughat prepares to avenge her brother's murder by washing and rouging herself, dressing up like a woman while hiding a knife and clothes of a "hero" underneath, and setting off to kill the warrior Yatupan.[11] Like Judith, Pughat plans to seduce the warrior and eventually kill him.

Like these other women, Ruth's primary weapon is her intelligence. Like the armor of a warrior preparing for battle, Ruth's physical dress prepares her for persuasion, seduction, and even "battle" in the sense of achieving her desired goal on the threshing floor. Yet later, Boaz will not remark upon her beauty or physical appearance; moreover, he does not even see her form clearly, as he only realizes her presence in the middle of the night. The seduction by clothing therefore proves unnecessary and subverts other narratives in which clothing is used as deception, including Tamar in Genesis 38 and Pughat in the Ugaritic story.[12] In the case of both Pughat and Tamar, physical clothing plays a role in their preparations, yet there is a similar lack of focus on the women's physical appearance. In Ruth's case, Naomi's emphasis is misplaced; she believes mistakenly that Ruth will achieve her goal through clothing or physical "props," while in reality, Ruth will achieve her goal through her words and intelligence.

Naomi's instructions to Ruth are also filled with sexual innuendoes as she prepares Ruth for the threshing floor. Naomi uses the word ידע, "to

11. "Tale of Aqhat," in *Ugaritic Narrative Poetry*, trans. Simon B. Parker, ed. Mark S. Smith and Simon B. Parker, WAW 9 (Atlanta: Scholars Press, 1997), 77; also *KTU* 1.19, 4:41-46. The tablet breaks off at the climax of the story, and we never know how the scene ends. David P. Wright proposes that washing and dyeing are part of preparations for going out to battle, based on Pughat and the goddess Anat, who similarly prepares herself before and after battle in "The Baal Cycle" (*KTU* 1.3, 2:38–3:2); see David P. Wright, *Ritual in Narrative: The Dynamics of Feasting, Mourning and Retaliation Rites in the Ugaritic Tale of Aqat* (Winona Lake, IN: Eisenbrauns, 2001), 206–8.

12. Other examples of biblical stories in which clothing is used as deception include Joseph's coat in Genesis 37:29-33, which his brothers use to deceive their father into thinking Joseph is dead, as well as Joseph's garment that he leaves in the hands of Potiphar's wife in Genesis 39:12-18.

know," twice (translated "make yourself known" in v. 3, and "observe" in v. 4), a word that is commonly connected to sexual knowledge in the Bible.[13] Naomi also utilizes the verb שכב, "to lie down," three times in verse 4, a word that is similarly connected to "lying with" someone in the sexual sense (e.g., Gen 19:33, 35 in the story of Lot and his daughters; also the Levitical codes, e.g., Lev 18:20, 22-23). Finally, the expression "uncover his feet" in verse 4 could mean that Ruth is meant to uncover Boaz's literal feet, the lower part of his body, or, more likely, his genitals (see "Translation Matters" on page 106).[14] In addition, the threshing floor itself is associated with prostitution and promiscuity. Hosea 9:1 reads, "Do not rejoice, O Israel! / Do not exult as other nations do; / for you have played the whore, departing from your God. / You have loved a prostitute's pay / on all threshing floors."[15] There is no question that Naomi's plan for Ruth is highly suggestive; she seems to be preparing Ruth to proposition Boaz in some way. Her directions to Ruth are therefore unconventional, risky, and even "outrageous."[16]

What will transpire between Boaz and Ruth on the threshing floor is left up to the interpretation of the reader, and the writer plays with the sexual undercurrents of Naomi's instructions while maintaining ambiguity in the threshing-floor scene that will unfold. Perhaps the greatest

13. Jack M. Sasson notes, however, that the *piel* of "to know" (v. 3) never refers to sexual knowledge (*Ruth: A New Translation with a Philological Commentary and a Formalist-Folklorist Interpretation* [Baltimore: Johns Hopkins University Press, 1979], 69).

14. Translators have pushed the plain reading of the text in various ways. Some have proposed that Ruth uncovers some unknown object at Boaz's feet: e.g., the LXX translates the text "reveal the (place) at his feet," while the Vulgate translates "remove the coverlet which hides the place at his feet." The Peshitta states, "draw near and lie down near his feet," and the Old Latin has "go there and cover yourself at his feet and sleep." The Hebrew lacks a direct object, and it is therefore most likely that Ruth is told to uncover the lower part of Boaz's body, perhaps only the feet but likely the genitalia. Some have also argued that Naomi is telling Ruth to uncover *herself* at Boaz's feet (e.g., Kirsten Nielsen, *Ruth*, OTL [Louisville: Westminster John Knox, 1997], 69–70; also Sasson, *Ruth*, 70), yet the Hebrew does not support the plain reading that Ruth takes off her own clothes on the threshing floor.

15. On the connection between the "threshing floor" and promiscuity, see Hubbard, *Book of Ruth*, 201; and Tod Linafelt and Timothy K. Beal, *Ruth and Esther*, Berit Olam (Collegeville, MN: Liturgical Press, 1999), 49.

16. Phyllis Trible refers to Naomi's scheme as "outrageous," "dangerous," and "delicate" (*God and the Rhetoric of Sexuality* [Philadelphia: Fortress, 1978], 182), while Tikva Frymer-Kensky states that it is "completely scandalous" (*Reading the Women of the Bible: A New Interpretation of Their Stories* [New York: Schocken Books, 2002], 248).

question is whether Naomi wishes Ruth to prostitute herself in some way and how we as readers handle this possibility (see also Rajkumar Boaz Johnson's contribution in the introduction, which engages with the question of prostitution in the book of Ruth from a South Asian perspective).[17] Biblical narratives often depict prostitution without judgment and even elevate women associated with prostitution as exemplars of faith; examples include Tamar, whom Judah mistakenly takes to be a prostitute (Gen 38:15), and Rahab in Joshua 2, who professes her belief in YHWH and demonstrates unconditional loyalty to the Israelite spies, even while their promise to save Rahab and her family is conditional (Josh 2:14, 17-21). Along with Ruth, both Tamar and Rahab become part of Matthew's genealogy that leads to Jesus in the New Testament (Matt 1:3, 5). Elsewhere, the great warrior Jephthah's mother is a prostitute (Judg 11:1), and Solomon resolves a dispute between two women (both prostitutes) over a son in a story meant to display Solomon's wisdom rather than judge the profession of the women (1 Kgs 3:16-28). Biblical narratives demonstrate little discomfort with the profession.

Unlike in the United States (besides parts of Nevada), prostitution was legal in ancient Israel. The Torah admonishes a father not to profane his daughter by making her a prostitute, yet there is no penalty for doing so (Lev 19:29); in the case of a priest's daughter, however, prostitution is taken seriously as a capital offense (Lev 21:9). The priests are held to higher standards and are told not to marry prostitutes, yet again there is no punishment for doing so. Moreover, the real issue is virginity and the holiness of the priestly line, which was understood to be genetic—alongside the ban on marrying prostitutes, priests are also told not to marry divorced women or widows (Lev 21:7, 14).

In our contemporary world, prostitution laws vary depending on the country. In many countries in which the act of prostitution is legal (i.e., the exchange of sex for money), related activities or organized prostitution such as brothels and pimping are illegal (e.g., much of Europe), even

17. According to Theodoret of Cyr, fifth-century Christian bishop of Cyrrus and theologian in the School of Antioch, Naomi tells Ruth to sleep at Boaz's feet, but she does not suggest that Ruth "sell her body . . . rather, she trusts the man's temperance and judgment" (in John R. Francke, ed., *Ancient Christian Commentary on Scripture: Old Testament*, vol. 4: *Joshua, Judges, Ruth, 1–2 Samuel* [Downers Grove, IL: InterVarsity Press, 2005], 187). According to the bishop, the subsequent actions corroborate Naomi's words and prove that nothing takes place on the threshing floor. See other interpretations below.

while such activities may remain prevalent. In many countries, prostitution and its related activities are illegal yet widespread and thriving; the United States is one such example (again, with the exception of parts of Nevada) as well as many countries in Africa, including Angola, the Democratic Republic of Congo, Egypt, Kenya, and South Africa. In Asia, where the legality of prostitution varies by country, the inconsistency between the laws and what happens in practice can be great.[18]

The case for the illegality of both prostitution and its related activities includes concerns with human trafficking and, more broadly speaking, the dignity of the human person; many people consider prostitution exploitative and demeaning to sex workers, and it can place individuals in risky, sometimes violent, situations. Yet the act of prostitution is a broad term, only a segment of which involves streetwalking; prostitution also includes high-end escorts, "call girls" and "rent boys," and those who advertise prostitution on the internet. It is unclear to what extent women and men "choose" prostitution in its various forms, and for every person there is a story. Some would even say that the profession is empowering.[19] A feminist perspective clearly condemns any situation in which a person is forced into prostitution against her or his will, which includes anything from difficult economic situations to human trafficking. Yet judgments against prostitution can lead to negative judgments against those who take part in the profession. Biblical narratives often turn these judgments upside down by presenting characters associated with prostitution as exemplars in some way and as characters with great wit, character, and courage.

18. For example, child prostitution is a serious problem in Asia, in particular Great Mekong (including Cambodia, Laos, Myanmar, Thailand, Vietnam, and Yunnan Province, China); see, e.g., "Child Trafficking Prevalent Throughout Southeast Asia," October 29, 2009, http://www.voanews.com/content/a-13-child-trafficking-prevalent-throughout-southeast-asia-67390462/382777.html; Katja Dombrowski, "Sex Tourism: Dubious Reputation," March 20, 2015, http://www.dandc.eu/en/article/cambodia-seen-heaven-paedophiles-and-sex-tourists; "Trafficking of Children for Prostitution and the UNICEF Response, 2016," http://asiasociety.org/trafficking-children-prostitution-and-unicef-response.

19. In 2008–2009, journalist Susannah Breslin embarked on a yearlong blogging project called "Letters from Working Girls" and "Letters from Johns," in which she received and posted letters from women who engaged in prostitution and men who hired them. The result is eye-opening; see http://lettersfromworkinggirls.blogspot.com/ and http://lettersfromjohns.blogspot.com/.

TRANSLATION MATTERS

The common word for "foot," רגל, is a euphemism for genitals in certain texts (e.g., Exod 4:25; Judg 3:24; 1 Sam 24:4 [= 24:3 in the NRSV]).[20] The rare denominative word "feet" or "at the feet," מרגלות, is attested only in Ruth 3:4, 7, and 14; and in Daniel 10:6. In Daniel 10:6, the term is used in a physical description that extends from the head down to the arms and legs, and is translated commonly as "legs." In Ruth, the expression מרגלות alone means something like "at the feet," and it is coupled with the verb גלה, "to uncover," the latter of which connotes nakedness or "uncovering one's nakedness." For example, Genesis 9:21 states that Noah drank wine and lay "uncovered" (גלה) in his tent, and Leviticus 20:18 sets forth a punishment for a man who "uncovers" (גלה) a woman's nakedness while she is menstruating.[21]

The details of the plan (Ruth's physical preparations, hiding herself on the threshing floor, waiting until Boaz has eaten and is likely drunk before lying down and uncovering his "feet"), as well as Naomi's seeming preoccupation with finding Ruth "rest," all imply that Naomi has something particular in the short-term, yet with likely long-term results, in mind for what will transpire on the threshing floor. In these opening verses of chapter 3, Naomi describes Boaz only vaguely as a "kinsman" or "relative," without saying anything of his function as a גאל, "redeemer." It is Ruth who first uses this term in conjunction with Naomi's plan on the threshing floor (3:9), potentially taking Naomi's proposal for seduction a step further into a quest for finding a redeemer for the two women.[22] If Naomi is similarly connecting her plan with the possibility of redemption, she does not voice this explicitly here. All we know is that Naomi tells Ruth that Boaz "will tell you what you are to do." The most we can infer is that Naomi's goal is for Ruth to gain Boaz's assistance in one form or other.

20. For a range of meanings of the Hebrew רגל, "foot," see Tamara Eskenazi and Tikva Frymer-Kensky, *The JPS Bible Commentary: Ruth* (Philadelphia: Jewish Publication Society of America, 2011), 53–54.

21. See Ilona Rashkow, "Ruth: The Discourse of Power and the Power of Discourse," in *A Feminist Companion to Ruth*, ed. Athalya Brenner, FCB 3 (Sheffield: Sheffield Academic, 1993), 26–41, esp. 37–39.

22. See Adele Berlin, *Poetics and Interpretation of Biblical Narrative*, ed. David M. Gunn, BLS 9 (Sheffield: Almond Press, 1983), 90. According to Berlin, Ruth misunderstood Naomi's instructions: "Naomi sent her on a romantic mission but she turned it into a quest for a redeemer" (ibid.). Yet there is nothing romantic about the plans set out for Ruth on the threshing floor.

Naomi's concern for Ruth's "rest" also reflects a certain amount of self-interest, as demonstrated by what might seem to be a lack of concern for Ruth's short-term safety.[23] Naomi asks Ruth to carry out her plan under cover of night, placing Ruth in potential peril. Song of Songs hints at the danger of a woman alone at night: the female protagonist is found and beaten by the city watchmen when she is in search of her beloved (Song 5:6-7). Tamar in Genesis 38, who takes off her widow's garments and allows Judah to have sexual intercourse with her, places herself in a potentially dangerous situation, proven by her near-death escape when he learns that she is pregnant (and before he learns that the child is his).

Yet the narrative itself contains no judgment regarding Naomi's plans and Ruth's subsequent actions. Chapter 2 emphasizes Ruth's strength (as does the end of this chapter), and there is no reason why Naomi should be concerned about Ruth's ability to take care of herself now. The text therefore requires the reader to hold the risk factor and the strangeness of the plan in tension with the lack of judgment or foreboding from the text itself. Although the situation is daring, Naomi must trust, to some extent, that her daughter-in-law will succeed in this nighttime endeavor. Ruth is her best asset. If something were to happen to Ruth, who has thus far provided for her mother-in-law in Judah, Naomi would be left to work out her future on her own. Naomi is certainly quite capable—her walk from Moab to Judah has proven that—and we come to find out in chapter 4 that she owns property. Perhaps the community would also come to her aid, including even Boaz himself (or the "closer" kinsman in chapter 4). Yet there is no way of knowing any of this, and there is no hint that Naomi wants to get rid of Ruth, regardless of whether her motivations are selfish.

Naomi also demonstrates some trust in how Boaz will respond to Ruth on the threshing floor. Had she thought Boaz's motives for assuming responsibility for the women would be purely selfless, she likely would have chosen an alternative plan than setting up Ruth to seduce him. Yet if Naomi intuits that Boaz will commit himself to Ruth, then she is correct; moreover, the unfolding story line will demonstrate that it is Ruth who controls the threshing floor scene and guides Boaz according to her wishes. In addition, Boaz will state that Ruth's actions are valiant and even appropriate when he calls her a "woman of strength" (v. 11) and asks for YHWH's blessing upon her. It is yet to be determined whether we, as readers, agree with Boaz's judgment and the particular actions

23. Danna Nolan Fewell and David M. Gunn, *Compromising Redemption: Relating Characters in the Book of Ruth* (Eugene, OR: Wipf & Stock, 1990), 77. See also the discussion on Naomi in chapter 2.

for which he praises Ruth (namely, her loyalty; see below). Yet in the scene that unfolds, the narrative voice not only leaves aside judgment as to what transpires but even applauds Ruth's actions through Boaz's praise and Ruth's control on the threshing floor.

Ruth's agency is a crucial factor. In both chapters 1 and 2, she has defied Naomi or acted of her own accord. Phyllis Trible has observed that in chapter 1, Ruth ignores Naomi's concern to return home to find a husband. In chapter 2, Ruth's focus has been on physical survival. Now, in chapter 3, Ruth acts in accordance with Naomi's wishes. The movement, Trible writes, is from "dissent to perseverance to consent."[24] Some, including Surekha Nelavala (see below), see Ruth as helpless and vulnerable in following Naomi's commands. Yet we propose an alternative reading, that Ruth's seeming "consent" reflects her own quiet calculations in the plan to attract Boaz. It is possible that Ruth herself has been slowly manipulating Boaz since he noticed her in chapter 2, in order to succeed in seducing him on the threshing floor.[25] While Naomi tells Ruth that Boaz will "tell you what you are to do," and Ruth states that she will do everything Naomi tells her (v. 5), in reality Ruth will disrupt Naomi's instructions to wait for Boaz to act; instead she will act on her own initiative (see v. 9). There is also the question of whether Boaz would have any clue what to do without Ruth's prodding. Ruth's acquiescence to Naomi is therefore not simple consent, for she will enhance Naomi's expectations for what happens on the threshing floor.

Shame and Honor

Naomi, who loves and supports Ruth as a mother, is excited at the opportunity that she sees in Boaz's interaction with Ruth. While there is hope for her in Boaz's household, Ruth's vulnerability is increased by the fear of losing this opportunity very nearly within their grasp. Naomi pushes her to take the first step to get closer to Boaz, as Boaz has not made any advances during her time in his field. In a shame-and-honor society, it is shameful for a woman to approach a man. However, her vulnerability dominates her desire to seek honor, and so Ruth acts as Naomi tells her to do. Naomi offers a plan of

24. Trible, *God and the Rhetoric of Sexuality*, 182.

25. See Jon L. Berquist, "Role Differentiation in the Book of Ruth," *JSOT* 57 (1993): 23–37; also Carolyn J. Sharp, *Irony and Meaning in the Hebrew Bible*, ISBL (Bloomington: Indiana University Press, 2009), 117.

action in Ruth 3:3-4: "Wash and perfume yourself, and put on your best clothes. Then go down to the threshing floor, but don't let [Boaz] know you are there until he has finished eating and drinking. When he lies down, note the place where he is lying. Then go and uncover his feet and lie down. He will tell you what to do." After hearing her suggestion, Ruth, a modest woman, a trait required of an ideal woman, does not confront or question Naomi regarding this daring suggestion but instead agrees to Naomi's suggestion. Ruth's vulnerability and helplessness is evident, and in contradiction to the behavior of an ideal woman, she turns and assumes the role of trickster and temptress. In her low-status reality of being a widow and a foreigner, she approaches Boaz in a shameless manner. How did this sudden shift happen in the story? Ruth's character suffers the play of shame and honor. On the one hand, she plays a temptress role, where her honor is at stake; yet, there is a notion of maintaining sexual purity and thus guarding her honor.

Ruth gains complete honor when Boaz takes her to be his wife and when he bears him a son. Thus, at the conclusion, her idealness is reconstructed to match with the ideal man: Boaz who does all the right things as a redeemer of his kinsman's widow. Thus, an Indian feminist reading upholds the realistic elements of Ruth's story, recognizing her vulnerabilities, while being critical about the so-called ideal image that is unduly bestowed on her.

Surekha Nelavala

Ruth Solicits Boaz on the Threshing Floor (3:6-9)

When Ruth arrives on the threshing floor, she complies with Naomi's instructions. She spies on Boaz by waiting until he has eaten and drunk, is in a "contented mood," and is lying down. The "contented mood" likely translates to drunkenness,[26] which plays a large role in other biblical stories that parallel the threshing-floor scene. Noah, for all that his name is connected with the "security" or "rest" that Naomi desires, becomes drunk and passes out, at which point his son Ham accidentally sees his "nakedness," and his other two sons, Shem and Japheth, cover him (Gen 9:21-23); similarly, Ruth will soon uncover the "feet" (or nakedness) of Boaz on the threshing floor. Judith kills Holofernes after he has passed out from drunkenness (Jdt 13:1-10). When Ruth goes to Boaz

26. Elsewhere, the Hebrew construction יטב לב, "to be good in one's heart," is attested in connection to food and drink (Judg 19:6; 1 Kgs 21:7), though not necessarily drunkenness.

Ruth 3:6-9

6So she went down to the threshing floor and did just as her mother-in-law had instructed her. 7When Boaz had eaten and drunk, and he was in a contented mood, he went to lie down at the end of the heap of grain. Then she came stealthily and uncovered his feet, and lay down. 8At midnight the man was startled, and turned over, and there, lying at his feet, was a woman! 9He said, "Who are you?" And she answered, "I am Ruth, your servant; spread your cloak over your servant, for you are next-of-kin."

stealthily, or in "secrecy" and uncovers his "feet," the word for "secrecy" (לט) could be a play on the story of Lot (לוט).[27] Boaz's possibly drunken state recalls the story of how Lot's daughters make their father drunk, have intercourse with him, and give birth to their sons Moab (from the Hebrew "from my father") and Ben-ammi ("son of my people"), the ancestor of the Ammonites (Gen 19:30-38).

The account in Genesis is an etiology reflecting the fraught relationship between Israel and two of its closest neighbors, yet the story also demonstrates the resourcefulness and pragmatism of two women who think there is no one left on earth to perpetuate their line.[28] Ruth the Moabite is a descendant of this line, and her own situation with Boaz both imitates and contrasts with the story of Lot and his daughters.[29] Boaz also calls Ruth "my daughter," and his age relative to hers is similar to that of Lot and his own daughters. Like Lot's daughters, Ruth demonstrates initiative in soliciting Boaz at night. Some have grouped Ruth's actions with the story of Lot and his daughters, as well as with Tamar and Judah (Gen 38), according to the "bed-trick," in which the female characters trick the

27. Linafelt (*Ruth and Esther*, 52) proposes that the word לט is "carefully chosen" by the author to imply trickery or deceit. The word is also found in the story of Jael and Sisera (Judg 4–5), another story with sexual double entendres, when Jael approaches Sisera quietly or secretly (לט) and drives a tent peg through his temple (Judg 4:21). Berlin considers Ruth's "secrecy" to be the single point in which Ruth strays from Naomi's plan, which would account for Boaz jolting awake in the middle of the night rather than recognizing Ruth prior to falling asleep (*Poetics and Interpretation*, 90–91). Yet this is not true; Ruth's greatest point of deviance from Naomi's plan comes when she speaks to Boaz without waiting for him to tell her what to do first. (Had she waited for Boaz to make the first move, Ruth might still be waiting.)

28. See Peter W. Coxon, "Was Naomi a Scold? A Response to Fewell and Gunn," *JSOT* 45 (1989): 25–37, esp. 30–31.

29. See Levine, "Ruth," 88. Eskenazi and Frymer-Kensky argue that Ruth is offered as a "corrective" to the story of Lot and his daughters in *Ruth*, 55.

male characters into sexual intercourse.[30] Yet whereas Lot's daughters bear children from incest that become the unfavorable neighbors to Israel, Ruth moves from one of these countries to Israel, marries Boaz, and continues the line that leads to David. Anyone who has left her homeland for a new country, or has experienced the feeling of straddling different cultures, knows that Ruth will never feel entirely at home in Israel (nor would she ever feel entirely at home back in Moab, at this point, if she were to return) and that Ruth's background will always be part of her identity. Yet she carries this identity into the bloodline that leads to King David. While Lot is unfavorably contrasted with Abraham through their separate lineages (one is the father of Israel, while the other is the father of Moab and Ammon), the story of Ruth esteems the combined Israel-Moab line that descends from Ruth and Boaz.

Ruth then uncovers Boaz's feet and lies down. The words "to lie down" (שכב; vv. 7-8, 13-14) and "uncovered his feet" (גלה מרגלות) or simply "at the feet" (מרגלות) in verses 7, 8, and 14 carry over from the previous section to perpetuate the sexual undercurrents of the narrative. The language of secrecy and the nighttime scene further add to the sense that Ruth's actions are sexually suspect. The cover of darkness or "midnight" is the time when social boundaries are relaxed and undecided.[31] Ruth could not have acted this way in broad daylight, when people were watching and Boaz was awake and alert.

When Boaz awakes in the middle of the night, he does so in terror. The NRSV "startled" fails to convey the strength of the Hebrew חרד, which elsewhere indicates fear and trembling (e.g., Gen 27:33; Exod 19:16; 1 Sam 14:15; Ezek 26:16). The Septuagint describes Boaz as ἐξίστημι, "beside oneself," and as ταράσσω, "troubled," while the Targum adds, "his flesh [בשר] became soft like a turnip from fear." The turnip was a well-established crop in Hellenistic and Roman times, yet the metaphor is strange; turnips are hard rather than soft, and their strange coloring and round shape do not easily represent any part of the human body. The reader might interpret this metaphor to mean that Boaz's entire body grows white (or purple?) and shakes in fear, or perhaps that a particular portion of his body, such as his "feet," become limp.

30. Harold Fisch, "Ruth and the Structure of Covenant History," *VT* 32 (1982): 425–37; André LaCocque, *The Feminine Unconventional: Four Subversive Figures in Biblical Tradition* (Minneapolis: Fortress, 1990), 104–5.

31. Midnight is also a "time of reckoning" for significant events in the Bible (e.g., God strikes the Egyptians at this hour in Exod 11–12; Jacob wrestles with the mysterious figure at the Jabbok in Gen 32). See Sasson, *Ruth*, 74.

Ruth's Threshing Floor

Beneath the clutter of the grain
lies the floor, its surface strewn
with plenty.
Tradition covers the floor, as God
brings Israel her harvest.
Here, the seed, dropping into the
dirt below brings renewal.

Newness of life is born with each
threshing for God replenishes
the earth.
And newness of love is blessed
as two hearts unite as one amid
the bounty of the
threshing floor.

Sheila Clare DeLuca

We might label Ruth's actions in this scene as sexual harassment or worse. Had the roles been reversed and Boaz had come upon a sleeping Ruth, uncovered part of her body, and lain down beside her, we would not hesitate to charge him with such a crime. In the scene of Lot and his daughters, the daughters rape their father, yet we judge their actions based on incest; again, had the roles been reversed and it was their father who made them drunk and slept with them, we would more easily label him a perpetrator of sexual violence. Our perspective clearly changes based on the gender of the perpetrator. In the book of Ruth, we readers generally do not see Boaz as the one "at risk" in this scene. Rather, we may perceive him to be the lucky one (once he gets over his shock). Some would even say that Ruth fulfills male fantasies in how she acts on the threshing floor: she dominates Boaz. Yet from a feminist perspective, we *should* label Ruth's actions as sexual harassment. The irony is that while the reader's natural propensity might be to feel concern for Ruth in this scene, it is the woman who is in complete control and acts as the sexual aggressor. She is the "strange" or "foreign" woman in Proverbs 1–9 who dresses as a prostitute and preys upon young men in the dark hours of the night (Prov 7:5-22).

Boaz turns over or twists himself (see "Translation Matters" on page 113) to see the form of a woman, though he does not yet recognize her. In the darkness, all her clothing and physical preparations turn out to be irrelevant. In chapter 2, Boaz asks about Ruth's identity in relation to a third party: "To whom is this young woman?" (2:5). No longer viewing Ruth in relation to another person, he asks her directly: "Who are you?"[32]

32. Jennifer Koosed proposes that Boaz finds Ruth's identity "unsettled and unsettling," which is reflected in his questions regarding her identity in chapters 2–3 (*Gleaning Ruth: A Biblical Heroine and Her Afterlives*, Studies on Personalities of the Old Testament [Columbia: University of South Carolina Press, 2011], 2).

Ruth Rabbah,[33] followed by the eleventh-century commentator Rashi, interprets Boaz's fright as a mistaken identification of Ruth with a female demon similar to the Hebrew Lilith.[34] These female demons sought out men aggressively, mated with them (i.e., caused nocturnal emissions), and produced a breed of demonic offspring. Ruth is somewhat like Lilith in that she is seducing the man without his being aware. Other interpretations for Boaz's abrupt awakening include that he grew cold with his body exposed,[35] or that he woke up horrified, thinking he had had intercourse with Ruth.[36] Yet the simplest explanation is that Boaz awoke startled in the middle of the night, and the twisting motion is to be understood as an abrupt turning toward or away from the unknown person at his feet.

TRANSLATION MATTERS

The Hebrew לפת, "to twist, turn," is attested twice elsewhere in the Bible in the sense of "grasping" in the *qal* (Judg 16:29) and "twisting" or "turning aside" in the *niphal* (Job 6:18). An anonymous rabbinic commentary from the medieval period[37] described לפת as "twisting about" in the sense that Boaz stretched out his arms and legs, as is customary for men upon awakening.[38] Sasson interprets לפת as "twisting away," as in turning away from Ruth, and translates verse 8 as follows: "Around midnight, the man was shaken by fright; he twisted away—there was a woman lying close to him!"[39]

Ruth's response to Boaz's question is to state clearly her identity, "I am Ruth," using the Hebrew emphatic "I" (אנכי). Ruth then deviates from

33. According to Ruth Rabbah, Boaz first thought Ruth was a woman because he noticed that she had hair, and "spirits have no hair." He then asked her: "Who are you?, a woman or a spirit?" (Ruth Rab. 6.1).

34. See the discussion in Eskenazi and Frymer-Kensky, *Ruth*, 58.

35. Trible, *God and the Rhetoric of Sexuality*, 183.

36. Fewell and Gunn, *Compromising Redemption*, 80–87.

37. See Derek R. G. Beattie, *Jewish Exegesis of the Book of Ruth* (Sheffield: Sheffield Academic, 1977), 33. The rabbis are generally taken to be a combination of R. Joseph Qara, Rashbam, Dunash, and R. Menahem bar Helbo. Beattie prefers to attribute the commentary simply to "an anonymous rabbi," because the complete work is a composite of sources, of which very little appears to be written by the rabbis listed.

38. Ibid., 126.

39. Sasson, *Ruth*, 75–78.

Naomi's plan. Rather than wait for Boaz to tell her what to do (v. 4), she tells Boaz what to do. Had she not been the one to speak first, who knows where the conversation would have led; perhaps Boaz would have acknowledged that he was next-of-kin, as Ruth states in verse 9. Or perhaps he would have taken an alternate route that would have given him less long-term responsibility for Ruth's situation. As soon as Ruth speaks in verse 9, however, he responds in an overwhelmingly positive manner, and it is clear that Boaz will need no further prompting in the narrative.

First, Ruth refers to herself as Boaz's "servant" (אמה), a term that reflects subordination in relation to Boaz. She also subtly elevates her importance from the more servile self-designation שפחה in 2:13, possibly from a "slave" or "servant" to a concubine or even wife (the NRSV translates both Hebrew words as "servant").[40] She then tells Boaz to spread his "cloak" over her, that he is "next-of-kin" or גאל (see 2:20). The Hebrew word כנף, translated here as "cloak," literally means "wing." Ruth's instructions are clear; Boaz is not to view her as a sexual object but rather as someone requesting long-term protection.[41] As discussed earlier, the language of "spreading" one's "cloak" or "wing" is a clear metaphor for marriage and protection based on Ezekiel 16:8: "I passed by you again and looked on you; you were at the age for love. I spread the edge of my cloak over you, and covered your nakedness: I pledged myself to you and entered into a covenant with you, says the LORD God, and you became mine."[42]

The age difference between the male YHWH and the female Jerusalem in Ezekiel 16 is great; YHWH (the mature man) watches Jerusalem grow up from a baby into womanhood before entering into a covenant with

40. On the self-designations of "slave" or "servant," שפחה and אמה, note the discussion in this commentary on Ruth 2:13. See also Sakenfeld, *Ruth*, 57–58.

41. Contra Fewell and Gunn, who view Ruth as presenting Boaz with a choice: "see her as but an ephemeral sexual object ('extend your penis'), or see her as a person in need ('spread your wing/skirt'), a person who offers an enduring relationship, in which sexuality will have its home" (*Compromising Redemption*, 102–3). See also Linafelt, who quotes Fewell and Gunn and states that Ruth gives Boaz the power of decision in how to respond (*Ruth and Esther*, 55). Yet the connections to the relationship between YHWH and Jerusalem in the book of Ezekiel, as well as back to chapter 2, in which Boaz blesses Ruth and asks YHWH to protect and "spread his wing" over her, make it clear that Ruth is requesting long-term protection.

42. On the relationship between Ruth and Ezek 16:8-10, see Sasson, *Ruth*, 66; and Eskenazi and Frymer-Kensky, *Ruth*, 51.

her when she arrives at a marriageable age. However, whereas Jerusalem proves to be unfaithful in Ezekiel, the Moabite widow (though not a virgin!) is commended for her faithfulness. The age difference between Ruth and Boaz may also be great, and Ruth's statement alludes similarly to Boaz's protection and refuge as mirroring that of YHWH.[43] In 2:12, Boaz prays that YHWH, "under whose wing" Ruth sought refuge, would reward her. The metaphor of "wing" complicates any phallic allusion; here, Ruth shifts the responsibility by reminding Boaz that if he wants to speak of YHWH's refuge and reward, he should be prepared to act as the agent.[44] The Targum changes Ruth's words to the unequivocal statement: "Let your name be called over your servant [אמה] by taking me in marriage."[45] If we read with the Targum, Ruth is, in a sense, proposing to Boaz. She therefore indicates her own independence in determining her marriage partner.

Boaz Responds (3:10-15)

Ruth gives Boaz room to act, and act he does. If readers were anxious about how Boaz would react to Ruth's unconventional plan on the threshing floor, this concern should fade away with his words of praise and validation. As in 2:12, Boaz's praise invokes YHWH's blessing. He refers to Ruth as "my daughter," as he had when first addressing her in 2:8; the phrase reflects paternal protection and, possibly, social imbalance.[46] It also continues the analogy from Lot and his daughters and may speak to Boaz's older age. The expression heightens the sense of Boaz's concern for Ruth while obscuring his possible lust. Subsequent to 2:8, Boaz watched over Ruth in the fields, instructing her to reap with his female servants and eat beside him at mealtime. Now, Boaz similarly enfolds Ruth into his protection (though not in his arms; as far as we know, the two have yet to touch). He praises Ruth, telling her that this

43. See the discussion in Eskenazi and Frymer-Kensky, *Ruth*, 59–60. They propose that while Naomi's primary plan is highly sexual, Ruth "de-sexualizes" the encounter by calling Boaz to take responsibility for her. This may be the case based on 3:9 alone, yet too many of Ruth's actions on the threshing floor perpetuate the sexual undercurrents of the narrative, as discussed throughout this chapter.

44. See Berel Dov Lerner, "The Challenge of Ruth," *The Jerusalem Post* (May 22, 2015).

45. Tg. Ruth 3:9, see trans. D. R. G. Beattie, in *Targums of Ruth and Chronicles*, trans. J. Stanley McIvor and D. R. G. Beattie, ArBib 19 (Collegeville, MN: Liturgical Press, 1994).

46. See Linafelt and Beal, *Ruth and Esther*, 56.

Ruth 3:10-15

10He said, "May you be blessed
by the LORD, my daughter; this last in-
stance of your loyalty is better than the
first; you have not gone after young
men, whether poor or rich. 11And now,
my daughter, do not be afraid, I will do
for you all that you ask, for all the as-
sembly of my people know that you are
a worthy woman. 12But now, though it is
true that I am a near kinsman, there is
another kinsman more closely related
than I. 13Remain this night, and in the
morning, if he will act as next-of-kin for
you, good; let him do it. If he is not will-
ing to act as next-of-kin for you, then,
as the LORD lives, I will act as next-of-
kin for you. Lie down until the morning."
14So she lay at his feet until morning,
but got up before one person could rec-
ognize another; for he said, "It must not
be known that the woman came to the
threshing floor." 15Then he said, "Bring
the cloak you are wearing and hold it
out." So she held it, and he measured
out six measures of barley, and put it
on her back; then he went into the city.

"last instance" of her loyalty is even greater than the first (i.e., her loyalty to Naomi), for in this second instance, Ruth has gone after Boaz rather than after "young men, whether poor or rich."

The language of "going after" implies sexual interest. If Ruth is like Abraham, then Boaz's praise may be like Sarah's laughter in her old age, in response to the idea that she is about to experience sexual pleasure (עדנה) (Gen 18:12). Although the narrative alludes to the age difference between Ruth and Boaz throughout (see the discussion at 2:5), this is the only indication that Boaz's age could be a disincentive for Ruth to pursue him, at least as far as Boaz is concerned. Boaz's praise therefore underscores the importance of youth, and sexual appeal, over age and social standing. Depending on how "old" we understand Boaz to be, the scene could be humorous; we do not often consider that senior citizens have sexual urges. The church father Theodoret of Cyr (born ca. 393 CE, Antioch) interprets Boaz's praise to mean that Ruth chooses to deny her own sexual desire (or "voluptuousness," in his words) in order to go after Boaz, "the man who stands in place of a father."[47] Yet Boaz will not simply be a father figure to Ruth; the next chapter will prove his vitality when he and Ruth have a son together. Ruth is clearly pursuing Boaz, despite his age.

According to Boaz, Ruth acts primarily out of family loyalty to Naomi rather than her own desire for a young man, whether "poor" (i.e., someone who represents love or sexual desire) or "rich" (someone who pro-

47. See Francke, *Ancient Christian Commentary on Scripture*, 187.

vides economic security).[48] Oddly, however, Boaz fails to recognize, or does not acknowledge, that Ruth *is* choosing someone who is rich; he just happens not to be a "young man."[49] Boaz describes this act of loyalty or loving kindness, *ḥesed*, as even better than her "first" or former act of leaving her land and returning with Naomi to Judah (2:11-12). In both instances, Ruth acts out of a sense of responsibility to Naomi that goes beyond obligation.[50] Both acts of loyalty invoke Boaz's call for YHWH's blessing upon Ruth. The reality, however, is that Boaz is the particular person in the obvious position to fulfill his own request for YHWH's blessing upon Ruth.[51] Ruth's act of loyalty is a gift that Ruth has offered to Boaz, at least as Boaz sees it; from this point on, Boaz's actions will be based on an unswerving commitment to embrace this gift.[52]

While Boaz emphasizes Ruth's family loyalty, there are other possible factors behind Ruth's actions on the threshing floor. First, as just stated, Boaz is rich, which may be more important than youth to her. This would not be the first time that someone younger has gone after someone older for his or her wealth. The North American expression "gold digger" generally refers to a woman who cultivates a relationship with a man for his wealth ("gigolo," the closest male equivalent, has a less venal connotation). Ruth may also choose Boaz based on his previous demonstration of kindness, which perhaps indicated that he was interested in her and would be open to taking her as a wife. Ruth's own desire must at least partially coincide with Naomi's in pursuing Boaz. Otherwise, it seems unlikely that she would take matters into her own hands on the threshing floor. Yet to take Ruth seriously is to acknowledge that we have only Boaz's view of the situation and to hold open all possibilities for the full scope of reasons that prompt Ruth's actions.

In verse 11, Boaz responds to Ruth, echoing again her own words to Naomi in 3:5: "I will do for you all that you ask." Boaz emphasizes his

48. Hubbard, *Book of Ruth*, 214–15; also Eskenazi and Frymer-Kensky, *Ruth*, 62.

49. Carolyn J. Sharp proposes that Boaz's praise of Ruth for turning to him and not to younger men, "whether poor or rich," actually emphasizes, ironically, that Ruth *does* act for material gain in going after Boaz ("Feminist Queries for Ruth and Joshua," *JSOT* 28 [2014]: 229–52, esp. 244). However, it does not seem that Boaz himself is aware that Ruth goes after him for such a reason. As such, the irony may come from the narrator rather than from Boaz.

50. Katharine Doob Sakenfeld, *The Meaning of Hesed in the Hebrew Bible: A New Inquiry*, HSM 17 (Missoula, MT: Scholars Press, 1978), 42–43.

51. Ibid., 42.

52. See Ilana Pardes, *Countertraditions in the Bible: A Feminist Approach* (Cambridge: Harvard University Press, 1992), 114.

concern for Ruth's well-being alone and excludes Naomi through the singular "you." Throughout the scene, Ruth acts on behalf of herself and Naomi, while Boaz acts on behalf of himself and Ruth alone. Boaz's exclusion of Naomi is striking, considering that his primary relationship is with Naomi's family, not with Ruth. He also acknowledges the older woman when he commends Ruth for her loyalty to her mother-in-law, so he is clearly aware of Naomi's existence. Perhaps Boaz fails to include Naomi because of his attraction to Ruth, the younger woman. In other words, he acts selfishly. This would corroborate the idea that Naomi does not trust Boaz to claim his responsibility for the women from purely selfless motivations. However, Boaz may also focus primarily on Ruth simply because her actions are so meritorious that he simply loses sight of Naomi.

Although there is no indication that Ruth is afraid, Boaz nonetheless tells her not to fear. First, he attributes intention to her; now, he attributes emotion. His statement could be a reminder of both his concern for Ruth and the precarious situation in which Ruth has placed herself. Yet thus far, only Boaz has demonstrated fear on the threshing floor. Moreover, it is not clear exactly what Ruth has to lose by now, other than Boaz's loyalty, and we know by his previous exclamation of praise that the loss of his care is unlikely to occur at this point. In telling Ruth not to fear, Boaz perhaps regains some of the power that he lost in his previously vulnerable state by assuming the position of the one who will protect Ruth.

Boaz then refers to Ruth as a woman of "strength" or "virtue" (חיל; NRSV "worthy woman"). In 2:1, the narrator also calls Boaz a man of "strength" or "virtue" (חיל; NRSV "prominent rich man"). This phrase recalls the woman of "strength" or "virtue" in Proverbs, which is translated as "good wife" (Prov 12:4) or "capable wife" (Prov 31:10) in the NRSV. The English translation limits the woman's "strength" or "virtue" to the boundaries of marriage; descriptions of the "strong" or "virtuous" woman, then, have to do with her capabilities in the home, in regards to care of family and household. Not in the book of Ruth, however; Boaz calls Ruth, the unmarried woman, a woman of strength.[53] When the Hebrew חיל is used in relation to men, it is never translated in the NRSV as a "good" or "capable" husband, but rather as someone who is "strong" or "able-bodied" (e.g., Judg 3:29) or a man of "wealth" (e.g.,

53. Note also Elaine W. F. Goh, who points out that Boaz describes Ruth as a woman of strength while Ruth is unmarried (in contrast to the woman of strength who is married in Prov 31). See "An Intertextual Reading of Ruth and Proverbs 31:10-31, with a Chinese Woman's Perspective," in Havea and Lau, *Reading Ruth in Asia*, 73–87, at 86).

1 Sam 9:1, which is similar to the description of Boaz in Ruth 2:1). Often, it is used in relation to armies (e.g., "warrior" in Josh 6:2; 8:3; 10:7; Judg 6:12 and 11:1).

In Proverbs, attaining the woman (or wife) of strength is similar to the attainment of wisdom and knowledge of God. In the Tanakh, the book of Ruth directly follows the book of Proverbs and its final description of this woman of virtue. In referring to Ruth as a woman of "strength" or "virtue," Boaz places Ruth in the same category as the woman of Proverbs 31. Yet there is irony in this description, for Ruth can also be compared with the "foreign" woman or seductress in Proverbs 1–9 who is juxtaposed with the woman of virtue.[54] In Proverbs, all women are sexualized; the foreign woman tempts the young man away from Wisdom and knowledge of God and toward death (Prov 2:16-19), while Wisdom (Prov 8), the "woman of strength" (Prov 31), and the wife (Prov 5) represent "appropriate" desire that tempts the young man toward life, knowledge, and fear of God. Ruth's Moabite origin prevents her from fully escaping the stereotype of the dangerous woman, even as Boaz relabels her as a woman of strength.

By calling Ruth a woman of strength or virtue, Boaz judges that her actions on the threshing floor are nothing but admirable despite the sexual undertones. Although he does not state that coming to the threshing floor was among these admirable acts, nor does he ever recount the threshing-floor scene publically, Boaz's declaration of Ruth's good reputation among "all the assembly" (literally "all the gate of my people") in verse 11 then further rescues her character. In verse 11, the Septuagint uses the word "tribe" (φυλή) rather than "gate" (שער), while the Targum changes the expression from "all the assembly" to the "great Sanhedrin" and expands the issue to emphasize Ruth's conversion: the "great Sanhedrin" knows Ruth as a "righteous woman" who has the "strength [חיל] to bear the yoke of the commandments of YHWH." These translations emphasize Ruth's good reputation among the men who make decisions in the town and imply that it will not only be Boaz who determines Ruth's acceptability as a wife.[55] Rather, it is the men, as well as public opinion, that Ruth has to negotiate (see chap. 4 for more). The changes in the Targum increase Ruth's importance and reputation, and they eliminate any sexual concern that may remain from the threshing-floor encounter.

54. Koosed, *Gleaning Ruth*, 92.

55. Edward F. Campbell, *Ruth*, AB 7 (New York: Doubleday, 1975), 124.

Finally, Boaz affirms that he is a redeemer for Naomi and simultaneously discloses a second, "closer" redeemer (גאל) than himself. The root גאל is then repeated six times in verses 12-13. Suddenly, Ruth has *two* possibilities for redemption. Boaz reiterates three times that he will redeem Ruth, and Ruth alone (v. 13), which reminds the reader of the distance between Naomi and Boaz in the narrative; again, we see that Boaz is concerned only with Ruth and, perhaps, with himself. Boaz tells Ruth that if the other man will act as the redeemer, well and good. Yet if not, he pledges an oath to YHWH that he himself will act as the redeemer for Ruth. The nonchalance and suddenness with which he discusses this other redeemer suggest that Boaz is fairly confident that he will end up as the redeemer (which is exactly what happens).[56]

Thus far in the narrative, the word "marriage" has never arisen. As discussed earlier (see 2:20), "redemption" involved the duty of a male family member to redeem or maintain land within a family (Lev 25:25-55 and 27:9-33). The redemption laws were separate from levirate marriage (Deut 25:5-10; Gen 38) that was performed by the brother-in-law for his dead brother and brother's widow. In applying the laws to the story of Ruth, we do not know how Boaz is related to the family of Elimelech, though the fact that Boaz is not the "closest" redeemer indicates that he is likely a distant relation. Furthermore, we have yet to hear of land belonging to Elimelech, and the land itself will mysteriously appear only in chapter 4, which will cause us to reimagine the women's economic situation (perhaps they have been living on Naomi's land this whole time). Yet Naomi's concern throughout has been rest or security, focused on a man rather than land (1:9), and Naomi may never have been aware that the land existed, or perhaps it simply remains undisclosed information until the narrator deems it necessary. Similar to the existence of Boaz as a relative of Naomi in chapter 2, the land becomes part of the narrative's "selective representation." Chapters 2–4 continue to raise the issue of redemption (גאל), focused on women rather than land. The narrative therefore remains inconsistent in is portrayal of redemption; here, we unexpectedly learn of another redeemer, and in chapter 4, we

56. Others have proposed that Boaz's willing discussion about the closer redeemer implies that the "redemption" is primarily about land rather than marriage (Berlin, *Poetics and Interpretation*, 85–86; Eskenazi and Frymer-Kensky, *Ruth*, 64; contra Hubbard, *Book of Ruth*, 219–20). However, Naomi's focus throughout has been the redemption of the women and the "rest" or security of marriage, and the land itself is unmentioned until chapter 4.

will unexpectedly learn about the land that has thus far been undisclosed.[57] These disclosures throughout the narrative require us to read the previous chapters differently; whereas we may have thought Naomi and Ruth to be destitute in chapters 2–3, the land in chapter 4 forces us to reevaluate previous assumptions.

After Boaz divulges the information of a second redeemer, he seeks to protect Ruth. Or, at least, "protection" is what he would have Ruth think was his concern. Rather than risk her being seen or caught alone in the middle of the night, or perhaps because he wants to keep her for himself longer, Boaz tells Ruth to "remain" until daybreak. The verb translated "to remain," לין, literally means "to lodge" and is the same verb attested in 1:16, when Ruth states that she will "lodge" with Naomi wherever the older woman goes. Here, Boaz tells Ruth to "lodge" or stay with him. Unlike the word שכב, "to lie down" (used eight times in vv. 1-14, including twice in vv. 13-14), the verb לין carries no sexual undertones. Still, it is strange that Boaz tells Ruth to remain with him rather than escort her home or even let her go alone under the cover of darkness. Ruth is more likely to be noticed at daybreak than in the middle of night. Perhaps Boaz was still half-drunk and lacked the capabilities of reasoning in his state, yet he does not sound unreasonable in his conversation with Ruth. Perhaps the writer keeps Ruth on the threshing floor to continue to play with the sexual undercurrents of the narrative. The longer that she stays with Boaz under the cover of darkness, the greater the possibility that the two consummate their relationship. Indeed, the sexual ambiguity returns when Boaz tells Ruth to "lie down" (שכב) at his feet (v. 13), thus utilizing the same sexual language that began with Naomi's instructions to Ruth in the beginning of the chapter. Ruth complies and "lies" there, at his feet, until morning (v. 14). Ruth says nothing to deter Boaz's instructions, so we can imagine her to be a willing participant; or, she could be uncomfortable with the arrangement yet not wish to risk losing Boaz's favor by voicing her disagreement.

Ruth then arises before dawn in order to escape recognition. Again, she would be more likely to be seen at dawn than at midnight; in North

57. On the relationship between law and application, see Campbell, *Ruth*, 133–34; Irmtraud Fischer, "The Book of Ruth: A 'Feminist' Commentary to the Torah?," in *Ruth and Esther*, FCB 3, 2nd ser., ed. Athalya Brenner (Sheffield: Sheffield Academic, 1999), 24–49, esp. 40–41; and Leila Leah Bronner, *From Eve to Esther: Rabbinic Reconstructions of Biblical Women* (Louisville: Westminster John Knox, 1994), 77–79. See also the discussion at 2:20.

American college terminology, the walk home from who-knows-where in the morning is called "the walk of shame," *because* it is done in the full light of day and leaves little question as to what occurred the previous night. Should Ruth be seen the next day, after a full night away from her home, the possible negative ramifications to her reputation could complicate the redemption proceedings.

Despite the clear sexual allusions, the narrative is discrete as to what (if anything) happens the remainder of the night. Adrien Bledstein suggests that the relationship between Boaz and Ruth is consummated on the threshing floor as part of the act of marriage,[58] yet the narrative thrives on an ambiguity that neither states explicitly that the relationship has been consummated nor denies that it has. In the Genesis stories, the Bible is straightforward when sexual intercourse occurs outside of marriage (e.g., 16:4; 19:32-36; 38:16-18) and as a marriage act (24:67; 29:21-30), so biblical narratives clearly have the capacity to make explicit statements when so desired. Ruth's clandestine operation contains allusions to other biblical stories of danger and promiscuity, as discussed earlier, without ever explicitly stating that intercourse takes place.[59]

Although the text is silent on anything beyond dialogue, the reception history of the threshing-floor scene recognizes its consistent sexual undertones. Early on, the rabbis construct an elaborate dialogue in which Boaz refuses his "Evil Inclination" to have intercourse with Ruth,[60] while

58. Adrien J. Bledstein, "Female Companionships: If the Book of Ruth Were Written by a Woman . . . ," in *A Feminist Companion to Ruth*, ed. Athalya Brenner, FCB 3 (Sheffield: Sheffield Academic, 1993), 116–33, esp. 125–26.

59. Eskenazi and Frymer-Kensky write that the propriety of Ruth and Boaz "stands out more clearly because of the possibility for transgression" that we see in other biblical stories, such as those of Tamar and Lot and his daughters in Genesis (*Ruth*, 55). Nehama Aschkenasy finds the story is "laden with sexual connotations, but does not explicitly indicate that Boaz was actually seduced by Ruth" ("Language as Female Empowerment in Ruth," in *Reading Ruth: Contemporary Women Reclaim a Sacred Story*, ed. Judith A. Kates and Gail Twersky Reimer [New York: Ballantine Books, 1994], 111–24, esp. 122).

60. "R. Judah said: All that night his Evil Inclination contended with him, saying, 'You are unmarried and seek a wife, and she is unmarried and seeks a husband. Arise and have intercourse with her, and make her your wife.' And he took an oath to his Evil Inclination, saying, 'As the Lord liveth, I will not touch her'" (Ruth Rab. 6.4). This textual expansion increases Boaz's agency while decreasing that of Ruth by stating that the possibility of a sexual encounter is fully within Boaz's control.

the Targum explains that Boaz "restrained his desire and did not approach her."[61]

Contemporary commentators, such as Carolyn Sharp, have opened the space for alternate conclusions, including the possibility that Ruth's actions are similar to those of a prostitute.[62] She comes to the threshing floor in the middle of the night, uncovers a man in a manner that is highly sexually suggestive, lies down beside him, and stays through the night. She leaves in the morning, before anyone can see her, carrying away a gift. These actions are similar to those of a woman "who has traded sex for economic security."[63] Sharp's interpretation swings in the opposite direction of early rabbinic interpretations and plays with the possibilities in the narrative. If Ruth were indeed acting as a prostitute, then we would have to contend with the fact that the narrative labels her a woman of "strength" and later draws her into the line of David (and into the genealogy of Jesus in the Gospel of Matthew). This reality shifts, or complicates, any negative view of "prostitution" that we might have, as discussed earlier. Furthermore, this interpretation asks us to contend with the possibility that readers view Ruth differently, possibly more favorably, when we imagine her to be restrained and pious on the threshing floor. Simultaneously, however, Sharp's proposal that Ruth acts as a prostitute is similar to rabbinic interpretations in that she makes a particular interpretive choice that shuts down other possibilities in the narrative. This choice fails to honor the uncertainty that is so central to the narrative goals of the threshing-floor scene.

What matters most in the scene is that readers recognize Ruth's sexual agency and the openness in interpretation that the biblical text allows.[64] As an alternative perspective to the notion of honor and shame in Nelavala's contribution, the book of Ruth, like other biblical narratives, contains no particular sexual code of conduct.[65] Ruth's righteousness, like that of Boaz, has nothing to do with possible restraint from sexual

61. Tg. Ruth 3:8.

62. E.g., Sharp, *Irony and Meaning in the Hebrew Bible*, 117.

63. Ibid.

64. See Athalya Brenner, "Naomi and Ruth: Further Reflections," in Brenner, *A Feminist Companion to Ruth*, 141. Brenner writes that whether Ruth and Boaz consummate their relationship on the threshing floor can be left undetermined, so long as the reader realizes the importance of Ruth's sexuality in the scene.

65. Koosed, *Gleaning Ruth*, 90.

intercourse. The narrative even demonstrates playfulness in its allusions to sexuality on the threshing floor.

Before Ruth returns home, Boaz offers her a gift. Telling her to hold out the "cloak"[66] she is wearing, Boaz measures out "six barleys" (שש־שערים) and places it on her back. In 2:17, Ruth carried home to Naomi one ephah of barley, yet the measurement here is unclear. A mere six grains would not necessitate Boaz's help in placing it on her back. The amount is unlikely to be six ephahs, which would weigh between 175 and 285 pounds. Ruth Rabbah names the amount as six seahs, which is between 58 and 95 pounds[67] and would still require Ruth to "gird her loins like a man" in order to carry the grain home.[68] The text may be playing with the idea of Ruth as exceptionally strong: not only can she glean all day, but she can also lift very heavy weights. If this is the case, Ruth was in less danger than might be supposed.

Whatever the amount, it is meant to be an extravagant gift and a sign of Boaz's future support. Moreover, one could imagine that this gift would be quite conspicuous on the road home (particularly if it grows light while she is hauling her load), which undermines the desire for secrecy that kept Ruth on the threshing floor overnight and makes the reader question whether Boaz, in fact, wanted people to know that Ruth had been there. If so, and he were interested in having her as a wife, then the negative notice would discourage redemption by another, closer relative. Boaz's gift can also be understood as a metaphor for the "seed" or gift of procreation that will be given to Ruth at the end of chapter 4. Yet the Hebrew word "seed" first appears in 4:12, and the leap from "barley" (שערה) to procreation here may be forced.

At the end of both chapters 2 and 3, Ruth's encounter with Boaz leads to a gift of food and a promise that she will not "go away empty," Naomi's lament in 1:2.[69] Yet whereas Boaz indirectly provides the grain in chapter 2 by allowing Ruth to glean, here the grain is a direct gift. Boaz and Ruth are moving closer to each other. Ruth will bring this grain home

66. The Hebrew מטפחת, translated in v. 15 as "cloak," is attested only here and in Isa 3:22.

67. See Hubbard, *Book of Ruth*, 222.

68. Ruth Rab. 7.2. According to R. Simon, a certain Bar Kappara asked, "Is it then the custom of a king to betroth a wife with six grains of barley? Or is it the custom of a woman to be betrothed with six *se'ah* of barley?" The Targum augments the verse to read that YHWH gives Ruth "strength and power" to carry the barley home (3:15), thus envisioning how a human could carry such a heavy load.

69. See Trible, *God and the Rhetoric of Sexuality*, 186; also Nielsen, *Ruth*, 80.

to Naomi, providing for her as Boaz has provided for Ruth. Ruth's roles as both breadwinner and as the one being provided for remain fluid, just as she moves fluidly from home to threshing floor and back.[70] Boaz then goes immediately into the city to put his plan into motion.[71]

Home Again (3:16-18)

Thus far, each chapter in the book of Ruth is marked by a return. In chapters 2 and 3, the returns are parallel: in both cases, Ruth returns from an encounter with Boaz carrying grain from the threshing floor. This time, when Ruth returns, Naomi asks a pointed question: "How did things go with you, my daughter?" The NRSV fails to capture the Hebrew expression: "Who are you, my daughter?"[72] This is the same question Boaz asks Ruth (3:9), yet unlike Boaz's question, Naomi clearly knows the identity of Ruth, her "daughter." Thus, Naomi is asking a more specific question about Ruth's identity and the possible transformation that took place between Ruth's departure from the house and her return. Is Ruth still her "daughter"? Is she now an engaged woman? Does Ruth belong to Naomi or to Boaz, or perhaps to neither? Ruth's identity has been fluid throughout the narrative; she is variously a Moabite, a servant, a daughter, and a daughter-in-law. Always, her identity is in relation to another party, with the exception of the first part of her statement to Boaz in 3:9 "I am Ruth."

The rabbis explain Naomi's question by stating that what she means is, "Are you still a virgin or a married woman?" To this question, Ruth

70. Fewell and Gunn propose that Ruth acts as "wife" to Boaz and "husband" to Naomi; they therefore perpetuate gendered stereotypes of what constitute a "wife" and a "husband" (*Compromising Redemption*, 103).

71. While the Masoretic Text contains the third masculine singular "to go," various Hebrew manuscripts and the Peshitta contain the third feminine singular of the verb. In the case of the third feminine singular, it is Ruth, rather than Boaz, who "comes into the city." The JPS translation follows this reading, stating in 3:15b, "When she got back to the town." This alternative ending parallels 2:18, in which Ruth "comes into the city" after she had gleaned. In the case of the MT and the NRSV rendering, it is Boaz who places the barley on her back and then instantly goes into the town; for the MT and NRSV, Boaz is quite eager to put his plan of redemption into action, and the scene in chapter 4 may be happening in tandem with Naomi and Ruth's final conversation at the end of chapter 3.

72. In an attempt to deal with the strange Hebrew expression, some Greek manuscripts and one of four fragments from the Dead Sea Scrolls (4QRuth[b]) translate "How are you?" rather than "Who are you?"

Ruth 3:16-18

[16]She came to her mother-in-law, who said, "How did things go with you, my daughter?" Then she told her all that the man had done for her, [17]saying, "He gave me these six measures of barley, for he said, 'Do not go back to your mother-in-law empty-handed.'" [18]She replied, "Wait, my daughter, until you learn how the matter turns out, for the man will not rest, but will settle the matter today."

replies, "A virgin."[73] Given that Ruth was married for ten years in Moab (a marriage that is acknowledged in the rabbinic sources), this attempt to accentuate Ruth's piety and restraint goes a bit too far. Rather, their goal is to remind readers that Ruth and Boaz acted with restraint on the threshing floor.

Ruth's reply is not a statement of identity but rather an edited recounting of what Boaz had done for her. She ignores her own role in the encounter, including the fact that she veered from Naomi's instructions; thus she suppresses her own agency while focusing instead on Boaz's generosity. Lying to her mother-in-law, she states that the gift of grain had been specifically for her, so that Ruth would not return to her mother-in-law "empty" (ריקם). The word corrects Naomi's statement that she had gone away "full" but YHWH had brought her back "empty" (ריקם; 1:21). In her lament to the women of the town, Naomi had ignored Ruth's existence while attributing her emptiness to YHWH. Ruth's statement at the end of chapter 3 pointedly counters Naomi's grief. Human hands have brought fullness to Naomi. Ruth is the "fullness" of Naomi.[74]

Ruth's statement to Naomi is, however, a lie. Throughout the encounter on the threshing floor, Boaz's concern has been for himself and Ruth. He never mentions Naomi, neither when he speaks of redemption, nor when he loads the grain onto Ruth's back. Yet he does bless Ruth specifically for her loyalty to her mother-in-law, and one could infer that Boaz regards the grain as a gift for Naomi as well. Ruth's telling Naomi that Boaz intended the grain for her therefore enfolds Naomi into Boaz's promise.[75]

73. Ruth Rab. 7:4.

74. André LaCocque, *Ruth, A Continental Commentary*, trans. K. C. Hanson (Minneapolis: Fortress, 2004), 105.

75. Trible, *God and the Rhetoric of Sexuality*, 187; Linafelt and Beal, *Ruth and Esther*, 61; Danna Nolan Fewell and David M. Gunn, "'A Son Is Born to Naomi!': Literary Allusions and Interpretation in the Book of Ruth," *JSOT* 40 (1988): 99–108, at 101–2.

The end of chapter 3 offers a profound statement about Ruth's role, not as the bearer of children (at least not yet), but as breadwinner.[76] Even though the grain in chapter 3 is a "gift" rather than the result of working in the fields, the end of chapter 3 nonetheless parallels the end of chapter 2. It is Ruth's daring and resolve that allow her to provide for her mother-in-law in chapter 2 and then to bring Naomi's plan into action in chapter 3, actions that bring Naomi from emptiness to fullness. Ruth's choice to follow Naomi in chapter 1 has therefore resulted in her opportunity to provide for her mother-in-law economically. The child that Ruth will bear in chapter 4 will then become an extension of economic security, according to the text (see 4:15). In a contemporary context, children (especially when there are many) can become more mouths to feed that place additional pressure on the parents, yet this one son is an extension of Ruth's ability to care for Naomi.[77]

These are Ruth's last words in the book, after she has "left her home, risked attack in the fields, placed both herself and Boaz in a compromising position, and twice lied to Naomi."[78] As in chapter 2, Naomi has the last word. She tells Ruth to wait or "sit" (ישב; v. 18), a word that forms an inclusio with the invitation for Ruth to live or "sit" (ישב) in 2:23. Together, Ruth and Naomi will wait to see how the "matter turns out" (נפל דבר); literally "how the thing falls." As the story moves toward its resolution, the final verse in this chapter is a reminder that from here on, the women have little control over the events.[79] From now on, they will be dependent on Boaz, not because they do not have the power to act themselves, but because they choose to allow Boaz to do what he wants. To this point, the entire narrative arc demonstrates that the two women can act independently. Now, what holds them back may be social convention, in part, as well as the simple fact that Boaz has more leverage to address the legal situation. Yet Ruth had prepped Boaz for what will take place beginning in chapter 4.

Eskenazi and Frymer-Kensky, *Ruth*, 67. Sasson notes that the language of "emptiness" must come from Ruth, considering that Boaz was not a witness to Naomi's lament at the end of chapter 1 (*Ruth*, 101–2). Sakenfeld notes that Ruth's statement demonstrates how Boaz will show as much concern for Naomi as does "the loyal Ruth" (*Ruth*, 66).

76. Eskenazi and Frymer-Kensky, *Ruth*, 67–68, note that the text remains focused on "bread—on household economy, not procreation."

77. Ibid., 68. See also the discussion at 4:15.

78. Levine, "Ruth," 89.

79. Sakenfeld, *Ruth*, 66.

Power in the Book of Ruth

Who has power in the story of Ruth? If we take our cues from Rahab and Jezebel, stories about "foreign" biblical women reveal an unsettling correlation between compliance and survival. The foreign woman who is dangerous, like Jezebel and the "strange woman" of Proverbs, is the foreign woman who, with her militant allegiance to Baal or with her seductive promiscuity, defies Israelite control (1 Kgs 18:13, 19; Prov 2:16-17; 5:2-6). By contrast, Rahab, the "safe," indeed salvific, foreign woman, must align Israelite interests with her own to ensure her protection (Josh 2:8-14). Can this connection between compliance and survival be applied to Ruth, a foreign woman whose success depends on her conformity to Israel's levirate custom and her obedience to the directives of Israelite characters?

Ruth 3 can be read as yet another example of this correlation. In this chapter, Ruth receives a relentless series of commands. Through these commands, Ruth's feminine foreignness is corralled first by Naomi ("Wash!" "Anoint!" "Put On!" "Go!" "Do not let yourself be seen"), and then by Boaz ("Remain," "Lie Down"). Ruth obeys and, like Rahab, is rewarded with life and an illustrious lineage.

Yet Ruth's narrative does not submit to tidy categories of power and weakness. Strength, vulnerability, and compliance evade simple typecasting in this text. Ruth herself issues a command to Boaz: "Spread your cloak over me." Though this imperative essentially revoices Naomi's plans, she has also made it her own. Ruth's subtle initiative in this scene, mixed with Boaz's terror and his open-handed offer ("I will do for you all that you ask") complicates clear assignations of submission and control. In the wake of these considerations, we might ask: Was Ruth's pre-dawn departure from the threshing floor an act of benefaction, for the sake of Boaz's reputation, or of subordination? Is Ruth's relative quietness in this passage a sign of hapless assimilation, uncanny strength, or some elusive combination thereof?

This tale's complex dance of authority and compliance, agency and reward, invites us to assess the risks of too quickly equating silence and obedience with powerlessness. Ruth's story allows revelations of cooperation to sit—however uneasily—alongside those of coercion.

Laura K. Carlson

Ruth 4

Persevering in Loyalty

Contracting and Claiming: Men and Marriage (4:1-6)

The narrative scene has returned to the place where Naomi and Ruth had entered Bethlehem (1:19). It may be that while Naomi and Ruth are conversing (3:16-18), Boaz goes to the city gates, the actions occurring simultaneously rather than in succession.[1]

Whereas the women had been at the city gates at the time of Naomi and Ruth's arrival in Bethlehem and were the first in the narrative to speak (1:19), there is no mention of them during the negotiations between Boaz and Naomi's next-of-kin. However, the townswomen will function as an inclusio; they are the last people in the narrative to speak. They bless the Lord for providing Naomi a redeemer and they name the child (4:14-17). Otherwise, the words and actions of men dominate chapter 4. Neither Naomi nor Ruth speaks at all in the chapter. The narrator refers to Ruth by name in verse 13, the women refer to her in verse 14 as Naomi's "daughter-in-law," and then she disappears entirely. After verse 13 and the birth of Ruth's son, Naomi too fades before Elimelech's line and the genealogy that follows. Brenner describes this literary ending as part

1. Edward F. Campbell, *Ruth*, AB 7 (New York: Doubleday, 1975), 141-42.

Ruth 4:1-6

4:1No sooner had Boaz gone up to
the gate and sat down there than the
next-of-kin, of whom Boaz had spoken,
came passing by. So Boaz said, "Come
over, friend; sit down here." And he
went over and sat down. 2Then Boaz
took ten men of the elders of the city,
and said, "Sit down here"; so they sat
down. 3He then said to the next-of-kin,
"Naomi, who has come back from the
country of Moab, is selling the parcel
of land that belonged to our kinsman
Elimelech. 4So I thought I would tell you
of it, and say: Buy it in the presence of
those sitting here, and in the presence
of the elders of my people. If you will

of "the patriarchal framework" in which Ruth and Naomi operated.[2] This insight highlights the women's ability to act independently, despite patriarchy's values that could marginalize and silence them.

The boundaries of a city, what today we would refer to as "city limits," were determined by the city's walls, which also served for protection.[3] Built into the walls were gates, positioned in different directions that allowed people to travel north, south, etc. by way of the roads that lay outside the gates. People gathered at a city's gates, which were often the local seat of commerce; gates were places to say hello and goodbye as well as places to check out the newcomers. There at the gates, the city's inhabitants made agreements, swore oaths, and served as witnesses. For example, according to the biblical laws, if a man does not wish to marry his brother's childless widow, the widow appears before the city's gates to declare before all the elders that the man will not perform the duties of the brother-in-law, that is, levirate marriage (Deut 25:7);[4] Deborah's victory song tells YHWH's people to gather at the city gates (Judg 5:11); David is described as sitting between the two gates of the city (2 Sam 18:24); and Wisdom cries out, at a place brimming with activity, proclaiming her message at the city gates (Prov 1:21). That the husband of the

2. Athalya Brenner, *I Am . . .: Biblical Women Tell Their Own Stories* (Minneapolis: Fortress, 2005), 107.

3. Richard R. Losch refers to a Philistines garrison at Bethlehem in the pre-Israelite Canaanite period and the city itself as "a strategic military location," from which we can reasonably conclude that Bethlehem was a city with walls (*The Uttermost Part of the Earth: A Guide to the Bible* [Grand Rapids: Eerdmans, 2005], 51).

4. Bernard M. Levinson describes the village gate as "the traditional site of public justice in the ancient Near East" ("You Must Not Add Anything to What I Command You: Paradoxes of Canon and Authorship in Ancient Israel," *Numen* 50 [2003], 1–51, esp. 21).

redeem it, redeem it; but if you will not, tell me, so that I may know; for there is no one prior to you to redeem it, and I come after you." So he said, "I will redeem it." [5]Then Boaz said, "The day you acquire the field from the hand of Naomi, you are also acquiring Ruth the Moabite, the widow of the dead man, to maintain the dead man's name on his inheritance." [6]At this, the next-of-kin said, "I cannot redeem it for myself without damaging my own inheritance. Take my right of redemption yourself, for I cannot redeem it."

valiant woman of Proverbs 31 is known at the city gates (v. 23) and that the woman's own works praise her at the city gates (v. 31) give some idea of the social and serious roles gates played.

Now at the city gates, Boaz fortuitously meets Elimelech's next-of-kin and invites him to sit beside him. Physical proximity facilitated their conversation. The next-of-kin is not here named, and he remains nameless throughout the narrative. From his first introduction (3:12) we know only one thing about him: he is a closer relative to Naomi/Elimelech's family than Boaz. He is not the brother-in-law who, according to Deuteronomy 25:5-10, was to raise up a son for his deceased and childless brother. On the other hand, he is the family's closest male relative. And even if he were not, he has some moral and/or social responsibility to intervene on the widow's behalf (e.g., Deut 24:19-21; Isa 1:17; Jer 7:6; 22:3). He also has a legal obligation to redeem the land, according to Leviticus 25:25, "If any one of your kin falls into difficulty, and sells a piece of property, then the next-of-kin shall come and redeem what the relative has sold."

When the two men are seated, Boaz asks ten elders of the city to join them, and they do. In Jewish law and custom, ten is a symbolic number designating completion.[5] Boaz chooses elders, respected members of the community, as witnesses. He thus gathers together all of the constituencies necessary for the making of a legal decision regarding Elimelech's inheritance.

A conversation ensues as Boaz addresses the next-of-kin as פלני אלמני, a Hebrew phrase that means "such a one, so and so." The Hebrew phrase

5. Deuteronomy 4:13 and 10:4 speak, for example, of ten "words" or commandments, although there is variation in the determination of which laws are included in the ten. See Exodus 20:1-17 and 1 Samuel 1:8; 25:5. Christians also have understood ten as a symbolic number and one that signifies completion (e.g., Luke 17:11-19; 19:11-27). In both the Old and New Testaments twelve is another number that signifies completion.

is very uncommon, occurring only here and in 1 Samuel 21:2 and 2 Kings 6:8, where it designates a specific but unnamed place. The NRSV and several other versions[6] translate the term "friend," yet the Hebrew term for friend is distinct.[7] The New American Bible, Revised Edition (2011) translates, "Boaz called to him by name," which is inconsistent with the narrative's manner of naming in general.[8] He is important, but he will turn out to be not that important. In addressing the next-of-kin by his particularity, as his friend, Boaz may be trying to elicit trust, an intent that justifies the translation "friend"; he may also be insinuating that what he is about to say truly has the next-of-kin's best interests at heart.

Boaz proceeds to tell the next-of-kin that Naomi, who has returned from Moab, is selling the land that belonged to her husband Elimelech. This is news to the reader as well as to the next-of-kin. It may even be news to Naomi (unless she has merely forgotten about the land) since nothing has been said about land so far in the narrative. But why would she want to, or even be willing to, sell that land, which had belonged to her husband and now belongs to her? What she wants is a husband for Ruth and a grandson; she does not necessarily want to lose control of ancestral land (Josh 13:8–19:48), which she may very well need. The land may translate into food for the future. However, the land may be the price Naomi is willing to pay for a husband for Ruth and a grandson—and Ruth has sworn not to abandon her (1:16-17).

Elimelech's inheritance includes both property and family. The text confirms the situation detailed in Numbers 27 and 36 that women could, under certain circumstances, both inherit and sell property. If a father died without sons, as was the case with Zelophehad, his daughters could inherit their father's property (Num 27:7). However, his daughters were then required to marry within their own clan or tribe, so as to keep the land within the tribe (Num 36:6-9). Although Naomi's situation differs from that of Zelophehad's daughters, applying the practice, with variation, to Naomi's situation is reasonable. It was her husband, not her father, who had died. Even if Naomi were to marry again, and marry a member of her dead husband's tribe, that marriage would not result in offspring. She needed to find a way to prevent the land's leaving the tribe after her (or her husband's) death. For the land to remain securely in

6. E.g., the New American Standard Bible (1971), the Revised Standard Version (1977), and the New International Bible (1983).

7. The Hebrew term for friend is רעה (see Gen 38:12, 20; Exod 32:27; 33:11; 2 Sam 13:3; 16:16-17).

8. We have not yet learned the name of Ruth's deceased husband. See 4:10.

Elimelech's clan or tribe,[9] not only would a next-of-kin have to purchase it, but the next-of-kin would need progeny to keep the land within the tribe.

Boaz asserts that the "next-of-kin" is exactly that, Elimelech's next-of-kin, and as such, first in line to buy Elimelech's land. Boaz indicates his willingness that the next-of-kin "redeem" (גאל) the land, but he asserts that if the next-of-kin is unwilling, he wants to know; he is second in line. The presence of the elders as witnesses solemnizes the verbal exchange. What is committed to or agreed on is potentially binding.

Land was precious and was distributed proportionally in ancient Israel. Not only was it not to be sold outside the tribe, but only when a family was in dire economic straits could it be turned over to another. Even then it was to be returned at the time of jubilee (Lev 25). When King Ahab wanted to acquire Naboth's vineyard and turn it into a vegetable garden, even though Ahab offered "a better vineyard for it" (1 Kgs 21:2), Naboth rejected the offer. Naboth did not consider the vineyard his to sell: "The LORD forbid that I should give you my ancestral inheritance" (v. 3).[10] Thus the next-of-kin should want to redeem Elimelech's land: it was his familial and tribal duty to do so. In verse 5, he agrees to redeem (גאל) the land.

Only after the next-of-kin has agreed to buy Naomi's land does Boaz bring Ruth into the conversation. For the reader (and maybe for Boaz too) the conversation about the land has been a delay tactic. Boaz had told Ruth that he would settle her future (the next-of-kin or himself) that very day, and the reader has been waiting to see what Boaz will do. Either the next-of-kin, who is closer to Elimelech's family, or else Boaz himself will redeem her. The Hebrew verb translated here "redeem" is the same verb (גאל) used in Exodus 6:6 when YHWH says to Moses: "I am the LORD, and I will redeem you with an outstretched arm and with mighty acts of judgment." We anticipate Ruth's redemption.

The next-of-kin, who has agreed to purchase Naomi's land, is also both entitled and socially expected to buy the rest of Elimelech's inheritance, namely, Elimelech's daughter-in-law whose husband has died without fathering a son. The NRSV translates the same Hebrew verb as both "to buy" and "to acquire" (קנה), and the English translation therefore loses the point that Ruth is being purchased in the same way that the land is purchased. What more blatant indicator of patriarchy! The Decalogue does the same with respect to coveting: wife (Deut 5:20) and property

9. We do not know Elimelech's clan or tribe since he only appears in the book of Ruth; the same is true for Naomi.

10. Leviticus 25 describes the year of jubilee during which provision is made for returning land to the families that originally held it.

(v. 21) are equally the objects of the prohibition. In Exodus 20:17, the prohibition against coveting includes not only a neighbor's house and wife but even his "male or female slave, or ox, or donkey, or anything that belongs to your neighbor"; the neighbor's wife "belongs" to him.

Even today, in many families in the United States, a father "gives away" (as though he possessed) his daughter at her wedding, handing her off (literally) to her future husband. This exchange of goods is symbolized by the woman's relinquishing what had been her surname, her father's surname, in favor of her husband's surname. And up until the mid-twentieth century, when a widow married, she traditionally wore off-white, to acknowledge that she was not a virgin.

Though the next-of-kin is not a brother of Ruth's deceased husband, if he behaves as next-of-kin and buys the land, Boaz assures him that he also acquires/buys the childless widow. There are no other passages in the Old Testament where a man acquiring land also acquires a widow.[11] In addition, the land that the next-of-kin would be acquiring would not become part of his patrimony; it would become, as the property of Elimelech's family and Ruth's dead husband, the property of Ruth's first son. This should give the next-of-kin pause.

As if to further discourage the next-of-kin, Boaz identifies Ruth as "the Moabite." The land comes with baggage: Ruth. Ruth comes with baggage. She is not just a pre-menopausal woman of marriageable age; she is a widow, a foreigner, a Moabite. Boaz does everything he can to make the acquisitions less favorable in the eyes of the next-of-kin.

Re-creating Ruth

There is much in the story of Ruth that shows Boaz's attitude toward this immigrant refugee. The climax is seen in Ruth 4. Boaz calls the rightful גאל, guardian redeemer, to the city gate. (This is the place of wisdom, where all the wise justices of the community meet. This is also the place where the husband of the wise woman, the אשת חיל of Proverbs 31, is, because of her, recognized.) Boaz says to the guardian redeemer, "'The day you acquire the field from the hand of Naomi, you are also acquiring Ruth the Moabite, the widow of the dead man, to maintain the dead man's name on his inheritance.' At this, the next-of-kin said, 'I cannot redeem it for myself without damaging my own inheritance. Take my

11. David marries the widows Abigail (1 Sam 25:39-42) and Bathsheba (2 Sam 11:14-26); Onan takes his childless dead brother's wife Tamar (Gen 38:8-10).

right of redemption yourself, for I cannot redeem it'" (Ruth 4:5-6).

The translation "acquire" is rather unfortunate. The Hebrew קנה elsewhere in the Bible, as in Genesis 14:19, 22, describes the Creator or Maker of heaven and earth. In this story, Boaz is described as gracefully re-creating the woman Ruth to her original glory. His actions in Ruth 4 describe the re-creation of a new economy, redressing the hardships that have caused a family to fall into dire poverty. It also describes the re-creation of a new woman. This seems to be the core message of the story of Ruth and Boaz. It is a story that provides an alternative to the women's poverty and insecurity.

My mind goes back to so many Ruths who were trafficked from the slum where I was reared. I often ask the question, "Where are the Boazes who would courageously change the moral fiber of society?"

Rajkumar Boaz Johnson

Having to take Ruth and conceive a son with her for her dead husband changes everything. The next-of-kin thought he was buying land that would belong to him and that he would be able to pass on to his own sons. Apparently, he had either not heard about Ruth or had not thought through the implications of buying Naomi's land. How had it happened that he had not heard about Naomi's return with her daughter-in-law? Was the family estranged? Now he learns that the land he was buying would never belong to "his own" son—the first son he fathered with Ruth—because that first son would never be his own. And if he already had a wife[12] and son, his firstborn would not inherit the land. Though he was not the brother of Ruth's dead husband and therefore not required by levirate law to marry Ruth,[13] if he did so as next-of-kin, these expectations

12. The possibility of his already being married raises other questions. What would it be like if your husband brought home a stranger—to both you and to him—as a new wife? What would it be like, for Ruth, to be the second wife?

13. Roi Nu, considering her own social context of Myanmar, argues that the narrative of Ruth is not an example of the practice of the levirate law. She does so because the levirate law is still enforced among the Kachin society of Myanmar, comprised of approximately six hundred thousand Christians, much to the detriment of women ("A Reinterpretation of Levirate Marriage in Ruth 4:1-12 for Kachin Society," in *Reading Ruth in Asia*, ed. Jione Havea and Peter H. W. Lau, IVBS 7 [Atlanta: SBL Press, 2015], 57–72). "Levirate marriage" is still practiced in many parts of Asia and Africa. While the practice is identified as "levirate marriage," it seems to be "customary (traditional/tribal) law" among peoples who have a strong clan structure and among whom marriage outside the clan is forbidden. The Immigration and Refugee Board of Canada in February 2006

would fall on him.[14] They seemed too costly; perhaps he was not as wealthy as Boaz and buying the property that would not become part of his legacy would prevent him from buying other property that could. He might not have been able to do both. The next-of-kin therefore told Boaz that he would forego the land and his right to redeem it and, formally in the presence of the ten elders, he "handed over" his right to Boaz.

Bridal Customs

Traditional Indian culture shares similarities with the setting and scene described in the book of Ruth, where a young woman's achievement depends on her ability to find favor with a man. I once witnessed an arranged marriage event where a bride's family hosted the groom and his family in their home, and the potential bride dressed herself up, brought refreshments and served them while displaying her best and modest behavior, then left the room while the adults discussed formalities related to bridal gifts or dowry. After the bride's family had passed all the tests, the groom's family demanded the bride be checked privately to see if there were any skin or other related issues that might affect their marriage.

Even though it is a humiliating experience, young women are often made to believe that it is their fortune if the man's family agrees to marry. Like Ruth trying to catch the eye of Boaz, a young Indian woman makes considerable efforts to find favor with a man. Ruth attains honor for being noticed among others, and her honor increases because she finds favor in the eyes of a man of good standing. In their society, as in Indian society today, a woman's honor depends much on man's appreciation and affirmation of her in terms of her beauty or her character. It happens in Ruth 2:11-13, and Ruth continues to be pleasantly surprised by Boaz's attention and kind treatment.

Surekha Nelavala

---

documented the practice by three Nigerian tribes, including in its report the consequences for a man or woman who refused to participate as well as state protections for such refusal (http://www.refworld.org/docid/45f1478811.html). When Alice visited Kenya a few years ago, she learned firsthand that the levirate law was still observed in many small villages. This was particularly problematic because of the transmittal of AIDS.

14. Levinson addresses the question of how cultures with a tradition of prestigious and authoritative texts deal with the problem of literary and legal innovation. Based on the notion that God punishes wrongdoers to the third and fourth generation, he shows how later writers were able to replace that idea with the alternate notion of individual retribution. Such development allows for the adaptation of the sandal ritual ("You Must Not Add Anything," 1–51), and, by extension, the wider application of the levirate law.

"Acquiring" Land and a Wife: Boaz Triumphs (4:7-12)

According to verse 7, in order to confirm a transaction that involved exchanging or redeeming something(s), it was the custom that[15] the one "exchanging" or giving away took off a sandal and gave it to the one "redeeming." The solemnity of the exchange thus took the form of action as well as words.[16] The ritual as here described is attested nowhere else in the Old Testament. A variation of it occurs only once elsewhere, and the circumstances surrounding the ritual are slightly different. When a man refuses to observe the levirate law—marrying the widow of his deceased brother who died without fathering a son—"the elders of his town shall summon him and speak to him. If he persists, saying, 'I have no desire to marry her,' then his brother's wife shall go up to him in the presence of the elders, pull his sandal off his foot, spit in his face, and declare, 'This is what is done to the man who does not build up his brother's house' " (Deut 25:9-10).

The symbolism expressed in these actions—the widow uncovering the man's foot (3:7) and then spitting in his face—emasculates the man. The dual form of רגל, "foot," often replaces the plural form of רגלים, which can mean the lower parts or genitals (see the discussion in "Translation Matters" on 3:4); the one is used euphemistically for the other. Here, the woman, symbolically, uncovers her brother-in-law's genitals. Because he refuses to direct his water to her and ejaculate into her vagina, she directs her water (spit) toward him. The lack of reciprocal action that should lead to marriage and her pulling off his sandal signify the man's rejection of his sister-in-law and the custom's violation.[17]

By taking off his sandal, the next-of-kin indicates that he was not going to redeem Ruth. Since he was not the brother of Ruth's deceased husband, he would not have violated the levirate law, strictly speaking. Still, his behavior was dishonorable. He had just stated that he would redeem the land, and now he reneges, so he looks self-interested and unconcerned about the well-being of Ruth and Naomi. Nevertheless, by

15. According to Levinson, v. 7 is an editorial interpolation. It prepares the reader for the symbolic ritual that follows, which would not have been comprehensible to the original audience without some explanation. (See "You Must Not Add Anything," 22.)

16. Commitment to a promise also occurred when one placed his hand under another man's thigh, that is, on his testicles (from which comes the term "testimony"). See, for example, Gen 24:2, 9; 47:29.

17. "Spitting in one's face" is elsewhere a gesture that accuses one of wrongdoing (see Num 12:14).

Ruth 4:7-12

[7]Now this was the custom in former
times in Israel concerning redeeming
and exchanging: to confirm a transac-
tion, the one took off a sandal and gave
it to the other; this was the manner of
attesting in Israel. [8]So when the next-
of-kin said to Boaz, "Acquire it for your-
self," he took off his sandal. [9]Then Boaz
said to the elders and all the people,
"Today you are witnesses that I have
acquired from the hand of Naomi all
that belonged to Elimelech and all that
belonged to Chilion and Mahlon. [10]I
have also acquired Ruth, the Moabite,
the wife of Mahlon, to be my wife, to
maintain the dead man's name on his

pulling off his sandal, he solemnly attests, in the presence of Boaz and the elders, that he will not perform the duty of the next-of-kin.

After the next-of-kin foregoes his rights, Boaz publicly declares that he has bought the inheritance of Elimelech with the intention of marrying Ruth. In both verses 10 and 13, the expression for marriage is a Hebrew construction that translates literally, she is "to me for a woman" (לי לאשה).[18] The phrase is not uncommon; on the contrary, its usage begins in Genesis.[19] Here, it answers the question Boaz asked of his servant who was in charge of the reapers (2:5): "To whom does this young woman belong?" In 2:5 Ruth is a נערה, a young woman; here, she is referred to as an אשה, a woman/wife, first to Mahlon and then to Boaz (v. 10).

Only in verse 10 do we finally learn the name of Ruth's dead husband. Up until now, Ruth could have been Chilion or Mahlon's wife; neither of Naomi's sons had been named in connection with Ruth (or Orpah) in chapter 1. Rather, the women (and mainly Ruth) have been the characters in the foreground. Ruth has been wife and widow and daughter-in-law, while one of Naomi's sons had been Ruth's husband. In many cultures it is very important to call someone by name (see Isa 43:1); as long as Ruth's dead husband lacked a name, he lacked a real presence, even in the past. Only when Ruth is acquiring another husband, Boaz, does Mahlon emerge out of the shadows.

18. The grammatical construction is a "dative of possession," that is, the woman (אשה) who comes to belong to the man is his wife (אשה). In the Hebrew, the terms "woman" and "wife" are the same word; when the man possesses the woman, she becomes his wife.

19. The phrase occurs in Gen 16:3 although there it may refer to Hagar as Abram's concubine, rather than his wife; in Gen 20:12 Abraham acknowledges to Abimelech that Sarah is his wife.

inheritance, in order that the name of the dead may not be cut off from his kindred and from the gate of his native place; today you are witnesses." [11]Then all the people who were at the gate, along with the elders, said, "We are witnesses. May the LORD make the woman who is coming into your house like Rachel and Leah, who together built up the house of Israel. May you produce children in Ephrathah and bestow a name in Bethlehem; [12]and, through the children that the LORD will give you by this young woman, may your house be like the house of Perez, whom Tamar bore to Judah."

Naming Mahlon, differentiating him from his brother Chilion as Ruth's former husband, serves to allow Boaz to proclaim, with specificity, before the elders, that he is taking on the responsibilities of a levir. Boaz will acquire/buy (קנה) Ruth, who is here officially identified as the wife of Mahlon; he will maintain "the dead man's" name (Mahlon's name is not given here) on his inheritance so that "the name of the dead" (again excluding the name Mahlon) may not be cut off from his kindred and from the gate of his native place (v. 10). Although Mahlon is differentiated from his brother, the text provides the reader with no information about him other than that he was Ruth's husband and that he is dead. The reader knows nothing about Ruth's relationship with him.

Boaz not only buys the field (and Ruth), but he must also pay for the upkeep of all of Elimelech's inheritance, including the land, Ruth, and Naomi. After fathering a son, he must provide for the son too. Boaz had no legal obligation to redeem the land and marry Ruth, although the social customs of the day may have made his doing so praiseworthy. Since Ruth was not an Israelite, Boaz may even have been less bound, according to social custom, to marry her. He may even have been ignoring or resisting social norms.[20]

Boaz took a risk in marrying Ruth. While he may have earned the admiration of some, marrying and producing a son out of "a deeply felt sense of duty"[21]—to preserve Ruth's dead husband's name, to keep the land in the family, and to provide Naomi with stability and continuation—perhaps he was putting his reputation at risk by marrying a

20. Lau, "Another Postcolonial Reading of the Book of Ruth," in Havea and Lau, *Reading Ruth in Asia*, 20.

21. Brenner, *I Am . . .*, 106.

foreigner.[22] Yet because the Bible's perceptions of marriage to foreigners are mixed, this latter possibility is only that—a possibility. Moreover, there is nothing in the text itself that would suggest that Boaz marrying Ruth would be a problem to the community.

According to the judgment of Boaz, by becoming his wife, Ruth would be demonstrating *ḥesed*[23] in choosing to marry the older man who was Naomi's close relative. This marriage would bind her to her dead husband and to her mother-in-law's family. As discussed in chapter 3, we do not know Ruth's motivations in going after Boaz rather than a younger man, but we do know that she appears to be devoted to her mother-in-law. By marrying Boaz, Ruth becomes bound to Israelite society,[24] and she can fulfill the promise she made to Naomi (1:16-17).

Verse 11 reminds the reader that these proceedings are all taking place publicly. The exchange is made between Boaz and Elimelech's next-of-kin, but it takes place at the city gates with ten elders as witnesses, as well as in the presence of all of the people who were at the gate. They all testify to what they have heard and seen. We cannot help but notice the absence of Ruth and Naomi as others determine their destinies (Naomi's land and Ruth's future husband). We do not know whether Naomi was intending to sell the land; there had been no conversation between Naomi and Boaz about anything, let alone about the exchange of land. Boaz may assume that Naomi knows that the land and Ruth will go together to whomever acquires Ruth. Or Boaz may be surmising that Naomi will go along with the plan, if it means gaining a close relative as husband for her daughter-in-law. Maybe Boaz was setting up the closer next-of-kin—to have happen exactly what did happen—to expose the next-of-kin as desiring to buy the land but not wanting to acquire Ruth, and thus allowing Boaz to acquire both Ruth and the land. If such were the case, Boaz was using the land to increase his chances of acquiring Ruth.

The prayer uttered by all the witnesses, at least ten of whom were men, asks YHWH to make Ruth very fertile. They wish that she will be like

22. See Lau, who interprets Ruth in light of Deut 23:3-6, which conveys a less-than-positive attitude toward Moabites in addressing the exclusion of Moabites from the assembly of the Lord, even while this exclusion was probably irrelevant to Ruth's situation ("Another Postcolonial Reading of the Book of Ruth," 19). Lau also suggests that Boaz, if he were single, may have risked his own family line if Ruth were no longer fertile.

23. See the comments on the importance of *ḥesed* in our introduction and throughout the commentary.

24. Lau, "Another Postcolonial Reading of the Book of Ruth," 23.

Rachel and Leah,[25] who together with his slaves/Jacob's other wives/concubines produced at least thirteen children for Jacob, twelve sons and Dinah (Gen 34).[26] They pray that one Moabite woman, Ruth, will do what it took two Israelite matriarchs and their two "maids"[27] to accomplish.[28]

While the elders and all the witnesses compare Ruth with Rachel and Leah, asking for Ruth's fertility to be like theirs, they ignore the strained and competitive relationship between Rachel and Leah. In contrast, there is no competition between Naomi and Ruth. Naomi does not envy Ruth's fertility; her only wish is that Ruth takes advantage of it. Whereas Rachel's beauty (Gen 29:18) attracts Jacob, Ruth's *ḥesed* (3:10) attracts Boaz; or at least, this is what Boaz leads us to believe in chapter 3.

Continuing their prayer for Boaz, the elders and all the people at the gate ask that Boaz, according to the NRSV translation of עשה חיל, "produce children" (עשה חיל literally means "to do strength")[29] in Ephrathah and that he bestow (call) a name in Bethlehem. The reader is drawn back first to 3:11, where Boaz describes Ruth as a "woman of strength,"[30] and

25. Intertextuality is a prominent element of the postcolonial approach, often used to explore what ideologies or powers the world of, in this instance, the Ruth narrative might be resisting. Ruth turns out to be like Leah, not in the number of sons she bears, but in bearing a son who became the ancestor of David. In contrast to Rachel and Leah, she is not an insider, from the family so important to Rebekah and Isaac (Gen 28:2), but an outsider, a foreigner. Her Moabite identity that becomes so integral to Israelite identity is precisely how she resists the empire. See Lau, "Another Postcolonial Reading of the Book of Ruth," 17. Lau's article focuses on the intertexts that modify or reinforce the identities of the main characters in the Ruth narrative.

26. Genesis 37:35 records that "all [Jacob's] sons and *all his daughters* sought to comfort him" after Joseph's death, which suggests that the women bore more than one daughter.

27. While the NRSV refers to Bilhah and Zilpah as Rachel and Leah's "maids," respectively, a more accurate translation of שפחה is "slave."

28. Amy-Jill Levine, "Ruth," *Women's Bible Commentary*, ed. Carol A. Newsom and Sharon H. Ringe, exp. ed. (Louisville: Westminster John Knox, 1998), 84–90, esp. 89.

29. The phrase עשה חיל, "to do strength" or, more eloquently, "to do with virtue," is found in Ruth 4:11 as well as in Prov 31:29 in terms of the woman or wife of strength/virtue.

30. Elaine W. F. Goh recommends translating אשת חיל in Ruth 3:11 as "a woman of strength" rather than "a woman of worth" (NRSV) or a "valiant woman" (NKJV); she speaks from a Chinese woman's perspective. Goh believes that using the phrases "woman of worth" or "valiant woman," given the scene at the threshing floor, allows Ruth to be considered as a crafty seductress—strong-willed, self-serving, guileful. In contrast, the phrase "a woman of strength" connotes a woman who aspires to survive, albeit by shrewdness, a tough woman. She points out that Chinese women of strength

then to 1:2, where Elimelech's family is identified as Ephrathites from Bethlehem in Judah. Yet here, the language of "strength" is associated with Boaz. The witnesses therefore suggest that, similar to the matriarchs "building up the house of Israel" (see Deut 25:9), Boaz, through Ruth, will "produce children." Here, by again naming Ephrathah and Bethlehem, the townspeople pray for the fullest possible incorporation of Boaz and his family into Israel. Boaz is now recognized as part of Elimelech's line.

They ask also that Boaz's house be like Perez's, a reference that we will return to twice in verse 18 with respect to Perez's descendants. Here, the line or "house" of Perez is the focus of the people's prayer, even though it is Tamar who bore Perez to Judah (Gen 38). As we noted earlier, Tamar, like Ruth, is also a foreigner, and her situation is also a variation of the levirate law. She tricks her father-in-law into impregnating her because Judah refuses to give her his third son as a husband; she and Judah conceive twins, the firstborn of which is Perez. After Judah realizes what Tamar has done—tricking him into impregnating her—he acknowledges, "she is more in the right than I" (Gen 38:26). Judah did not trust YHWH; he likely feared that if he gave his third and last son to Tamar as a husband, he too would die before producing a son and Judah's line would be lost. Tamar, the foreigner, on the other hand, was intent on fulfilling the levirate law the only way she knew how. Without indicating how many children Perez fathered (see Gen 38:27; 46:12), the women nevertheless know that his line has endured. Five generations later, Boaz enters the genealogy, and they pray that Boaz's offspring will also produce a lasting line.

Ruth is unnamed in this scene. Rather, she is designated first as "the woman who is coming into your house" (v. 11) and then as "this young woman" (נערה, v. 12), the same phrase Boaz used for Ruth before they ever exchanged words (2:5). The shift in language takes the emphasis from her as a named subject and emphasizes her role as a fertile young woman, in relation to Boaz and offspring. This marriage is clearly about

---

were identified throughout history, and even today. They run households smoothly, provide food, and make possible a secure future for their families. She attests that Ruth possesses that strength ("An Intertextual Reading of Ruth and Proverbs 31:10-31, with a Chinese Woman's Perspective," in Havea and Lau, *Reading Ruth in Asia*, 73–87, esp. 76-77). See also the discussion at 3:11 regarding the translation of אשת חיל as "woman of strength." See Naomi Seidman's "A New Garb for the Jewish Soul: The JPS Bible in the Light of the King James Bible," in *Assessing the Genius of the King James Version as Bible Translation and Literary Influence*, ed. David Burke, John Kutsko, and Philip Towner (Atlanta: SBL Press, 2013), 475–98.

children, yet at this point it is all about Boaz rather than Mahlon. While verse 10 identifies Mahlon as Ruth's dead husband whose inheritance and name Boaz promises to protect, Mahlon is then "buried" (pun intended) under the well wishes for Boaz and Ruth's marriage, children, and well-being. In fact, his name, for all intents and purposes, is cut off from both his kindred (vv. 17, 18-22) and the gate of his native place. Once Boaz makes the public proclamation of his intent to act as a levir, Mahlon disappears, never to return.

Throughout, the Ruth narrative parallels Genesis 38: sons die, the sons of Judah and his wife, the daughter of Shua, that is, Er and Onan, as well as the sons of Elimelech and Naomi, that is, Mahlon and Chilion; in both narratives a spouse dies, the unnamed daughter of Shua, Judah's wife, and Elimelech. Tamar and Ruth both refuse to remain in or return to their parents' houses after being widowed; both women produce children who continue the threatened family line. The people at the city gates would recognize the similarities between Tamar and Ruth and wish that Ruth, like Tamar, would bear a son (or sons) to carry on the family line.

But there are more similarities: the older man/younger woman pairing in the relationships between Tamar and Judah, Ruth and Boaz, and the fact that both Tamar and Ruth are proactive with respect to men. While Tamar is deceptive, Ruth is seductive. Ruth is a Moabite who enters into Israel; Tamar may also be a non-Hebrew. Both are described as being either "more righteous" (Tamar) or "more (valuable)" (Ruth) than others. On her side, Tamar took a great risk in deceiving Judah; while her motive is not expressly stated, Judah assumes that her motivation is to accomplish, to the extent that she can, a variation of the levirate law for her deceased husband. On the other side, Ruth risks her future in marrying an older wealthy man who is Naomi's relative, and the women praise her (if not explicitly) for executing a variation of the levirate law, or at least for bearing Naomi a son. Just as Tamar, according to Judah, is "more" in the right than he, Ruth, according to the women of Bethlehem, is "more" (to Naomi) than seven sons. The objects of comparison—Judah's righteousness (which he at least presumes he possesses) and seven sons—are of unquestionable value, and yet the behavior of the two women exceeds them.

Finally, the women name what Ruth has done for Naomi (what Tamar had done for Judah): Ruth (and Tamar) had borne a son. But neither of the women, though they become mothers, bears sons who are, in themselves, famous (Perez and Obed, respectively); in contrast to many other mothers in the Old Testament, these women become famous because of other things they do (i.e., taking a risk and acting courageously)—as well as being mothers.[31] In both cases the younger women, who are both probably non-Hebrews and sexually assertive, take the initiative and act when men do not; their fates as well as their motivations are unrecorded.[32] Some readers will take the women's behaviors to be morally problematic, while others will see the women as acting shrewdly and courageously in situations where the culture limited their options.

Mothering and Silencing: The Women's Story (4:13-17)

Verse 13 declares the marriage between Boaz and Ruth. The action is reciprocal, though the verbs betray the agency of Boaz (לקח, "took," taking a direct object) and the alteration in Ruth's identity (היה, "to become," an intransitive verb). In addition, Boaz takes the sexual initiative: what the English translates as "they came together" is really "he comes to her" in Hebrew, בוא אליה.

Those readers who consider the biblical text to be inspired may see YHWH as dominating the entire narrative, yet direct intervention is explicitly mentioned only twice: YHWH acts to end the famine in Israel (1:6), and YHWH intervenes so that Ruth conceives (4:16). The text here therefore shifts from the actions of Ruth and the other characters (chaps. 2–3) to YHWH's agency in literally "giving" Ruth conception. Elsewhere, the Bible often credits YHWH with conception. YHWH opens the wombs of women who have not yet conceived (e.g., Rachel, Gen 29:31; 30:22)[33] and of women who apparently had ceased from childbearing (e.g., Leah, Gen 29:31). YHWH also closes the womb (e.g., of the house of Abimelech in Gen 20:18; and of Hannah in 1 Sam 1:5-6). The Israelites did not understand how conception took place scientifically, nor, as intelligent and observant as they were, could they control the process. Therefore, YHWH makes Ruth conceive by literally giving her pregnancy/conception.[34]

So far as we know, Ruth did not have a child in the ten years she was married to Mahlon, and now she is pregnant. Whether a woman con-

31. The reason for the inclusion of Tamar and Ruth into Matthew's genealogy (Matt 1:1-17) may be because they are both non-Hebrews and mothers, but they are also women who have stories of their own.

32. Levine, "Ruth," 90.

33. See Isa 44:2-24; 49:5; 66:9; Jer 1:5; Job 10:18; 31:15.

34. The noun הריון, meaning pregnancy (v. 13), is very rare, occurring only in Gen 3:16 and Hos 9:11. In Gen 3:16, God curses the woman by including pain in childbearing; Hos 9:11 depicts a time of no conception.

Ruth 4:13-17

[13]So Boaz took Ruth and she became his wife. When they came together, the LORD made her conceive, and she bore a son. [14]Then the women said to Naomi, "Blessed be the LORD, who has not left you this day without next-of-kin; and may his name be renowned in Israel! [15]He shall be to you a restorer of life and a nourisher of your old age; for your daughter-in-law who loves you, who is more to you than seven sons, has borne him." [16]Then Naomi took the child and laid him in her bosom, and became his nurse. [17]The women of the neighborhood gave him a name, saying, "A son has been born to Naomi." They named him Obed; he became the father of Jesse, the father of David.

ceives or not is in YHWH's hands, and the Bible does not treat issues of conception (whether due to infertility or menopause) as punishment for sin or grounds for judgment.[35] Consider, for example, Sarah and Abraham, Rebecca and Isaac, Rachel and Jacob, Hannah and Elkanah; none of these characters is blamed for having problems with conception. Similarly, Ruth's infertility during her ten-year marriage to Mahlon suggests nothing about her sinfulness, or even her own fertility. Given Ruth's apparently quick conception of her son, the likeliest explanation for her earlier, childless marriage was that Mahlon was infertile.

Ruth does not tell the reader whether she wanted a son, but she does indicate, in the larger context of the narrative and on the threshing floor, her willingness to marry. Knowing how much Naomi wanted her to be married and find "rest," she consented. Boaz came to her for sexual relations, and then YHWH gave Ruth the pregnancy. We do not know if Boaz and Ruth continued to have a sexual relationship after the pregnancy or whether, like Judah with Tamar, Boaz did not continue to have such relations with Ruth.

The narrator follows conception with birth straightaway. There is no sense of nine months' duration and what Ruth experienced during that time—a hard pregnancy, an easy pregnancy, or complications during the pregnancy or with childbirth. This may be our best indication that the author of the narrative was a man or at least not a mother, a person who had no experience of carrying another body within her own body for an extended period of time. Even if the author, male or female, were simply uninterested in detailing Ruth's pregnancy or in defining Ruth

35. See Candida R. Moss and Joel S. Baden, *Reconceiving Infertility: Biblical Perspectives on Procreation and Childlessness* (Princeton: Princeton University Press, 2015).

in relation to her son, "the final outcome is the traditional patriarchal ideal of a mother with a son on her lap."[36]

"They Called Him Obed"

The tale ends with a finale from God. The creator has brought Israel a future as a baby is born of Ruth. This child brings comfort to those who had suffered and brings hope to those who await the glory of God.

The coming of a child is the shining work of God and his divine design for women. Ruth was one among many fearless women of the Old and New Testaments chosen to bring God's people their heroes and heroines. In this story, and throughout the Word, women inhabited the natural essence of God's goodness and mercy. And they exhibited these qualities in the name of faith, with a quiet voice of truth to lead them. Innately, they proceeded as the Lord willed into roles that were specific to them and specific to the history of the Christian world.

I read that a tree glorifies God by "being" as designed, or by being "just" a tree. The tree has no voice in its design but exists as created, beautifully. If we are to believe in the purposeful design of God, then we too were created to glorify God by our very existence. Feminine attributes have impacted the history of faith with the same gravity of any male attributes. Since God's love is written and taught as the one true unconditional and whole love, then each creation shares equally in his divinely mystical agape being. This illustrates the ever-inclusive access to live and love as willed by God, as we are called to fulfill the destiny of humankind to the glory of the Lord, the God of Israel.

Sheila Clare DeLuca

A feminist eye[37] notes the ambiguity in verses 14-17. Similar to chapter 1, the women exclude Ruth when they speak to Naomi (1:19). The women bless YHWH who has provided Naomi with a next-of-kin (גאל), even though 2:1 identified Boaz vaguely as a relative (מידע; see the discussion of מידע at 2:1). But given the development of events through chapters 2–3 and in the beginning of chapter 4, the reader now knows that the next-

36. Irmtraud Fischer, "The Book of Ruth: A 'Feminist' Commentary to the Torah?," in *Ruth and Esther*, FCB 3, 2nd ser., ed. Athalya Brenner (Sheffield: Sheffield Academic, 1999), 24–49, at 33.

37. Ibid., 32. Fischer concludes that the statement by the women confirms Ruth's solidarity with Naomi rather than with her husband. This may be a bit of a stretch.

of-kin, the גאל, is Boaz. Because he married Ruth and has a son with her, he has provided for Ruth as next-of-kin; only indirectly does he provide for Naomi. Similarly, the women pray that "his" name will be renowned in Israel, which sounds as if they are referring to Boaz because of what precedes (and also v. 11), but, because of what follows, they may also be referring to Obed.[38] The narrator is talking about Naomi but including Ruth, and Obed but including Boaz. The women are talking to Naomi but including/implying Ruth, and about Boaz but including/implying Obed. The next-of-kin also becomes an inclusive term; whereas it describes the man who chose not to acquire Ruth, it now properly designates Boaz.

The women describe this next-of-kin as a "restorer of life" and as a "nourisher" of Naomi's old age. In many cultures, grandparents gain new life at the birth of grandchildren, and often grandchildren, as they grow, rejuvenate grandparents. In situations where parents are working and grandparents are retired, the bond that can develop between them is strong. Of course, in certain situations grandchildren may sap the life of grandparents rather than restore it, particularly in situations where grandparents become the primary caretakers or even guardians of the grandchildren. In other situations, grandparents simply cannot care for their grandchildren because they themselves work (perhaps they work to care for their children as well as their grandchildren). But whatever the circumstances, children signify new life; here, the child signifies new life to Naomi.

The women continue their blessing of Naomi. They identify Ruth as Naomi's "daughter-in-law" (back to 1:7) and describe her in relation to Naomi: she loves Naomi; she is more to Naomi than seven sons; she has borne a son. Despite Ruth's attestations of loyalty to Naomi, Naomi had never voiced "love" or particular appreciation for Ruth. Yet here the townswomen reclaim Ruth from Naomi's silence (1:18) with their praise. They are not necessarily critiquing Naomi, just offering the praise they believe is Ruth's due.

Readers may accept Ruth's exclusion from the conversation. The women know Naomi, so it makes sense that they would talk with her; they would naturally speak of Ruth in the third person, even as they say nice things about her. On the other hand, readers may resist the women's foregrounding of Naomi rather than Ruth. Ruth has shown Naomi love; Ruth has done what Naomi wanted, married a next-of-kin, and borne

38. Levine points out the ambiguity contained in vv. 14-15: Is Naomi's redeemer Boaz or Obed? ("Ruth," 90). Sasson compares the image of Obed on Naomi's lap and at her breast, surrounded by the neighborhood women, to other ancient Near Eastern images in which goddesses suckle human infants who become future kings (*Ruth*, 235).

a child; Ruth has fulfilled her profession of loyalty (1:16-17). Either the women or Naomi or, preferably both, should be addressing Ruth. Is there a reason the women do not address Ruth? Is it because she is a Moabite, because the women who may never have left Judah are xenophobic? Or, one could imagine a group of older women doting over a friend's grandson, during which time they praise Ruth as a third party when she is simply not present. Boaz is similarly absent; perhaps the two of them are taking a break from their child. The text doesn't answer these questions.

The only time the narrative uses the word "love," אהב, is here in verse 15, with the women's affirmation of Ruth's love for Naomi. Whether the women understand this "love" as personal affection or covenant faithfulness is ambiguous; it could be either or both. Ruth committed herself to Naomi (1:16-17) and has followed through on that promise. From the women's perspective, Ruth has accomplished the levirate law insofar as it was possible under the circumstances. When Jonathan professes his love (אהב) for David, it is within the context of covenant faithfulness (1 Sam 20:16-17). Most occurrence of the term אהב refer not to personal love but to a posture toward the other that involves covenant fidelity.[39]

The women attest that Naomi's daughter-in-law is worth more to her than seven sons.[40] As discussed above, this is the kind of love expressed between husband and wife when Elkanah asks Hannah, "Am I not more to you than ten sons?" (1 Sam 2:8). The text does not provide us with Hannah's answer to Elkanah, yet the text speaks to the agony of a woman who wants to bear children but cannot. While neither Hannah nor Naomi could bear a child, a significant other (Elkanah in Hannah's case and Ruth in Naomi's case) could mean more than a plenitude of children. Elkanah beseeches Hannah in her pain to see him as more to her than ten sons, while the women tell Naomi—Naomi does not tell Ruth—that Ruth is worth more to Naomi than seven sons. The similarity between the two verses, 1 Samuel 2:8 and Ruth 4:15, is obvious; in each case a personal relationship is of greater value than multiple children. The difference between the two verses is astounding: Elkanah draws the comparison

39. The covenant faithfulness included in the verb "love" is explored in William L. Moran, "Ancient Near Eastern Background of the Love of God in Deuteronomy," *CBQ* 25 (1963): 77–87. While the title of the article specifies "of God" and "Deuteronomy," the article makes the case more broadly.

40. C. F. Keil and Franz Delitzsch, *Commentary on the Old Testament*, vol. 2: *Joshua, Judges, Ruth, 1–2 Samuel* (Grand Rapids: Eerdmans, 1978), 492, remark, "Seven, as the number of the works of God, is used to denote a large number of sons of a mother whom God has richly blessed with children."

with a question, while in Ruth's case, the generic "women" make an assertion. Like the numbers ten and twelve, seven implies completion and wholeness and signifies that the women value Ruth to the fullest extent. Perhaps the women assume that Naomi similarly values Ruth, or perhaps they are reminding her that she should.

Where is Naomi in all of this? Verse 15 brings us back to Naomi's silence in the face of Ruth's pledge of loyalty, and it forces the reader to ask again: To what extent is the relationship between Naomi and Ruth one-sided? Perhaps Ruth's attraction to Naomi is unreciprocated. Just as the narrator deprives us of knowing the characters' motivations, we are also deprived of knowing feelings. We do not know what Naomi thinks when the women exclaim that Ruth is more than seven sons, particularly after losing the two sons whom she bore. No matter how much Naomi cares for Ruth, Ruth cannot replace Naomi's dead sons. As sometimes happens in conversation, when one is trying to be affirming of another but does not grasp the whole context, one's words can be heart wrenching to the other.

At the end of the women's prayer, Naomi acts (v. 16). The women have assured Naomi of what Ruth has done for her, but again, Naomi gives no indication of her appreciation of Ruth. Naomi takes the child, places him in her bosom, and nurses (literally, became to him for a nurse, אמנת). Is this gesture itself, this claiming of the child, Naomi's expression of appreciation to Ruth? Although other women can function as nurses for birth mothers in the biblical texts (Exod 2:7; 2 Kgs 11:23; 2 Chr 22:11), the record is not strong.[41] Stronger is the record of mothers nursing their own children. Sarah nurses her son Isaac (Gen 21:7); Moses' mother nurses him (Exod 2:8-9); the woman claiming the living child speaks of nursing it (1 Kgs 3:21); Hannah nurses her son Samuel (1 Sam 1:23); and the female speaker in Song 8:1 identifies her brother as having the same mother-nurse as she.

In addition, mothers name their offspring as often as fathers do,[42] but nowhere else in the biblical text is naming done by a group. In the

41. Post-menopausal women can breastfeed, and even women who lack a uterus and ovaries can breastfeed; physically, all that is needed to breastfeed are breasts and a functioning pituitary gland. However, the participle used as a substantive here, אמנת, meaning "foster-mother" or "nurse," is derived from the verb meaning "confirm, support" and occurs only here and in 2 Sam 4:4. It may or may not imply lactation. The more common verb for breastfeeding/nursing is ינק.

42. In Genesis alone, six women name their sons as do six fathers: Eve names her son Seth (4:25); Lot's daughters name their sons Moab and Ben-ammi, respectively (19:37-38); Leah names her sons Reuben (29:32), Simeon (v. 33), Judah (v. 35), Dan (30:6), Naphtali (v. 8), Gad (v. 11), Asher (v. 13), Issachar (v. 18), Zebulun (v. 20), and her daughter Dinah (v. 21). Rachel names her sons Joseph (30:24) and Ben-oni (35:18);

naming, Ruth is displaced, this time not by Naomi but by "the women of the neighborhood." The women assert that a son has been born to Naomi (v. 17), even though physically, Ruth has born the child. The statement implies that Ruth has acted as next-of-kin rather than as mother, in order to give Naomi offspring who will continue her husband's line.[43] By bearing a son, Ruth has provided a future for both women. The women then name the child Obed,[44] which further binds the child not only to Ruth or Naomi but rather to the entire community: "they named him Obed."

The child's name is ambiguous. It can mean "servant of YHWH" or "the serving one." Keil and Delitzsch prefer the second rendering because, given the context, the boy will serve his grandmother.[45] Yet as much as the boy will restore Naomi's life and provide comfort to her in her old age, his service will also extend beyond the life of a single individual. Verse 17 states what will be repeated in the genealogy in 4:18-22, namely, the child who has been born to Naomi (through Ruth) will lead to David.

A contrast occurs between the first three chapters of the narrative and chapter 4. Ruth, through her agency in word and deed, dominates the first three chapters, while the only thing she does in chapter 4 is bear a son. She is not even spoken *about* after verse 14. We could conclude that she died in childbirth;[46] that would explain why Naomi became Obed's nurse. It would also explain why the women, who hardly knew Ruth, would be so generous in their praise of her. And not commenting on Ruth's death would not be so unusual insofar as the only biblical reference to a particular woman's death in childbirth is Rachel's (Gen 35:18; in 1 Sam 4:19-20, the wife of Phineas dies after giving birth, although her death may be prompted less by the birth itself than by the news that the ark had been captured and that her father-in-law and husband had died). However, not commenting on Ruth's death in childbirth would be

---

Shua names her sons Onan (38:4) and Selah (38:5). Fathers also take this role, e.g., Seth names his son Enosh (4:26); Lamech names his son Noah (5:29); Abraham names his son Ishmael (16:15); Judah names his son Er (38:3); Joseph names his firstborn Manasseh (41:51) and his second son Ephraim (v. 52). Both Eve and Adam name Seth (4:25 and 5:3); while Rachel names her son Ben-oni, Jacob names him Benjamin (35:18).

43. Delitzsch comments, "Naomi has become the tribe-mother of a numerous and flourishing family" (*Commentary on the Old Testament*, 2:492).

44. Naming the child is not incidental; his name is his identity. When Solomon prays at the dedication of the temple that YHWH's name be present there (1 Kgs 8:29), he is asking for YHWH to be present. The name stands for the person.

45. Keil and Delitzsch, *Commentary on the Old Testament*, 2:492.

46. According to medieval Jewish tradition, Boaz died the night Obed was conceived (Ruth Zuta 4.14).

inconsistent with the rest of the narrative, which depends on the deaths of Elimelech and his and Naomi's two sons to move forward.

It is also possible that Ruth's status as a foreigner contributes to the silence in chapter 4. The narrative's author shifts the emphasis from Ruth to her descendants, perhaps relegating to the shadows the fact that the ancestor of the men named in the genealogy was a Moabite. Ruth will never become fully incorporated into Israel, even through her marriage and her child. However, this view is inconsistent with other stories of foreign women in the Bible, whose outsider status matters little for their potential to give birth to great men: consider Tamar in Genesis 38 and Bathsheba in 2 Samuel 12 (the wife of a Hittite [2 Sam 11:3], who in 2 Sam 23:34 is identified as the "son of Ahithopehl the Gilonite"). In the New Testament, Matthew's gospel similarly recounts Tamar, Bathsheba (literally "the wife of Uriah"), and Ruth, along with Rahab the Canaanite, as contributors to the line of David and Jesus. In the case of Ruth, it seems that the narrative glories in the fact that Ruth the Moabite is part of the line of David.[47]

A Communal and Egalitarian Ending

There are a couple of disconcerting issues in the conclusion of Ruth. First, why are Naomi and Ruth silent (or silenced) and only the women of the neighborhood speak? Their silence parallels the beginning of the story in chapter 1 where the women who addressed Naomi now exult with her. But while both Naomi and Ruth spoke movingly in the beginning, they are now voiceless. I propose two possibilities as to why the narrative ends by focusing on the neighborhood rather than the individual: first, to show that addressing individuals' needs will have positive repercussions for the community, and, second, because honor in a collectivist society is bestowed by the community at large.

We note that Boaz is also silent, and only the group of male elders spoke at the end, wishing God's blessing on him that his house may be like Perez's. They recognized his sacrificial act as redeemer for one member of the tribe, and the hope is that this act will expand the tribe like Tamar did for Judah. Similarly, Naomi's initiative on behalf of Ruth and Ruth's risk-taking on behalf of Elimelech's lineage became a joyful testimony to

47. Contra Cynthia R. Chapman, who argues that Naomi taking the child as symbolic wet nurse clarifies his "insider Judean ethnicity," while Ruth remains an outsider (*The House of the Mother: The Social Roles of Maternal Kin in Biblical Hebrew Narrative and Poetry*, AYBRL [New Haven: Yale University Press, 2016], 143–49).

the neighborhood of God's *ḥesed*. It was a testimony that extended beyond that particular community's space and time, leading ultimately to the messianic Davidic kingship for the nation.

Second, in a collectivist society, like those in the Mediterranean and Asian regions, the culture discourages praising oneself because that would be seen as shameless boasting. One can certainly give thanks to God, which Naomi had done in 2:20. But the superlative praise of Ruth for being better than seven sons was put in the mouths of other women, not in Ruth's or Naomi's own mouths. This is a fitting way to honor Ruth: despite being a Moabite, her worth is publicly recognized by all around her.

Another issue often highlighted is that despite the feminist focus on Naomi and Ruth, the narrative seems to end with an androcentric emphasis on women playing their role merely as mothers supporting the male hero—in this case a son, Obed, and ultimately a male king, David. All the women's sufferings, supporting, and shrewd planning were simply to produce a man who could save them all. That is one way of reading the narrative, but I would offer a more egalitarian perspective that subverts the patriarchal domination.

In the first place, the news of Obed's birth is brought to Naomi in 4:17 using the same formula as when a son is announced to a father, e.g., Jeremiah 20:15, i.e., "A son is born to/for [preposition לְ] 'personal name or pronoun.'" Here in the book of Ruth, a woman is given as much honor as a man. In the second place, the name Obed is a participle of the verb עבד, "serve/worship." When reading backward from 4:17, the idea of serving is appropriate, for Naomi's grandson will serve as her "restorer of life and nourisher of her old age" (4:15), just as Naomi will serve him as his nurse/foster mother (4:16). At the same time, as one reads forward to the rest of 4:17 and discovers that Obed is the grandfather of David, then the idea of worshiping God is also a suitable double meaning because David is known as a worshiper *par excellence*. Bringing the two ideas together, a true king and worshiper of God is one who serves, and he is especially to support those whom circumstances have deprived of material or social well-being, are disenfranchised, including women, widows, the elderly, and the aliens.

Third, even though the book ends with a patrilineal record, the reader can look back and realize that without the cooperation of widows and alien women, there would be no male genealogy to speak of. It is the concern and courage of women that made a difference to the kingdom of God in both the Old and New Testaments. God defends and effects God's will through the weak and powerless. Without the women there would be no messianic king, even though that king may have to be male in a patriarchal world. This does not elevate women over men or vice versa, for as much as women serve the men, so are men to serve the women. What matters in the end is not his or her kingdom but God's kingdom, a kingdom that should reflect the character of God revealed through the book of Ruth.

Maggie Low

The genealogy that follows and that concludes the narrative, like most of the genealogies in the Old Testament, does not list any non-Israelites or any women.[48]

All-Male, Israelite Genealogy: Does Tradition Triumph? (4:18-22)

In the final verses of the narrative, the characters cease to speak and the narrator concludes with a genealogy. The book of Ruth begins with a patriarchal framework, three men and a woman; Elimelech makes the decision to go (and bring his family) to Moab. Now, the narrative returns in verses 18-22 to a traditional patriarchal conclusion. Ruth 1:1-7 records the deaths of several men; 4:18-22, documenting the family line, records the births of several men. There is almost unanimous agreement among historical-critical scholars that verses 18-22 are an appendix to the Ruth narrative and not an original part of it.[49] In contrast to this view, Adele Berlin—on literary grounds, in seeking to understand the poetic function of the verses—sees the genealogy not as an addition but as an integral part of the narrative.[50] She notes that the characters and events in Ruth are independent of the characters and events in Genesis through

48. Levine, "Ruth," 85 and 90.

49. See, for example, Campbell, *Ruth*, 172; Jeremy Schipper, *Ruth: A New Translation with Introduction and Commentary*, AYBRL 7D (New Haven: Yale University Press, 2016), 186; Sasson, *Ruth*, 178–87, who digests the analyses of L. P. Smith ("Introduction and Exegesis of the Book of Ruth," *Interpreter's Bible*, vol. 2, ed. George Arthur Buttrick [Nashville: Abingdon 1953], 851); H. H. Rowley, *The Servant of the Lord and Other Essays on the Old Testament*, 2nd ed. (Oxford: Blackwell, 1965), 192–94, and others.

50. Adele Berlin, *Poetics and Interpretation of Biblical Narrative*, ed. David M. Gunn, BLS 9 (Sheffield: Almond Press, 1983), 110.

Ruth 4:18-22

[18]Now these are the descendants
of Perez: Perez became the father of
Hezron, [19]Hezron of Ram, Ram of Am-
minadab, [20]Amminadab of Nahshon,
Nahshon of Salmon, [21]Salmon of Boaz,
Boaz of Obed, [22] Obed of Jesse, and
Jesse of David.

Kings and that the genealogy situates the characters and events in Ruth among the body of known personalities. She even points out that Boaz is highlighted as the seventh in the genealogical line (Perez, Hezron, Ram, Amminadab, Nashon, Salmon, and then Boaz). However, Berlin's argument could also account for the genealogy as an addition, in that it would create a link between an otherwise independent account and a broader biblical cast of characters.

Both perspectives, that the verses are an appendix and that they are part of the original narrative, have merit. Whereas verse 17 presents a shortened genealogy and also traces David back to Obed, the additional verses expand the genealogy while also repeating key components. Perhaps the repetition is all part of the core story (the narrative often repeats significant information—Bethlehem, Moabite, and so on); however, one could also imagine a process of textual expansion to the ending of the story. In this latter case, verse 17 could be the original ending, or perhaps even a first stage of expansion, followed by the longer genealogy.

Genealogies are not uncommon in the Old Testament, although, as Koosed points out, in Hebrew narrative a genealogy usually begins rather than ends a story.[51] Genesis 5 traces the descendants of Adam from creation to the sons of Noah. Genesis 10 traces the descendants of Noah's three sons—Shem, Ham, and Japeth—"by their families, their languages, their lands, and their nations." The final verse of chapter 10 indicates that the families of Noah's sons "spread abroad on the earth after the flood" (Gen 6–9). First Chronicles 1–9 contains the longest biblical genealogy, tracing humankind from Adam through all the families

51. Jennifer Koosed, *Gleaning Ruth: A Biblical Heroine and Her Afterlives*, Studies on Personalities of the Old Testament (Columbia: University of South Carolina Press, 2011), 120. Koosed's examples include 1 Sam 1:1; Esth 2:5; 1 Chr 1–9. The New Testament limits its genealogies to Matt 1:1-17, which traces Jesus back to Abraham, and to Luke 3:23-38, which traces Jesus back to Adam.

of the twelve tribes of Israel.[52] First Chronicles 2:5-12 repeats with slight expansion most of the genealogy found in Ruth 4:18-22.[53]

Insofar as verses 18-22 comprise a genealogy, the passage is traditional (father to son). What makes the genealogy special is not simply the men who are named but rather the women who make the genealogy happen. The genealogy begins with the descendants of Perez; Perez is the son of Tamar. It continues through Boaz, the husband of Ruth; Obed, the son of Ruth; Jesse, the grandson of Ruth; and David, the great-grandson of Ruth. While the genealogy does not name either Tamar or Ruth, the genealogy would not exist without these two important female characters.

Peter Lau argues that genealogy is not central to Israelite identity in the same way that *ḥesed* is,[54] though neither should one dismiss genealogies in order to highlight the integral role of *ḥesed* in Israelite self-understanding. The Bible highlights the importance of lineage in the continuation of the Israelite people, who descended from a long line of ancestors united under a particular covenant with YHWH, the God of Israel. Whether or not all the names listed in the genealogies are historical personalities, cumulatively they represent the past of a people while bringing the people and community into the present. Narratively, genealogies function as chains, connecting one major period or series of events to another. Often they are long and consist mostly of names that contain few if any identifying features.[55]

The final five verses of the book of Ruth are a case in point. While some names are referenced elsewhere in the Bible, others occur only here. All

52. A short postexilic genealogy can be found in Nehemiah 12:10-11—from Jeshua to Joiakim, to Eliashib, to Joiada, to Jonathan, to Jaddua.

53. Campbell (*Ruth*, 170) notes that the opening of the Ruth genealogy is similar to that of the P genealogies in Genesis (chaps. 5 and 10) and to Numbers 3:1, even though it corresponds to the content of the genealogy of 1 Chronicles 2.

54. Lau, "Another Postcolonial Reading of the Book of Ruth," 24. Lau's perspective is distinctly Christian; Jews may not agree with this perspective, based on the importance of lineage to Jewish identity as a people. For traditional Judaism, the "children of Israel" are, literally, the children of Jacob/Israel.

55. This is true also of the genealogies in the New Testament. In tracing Jesus back to Adam (and God, Luke 3:23-38), or tracing forward from Abraham to Jesus (Matt 1:2-16), the goal is to provide a pedigree for Jesus. The Old Testament provides no information about some of the named men and, therefore, readers of the Bible know nothing about them. Whereas Jews read the genealogies as part of annual or triennial Torah readings, Christians do not read the Old Testament genealogies at their liturgies.

we know is that this person was a "place marker" between the man who preceded him and the man who followed, as part of the same family line.

For Lau, because Ruth is a Moabite, she is outside the genealogy; her parents were not Israelites and therefore she can never be within the genealogical line of Israel.[56] Despite her best efforts to assimilate into Israelite society (e.g., caring for her widowed mother-in-law, gleaning) and even the public recognition of her change in status to an Israelite (Ruth 4:11-12), she still maintains elements of her Moabite origin.[57] In recognizing Ruth's Moabite-Israelite identity, early Jewish interpretation of the text made Ruth the role model of conversion.[58]

Then, as now, there, as here, immigration and intermarriage do not and cannot erase one's past. Nor should they. Ruth will always have been born a Moabite and will have lived and married in Moab. She was not born in Judah, nor did she live her early years or marry her first husband in Judah. That will never change. If genealogies are about bloodlines, it is not surprising that she is omitted. But the question that Lau addresses, the question that must be asked today, is whether bloodlines should justify exclusion from belonging. For example, in Jewish tradition today as in antiquity, converts become members of the people Israel. Lau's conviction that there are more important elements to belonging than bloodlines is what, for him, identifies Ruth as a true Israelite. She integrated into Israel by adopting Israel's commitment to *ḥesed*, which she practices in choosing to adopt Naomi's land and people and even her God (1:8, 16-17). Therefore, she becomes incorporated, to the extent she is able, into the Israelite people. Ruth's execution of *ḥesed*, that posture of behavior attributed to Israel's YHWH and associated with the Israelites' best behavior and highest ideals, has priority over her ethnicity and, even though it does not eliminate her ethnicity, it allows Ruth entrance into the Israelite community.

Many immigrants to the United States become citizens by embracing the values of the US Constitution. Many other immigrants are deprived of the opportunity "to convert to citizenship," no matter how many years

56. E.g., although 1 Kgs 14:21 identifies Naamah, an Ammonite, as the mother of Rehoboam, the verse does not occur in a genealogy.

57. Lau, "Another Postcolonial Reading of the Book of Ruth," 24–25.

58. Leila Leah Bronner, *From Eve to Esther: Rabbinic Reconstructions of Biblical Women* (Louisville: Westminster John Knox, 1994), 63–67 cites b. Yebam. 47a-b; Ruth Rab. 2.22; cf. 2.12; 5.12; b. Sanh. 56a; Ruth Zuta 49, vs. 44, and Maimonides, *Mishneh Torah, Sefer Shoftim, Hilkhot Melakhim* 8:10; 10:12 with respect to Ruth's conversion.

they have lived and worked in the United States and no matter how deep their commitment to the values of the US Constitution, because they are undocumented. Strict adherence to current law or Executive Order will result in their deportation, ignoring their time-proven commitment to the country and its values.

Complementing the importance of *ḥesed* is the genealogy contained in the final four verses of the narrative. Therefore, *ḥesed* and genealogy work together. Verse 18 declares what the following verses will do: enumerate the descendants of Perez. The genealogy goes back only as far as Perez; he was the founder of the family of Judah, to which Elimelech and Boaz belonged.[59] Perez, as the reader will recall, was the son of Tamar and her father-in-law (Gen 38:29). When Judah failed to fulfill the requirement of levirate law by giving Tamar his third son Shelah, Tamar took matters into her own hands. Knowing that Judah was going up to Timnah, she took off her widow's garments, wrapped herself in a veil,[60] and sat down at the entrance of a town en route to Timnah. When Judah came by, he read the fact that she was sitting at the town's entrance as a sign that she was a prostitute and propositioned her. By covering her face with her veil, Tamar was able to hide her identity and could thus "play the prostitute." She conceived and bore Perez as well as his twin, Zerah. Zerah's hand came out of Tamar's womb first but then receded and Perez came out, for which reason the midwife named the child Perez, meaning "breach."[61]

There are ten other references to Perez in the Old Testament,[62] all in genealogies. While the quantity of references does not guarantee that

59. Keil and Delitzsch, *Commentary on the Old Testament*, 2:492.

60. When Rebekah, having not yet met Isaac, learns that he is the man in the field, she wraps herself in her veil (Gen 24:65), perhaps as a gesture of modesty or perhaps to enhance her beauty, or perhaps even as a sign of availability. For Tamar to encounter Judah, she takes off her widow's clothing and dons a veil. After her encounter with Judah, she removes the veil and again dons the garments of widowhood (Gen 38:19). The unavailable who had made herself available is no longer available.

61. Sasson, *Ruth*, 187.

62. Genesis 46:12 lists the names of Judah's sons, including Perez, and his offspring who came to Egypt. Numbers 26:20-21 lists descendants of the sons of Jacob, including Perez, who came out of Egypt. First Chronicles 2:4 forefronts Tamar, while v. 5 names Perez's sons. First Chronicles 4:1 lists five sons of Judah, including Perez. First Chronicles 9:4 and Nehemiah 11:4 list a few of Perez's descendants who lived in Jerusalem after the exile while v. 6 adds that they numbered 468 valiant warriors. First Chronicles 27:3 identifies Jashobeam, a descendant of Perez who served King David as "chief of all the commanders of the army for the first month."

he is a historical person, it does suggest that he is a known one, if only by the repetition with which he is named. This technique of repetition fosters the idea that Perez is valuable, and a key purpose of the genealogy in Ruth is to establish the line of David through Perez.

Where Perez is listed in the genealogy of 1 Chronicles (2:4), the text also names Tamar: "His [Judah's] daughter-in-law Tamar also bore him Perez and Zerah." This is the only genealogy in the Old Testament to name Tamar, and the inclusion of any woman in an Old Testament genealogy is very rare.[63] The genealogy of Moses and Aaron names Aaron's wife and Nadab's mother, Elisheba (Exod 6:23), and a census lists Jochebed as the wife of Amram and the mother of Moses, Aaron, and daughter Miriam (Num 26:59). Just as the women who bore Nadab and Moses, Aaron and Mirian are not to be discounted, neither is the woman who bore Perez. We should also recall the genealogy in Judith 8:1, which begins with Judith and traces her lineage back multiple generations to "Israel."

In addition to the inclusion of Perez and Hezron here in verse 18, they are listed in two genealogies in the New Testament. Matthew 1:2-16 begins with Abraham and traces his descendants through Perez and Hezron (v. 3) and David (v. 6) to Jesus; Luke 3:23-38 traces Jesus back through David (v. 31) and Hezron and Perez (v. 33) to Adam.

Hezron,[64] named in Genesis 46:12; Numbers 26:21; and 1 Chronicles 2:5 as the son of Perez,[65] is also named in 1 Chronicles 2:9 and likely also in 1 Chronicles 2:18, 21, 24, 25. These verses are all part of genealogies. We know nothing about him except who his father was and the name of his son. As an individual, he contributes nothing to the Ruth narrative; however, he provides the necessary genealogical link that takes David back to Judah, the son of Jacob the "patriarch." His name means "to be green,"[66] which may foretell fertility.

63. In the New Testament, the inclusion of women in genealogies is also rare; Luke's genealogy of Jesus contains no women, and Matthew's long genealogy contains only four: Tamar, Rahab, Ruth, and the wife of Uriah (Matt 1:3-6).

64. In some ancient manuscripts his name is Hezrom but the final letters (on/om) are interchangeable in other Hebrew names, e.g., Gershon/Gershom, and as far as we know, the difference is not of significance. See Sasson, *Ruth*, 187; see also Campbell, *Ruth*, 170.

65. In addition to Hezron, the son of Perez, Reuben's son is also named Hezron (Gen 36:9; Exod 6:14; Num 26:6, and 1 Chr 5:3). First Chronicles 4:1 seems to confuse the two men. In Joshua 15:3 Hezron refers to a place.

66. Sasson, *Ruth*, 187.

In addition to his occurrence in Ruth 4:19, Ram,[67] the second son of Hezron, appears in only three other places in the Old Testament: in 1 Chronicles 2:9; 1 Chronicles 2:10;[68] and Job 32:2, where the reference is to the family of which Ram is an ancestor. His name means "lofty,"[69] which may justify his place in a lofty genealogy.

Amminadab, Ram's son, appears with his father in 1 Chronicles 2:9; in 1 Chronicles 2:10 he is identified as both Ram's son and Nahshon's father.[70] In contrast to Perez, Hezron, and Ram, Amminadab's name emerges in narrative as the father of Nahshon (Num 1:7; 2:3; 7:12, 17; 10:14). Amminadab is a combination of two Hebrew words meaning "uncle or kinsman" and "to be generous, noble, munificent,"[71] a name also consistent with the genealogy in which he is included.

Campbell's commentary[72] identifies Amminadab in Exodus 6:23 as "Aaron's father-in-law" while the biblical text actually identifies him as Elisheba's father (Elisheba is Aaron's wife). This is one of only three verses in the entire Old Testament in which a woman appears in a genealogy. Not surprisingly, then, Campbell replaces the female name with a male. Looking at the texts from a feminist perspective, however, we recognize how often women's experiences have been left out, later attributed to men, or in other ways been rendered invisible.

Nahshon, Amminadab's son, appears in 1 Chronicles 2:10-11 and with his sister as Elisheba's brother in Exodus 6:23. Nahshon's name has several possible sources; it could mean "bronze," "to practice divination," or "to be full, healthy." Sasson suggests that it comes from the noun "serpent," based on the fact that other Old Testament names are also derived from snakes (i.e., Levi and Saraph).[73] Whether the name alludes

67. Variations of the name Ram, Arran and Aram, are found in LXX versions. See Campbell, *Ruth*, 171; Sasson, *Ruth*, 187–88.

68. The name Ram appears in 1 Chronicles 2:25 and 27 also, but there the reference is to a later descendant.

69. Sasson, *Ruth*, 188.

70. The Amminadab identified in 1 Chronicles 6:22 is a son of Kohath of the tribe of Levi. The Amminadab identified in 1 Chronicles 15:10 and 11 is a contemporary of David.

71. Sasson, *Ruth*, 189.

72. Campbell, *Ruth*, 171. Campbell also identifies Bathsheba as the not-unwilling adulteress (*Ruth*, 173) though many feminists, recognizing the power differential between Bathsheba and the king, question her willingness. Still others see her as seducing David and so as the active agent.

73. Sasson, *Ruth*, 189.

to the bronze serpent that Moses made in the desert (Num 21:9), or to something godly or healthy, the implications are all positive.

Nahshon is the first among the persons listed in this genealogy to appear as a narrative character. Although he does not speak, he acts: he assists in taking the census (Num 1:7); he leads the people of Judah when they camp (Num 2:3); he presents his offerings first, at the time of the altar's dedication (Num 7:12, 17); and he heads the whole company of Judah when they depart from Sinai (Num 10:14). Rabbinic tradition credits Nahshon with exceptional courage at the Red Sea during the exodus. According to the Midrash, Nahshon was the first Israelite to enter the sea; only after he entered did the waters part so that the Israelites felt safe to cross. He was also the first to bring dedicatory offerings to the tabernacle, acting as a leader and role model.[74] One might conclude that Nahshon's activities merit remembrance, except that Nahshon's son hardly appears. Apart from the genealogy in Ruth, Nahshon's son and Boaz's father, Salmon, appears only in 1 Chronicles 2:11, where his name is "Salma."[75] According to Matthew 1:5, Rahab is the wife of Salmon and therefore the mother of Boaz.

Boaz,[76] Salmon's son, is found only here and in the genealogy of 1 Chronicles 2 (vv. 11 and 12). The genealogy in 1 Chronicles 2, like the genealogies in Ruth, names Boaz and not Mahlon (who is not named in any genealogy) as the father of Obed. While Ruth's absence from the genealogies can be attributed to her being a woman, or to her being a foreigner, or both, one might expect Mahlon to appear as Obed's father if Boaz were fulfilling a variation of the levirate law. On the other hand, no Old Testament genealogy contains the name of a dead husband whose widow has given birth according to the law. There is no provision in the law that requires such an inclusion.

Boaz's son, Obed, who represents an end to which the entire narrative has been moving (see v. 17), is Ruth's son as well. Obed becomes

74. B. Soṭah 37a and Num. Rab. 13:9. See Tamara Eskenazi and Tikva Frymer-Kensky, *The JPS Bible Commentary: Ruth* (Philadelphia: Jewish Publication Society of America, 2011), 94–95.

75. Campbell points out the variations on the name of Nahshon's son, even in Hebrew: Salmon, Salmah, Salma. Since the name, variations withstanding, does not appear often in the biblical text, an attempt to determine the more accurate rendering is futile (*Ruth*, 171–72). Determining the meaning of his name, according to Sasson, is likewise futile (*Ruth*, 190).

76. On the derivation of Boaz's name, see the discussion at 2:1. Matthew 1:5 identifies Rahab as Boaz's mother.

the ancestor of King David, yet he appears only three times in the entire Old Testament: in Ruth (4:17, 21) and in 1 Chronicles 2:12.[77]

Obed becomes the father of Jesse. The name Jesse can mean "being, existence" if it is derived from the particle יש, or "to resemble, be equal to" if it is derived from the root ישה.[78] Jesse, like Nahshon, appears not only in genealogies (e.g., here and in 1 Chr 2:12-13) but also in 1–2 Samuel, 1 Kings, 1–2 Chronicles, Psalm 72:20, and Isaiah 1:1, 10. When the Lord sends Samuel to Jesse to anoint one of his sons king, Jesse presents all of his sons and then, finally, the youngest, David (1 Sam 16:1, 3, 5, 8-11). Jesse is instrumental in David's meeting Saul (1 Sam 16:18-20, 22), which leads to David playing the lyre for Saul; Jesse is recognized as David's father after David kills Goliath (1 Sam 17:12-13, 17, 20, 58).[79] The reader might presume that Jesse is a man of some status in the society: he is a descendant of Boaz, and the Lord sends Samuel to seek out one of his sons to be king. On the other hand, the fact that the Lord chooses the least likely, the youngest son, David, a shepherd who lacks heavy armor and who kills Goliath with a slingshot, may indicate that Jesse was a man of more modest means. In any case, though Jesse speaks twice (1 Sam 16:11 and 17:17), he is never presented as his own person. Everything he does is in relationship to his son, the future King David.

The last few paragraphs have provided details about the men in the genealogy at the end of the book of Ruth. They are not particularly feminist in any way—*except that* they serve, by their detail, to reinforce the patriarchal contents of genealogies in general and of a society that documents men and men's roles and accomplishments (even when they are not significant), and thereby erases women and their accomplishments. That kind of society feminists seek to resist and reject.

77. Obed occurs three times in the New Testament: twice in v. 5 of Matthew's genealogy (1:5) and once in Luke's (3:32). The name Obed appears in 1 Chronicles 2:37, 38, and again in 1 Chronicles 11:47 and 26:7, and in 2 Chronicles 23:1, but none of these references is to the Obed who is Boaz's son and Jesse's father. Two of the references are to a contemporary of David, and the other seems to be to a descendant of David.

78. Sasson, *Ruth*, 190.

79. When Saul is angry with David he refers to him as the "son of Jesse" rather than calling him by name (1 Sam 20:27, 30-31; 22:7-9, 13). "Son of Jesse" stands as a synonym for David (1 Sam 25:10; 1 Kgs 12:16; 1 Chr 12:18; 2 Chr 10:16; Isa 11:1) as does "root of Jesse" (Isa 11:10). Jesse is identified as the father of David in 2 Samuel 20:1; 23:1; 2 Chronicles 10:14; 29:26; Psalm 72:20. In 2 Chronicles 11:18 Mahalath, Rehoboam's wife, is identified as David's granddaughter (daughter of David's son Jerimoth) and Jesse's great-granddaughter also (daughter of Abihail who was daughter of Eliab who was a son of Jesse).

The final descendant of Perez named in the genealogy is David himself. The ending is stark: Jesse [became the father] of David. Yet if we were to trace references to David throughout the Old Testament, one would find them, beginning in 1 Samuel, almost everywhere. The issue in the book of Ruth is not what David says and does or what he becomes. It is that he is born, and he is indebted to Ruth for his birth.[80] Any audience for the book of Ruth, whether living in the preexilic period or only later in the Persian Period, could fill in what the text does not elaborate.

Whereas our book concludes with five verses of male genealogy that effectively exclude women, a feminist commentary cannot. Ruth may be excluded from the final genealogy, but she is responsible for the lives of the last names within it. Not knowing how conception takes place, people in antiquity concluded, incorrectly, that male ejaculation provided that which becomes a human being. Males then father children while women nourish the seed until birth, but what is born, whether male or female, is a nourished male seed. This biological view makes male genealogies make sense. It was millennia after these texts were produced before people came to understand the role of the egg in human biology. Slowly genealogies have been changing. Ancestry.com is as interested in female ancestors as in male ancestors, but this is again another millennium removed from the writing of Ruth. We cannot deny the limitations of knowledge millennia ago, but neither should we repeat them.

80. Many feminist theologians have commented on the disconnect, that a woman gave birth to Jesus, that Mary brought Jesus into the world, but yet a woman is, to this day, not able to celebrate the Eucharist in the Roman Catholic Church or Eastern Orthodoxy or many conservative Protestant denominations.

Afterword

The biblical book of Ruth tells the story of one family and, in so doing, uncovers for its readers many aspects of the rich world of ancient Israel while introducing us to the lived expression of some of the peoples' values and customs. A famine causes the family to emigrate from Bethlehem of Judah and immigrate to the neighboring country of Moab, where they settle and live for many years. There, the two Israelite sons marry Moabite women. But after the deaths of Naomi's husband and sons, she desires to go home. While Orpah, one of her daughters-in-law, stays in Moab, Ruth emigrates from Moab and accompanies Naomi back to Judah. We witness Ruth's concrete expressions of loyalty and perseverance, including gleaning in the fields, a practice that Israelite law allowed the poor, and her willingness to marry a next-of-kin to Naomi (perhaps a variation of the levirate law) in order to provide a son for her dead husband and preserve the family line. We witness the women's courage in the face of hardship and loss, their agency, perseverance, ingenuity, and risk-taking. The three women—Naomi, Ruth, and Orpah—make decisions that affect their and others' futures. And, of course, there is Boaz, the person of privilege, who also expresses concrete acts of loyalty and care. He sees, listens, and responds to the one who needs his help.

It is hoped that women and men today can identify with the characters in the book. While not all of us have been forced to leave our land because of famine and poverty, some of us have, and others have been forced to flee because of war. Still others leave in search of a better life, if not for themselves, then for their children. Contemporary women and men share Naomi's and Ruth's pain; they know the mixed feelings, the sense of loss, of not feeling welcome, of not fully belonging. Still others, like Orpah, choose to stay while watching loved ones leave. Even those of us who have not emigrated from our country can identify with the feeling of leaving home and moving away, of feeling like the alien in a foreign land. We can identify with loss that comes from separation and death and with difficult decisions in which we choose one path over another. Like Ruth and Naomi, sometimes we are those on the margins, who struggle to stay afloat, while at times we are those in positions of power like Boaz, whose responsibility it is to stop, listen, and respond, to love the neighbor and the stranger as ourselves. No matter what a person's circumstances, the Ruth narrative provides role models of strong character.

Our commentary, and the bibliography at its end, is replete with women (and men) who have added to our knowledge of the Ruth narrative, who have shared feminist wisdom regarding the text's continued vitality, and who have challenged accepted interpretations. We have tried to provide, in the introduction, in the body of the commentary, and in the footnotes, insights from the history of interpretation as well as insights from our contemporaries. Our work leads us to conclude that while the book of Ruth can be read as reinforcing the stereotype of a woman's happiness resting in marriage and motherhood, it doesn't have to be. Rather, it can also be read as revealing a strong and independent woman who is clearly responsible for her own decisions, who practices loving kindness, who is an agent of her own history and of the history of the people of Israel. Whether Mahlon and Chilion "raped" Ruth and Orpah, as some have suggested, or whether Ruth was sexually attracted to Naomi or the two women were in love with each other, as suggested by others, we do not know nor can we ever know. Yet our colleagues have helped us to see hints in the texts that make these suggestions possible. By so doing, they have opened up the text in new and important ways. Viewing the text through a feminist lens is meant to be inclusive and liberating, and we have tried to do this. We hope you have found the contributions of the diverse voices represented here helpful in the journey toward understanding, integration, and inclusivity.

Bibliography

Ackerman, Susan. *When Heroes Love: The Ambiguity of Eros in the Stories of Gilgamesh and David.* GTR. New York: Columbia University Press, 2005.

Aelred of Rievaulx. *On Spiritual Friendship.* Translated by Marsha L. Dutton and Lawrence C. Braceland. CF 5. Collegeville, MN: Cistercian Publications, 2010.

Alexander, T. Desmond, and Brian S. Rosner, eds. *New Dictionary of Biblical Theology.* Leister: Inter-Varsity Press, 2000.

Allam, Schafik. "Women as Owners of Immovables in Pharaonic Egypt." In *Women's Earliest Records from Ancient Egypt and Western Asia,* edited by Barbara S. Lesko, 123–35. BJS 166. Atlanta: Scholars Press, 1989.

Alonso-Schökel, Luis. *The Inspired Word: Scripture in the Light of Language and Literature.* New York: Herder and Herder, 1965.

Alter, Robert. *The Art of Biblical Narrative.* Rev. ed. New York: Basic Books, 2011.

Alter, Robert, and Frank Kermode, eds. *The Literary Guide to the Bible.* Cambridge: Harvard University Press, 1987.

Aschkenasy, Nehama. "Language as Female Empowerment in Ruth." In *Reading Ruth: Contemporary Women Reclaim a Sacred Story,* edited by Judith A. Kates and Gail Twersky Reimer, 111–24. New York: Ballantine Books, 1994.

Astour, Michael C. *Hellenosemitica: An Ethnic and Cultural Study in West Semitic Impact on Mycenaean Greece.* Leiden: Brill, 1967.

Avruch, Sheila, and Alicia Puente Cackley. "Savings Achieved by Giving WIC Benefits to Women Prenatally." *Public Health Records* 110 (1995): 27–34.

Bach, Alice, ed. *Women in the Bible: A Reader.* New York: Routledge, 1998.

Bailey, Randall C., Tat Siong Benny Liew, and Fernando F. Segovia, eds. *They Were All Together in One Place? Toward Minority Biblical Criticism.* SemeiaSt 57. Atlanta: SBL Press, 2009.

Batcher, Dennis. "Hebrew Calendar of the Old Testament." www.crivoice.org/calendar.html.

Beattie, Derek R. G. *Jewish Exegesis of the Book of Ruth.* Sheffield: Sheffield Academic, 1977.

Beattie, Derek R. G., and J. Stanley McIvor, trans. *Targums of Ruth and Chronicles.* ArBib 19. Collegeville, MN: Liturgical Press, 1994.

Berlin, Adele. *Poetics and Interpretation of Biblical Narrative.* Edited by David M. Gunn. BLS 9. Sheffield: Almond Press, 1983.

———. "Ruth and the Continuity of Israel." In *Reading Ruth: Contemporary Women Reclaim a Sacred Story*, edited by Judith A. Kates and Gail Twersky Reimer, 255–60. New York: Ballantine Books, 1994.

Berquist, Jon L. "Resistance and Accommodation in the Persian Empire." In *In the Shadow of Empire: Reclaiming the Bible as a History of Faithful Resistance*, edited by Richard A. Horsley, 41–58. Louisville: Westminster John Knox, 2008.

———. "Role Differentiation in the Book of Ruth." *JSOT* 57 (1993): 23–37.

Bledstein, Adrien J. "Female Companionships: If the Book of Ruth Were Written by a Woman . . . ." In *A Feminist Companion to Ruth*, edited by Athalya Brenner, 116–33. FCB 3. Sheffield: Sheffield Academic, 1993.

Brenner, Athalya. "Female Social Behaviour: Two Descriptive Patterns within the 'Birth of the Hero' Paradigm." *VT* 36 (1986): 257–73.

———. *I Am . . .: Biblical Women Tell Their Own Stories.* Minneapolis: Fortress, 2005.

———. "Naomi and Ruth." In *A Feminist Companion to Ruth*, edited by Athalya Brenner, 70–84. FCB 3. Sheffield: Sheffield Academic, 1993.

———. "Naomi and Ruth: Further Reflections." In *A Feminist Companion to Ruth*, edited by Athalya Brenner, 140–45. FCB 3. Sheffield: Sheffield Academic, 1993.

———. "Ruth as a Foreign Worker and the Politics of Exogamy." In *Ruth and Esther*, edited by Athalya Brenner, 158–62. FCB 3, 2nd ser. Sheffield: Sheffield Academic, 1999.

———, ed. *A Feminist Companion to Ruth.* FCB 3. Sheffield: Sheffield Academic, 1993.

———, ed. *Ruth and Esther.* FCB 3, 2nd ser. Sheffield: Sheffield Academic, 1999.

Brenner, Athalya, and Fokkelien van Dijk-Hemmes. *On Gendering Texts: Female and Male Voices in the Hebrew Bible.* Leiden: Brill, 1993.

Brenner, Athalya, and J. W. van Henten, eds. *Food and Drink in the Biblical Worlds.* Atlanta: SBL Press, 1999.

Breslin, Susannah. "Letters from Johns." http://lettersfromjohns.blogspot.com/. 2008–2009.

———. "Letters from Working Girls." http://lettersfromworkinggirls.blogspot.com/. 2008–2009.

Bright, John. *A History of Israel.* 4th ed. Louisville: Westminster John Knox, 2000.

Bronner, Leila Leah. *From Eve to Esther: Rabbinic Reconstructions of Biblical Women.* Louisville: Westminster John Knox, 1994.

———. "A Thematic Approach to Ruth in Rabbinic Literature." In *A Feminist Companion to Ruth*, edited by Athalya Brenner, 146–69. FCB 3. Sheffield: Sheffield Academic, 1993.

Brown, Francis, S. R. Driver, and C. A. Briggs. *Hebrew and English Lexicon of the Old Testament*. Oxford: Oxford University Press, 1972.

Brown, Raymond E. *The Birth of the Messiah: A Commentary on the Infancy Narratives in the Gospels of Matthew and Luke*. New York: Doubleday, 1977.

Bush, Frederic W. *Ruth, Esther*. WBC 9. Dallas: Word Books, 1996.

Campbell, Edward F., Jr. *Ruth*. AB 7. New York: Doubleday, 1975.

Caspi, Mishael Maswari, and Rachel S. Havrelock. *Women on the Biblical Road: Ruth, Naomi, and the Female Journey*. Lanham, MD: University Press of America, 1996.

Chan, Man Ki. *A Comparative Study of Jewish Commentaries and Patristic Literature on the Book of Ruth*. PhD diss., University of Pretoria, 2010.

Chapman, Cynthia R. *The House of the Mother: The Social Roles of Maternal Kin in Biblical Hebrew Narrative and Poetry*. AYBRL. New Haven: Yale University Press, 2016.

Cohen, Jonathan. "Why Milk and Honey." www.uhmc.sunysb.edu/surgery/m&h.html.

Collins, C. John. "Ambiguity and Theology in Ruth: Ruth 1:21 and 2:20." *Presbyterion* 19 (1993): 97–102.

Commager, Henry Steele. *The Blue and the Gray*. New York: Wings Books, Random House, 1996.

Counihan, Carole, and Penny Van Esterik, eds. *Food and Culture: A Reader*. 2nd ed. New York: Routledge, 2008.

Coxon, Peter W. "Was Naomi a Scold? A Response to Fewell and Gunn." *JSOT* 45 (1989): 25–37.

Crowell, Bradley. "Postcolonial Studies and the Hebrew Bible." *CurBR* 7 (2009): 217–44.

Culley, Robert C. *Studies in the Structure of Hebrew Narrative*. SemeiaSup 62. Philadelphia: Fortress, 1976.

Darr, Kathryn P. *Far More Precious than Jewels: Perspectives on Biblical Women*. Gender and the Biblical Tradition. Louisville: Westminster John Knox, 1991.

Day, Linda, and Carolyn Pressler, eds. *Engaging the Bible in a Gendered World: An Introduction to Feminist Biblical Interpretation; In Honor of Katharine Doob Sakenfeld*. Louisville: Westminster John Knox Press, 2006.

Dombrowski, Katja. "Sex Tourism: Dubious Reputation." March 20, 2015. http://www.dande.eu/en/article/cambodia-seen-heaven-paedophiles-and-sex-tourists.

Donaldson, Laura E. "The Sign of Orpah: Reading Ruth through Native Eyes." In *Vernacular Hermeneutics*, edited by R. S. Sugirtharajah, 20–36. Atlanta: SBL Press, 2001. And in *Ruth and Esther*, ed. Athalya Brenner, 130–44. FCB 3, 2nd ser. Sheffield: Sheffield Academic, 1999.

Dube, Musa A. *Postcolonial Feminist Interpretation of the Bible*. St. Louis: Chalice, 2000.

———, ed. *Other Ways of Reading: African Women and the Bible*. Atlanta: SBL Press, 2001.

———. "The Unpublished Letters of Orpah to Ruth." In *Ruth and Esther*, edited by Athalya Brenner, 145–50. FCB 3, 2nd ser. Sheffield: Sheffield Academic, 1999.

Duncan, Celine. "The Book of Ruth: On Boundaries, Love and Truth." In *Take Back the Word: A Queer Reading of the Bible*, edited by Robert E. Goss and Mona West. Cleveland: Pilgrim Press, 2000.

Eskenazi, Tamara, and Tikva Frymer-Kensky. *The JPS Bible Commentary: Ruth*. Philadelphia: Jewish Publication Society of America, 2011.

Exum, J. Cheryl. *Plotted, Shot, and Painted: Cultural Representations of Biblical Women*. Sheffield: Sheffield Academic, 1996.

Fewell, Danna Nolan, ed. *Reading Between Texts: Intertextuality and the Hebrew Bible*. Literary Currents in Biblical Interpretation. Louisville: Westminster/John Knox, 1992.

Fewell, Danna Nolan, and David M. Gunn. "Boaz, Pillar of Society: Measures of Worth in the Book of Ruth." *JSOT* 45 (1989): 45–59.

———. *Compromising Redemption: Relating Characters in the Book of Ruth*. Eugene, OR: Wipf & Stock, 1990.

———. "Is Coxon a Scold in Responding to the Book of Ruth?" *JSOT* 45 (1989): 39–43.

———. "'A Son is Born to Naomi!': Literary Allusions and Interpretation in the Book of Ruth." *JSOT* 40 (1988): 99–108.

Fisch, Harold. "Ruth and the Structure of Covenant History." *VT* 32 (1982): 425–37.

Fischer, Irmtraud. "The Book of Ruth: A 'Feminist' Commentary to the Torah?" In *Ruth and Esther*, edited by Athalya Brenner, 24–49. FCB 3, 2nd ser. Sheffield: Sheffield Academic, 1999.

Foskett, Mary A., and Jeffrey Kah-Jin Kuan, eds. *Ways of Being, Ways of Reading: Asian American Biblical Interpretation*. St. Louis: Chalice, 2006.

Francke, John R., ed. *Ancient Christian Commentary on Scripture*. Vol. 4: *Joshua, Judges, Ruth, 1–2 Samuel*. Downers Grove, IN: InterVarsity Press, 2005.

Friedan, Betty. *The Feminine Mystique*. New York: W. W. Norton, 1963. Repr., New York: W. W. Norton, 2001.

Frymer-Kensky, Tikva. *Reading the Women of the Bible: A New Interpretation of Their Stories*. New York: Schocken Books, 2002.

Fuchs, Esther. "Status and Role of Female Heroines." *The Mankind Quarterly* 23 (1982): 149–60.

———. "Structure and Patriarchal Functions in the Biblical Betrothal Type-Scene." In *Women in the Hebrew Bible: A Reader*, edited by Alice Bach, 45–51. New York: Routledge, 1999.

Gafney, Wil. "Ruth." In *The Africana Bible*, edited by Hugh R. Page Jr., 249–54. Minneapolis: Fortress, 2010.

Giannarelli, Elena. "Ruth in the Church Fathers." *SIDIC* 23 (1990): 12–15.

Glueck, Nelson. *Hesed in the Bible*. Translated by Alfred Gottschalk. Cincinnati: Hebrew Union College, 1967.

Goh, Elaine W. F. "An Intertextual Reading of Ruth and Proverbs 31:10-31, with a Chinese Woman's Perspective." In *Reading Ruth in Asia*, edited by Jione Havea and Peter H. W. Lau, 73–88. IVBS 7. Atlanta: SBL Press, 2015.

Goss, Robert E., and Mona West. *Take Back the Word: A Queer Reading of the Bible.* Cleveland: Pilgrim Press, 2000.

Grebe, William. *Meal, Metaphor, and More: Food in the Old Testament.* Honors thesis, College of the Holy Cross, 2011.

Grossman, Jonathan. "'Gleaning Among the Ears'—'Gathering Among the Sheaves': Characterizing the Image of the Supervising Boy (Ruth 2)." *JBL* 126 (2007): 703–16.

Gunkel, Herman. *Reden und Aufsaetze.* Gottingen: Vandenhoeck & Ruprecht, 1913.

Havea, Jione. "Stirring Naomi: Another Gleaning at the Edges of Ruth 1." In *Reading Ruth in Asia*, edited by Jione Havea and Peter H. W. Lau, 111–24. IVBS 7. Atlanta: SBL Press, 2015.

Havea, Jione, David Neville, and Elaine Wainwright, eds. *Bible, Borders, Belonging(s): Engaging Readings from Oceania.* SemeiaSt 75. Atlanta: SBL Press, 2014.

Havea, Jione, and Peter H. W. Lau, eds. *Reading Ruth in Asia.* IVBS 7. Atlanta: SBL Press, 2015.

———. "Reading Ruth Again, in Asia." In *Reading Ruth in Asia*, edited by Jione Havea and Peter H. W. Lau, 1–14. IVBS 7. Atlanta: SBL Press, 2015.

Holmstedt, Robert D. *Ruth: A Handbook on the Hebrew Text.* Waco, TX: Baylor University Press, 2010.

Horsley, Richard A., ed. *In the Shadow of Empire: Reclaiming the Bible as a History of Faithful Resistance.* Louisville: Westminster John Knox, 2008.

Hubbard, Robert L. *The Book of Ruth.* Grand Rapids: Eerdmans, 1988.

Hurvitz, A. "The Chronological Significance of 'Aramaisms' in Biblical Hebrew." *IEJ* 18 (1968): 234–40.

James, Carolyn Custis. *The Gospel of Ruth: Loving God Enough to Break the Rules.* Grand Rapids: Zondervan, 2011.

Japhet, Sara. "Was David a Judahite or an Ephraimite? Light from the Genealogies." In *Let Us Go Up to Zion: Essays in Honour of H. G. M. Williamson on the Occasion of His Sixty-Fifth Birthday*, edited by Iaian Provan and Mark Boda, 297–306. VTSup 153. Leiden: Brill, 2012.

Jefferson, Thomas. *Notes on the State of Virginia.* Edited by Frank Shuffelton. New York: Penguin Putnam. 1999.

Johnson, Rajkumar Boaz. "Pandita Ramabai's Translation and Use of Proverbs 31." In *Global Perspectives on the Old Testament*, edited by Mark Roncace and Joseph Weaver, 168–69. Boston: Pearson Education, 2014.

Joüon, Paul. *Ruth: Commentaire Philologique et Exégétique.* Rome: Pontifical Biblical Institute, 1924.

———. *A Grammar of Biblical Hebrew.* Translated and revised by T. Muraoka. SubBi 14/I-II. Rome: Pontifical Biblical Institute, 1996.

Kalmanofsky, Amy. *Dangerous Sisters of the Hebrew Bible*. Minneapolis: Fortress, 2014.

Kates, Judith A., and Gail Twersky Reimer, eds. *Reading Ruth: Contemporary Women Reclaim a Sacred Story*. New York: Ballantine Books, 1994.

Keil, C. F., and Franz Delitzsch. *Commentary on the Old Testament*. Vol. 2: *Joshua, Judges, Ruth, 1–2 Samuel*. Grand Rapids: Eerdmans, 1978.

Kinukawa, Hisako, ed. *Migration and Diaspora: Exegetical Voices of Women in Northeast Asian Countries*. IBVS 6. Atlanta: SBL Press, 2014.

Koblin, John. "Sarah Paulson on Playing the Bruising Role of Marcia Clark." http://www.nytimes.com/2016/03/09/business/media/sarah-paulson-on-playing-the-bruising-role-of-marcia-clark.html?_r=0.

Kohler, K. "The Sabbath and Festivals in Pre-Exilic and Exilic Times." *JAOS* 37 (1917): 209–23.

Koosed, Jennifer. *Gleaning Ruth: A Biblical Heroine and Her Afterlives*. Studies on Personalities of the Old Testament. Columbia: University of South Carolina Press, 2011.

Kristeva, Julia. *Strangers to Ourselves*. Translated by L. S. Roudiez. New York: Columbia University Press, 1991.

Kuhn, Thomas. *The Structure of Scientific Revolutions*. 50th ann. ed. Chicago: University of Chicago Press, 2012.

Kuhrt, Amelie. "Non Royal Women in the Late Babylonian Period: A Survey." In *Women's Earliest Records from Ancient Egypt and Western Asia*, edited by Barbara S. Lesko, 215–39. BJS 166. Atlanta: Scholars Press, 1989.

Kwok, Pui-lan. *Postcolonial Imagination and Feminist Theology*. Louisville: Westminster John Knox, 2005.

LaCocque, André. *The Feminine Unconventional: Four Subversive Figures in Biblical Tradition*. Minneapolis: Fortress, 1990.

———. *Ruth, A Continental Commentary*. Translated by K. C. Hanson. Minneapolis: Fortress, 2004.

Laffey, Alice L. *Appreciating God's Creation through Scripture*. New York: Paulist, 1997.

———. "Feminist Biblical Studies as a Discipline and the Responsibilities of a Catholic Feminist Biblical Scholar." In *Themes in Feminist Theology for the New Millennium (IV)*, edited by Gaile M. Pohlhaus, 25–52. Villanova: Villanova University Press, 2006.

———. "The Influence of Feminism on Christianity." In *Daughters of Abraham*, edited by Yvonne Yazbeck Haddad and John L. Esposito, 50–64. Gainesville: University Press of Florida, 2001.

———. *An Introduction to the Old Testament: A Feminist Perspective*. Philadelphia: Fortress, 1988.

———. "A Liberation Perspective: Patriarchy, Monarchy and Economics." In *Pluralism and Oppression: Theology in World Perspective*, edited by Paul F. Knitter, 221–35. The 1988 Annual Publication of the College Theology Society 34. Washington, DC: University Press of America, 1991.

———. "Naming the Unnamed: Toward a Feminist Reconstruction of the Old Testament." Abstract published in *AAR/SBL Abstracts*, 1985.

———. *The Pentateuch: A Liberation-Critical Reading*. Minneapolis: Fortress, 1999.

———. "Ruth." In *The New Jerome Biblical Commentary*, edited by R. Murphy, R. Brown, and J. Fitzmyer, 553–57. New Jersey: Prentice-Hall, 1989.

———. "Ruth," *One-Volume Bible Commentary*. New Jersey: Paulist, forthcoming.

Lambdin, Thomas O. *Introduction to Biblical Hebrew*. New York: Scribner's Sons, 1971.

Lau, Peter H. W. "Another Postcolonial Reading of the Book of Ruth." In *Reading Ruth in Asia*, edited by Jione Havea and Peter H. W. Lau, 15–34. IVBS 7. Atlanta: SBL Press, 2015.

———. *The Book of Ruth*. Singapore: Armour Publishing, 2012.

Lee, Eunny P. "Ruth the Moabite: Identity, Kinship, and Otherness." In *Engaging the Bible in a Gendered World: An Introduction to Feminist Biblical Interpretation in Honor of Katharine Doob Sakenfeld*, edited by Linda Day and Carolyn Pressler, 89–101. Louisville: Westminster John Knox, 2006.

———. "Women's Doings in Ruth: A Feminist Biblical Theology of Providence." *JFSR* (forthcoming).

Lee, Yoon Kyung. "Postexilic Jewish Experience and Korean Multiculturalism." In *Migration and Diaspora: Exegetical Voices of Women in Northeast Asian Countries*, edited by Hisako Kinukawa, 3–18. IVBS 6. Atlanta: SBL Press, 2014.

Leonard-Fleckman, Mahri. *The House of David: Between Political Formation and Literary Revision*. Minneapolis: Fortress, 2016.

Lerner, Berel Dov. "The Challenge of Ruth." *The Jerusalem Post*. May 22, 2015.

Lesko, Barbara S., ed. *Women's Earliest Records from Ancient Egypt and Western Asia*. BJS 166. Atlanta: Scholars Press, 1989.

Levine, Amy-Jill. "Ruth." In *Women's Bible Commentary*, exp. ed., edited by Carol A. Newsom and Sharon H. Ringe, 84–90. Louisville: Westminster John Knox, 1998.

Levinson, Bernard M. "You Must Not Add Anything to What I Command You: Paradoxes of Canon and Authorship in Ancient Israel." *Numen* 50 (2003): 1–51.

Lichtheim, Miriam, trans. *Instruction of Amenemope* 26.9. COS 1:121.

Lin, Yan. "'Who Is More to You than Seven Sons': A Cross-Textual Reading Between the Book of Ruth and A Pair of Peacocks to the Southeast Fly." In *Reading Ruth in Asia*, edited by Jione Havea and Peter H. W. Lau, 47–55. IVBS 7. Atlanta: SBL Press, 2015.

Linafelt, Tod. "Taking Women in Samuel: Readers/Responses/Responsibility." In *Reading Between Texts: Intertextuality and the Hebrew Bible*, edited by Danna Nolan Fewell, 99–113. LCBI. Louisville: Westminster John Knox, 1992.

Linafelt, Tod, and Timothy K. Beal. *Ruth and Esther*. Berit Olam. Collegeville, MN: Liturgical Press, 1999.

Losch, Richard R. *The Uttermost Part of the Earth: A Guide to the Bible.* Grand Rapids: Eerdmans, 2005.

MacDonald, Nathan. *Not Bread Alone: The Uses of Food in the Old Testament.* New York: Oxford University Press, 2008.

Masenya, Madipoane. "Ruth." In *The Global Bible Commentary*, edited by Daniel Patte, 86–91. Nashville: Abingdon, 2004.

Mathews, Jeanette. "Deuteronomy 30: Faithfulness in the Refugee Camps of Moab, Babylonia, and Beyond." In *Bible, Borders, Belonging(s): Engaging Readings from Oceania*, edited by Jione Havea, David J. Neville, and Elaine M. Wainwright, 157–70. SemeiaSt 75. Atlanta: SBL Press, 2014.

May, H. G. "Ruth's Visit to the High Places at Bethlehem." *JRAS* 75 (1939): 75–78.

McCarthy, Dennis J. "God as Prisoner of Our Own Choosing: Critical-Historical Study of the Bible, Why and Wither." In *Historicism and Faith: Proceedings of the Fellowship of Scholars*, edited by Paul L. Williams, 17–47. Scranton, PA: Northeast Books, 1980.

McCaslin, Susan. "Persephone Finds Ruth on the Threshing Floor." *JFSR* 28 (2010): 101–2.

McKinley, Judith E. *Reframing Her: Biblical Women in Postcolonial Focus.* Sheffield: Sheffield Phoenix, 2004.

Metzger, Bruce, and Bart Ehrman. *The Text of the New Testament: Its Transmission, Corruption, and Restoration.* 4th ed. New York: Oxford University Press, 2005.

Meyers, Carol, "The Roots of Restriction: Women in Early Israel." *BA* 41 (1978): 91–103.

———. "'Women of the Neighborhood' (Ruth 4.17): Informal Female Networks in Ancient Israel." In *Ruth and Esther*, edited by Athalya Brenner, 110–27. FCB 3, 2nd ser. Sheffield: Sheffield Academic, 1999.

Miller, J. Maxwell. A *History of Ancient Israel and Judah*. 2nd ed. Louisville: Westminster John Knox, 2006.

Millgram, Hillel I. *Four Biblical Heroines and the Case for Female Authorship: An Analysis of the Women of Ruth, Esther and Genesis 38*. Jefferson, NC: McFarland & Company, 2008.

Mohanty, Chandra Talpade. "Under Western Eyes: Feminist Scholarship and Colonial Discourses," *Feminist Review* 30 (Autumn 1988): 60–88.

Moran, William L. "The Ancient Near Eastern Background of the Love of God in Deuteronomy." *CBQ* 25 (1963): 77–79.

Moss, Candida R., and Joel S. Baden. *Reconceiving Infertility: Biblical Perspectives on Procreation and Childlessness.* Princeton: Princeton University Press, 2015.

Mother Teresa. *Come Be My Light: The Private Writings of the Saint of Calcutta.* Edited by Brian Kolodiejchuk. New York: Image Books, 2009.

Na'aman, Nadav. "Ephraim, Ephrath and the Settlement in the Judean Hill Country." *Zion* 49 (1984): 325–31.

Nadar, Sarojini. "A South African Indian Womanist Reading." In *Other Ways of Reading: African Women and the Bible*, edited by Musa W. Dube, 159–75. Atlanta: SBL Press, 2001.

Nelavala, Surekha. "Patriarchy, a Threat to Human Bonding: Reading the Story of Ruth in the Light of Marriage and Family Structures in India." In *Reading Ruth in Asia*, edited by Jione Havea and Peter H. W. Lau, 89–98. IVBS 7. Atlanta: SBL Press, 2015.

Newsom, Carol A., and Sharon H. Ringe, eds. *Women's Bible Commentary*. Exp. ed. Louisville: Westminster John Knox Press, 1998.

Nielsen, Kirsten. *Ruth: A Commentary*. OTL. Louisville: Westminster John Knox, 1997.

Noth, Martin. *History of Israel*. 2nd ed. New York: HarperCollins College Edition, 1960.

Nu, Roi. "A Reinterpretation of Levirate Marriage in Ruth 4:1-12 for Kachin Society." In *Reading Ruth in Asia*, edited by Jione Havea and Peter H. W. Lau, 57–72. IVBS 7. Atlanta: SBL Press, 2015.

O'Connor, Kathleen. *Jeremiah: Pain and Promise*. Minneapolis: Fortress, 2012.

———. *Lamentations and the Tears of the World*. New York: Orbis Books, 2002.

Page, Hugh R., Jr., ed. *The Africana Bible*. Minneapolis: Fortress, 2010.

Pardes, Ilana. *Countertraditions in the Bible: A Feminist Approach*. Cambridge: Harvard University Press, 1992.

Parker, Simon P., trans. *Ugaritic Narrative Poetry*. WAW 9. Atlanta: Scholars Press, 1997.

Pattel-Gray, Anne. *Through Aboriginal Eyes: The Cry from the Wilderness*. Geneva: WCC Publications, 1991.

Perlitt, Lothar. *Bundestheologie im Alten Testament*. WMANT 36. Neukirchen-Vluyn, DE: Neukirchener Verlag, 1969.

Pritchard, James A. *The Ancient Near East: An Anthology of Texts*. Princeton: Princeton University Press, 2010.

Plumer, Brad. "Food Stamps Will Get Cut by $5 Billion This Week—and More Cuts Could Follow." *The Washington Post*. October 28, 2013. https://www.washingtonpost.com/news/wonk/wp/2013/10/28/food-stamps-will-get-cut-by-5-billion-this-week-and-more-cuts-could-follow/.

Rao, Naveen. "The Book of Ruth as a Clandestine Scripture to Sabotage Persian Colonial Agenda: A Paradigm for a Liberative Dalit Scripture." *Bangalore Theological Forum* 41 (2009): 114–34.

Rabinowitz, L., trans. *Ruth Rabbah*. Vol. 8 of *Midrash Rabbah*. London: Soncino, 1939. Reprinted 1971.

Rashkow, Ilona. "Ruth: The Discourse of Power and the Power of Discourse." In *A Feminist Companion to Ruth*, edited by Athalya Brenner, 26–41. FCB 3. Sheffield: Sheffield Academic, 1993.

Rauber, D. F. "Literary Values in the Bible: The Book of Ruth." *JBL* 89 (1970): 27–37.

Rebera, Basil. "Yahweh or Boaz? Ruth 2:20 Reconsidered." *BT* 36 (1985): 317–27.

Reinhartz, Adele. *"Why Ask My Name?" Anonymity and Identity in Biblical Narrative*. New York: Oxford University Press, 1998.

Roncace, Mark, and Joseph Weaver, eds. *Global Perspectives on the Old Testament*. Boston: Pearson Education, 2014.

Rowley, H. H. *The Servant of the Lord and Other Essays on the Old Testament*. 2nd ed. Oxford: Blackwell, 1965.

Sakenfeld, Katharine Doob. *The Meaning of Hesed in the Hebrew Bible: A New Inquiry*. HSM 17. Missoula, MT: Scholars Press, 1978.

———. *Ruth*. Interpretation: A Bible Commentary for Teaching and Preaching. Louisville: Westminster John Knox, 1999.

Sasson, Jack M. *Ruth: A New Translation with a Philological Commentary and a Formalist-Folklorist Interpretation*. 2nd ed. Sheffield: Sheffield Academic, 1995.

———. "Ruth." In *The Literary Guide to the Bible*, edited by Robert Alter and Frank Kermode, 320–28. Cambridge: Harvard University Press, 1987.

Schipper, Jeremy. *Ruth: A New Translation with Introduction and Commentary*. AYBRL 7D. New Haven: Yale University Press, 2016.

Schneiders, Sandra. *The Revelatory Text: Interpreting the New Testament as Sacred Scripture*. Collegeville, MN: Liturgical Press, 1999.

Scholz, Susan. *Introducing the Women's Hebrew Bible*. New York: T & T Clark, 2007.

Schüssler Fiorenza, Elisabeth. *Bread Not Stone: The Challenge of Feminist Biblical Interpretation*. Ann. ed. Boston: Beacon Press, 1995.

———. *In Memory of Her: A Feminist Theological Reconstruction of Christian Origins*. New York: Crossroad, 1994.

Segovia, Fernando F., and Mary Ann Tolbert, eds. *Teaching the Bible: The Discourses and Pedagogy of Biblical Theology*. Maryknoll, NY: Orbis Books, 1998.

Seidman, Naomi. "A New Garb for the Jewish Soul: The JPS Bible in the Light of the King James Bible." In *Assessing the Genius of the King James Version as Bible Translation and Literary Influence*, edited by David Burke, John Kutsko, and Philip Towner, 475–98. Atlanta: SBL Press, 2013.

Sharp, Carolyn J. "Feminist Queries for Ruth and Joshua." *SJOT* 28 (2014): 229–52.

———. *Irony and Meaning in the Hebrew Bible*. ISBL. Bloomington: Indiana University Press, 2008.

Smith, Lesley, trans. *Medieval Exegesis in Translation: Commentaries on the Book of Ruth*. Kalamazoo: Western Michigan University, 1996.

Smith, L. P. "Introduction and Exegesis of the Book of Ruth." In *Interpreter's Bible*. Vol. 2. Edited by George Arthur Buttrick. Nashville: Abingdon, 1953.

Smith, Mark S. "Your People Shall Be My People: Family and Covenant in Ruth 1:16-17." *CBQ* 69 (2007): 242–58.

Soler, Jean. "The Semiotics of Food in the Bible." In *Food and Culture: A Reader*, edited by Carole Counihan and Penny Van Esterik, 57–66. 2nd ed. New York: Routledge, 2008.

Spurgeon, Charles. *Spurgeon's Sermons on Ruth*. Apollo, PA: Ichthus Publications, 2014.

Stanton, Elizabeth Cady. *The Woman's Bible*. Seattle: Coalition Task Force on Women and Religion, 1981 (orig. pub. in 2 vols.: 1895 and 1898).

———. The Project Gutenberg eBook. Produced by Carrie Lorenz and John B. Hare. wattpad.com/13271-the-woman%275-bible.

Steinberg, Yehuda Y. *Harvest of Kindness: Megillas Rus and the Power of Chesed.* Southfield, MI: Targum Press, 2010.

Sugirtharajah, R. S. *Asian Biblical Hermeneutics and Postcolonialism: Contesting the Interpretations.* Maryknoll, NY: Orbis Books, 1998.

———, ed. *The Postcolonial Bible.* Sheffield: Sheffield Academic, 1998.

———, ed. *Vernacular Hermeneutics.* Sheffield: Sheffield Academic, 1999.

Thompson, Michael E. W. "New Life Amid the Alien Corn: The Book of Ruth." *EvQ* 65 (1993): 197–210.

Tong, Sin-lung. "The Key to Successful Migration? Rereading Ruth's Confession (1:16-17) through the Lens of Bhabha's Mimicry." In *Reading Ruth in Asia*, edited by Jione Havea and Peter H. W. Lau, 35–46. IVBS 7. Atlanta: SBL Press, 2015.

Trible, Phyllis. *God and the Rhetoric of Sexuality.* Philadelphia: Fortress, 1978.

Turner, Karen Gottschang with Phan Thanh Hao. *Even the Women Must Fight: Memories of War from North Vietnam.* New York: Wiley, 1999.

Vamosh, Miriam Feinberg. *Food at the Time of the Bible.* Herzlia, Israel: Palphot Ltd., nd.

van Dijk-Hemmes, Fokkelien. "Ruth: A Product of Women's Culture?" In *A Feminist Companion to Ruth*, edited by Athalya Brenner, 134–39. FCB 3. Sheffield: Sheffield Academic, 2001.

Wafula, R. S. *Biblical Representations of Moab: A Kenyan Postcolonial Reading.* New York: Lang, 2014.

Walker, Alice. *The Color Purple.* Chicago: Houghton Mifflin Harcourt, 1985.

Walthall, Comea M. "Ruth's Relevance to the Same-Sex Marriage Debate." In *Global Perspectives on the Old Testament*, edited by Mark Roncace and Joseph Weaver, 195–96. Boston: Pearson Education, 2014.

Weems, Renita. *Just a Sister Away.* San Diego: LuraMedia, 1988.

Westbrook, April D. *'And He Will Take Your Daughters . . .' Woman Story and the Ethical Evaluation of Monarchy in the David Narrative.* London: Bloomsbury T & T Clark, 2015.

Williams, Paul L. *Historicism and Faith: Proceedings of the Fellowship of Catholic Scholars.* Scranton, PA: Northeast Books, 1980.

Williams, Sherley Anne. *Dessa Rose.* New York: HarperCollins, 1986.

Wong, Wai Ching. "Identity and Hybridity: Ruth in the Genealogy of Jesus: Matthew 1:1-17; Ruth 1–4." *Theologies and Cultures* 6 (2009): 98–109.

Wright, David P. *Ritual in Narrative: The Dynamics of Feasting, Mourning and Retaliation Rites in the Ugaritic Tale of Aqat.* Winona Lake, IN: Eisenbrauns, 2001.

Yee, Gale A. "'She Stood in Tears amid the Alien Corn': Ruth, Perpetual Foreigner and Model Minority." In *They Were All Together in One Place? Toward Minority Biblical Criticism*, edited by Randall C. Bailey, Tat-Siong Benny Liew, and Fernando F. Segovia, 119–40. Atlanta: SBL Press, 2009.

Yoo, Yani. "Ruth as a Marriage Migrant." In *Global Perspectives on the Old Testament*, edited by Mark Roncace and Joseph Weaver, 193–95. Boston: Pearson Education, 2014.

Younger, K. Lawson, Jr. *Judges, Ruth.* NIV Application Commentary. Grand Rapids: Zondervan, 2002.

Zevit, Ziony. "Dating Ruth: Legal, Linguistic and Historical Observations." *ZAW* 117 (2005): 574–600.

Index of Scripture References and Other Ancient Writings

Index of Subjects

General Editor

Barbara E. Reid, OP, is a Dominican Sister of Grand Rapids, Michigan. She holds a PhD in biblical studies from The Catholic University of America and is vice president and academic dean and professor of New Testament studies at Catholic Theological Union, Chicago. Her most recent publications are *Wisdom's Feast: An Invitation to Feminist Interpretation of the Scriptures* (2016) and *Abiding Word: Sunday Reflections on Year A, B, C* (3 vols.; 2011, 2012, 2013). She served as president of the Catholic Biblical Association in 2014–2015.

Volume Editor

Amy-Jill Levine is university professor of New Testament and Jewish Studies, Carpenter Professor of New Testament Studies, and professor of Jewish Studies at Vanderbilt Divinity School and College of Arts and Science; she is also affiliated professor, Centre for the Study of Jewish-Christian Relations, Cambridge, United Kingdom. Her recent publications include *The Misunderstood Jew: The Church and the Scandal of the Jewish Jesus* (2006) and *Short Stories by Jesus: The Enigmatic Parables of a Controversial Rabbi* (2014). Dr. Levine is also coeditor of the *Jewish Annotated New Testament* (2011).

Authors

Alice L. Laffey taught the Old Testament for thirty-five years at the College of the Holy Cross in Worcester, Massachusetts, before retiring in May 2016. She is the author of many articles as well as *Introduction to the Old Testament: A Feminist Perspective* (Fortress, 1988), *Appreciating God's Creation through Scripture* (Paulist, 1997), *The Pentateuch: A Liberation-Critical Reading* (Fortress, 1998), and *1–2 Kings* in the New Collegeville Bible Commentary series (Liturgical Press, 2012).

Mahri Leonard-Fleckman is assistant professor of Hebrew Bible in the Theology Department at Providence College (Providence, RI). She earned her PhD in 2014 from New York University in Hebrew and Judaic Studies, with a focus on Hebrew Bible and ancient Near Eastern Studies. She is author of *The House of David: Between Political Formation and Literary Revision* (2016). Before coming to Providence College, Leonard-Fleckman was an assistant professor in the Department of Theology and Religious Studies at the University of Scranton (Scranton, PA).